Learning Web Design
with Adobe® CS3

Dreamweaver® ▪ Fireworks® ▪ Flash®

Katherine Murray

PEARSON

Prentice
Hall
DDC

Credits and acknowledgements borrowed from other sources and reproduced, with permission, in this textbook are as follows:

Adobe® Dreamweaver®, Fireworks®, and Flash® CS3 are either registered trademarks or trademarks of Adobe Systems Incorporated in the United States and/or other countries.

PEARSON

Prentice
Hall
DDC

ISBN-13: 978-0-13-362570-7

ISBN-10: 0-13-362570-2

1 2 3 4 5 6 7 8 9 10   11 10 09 08 07

Table of Contents

Introduction

Learning Web Design with Adobe CS3 shows you how to use Adobe Dreamweaver, Adobe Fireworks, and Adobe Flash to create high-quality Web sites complete with graphics, animations, buttons, and more. In this book, you learn to design and create attention-getting, interactive sites that businesses, governments, schools, and virtually every organization needs to communicate.

WHO SHOULD READ THIS BOOK?

▪ *Learning Web Design with Adobe CS3* is written for beginning Web page designers, graphics artists, and media producers. The book assumes the reader has a working knowledge of the Internet, basic design elements, and common Windows navigation.

▪ This book is for everyone who needs to know how to add solid design and interactivity to his or her Web site. You can use this book as an exercise-by-exercise tutorial on many Dreamweaver, Fireworks, and Flash features or refer to it on an as-needed topical basis.

▪ You should read this book if you need to design, manage, and modify a Web site and want to learn how to add interactive and advanced elements—including buttons, menus, and animations—to its pages.

WHAT YOU NEED

To gain the most from this book, you will need:

▪ Knowledge of fundamental Windows navigation and terminology.

▪ Intel® Pentium® 4, Intel Centrino®, Intel Xeon®, or Intel Core™ Duo (or compatible) processor.

▪ Microsoft® Windows® XP with Service Pack 2 or Windows Vista™ Home Premium, Business, Ultimate, or Enterprise (certified for 32-bit editions).

▪ 512MB of RAM.

▪ 1GB of available hard-disk space (additional free space required during installation).

▪ 1,024 × 768 monitor resolution with 16-bit video card.

▪ Adobe CS3, including Dreamweaver, Fireworks, and Flash.

▪ An Internet browser such as Microsoft Internet Explorer, Netscape, Mozilla, or Mozilla Firefox that supports multimedia, animation, and advanced interactive features.

▪ For the best results, Microsoft Internet Explorer 6.0 or 7.0 should be used.

INTEGRATED APPROACH

- Because Adobe Web CS3 is a suite of powerful applications—Adobe Dreamweaver CS3, Adobe Fireworks CS3, and Adobe Flash CS3—this course includes exercises that incorporate tasks and features from each of the three programs to give you a comprehensive understanding of the suite.

- The following colors are used to help you know which application to use in a specific exercise:

  Green lets you know to use Dreamweaver for that exercise.

  Gold is used for Fireworks exercises.

  Red indicates Flash exercises.

- The lessons and exercises are designed to replicate the steps you take when you create a new site for a client. You start with creating the site in Dreamweaver, adding pages and page elements, and then move to Fireworks to create and enhance graphics for the site. After you add the graphics to the Web site in Dreamweaver, you move to Flash to learn how to create simple animations for the site. This integrated approach helps you get the feel for the different programs and learn to use them together easily.

HOW THIS BOOK IS ORGANIZED

This book is organized into eight lessons that begin with Web site basics and then move to advanced features.

- **Lesson 1—Get Started with Dreamweaver.** This lesson introduces the program and its workspace. You learn how to start and exit the program and create a new site using the Site Definition wizard. You also learn how to create and save Web pages and view site files. Finally, you are introduced to HTML structure and syntax and the importance of adding keywords to a site. You learn how to add text to a Web page and view page content in both Design and Code views, as well as how to switch from one Dreamweaver site to another.

- **Lesson 2—Work with Web Page Text and Links.** This lesson focuses on creating Web page text content. It discusses how to enter text and import text from Microsoft Office documents, as well as how to find and replace text, check spelling, and insert special characters. You learn how to format text in many ways: change text fonts, sizes, styles, and colors; change text alignment; and create lists. You explore the Dreamweaver Code view and other options for viewing and modifying HTML and other kinds of Web page code. You also learn how to use the History panel to repeat or undo tasks. This lesson introduces links, the means by which visitors navigate a Web site. You learn how to create relative links within a site, absolute links to other sites, links to named anchors on a page, and links to e-mail addresses. You preview your site files in a browser, explore the new Device Central interface for viewing files in mobile devices, learn more about the Files panel's expanded window, and learn how to view and modify the site map.

- **Lesson 3—Work with Graphic Elements and Templates.** This lesson explores Dreamweaver's graphic capabilities and introduces you to creating art using Fireworks. You begin by applying background page colors in Dreamweaver and then move to Fireworks to learn how to use the various tools, create and work with bitmap and vector objects, control colors, add graphic text, and work with layers. This lesson also introduces you to Adobe Bridge, an application that makes it easy to organize graphic files. You learn how to create rollover images that change when the mouse pointer rolls over the graphic or navigation bar. You create image maps that contain hotspots to link pages in a site. You create and use a template to give pages a consistent look. After you store items in the Library, you insert them throughout the Web site. You also learn how to create design notes for pages in the site.

- **Lesson 4—Work with Tables and Forms.** This lesson introduces you to tables, which can be used to organize information or an entire Web page. You create and format a table to hold data on a page and structure a Web page using Dreamweaver's Layout mode features. You also learn how to import tabular data into a table, sort table content, and insert table-related tags. This lesson introduces forms, and you have the opportunity to create an accessible form by inserting various types of form fields: text boxes, radio buttons, checkboxes, list-menu boxes, and buttons.

- **Lesson 5—Work with AP Elements, Frames, and Styles.** Dreamweaver AP elements include absolutely positioned objects and AP divs that can hold any HTML content. You learn how to create, resize, position, and format AP divs to add visual impact to a page. This lesson shows you how to create frames on a Web page to open specific Web page content. You learn how to set up and modify frames in a frameset and how to specify target frames for links. Finally, you explore styles and style sheets, used to apply consistent formats throughout a Web site. You learn how to create internal styles and an external style sheet that can be applied to all pages in a site.

- **Lesson 6—Create Dynamic and Interactive Pages.** You begin this lesson by exploring the new Spry framework that allows you to insert interactive elements on Web pages. Spry Validation widgets, menu bars, and collapsible panels enhance Web pages and make them more useful as well. You then switch to Flash to learn the basics techniques for animation and discover how to create objects, add and work with keyframes, and preview an animation. Next you learn about creating symbols and using tweening to create animation effects quickly and easily. You learn to test and publish the movie in Flash, and then move to Fireworks to create interactive buttons and slices.

- **Lesson 7—Advanced Graphics and Animation.** This lesson shows you how to optimize your graphics so that they download quickly and have the best possible quality with the lowest possible file sizes. You learn to choose different color palettes, compress and create interlacing GIF files, and adjust JPEG quality and compression. In Flash, you find out how to create movie clips you can use over and over on your sites and work with the Movie Explorer and Timeline Effects to simplify animations for your pages.

- **Lesson 8—Manage and Publish a Web Site.** This lesson explores some regular site maintenance operations, such as testing a site using one or more target browsers, checking and modifying links, and running various kinds of reports that can help you make your site more accessible and locate problems such as untitled documents. You also learn how to put (publish) files on an FTP, WebDAV, or local server and how to use the Check In/Out feature to control access to sites maintained by a team.

Learning Web Design with Adobe CS3 is designed to make your learning experience easy and enjoyable. Lessons are comprised of short exercises designed to help you learn how to use Adobe CS3 in real-life settings. Every application exercise is made up of eight key elements:

- **Software Skills.** Each exercise starts with a brief description of how you would use the features of that exercise in the workplace.

- **Design Skills.** The key to a good Web site is a good design. Important design skills are outlined before you begin the exercise.

- **Application Skills.** A scenario is set to put the program features into context.

- **Terms.** Key terms are included and defined at the start of each exercise, so you can quickly refer back to them. The terms are then highlighted in the text.

- **Notes.** Concise notes aid in learning the computer concepts.

- **Procedures.** Hands-on mouse and keyboard procedures teach all necessary skills.

- **Application Exercise.** Step-by-step instructions put your skills to work.

- **On Your Own.** Each exercise concludes with a critical thinking activity that you can work through on your own. You are frequently challenged to provide your own Web page content. The "On Your Own" sections can be used as additional reinforcement, for practice, or to test skill proficiency.

Enhanced End-of-Lesson material puts skills to the test:

- **Summary Exercise.** Comprehensive exercises that touch on most skills covered in the lesson. Step-by-step directions guide you through the exercises.

- **Application Exercise.** The level of difficulty starts to ramp up with the application exercises. These summary exercises do not contain detailed steps.

- **Curriculum Integration.** Integrate other subject areas into the computer course with the curriculum integration exercises. Topics include math, English, social studies, and science.

- **Critical Thinking.** These challenging exercises are scenario-based—no specific steps are given.

WORKING WITH DATA AND SOLUTION FILES

As you work through the exercises in this book, you'll be creating, opening, and saving files. You should keep the following instructions in mind:

- You will create much of the content of your Web sites on your own, but a number of data files are included to provide specific types of Web site content, such as images, multimedia objects, and page text that would be time consuming to type.

- Unless the book instructs otherwise, use the default settings when creating a file.

- When the application or On Your Own exercise includes a file name and a CD icon ⊙ , you can open the file provided on the CD that accompanies this book.

- You will be building several sample Web sites as you work through the examples in this book. Often exercises assume you are working with these sites, which have been saved on your system. As needed, you will be provided with additional data files and Web pages on the CD that accompanies this book. The Directory of Files on page xv lists the Web sites and data files from the CD that are used with various exercises.

- Make sure you save all new materials to the Web site you are currently working on.

- When you see _xx in any instructions in this book, it means that you should type an underscore followed by your own initials—not the actual text "_xx". This will help your instructor identify your work.

COPY DATA FILES

You can copy data files from the CD-ROM to a hard drive.

1. Open Windows Explorer. (Right-click the [start] / ⊛ button and click **Explore**.)

2. Be sure that the CD is in your CD-ROM drive. Select the CD-ROM drive letter from the All Folders pane of the Explorer window.

3. Click to select the **Data** folder in the Contents of (CD-ROM drive letter) pane of the Explorer window.

4. Drag the folder onto the letter of the drive to which you wish to copy the data files (usually C:) in the All Folders pane of the Explorer window.

USE THE WINDOWS IIS WEB SERVER

- If you are running the Windows 2000, XP Professional, or Vista operating system, you can publish your Web sites to the IIS personal Web server available on those operating systems.

- For more information on installing the personal Web server, consult Help (Start>Help). Search for IIS and click the topic *IIS Installation*. You use the Add/Remove Windows Programs feature to install IIS components. You may need your Windows CD to install this feature.

DIRECTORY OF FILES ON CD

Use the following table to locate the files you use in exercises throughout this book. In the FILE NAME column, folder names appear before the backslash (for example, lillysgarden\index.html indicates that the file index.html is inside the lillysgarden folder). You are prompted in the text when to open the needed files from the CD. The USE EXISTING SITE column shows you which Web site to open on your system (this assumes that you have been creating the sites and following along with the examples throughout the book.)

LESSON NO.	EXERCISE NO.	FILE NAME	USE EXISTING SITE(S)
1	1	lillysgarden\index.html	
	3	gardenscape\index.html	
		gardenscape\contactus.html	
		gardenscape\gardenscape_text.txt	
2	8	aboutus.html	GardenScape
		articles.html	YardArt
		indextext.doc	
		newtext.doc	
	9	returntext.doc	GardenScape
			Java2Go
	10	glossary.html	GardenScape
		recipe.html	Java2Go
	11	tierraverde\index.html	GardenScape
		tierraverde\events.html	Tierra Verde
		tierraverde\for_parents.html	
		tierraverde\schedule.html	
	12	webspecials.html	GardenScape
			Tierra Verde
	13	registration.html	Tierra Verde
		revistrationform.doc	
	14	groupstxt.doc	Classmate Connections
3	17	designers.html	GardenScape
	18	18_logo.png	
	19	19_tree.png	
	20	sitka_spruce.png	
	22	22_gslogo.png	
		flower.png	
		22_javalogo.png	
	23	23_tierraverde.png	
		23_treeline.png	
	24	gslogo.png	GardenScape
		terrace.jpg	
		lotus.jpg	
		butterfly.jpg	
		javalogo.jpg	Java2Go
		muffins.jpg	
		threeberry.jpg	

LESSON NO.	EXERCISE NO.	FILE NAME	USE EXISTING SITE(S)
3 (cont.)	25	gsarticles_ovr.png	GardenScape
		gsarticles_up.png	
		gscontact_up.png	
		gscontact_up.png	
		gsdesigners_ovr.png	
		gsdesigners_up.png	
		gshome_ovr.png	
		gshome_up.png	
		gsservices_ovr.png	
		gsservices_up.png	
		jcontact_ovr.png	Java2Go
		jcontact_up.png	
		jhistory_ovr.png	
		jhistory_up.png	
		jhome_ovr.png	
		jhome_up.png	
		jlocations_ovr.png	
		jlocations_up.png	
		jrecipes_ovr.png	
		jrecipes_up.png	
	26	daffodils.jpg	YardArt
		splatter.jpg	
		squares.jpg	
		ya_about_ovr.png	
		ya_about_up.png	
		ya_contact_up.png	
		ya_contact_up.png	
		ya_favorites_ovr.png	
		ya_favorites_up.png	
		ya_home_ovr.png	
		ya_home_up.png	
	27	gsspecialties_ovr.png	GardenScape
		gsspecialties_up.png	
	28	background.jpg	Tierra Verde
		cabin.jpg	
		t_contact_ovr.png	
		t_contact_up.png	
		t_home_ovr.png	
		t_home_up.png	
		t_info_ovr.png	
		t_info_up.png	
		t_news_ovr.png	
		t_news_up.png	

LESSON NO.	EXERCISE NO.	FILE NAME	USE EXISTING SITE(S)
3 *(cont.)*	29	addme_form.doc	
		c_addme_ovr.png	
		c_addme_up.png	
		c_groups_ovr.png	
		c_groups_up.png	
		c_home_ovr.png	
		c_home_up.png	
		c_links_ovr.png	
		c_links_up.png	
		c_pages_ovr.png	
		c_pages_up.png	
		class01.jpg	
		class02.jpg	
		home_class.jpg	
4	32	rose.jpg	GardenScape
	33	contact.txt	GardenScape
		favorites.txt	
		flowers.jpg	YardArt
	34	lafter.jpg	GardenScape
		streisand.jpg	
		new.gif	
	36	beachtext.doc	Tierra Verde
		calendar.txt	
5	40	projects.html	GardenScape
	42	sports_info\basketball.html	Classmate Connections
		sports_info\football.html	
		sports_info\home.html	
		sports_info\soccer.html	
		sports_info\basketball.jpg	
		sports_info\football.jpg	
		sports_info\links.html	
		sports_info\soccer.jpg	
	43	index.html	
		products.html	
		reflectivepool.jpg	
6	49	articletxt.html	GardenProjects
		index.html	
		news.html	
		products.html	
		tutorials.html	
	52	52garden.fla	
	53	53tierra.fla	
	54	54garden.fla	
		SO_54myfile.fla	

LESSON NO.	EXERCISE NO.	FILE NAME	USE EXISTING SITE(S)
6 *(cont.)*	55	intro.html	GardenProjects
		garden.swf	
		enter.swf	Gardentutorial
	57	57landscape.jpg	
	58	star.fla	Tierra Verde
	59	montage.png	
7	62	seeds.png	
	63	garden.gif	
	64	daffodils.jpg	
	65	65bee.fla	
		walking.fla	
	66	66flowers.fla	
	69	jung.jpg	
		jung.tif	
		jung2.jpg	
		jungAA_jpg	
8	71		GardenScape
			GardenProjects
	72		GardenScape
			GardenProjects
	73		GardenScape
			YardArt
	74		Tierra Verde
	75		Classmate Connections

Lesson | 1

Get Started with Dreamweaver

Skills Covered

- About Adobe Dreamweaver CS3
- Start Dreamweaver
- Open a Web Page
- Dreamweaver Workspace
- Work with Panels and Panes
- Close and Exit Dreamweaver

Software Skills Dreamweaver has many innovative features to make designing, creating, editing, managing, and publishing your new Web site easier and more intuitive.

Design Skills Starting out, a Web designer needs to know where to find and how to use basic design tools. Preparing your workspace and arranging tools the way you want them will help you get ready to create.

Application Skills In this exercise, you learn how to open a site and then explore and arrange the Dreamweaver workspace to become familiar with menus, toolbars, and panels.

TERMS

Cascading Style Sheet (CSS) A group of formatting instructions that enable you to easily apply formats to specific items on your Web pages.

Expander arrow The small arrow icon at the bottom right of the Property inspector that, when clicked, enlarges the panel to reveal additional properties.

Floating panel A Dreamweaver container for tools and properties that is undocked and can be repositioned anywhere in the workspace or closed if desired.

HTML (Hypertext Markup Language) The code used to create all Web pages.

Insert bar A toolbar in the Dreamweaver window that shows categories from which to insert objects into a Web page, including graphics, text features, tables, multimedia objects, etc.

Object An element such as a form, image, or multimedia file added to a Web page.

Panel A Dreamweaver container for tools and properties that appears in the Dreamweaver window either alone or as part of a panel group. Panels can be undocked and repositioned anywhere in the workspace or closed if desired.

Panel groups pane The panel on the right side of the Dreamweaver workspace where panels appear by default.

Property A characteristic that defines the value, appearance, and/or state of an object.

Property inspector A Dreamweaver panel that displays properties for the currently selected object.

Web page A single file in a collection of files that make up a Web site.

Web site A collection of Web pages and other objects, such as images, that are linked to create a resource dedicated to a particular subject.

Workspace In Dreamweaver, the desktop area where the Document window and panels appear.

NOTES

About Adobe Dreamweaver CS3

- Adobe Dreamweaver has been one of the most widely used Web site design programs for many years. Combining sophisticated design tools with an easy-to-use interface, Dreamweaver makes it simple for anyone to create and manage many types of Web sites.

- Dreamweaver offers design environments that are friendly to both new and experienced designers. A new user does not have to be **HTML** literate to create a Web site in Dreamweaver. Dreamweaver's Design view, Code view, and Code and Design view give you different ways to view your work and enable you to create pages using familiar word processing–type tools to format text and insert images.

- For designers who customarily work directly in HTML, Dreamweaver's Code view and many code features speed the process of inserting and troubleshooting HTML code.

- For designers who are familiar with **cascading style sheet (CSS)** formatting, Dreamweaver's integrated CSS panel enables them to create, apply, and manage CSS styles almost effortlessly. The new Spry framework combines HTML, CSS, and JavaScript to create a number of interactive and dynamic features that can really spark up a Web page.

- Using Dreamweaver CS3, it is easier than ever to construct a Web site and manage files. For example, a designer can now modify image files right in Dreamweaver rather than have to work in an outside graphics program. Integration with Adobe Photoshop allows a designer to insert Photoshop images directly onto a Web page and then edit the image if desired in Photoshop. Improved and expanded templates allow a designer to create many types of pages and apply cascading style sheets at the same time.

- Dreamweaver CS3 also allows a designer to preview files not only in a number of browsers but in simulated mobile devices. Adobe's Device Central includes an emulator that displays popular cell phone models and shows how your Web page will look when viewed on each particular brand of phone.

- Easy integration with the other applications in the Adobe CS3 suite make it easy to add special elements to your site, such as animations from Adobe Flash CS3 and high-quality graphics you create in Adobe Fireworks CS3.

- You will learn about these features and many more as you work through this course.

Start Dreamweaver

- Start Dreamweaver by clicking the ▰ start / ◉ button on the Windows taskbar, clicking All Programs, and navigating to the folder that contains Dreamweaver CS3.

  ✔ *The folder name will depend on whether Dreamweaver is installed as a standalone product or as part of the Web Design suite.*

- Click the folder and then click Adobe Dreamweaver CS3 on the list to open the Dreamweaver workspace.

- Dreamweaver opens the Start page shown in the following illustration. In this page, you can choose to open an item you have recently worked on; create a new page or site from scratch; or create a new page from sample style sheets, framesets, or page designs. For Dreamweaver novices, the Starter pages offer simple, attractive designs that can be customized to create a wide variety of Web sites.

Dreamweaver Start page

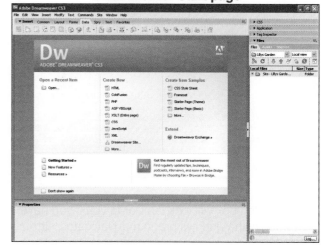

- Click the Dreamweaver Exchange option to jump to a site where you can buy or download programs designed to extend Dreamweaver's usefulness. This is the place to go to find customized navigation buttons, table layouts, and scripts that perform various functions.

- If you are new to Dreamweaver, you may want to use the options at the lower left of the dialog box to take a tour of the new features or run a tutorial to help you get up to speed.

Open a Web Page

- When Dreamweaver starts, it automatically opens the **Web site** that was active the last time the program was used. For each Web site you intend to create or work with in Dreamweaver, you must define the Web site so that Dreamweaver knows where to locate the site files.

  ✔ *You will learn how to create a site in the next exercise.*

- You can open any Web page in Dreamweaver, even if you have not created a site related to the page. A **Web page** is a single file in a Web site, usually devoted to one part of the Web site's topic.

- To open a Web page from the Start page, click **Open...**. Or, to open a Web page while you are working in a Dreamweaver session, use the File>Open menu command to display the Open dialog box, shown in the following illustration.

Dreamweaver's Open dialog box

- This dialog box will look familiar to you if you have worked with Windows programs. Navigate to the location of the Web page to open, select it, and click **Open** to display the page in Dreamweaver.

- The **Site Root** button in the lower-left corner of the Open dialog box allows you to open the root folder of the current Dreamweaver site without having to navigate through a number of folders.

Dreamweaver Workspace

- The Dreamweaver **workspace** is the part of the window where you create, work with, and save Web pages. The Dreamweaver workspace is divided into several sections, as shown in the following illustration.

Default Dreamweaver CS3 workspace

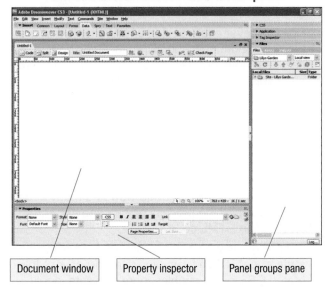

| Document window | Property inspector | Panel groups pane |

- The largest area in the workspace is the Document window. You use the Document window to create page content.

- The **panel** at the bottom of the screen named Properties is known as the **Property inspector** because it allows you to look at the settings, or properties, of the currently selected object. You will use this panel constantly as you create and modify Web pages.

- The pane at the right side of the screen contains a number of other panel groups. By default, only the Files panel group is open, as you see in the previous illustration.

- The workspace also contains a menu bar, a status bar, and two toolbars that provide easy access to commonly used tools: the Insert bar and the Document toolbar. You will learn more about parts of the workspace in the following sections.

Property Inspector

- When you click an element on a Web page—for example, a text paragraph or a picture—the Property inspector displays information, or *properties,* about the selected element. Dreamweaver considers a **property** to be an HTML or other Web code characteristic, such as alignment or size, that you can assign to an element in your project.

- Use the Property inspector to make formatting choices and position items precisely on the Web page.

- The properties displayed in the Property inspector depend on the item that is currently selected in the document. The following illustration shows HTML properties for a heading.

Property inspector showing properties for a heading

Expander arrow

- The most common properties are displayed in the panel's fields. If your monitor is large enough, you will see all available fields. On a smaller monitor, you may need to click the **expander arrow** at the lower-right corner of the Property inspector to display additional fields.

Insert Bar and Document Toolbar

- The **Insert bar** (see the following illustration) is a toolbar divided into tabs that contain buttons for creating all sorts of Web page objects. **Objects** are elements you add to a Web page. Forms, images, animation files, sound files, text paragraphs, and so on are objects.

Insert bar showing Common tab

- The Insert bar displays the Common tab's buttons by default. To display buttons for other tabs, click the tab name.

  ✔ *The Insert bar's tabs can also be displayed as a menu by clicking the Options menu at the far right of the toolbar and selecting Show as Menu.*

- To identify a button on the Insert bar, rest the mouse pointer on the tool. Dreamweaver displays the name of the button in a tooltip.

- The Document toolbar (see the following illustration) appears at the top of the Document window directly above the window's contents. The toolbar displays Code, Split, and Design buttons that you can use to toggle between Code view, Code and Design view, and Design view. You will learn more about these and other view options later in the course.

Document toolbar

- The Document toolbar also shows the title of the current page and gives you easy access to tools that enable you to check browser compatibility, preview the page, and modify the display of page content.

- Dreamweaver also offers a Standard toolbar with tools for creating new pages; saving; and cutting, copying, and pasting. This toolbar does not display by default, but it is very useful. If your screen is large enough, you may want to display this toolbar all the time. To display the Standard toolbar, choose the View>Toolbars menu command and click Standard. The following illustration shows the Standard toolbar, located below the Document toolbar.

Standard toolbar

Status Bar

- Every Web page document features a status bar underneath it (see the following illustration) that displays information about the Web page, such as the type of coding it contains, the window size, and how long it takes to download on different kinds of modem and broadband connections.

Status bar

Status bar

- You can click the HTML coding symbols such as `<body>` and `<p>` to select their associated objects on the page.

- The Set Magnification setting enables you to zoom in or out on the page.

- The Window Size list box can be used to change the window size of your Web page.

- The default connection speed at which your Web pages are downloaded by users is 56kbps. You can change the connection speed shown in the status bar by clicking Edit>Preferences>Status Bar and selecting the desired connection speed in the Connection speed list box.

Work with Panels and Panes

- Dreamweaver opens with the panel groups you need to begin creating a Web page. (The panels that you see depend on which panels were open during Dreamweaver's last session and any changes made to the default Preferences settings.)

- A *panel group* contains several related panels. As you see in the following illustration, the Files panel group contains the Files panel, the Assets panel, and the Snippets panel. To switch from one panel to another in a group, simply click the panel's tab.

Files panel group

Expander arrow

- Panel groups can be opened and closed as you require. To open a panel group, click the expander arrow (the small black triangle to the left of the panel name) so that it points downward. To close a panel group, click the expander arrow so that it points to the right.

- You can drag a panel group away from its default location by clicking the ▦ gripper in the panel group's title bar. The mouse pointer becomes a four-headed arrow. Hold down the mouse button to drag the panel group to a new location. If you leave the panel group undocked in the workspace, you have created a **floating panel** group.

  ✔ *Floating panel groups are helpful when you want to view the contents of several panels at the same time.*

- You can return the panel group to its previous position in a pane by dragging it by the gripper until a heavy black bar displays. When you release the mouse button, the panel group docks at the location of the black bar.

- To access additional options for an open panel group, click its ▤ Options menu to display a drop-down menu. Commands on the Options menu always include an option to close the panel group.

- You can give the Document window more room on the screen by hiding the panes that contain panel groups—the pane at the bottom of the screen that contains the Property inspector and the pane at the right of the screen that contains the CSS, Application, and Tag inspector, as well as other panel groups. To show or hide these panes, use the Collapse/Expand button attached to the edge of the pane. This button can be horizontal, like the one ⬛▼⬛ in the Property inspector, or vertical, such as the one for the right panel group pane.

- You can close floating panel groups and the Document window by clicking the ⊠ or ✖ Close button.

- Dreamweaver "remembers" the workspace setup from its last session. If you close panels, they will not display when you next start Dreamweaver. To open a panel that has been closed, select the name of the panel from the Window menu.

- If you work frequently with the same panels and want an easy way to display them, you can save a workspace layout. Open and position the panels where you want them and then choose the Window>Workspace Layout>Save Current menu command. Provide a name for the layout and click OK. The new layout name will appear at the top of the list of default layouts on the Workspace Layout submenu.

  ✔ *Save different workspace layouts for each of the projects you work on so that you have easy access to the panels you need for the project you open.*

Close and Exit Dreamweaver

■ After completing work on a Web page or site, close all open documents and then exit Dreamweaver. You can use File menu commands to close documents and exit the program or use the ☒ Close button in the program's title bar.

Web Design Connection

About Web Design

Web design is the process of creating and arranging Web pages that make up a Web site. Good Web design considers the importance of page content, appearance, usability, and visibility.

Investigate Web Design

Search online to find Web pages with designs that you like and save them as Favorites in your Web browser. Throughout this course, you can return to those pages to see which elements of page design they reflect.

PROCEDURES

Start Dreamweaver

1. Click `start` / 🪟 on the Windows taskbar...........................⊞
2. Click **All Programs**...............Ⓟ
3. Click the folder that contains Dreamweaver.
4. Click **Adobe Dreamweaver CS3**.

Open a Web Page (Ctrl + O)

1. Click 📂 Open... on the Start page.

   OR
   a. Click **File**..................Alt + F
   b. Click **Open**...............Ⓞ, Enter
2. Click the **Look in** arrow......................Alt + I, ↓
3. Select the drive or folder.

   ✔ If necessary, double-click the folder name.
4. Click a file name to select it.
5. Click | Open |.

Open a Panel

■ Click the expander arrow to the left of the panel group name to point downward.

Choose a Different Panel in a Panel Group

■ Click the tab of the panel you want to display in the panel group.

Close a Panel

■ Click the expander arrow to the left of the panel group name to point to the right.

   OR
■ Click the panel group's 🗏 Options menu and click **Close panel group**.

   OR
■ Click **Close** button ☒ in the panel group or inspector.

Move Panels

1. Click the ⠿ gripper in the panel title bar.
2. While holding down the mouse button, drag the panel (or panel group) to new location.

Hide/Show All Panels (F4)

1. Click **View**....................Alt + V
2. Click **Hide/Show Panels**......Ⓟ

Close a Document (Ctrl + W)

1. Click **File**.......................Alt + F
2. Click **Close** ....Ⓒ

   ✔ Click Yes or No as desired if asked to save the document.

Exit Dreamweaver (Ctrl + Q)

1. Click **File**.......................Alt + F
2. Click **Exit**.............................Ⓧ

   OR
■ Click **Close** button ☒ in the Dreamweaver title bar.

EXERCISE DIRECTIONS

1. Start Dreamweaver.
2. Open a Web page as follows:
   - Issue a command to open a file in Dreamweaver.
   - Navigate to the location of the Data files for this course.
   - Open the Lesson01 folder.
   - Open the Exercise1 folder
   - Open the lillysgarden folder.
   - Select and open the ⊙ index.html file.

   ✔ *This Web page is the home page for a Web site under construction. Note that, depending on your computer's settings, you may not see the .html extension.*

3. Locate the following items in the workspace:
   - Document window
   - Menu bar
   - Insert bar
   - Document toolbar
   - Property inspector

   ✔ *If some of these items are not displayed in the workspace, open them from the Window or View menu.*

4. Click in the *Lilly's Garden* heading and view the properties shown for this heading in the Property inspector. Also notice the HTML tags for the heading in the status bar.
5. Collapse the Property inspector and all panels at the right side of the screen.
6. Use the Window menu to open the Property inspector by choosing the Properties command. Use the Collapse/Expand button to redisplay the panels at the right side of the screen.
7. Rearrange the workspace by dragging the Property inspector into the Document window and docking the Files panel at the bottom of the Property inspector.
8. Drag and redock both the Property inspector and Files panel in their original positions.
9. Close the current document without saving it and exit Dreamweaver.

ON YOUR OWN

1. Start Dreamweaver.
2. In the Start page, locate the file you opened in the Exercise Directions, ⊙ lillysgarden/index.html.
3. Explore this simple Web site as follows:
   - On the Document toolbar, locate the button that allows you to preview/debug the current page in the browser.
   - Select your browser from the list.
   - Click the links above and below the text on the page. (The links are functional but they take you to a secondary page instead of additional site pages.)
   - Close the browser when you have finished testing the site.

4. View the different categories of buttons available in the Insert bar.
5. Click in the *About Us* link above the main heading and view the properties for this object in the Property inspector and the status bar.

   ✔ *Note that this and the other links are inserted in table cells. You will learn how to use tables to organize Web page objects in Lesson 4.*

6. Open each of the panel groups in the right pane to see the different information displayed in each.
7. Close the current document and exit Dreamweaver.

Skills Covered

- **Create a New Site**
- **Create Web Pages**
- **View Site Files**
- **Web Design Guidelines**

Software Skills In this exercise, you get ready to create your first Web site in Dreamweaver. Before you create the site and add pages, it is important to set up the Web site properly so you can manage the site easily later in the process.

Design Skills Preparing your tools and planning the outcome of your work is an important first step in any design process. This exercise shows you how to take care of all preparatory steps so you'll be ready to add content to your pages.

Application Skills In this exercise, you set up a site for GardenScape, a landscaping company. You define the site, add multiple Web pages, and use the Files panel to view the files in the site.

TERMS

Browser A program that enables a user to view and move among pages on the World Wide Web. Examples of popular Web browsers include Internet Explorer, Firefox, Netscape, Mozilla, Opera, and Safari.

Home page The first page of a Web site, displayed when a Web site is accessed. The home page typically includes an easy-to-locate navigation panel with links to all main pages on the site.

Remote server A server, such as an FTP or WebDAV server, on which you put or publish your Web site. The remove server is typically the server where the files used to display your Web site are stored.

Wizard An automated process that provides you with the steps for completing a specific program task. (For example, you will use the Site Definition wizard to set up a new Web site in Dreamweaver.)

NOTES

Create a New Site

- When you set up a new Web site in Dreamweaver, you name the site and its folder, select your server, and specify where the site folder will be stored. Dreamweaver provides a **wizard** to walk you through the process. It is important to set up your site properly to ensure that all files used to create your Web site are stored together in the site folder. Otherwise, your site might not display properly.

- Before you begin, you will find it helpful to plan your Web site. Identify the number of pages you need and do a simple sketch to show how the pages are linked and what content they will provide. This sketch will serve as a map as you begin creating your site.

- ✔ Dreamweaver makes it easy to create a simple one-page site or to expand an existing site. You can also create a new site based on an existing site. By thinking through your idea for the site, you will get a sense of how many pages you need, how they are related, and which topics visitors to your site will most want to see.

- The quickest way to define your Web site is to start Dreamweaver and click the [Dreamweaver Site...] option in the Create New column of the Start page. If you are already working in Dreamweaver, click the Site>New Site menu command.

- Either action opens the Site Definition dialog box, shown in the following illustration. By default, the Basic tab is selected. The Basic steps offer the quickest way to set up a new site.

✔ *If you are familiar with site settings and server setup and have the information you need to set up your site, you can click the Advanced tab and enter that information, bypassing the Site Definition wizard. Be sure to check with your instructor before setting up the site using the Advanced settings.*

Site Definition wizard—naming the site

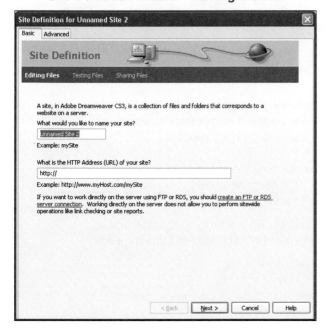

- The first step in the Site Definition wizard occurs on the Editing Files screen. Here you give your site a name in the *What would you like to name your site?* text box. If you know the URL of your site, you can supply it in this dialog box. Then click Next to move to the next screen as you complete your entries.

  ✔ *At any point while you work with the Site Definition wizard, you can click the Back button to return to a previous wizard screen.*

- When you choose a name for your Web site, think about where you intend to publish the Web site. Most Web servers use UNIX-based operating systems and have specific limitations for file names.

- If you know that your ISP or Web server is UNIX-based, remember the following file-naming rules for the site names, page names, and the names used for other objects that the server stores:

  - The underscore (_) is the only special character allowed.

  - No spaces are allowed.

  - UNIX file names are case sensitive. As a general rule, use lowercase for page and other object files.

- Recognizing these rules before designing your site will save you hours of frustration that can result if you use names your server will not recognize.

Select a Server Technology

- In the Editing Files, Part 2 screen, you have the option of selecting a server technology. If your site will feature a Web application such as a form for entering data, you can select the desired server technology to support different kinds of dynamic (interactive) content.

- If you are not sure, select No. You can change this option at any time by editing your site definition.

- If you know the server technology that you will use, select Yes and then select the desired server technology from the drop-down list (see the following illustration).

Selecting a server technology

✔ *Ask your instructor, Web server administrator, or ISP which server technology you should choose for a new site.*

Where to Store Your Web Site

- In the third screen, Editing Files, Part 3, you select how you want to work with your files. You can choose to store your Web folder and files locally on your hard drive and then upload the files to the server when you're ready to publish the site.

- You can also choose to create and edit your Web site directly on the server.

- If you selected a server technology in Editing Files, Part 2, the options you see are slightly different. You can edit and test the site on your local system, edit locally and upload to the server, or edit directly on the server.

- As you are learning Dreamweaver, you will probably want to create your Web site locally before uploading the site to the server.

- A default path is displayed in the *Where on your computer do you want to store your files?* text box (see the following illustration).

Selecting a storage location

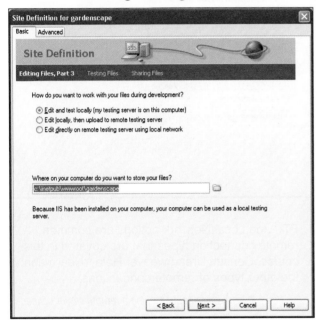

- By default, Dreamweaver will name the folder in which you store your files with the name you entered for your Web site. This folder is also called the *root folder* for the site.

- You can leave this location or choose a new one by clicking the 🗀 Folder button and selecting a new folder in the Choose local root folder for site dialog box.

- If you want to change the default location, click the 🗀 Folder button and navigate to a desired location in the Choose local root folder for site [name of site] dialog box, and then click Select.

- If you select an FTP or RDS server, you will need additional information to set up the FTP host, host directory, login, and password. If needed, ask your instructor, network administrator, or ISP for the required information.

  ✔ *FTP techniques and requirements are discussed in Lesson 8.*

Test Your Web Site

- If you selected a server technology, you will also see the Testing Files screen of the Site Definition wizard. You can select the URL (the Web address your browser uses) to open the Web site for testing purposes.

- The default choice for the URL is the name of the local or remote host and the root folder in which you have stored your files (see the following illustration).

Setting a root URL

- Typically, you will want to keep the URL provided by Dreamweaver. You should also take this opportunity to test it.

- Click the [Test URL] button. If the test is successful, a message box will appear. If it is unsuccessful, you will need to consult with your instructor, network administrator, or ISP to obtain the correct URL, which you can enter in the *What URL would you use to browse to the root of your site?* text box.

  ✔ *If you did not enter an HTTP address for the site in the first Site Definition window, you may receive a warning message that the URL you specify in the Testing Files window does not match the HTTP address. You can ignore this warning while defining the site.*

Select a Remote Server

- In the next screen of the Site Definition wizard, you can select the option for setting up your **remote server** site (see the following illustration). The remote server is the server where your published Web site will be saved so that users can access the site with their Web browsers.

A remote server is where users will browse your site

- In the Sharing Files, Part 2 screen, click the *How do you connect to your remote server?* list box arrow and select the type of remote server that you will use to publish your Web site (see the following illustration).

  ✔ *You may not see the Sharing Files, Part 2 screen if you chose not to use a server technology in the previous step.*

- Many Internet Web sites are stored on FTP servers. Choosing the FTP option displays the screen shown in the following illustration.

- After you enter the appropriate information for an FTP remote site—including any login name and password—test the connection by clicking the `Test Connection` button

- If you selected Local/Network in the *How do you connect to your remove server?* list box, you can enter the file path in the space provided, or click the 🗀 Folder button and navigate to the desired location in the Choose remote root folder for site [name of site] dialog box.

Select your remote server

- FTP and Local/Network options are common remote connection types that are covered in this course. Consult Dreamweaver Help to learn about the other types of remote connections.

  ✔ *You will learn more about making a remote server connection in Lesson 8.*

Check In/Check Out Feature

- In the Sharing Files, Part 3 screen, you make choices about whether to turn on the check in/check out feature. This allows you to set up procedures so that no member of your Web design team can edit a file while another member is editing the same file. This keeps you from accidentally creating multiple versions of the same file. When you select the *Yes, enable check in and check out* option, all team members can see which files are checked out by team members (and also see who is working on the files).

- When you open a file, you can have Dreamweaver check it out to you (this is the default option). In this case, the file is opened on your desktop and you can make changes as needed

- If you simply want to review files (but not edit them), you can choose *I want to view a read-only copy*. Choosing this option doesn't check out the file; rather, you can simply review the file, but not make any changes.

- The *What is your name?* text box records the name you want to be displayed when the file is checked out. You can also add your e-mail address so that other members of the team can communicate with you when a file is checked out to you.

Enabling the check in/out feature

Finish the Site Setup

- The Summary screen in the Site Definition wizard lists the local and remote information about your Web site as well as other options that you have selected (see the following illustration). Review these options and change any if necessary by clicking the Back button to return to the desired tab. If you are finished defining your site, click [Done].

Summary of a newly created Web site

- Your new site—shown as a green folder—is listed in the Files panel in the panel group on the right side of the screen (see the following illustration). The Files panel is where you work with all the files you need as you design your site.

Files panel for the new Web site

Create Web Pages

- Your Web site content appears on documents stored within the Web site. These documents become the Web pages that visitors open when the Web site is published on a Web server.

- You can create new Web pages from the Start page if you have no other pages open in a site. To start a new page, select a type of page from the Create New section. The most common selection is the HTML option. Choosing this selection creates a blank page that uses XHTML to display page elements. Some types of Web content, such as content that changes dynamically based on certain controls on the page, require different selections.

The Dreamweaver Start page

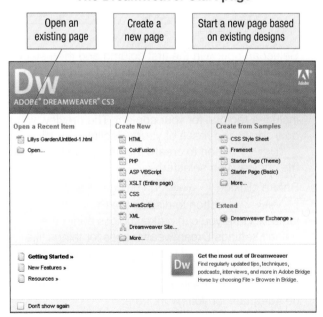

- You can also choose to create a new page based on samples. Samples are like templates in a word processing program. You can create a new page already formatted with a cascading style sheet (CSS), create a frames page, or create a page based on an existing page design.

  ✔ *You will learn more about cascading style sheets and frames pages later in this course.*

- The Start page also gives you the ability to open existing pages you've created in Dreamweaver. To open a page, click it in the Open a Recent Item list or click Open to display the Open dialog box, navigate to the folder containing the page you want, click the file, and click Open.

- When you have a page open in a site, you can create a new page using the File>New command, or you can click the 🖹 New button on the Standard toolbar. The New Document dialog box opens, as shown in the following illustration.

New Document dialog box

- Select an option in the first column and then select the desired page type in the second column. The third column lists a large collection of default CSS layouts. You can choose one to set up a page that includes regions for your content. The preview window shows the result of your selection. You click the [Create] button to create the new page based on the choices you selected.

- Before clicking [Create], you can click the [Preferences...] button to display the Preferences dialog box. Here you can make choices about the default settings Dreamweaver uses for things like font choice, copy and paste options, editing options, and more. For the most part, the default settings in effect when you begin using Dreamweaver should be adequate for your work here.

- Before you begin adding content to a new page, you need to save it. Use the File>Save (or Save As) command to save the new document.

- You can also right-click the untitled document's tab in the upper-left corner of the Document window and select Save or Save As from the shortcut menu.

- The process of saving a document in Dreamweaver is very similar to saving files in any Windows program: Give the new file a name and specify the location where it will be stored and the file type (see the following illustration).

Save new document in site folder

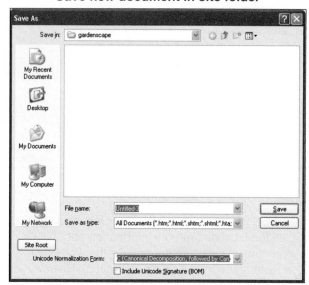

- The Site Root button in the Save As dialog box makes it easy to jump right to the folder that contains your site files. This is especially handy when you are opening an existing file from a location outside your site and saving it to your root folder.

- Note in the previous illustration that Dreamweaver supplies the *.html* extension by default. You can, if desired, change the default extension to *.htm* or to another extension based on the types of pages you create most often.

- After you save a page, the title bar shows the file folder and file name in parentheses.

- As you add pages or open existing pages, each page is opened in a tab in the Document window. Click a page tab to select the page so that you can work with it.

- Many servers expect the home page of a Web site to be named *index.htm* or *index.html*. The Microsoft IIS server can use either *default* or *index* as the file name for the **home page**. To make sure your Web pages are published without error, use the appropriate name for your home pages.

- The home page is the first page that opens in a Web site. This page usually gives general information about the site and includes links to other pages in the site.

- You can designate one of the site's pages as the home page by right-clicking the page in the Files panel and selecting the Set as Home Page command on the shortcut menu.

- As part of the page creation process, you should also give each page a title. A page's title appears in the title bar of the **browser** when the page is opened.

- Use the Modify>Page Properties menu command or the [Page Properties...] button in the Properties inspector to open the Page Properties dialog box. If you don't see the [Page Properties...] button, click the expander in the lower-right corner of the Properties inspector. Click the Title/Encoding category on the left. You can type the page's title in the Title text box (see the following illustration). Or, type the page title right in the Document toolbar's Title box.

Add a page title to a saved document

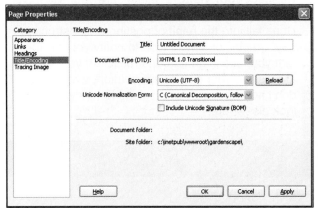

- ✔ Both page names and page titles can be changed later from the Files panel or the Document window.

- To create additional pages for a Web site, use the File>New command to select and create a new, blank document in the New Document dialog box.

  - ✔ You can also use the New button on the Standard toolbar to create the new page.

- If you select Close before you have saved a new page, you will be prompted to save the page if you have made any changes to the page.

View Site Files

- The Files panel gives you easy access to your Web site and its files and folders. The Files panel group also includes the Assets panel, which allows you to track colors, images, and objects used in a site, and the Snippets panel, which provides a variety of small coded programs you can insert in your Web pages.

  - ✔ You will learn more about the Assets and Snippets panels later in this course.

- As you add pages and other files to a Web site, you may need to see a more detailed and expanded view of your site than the Files panel's small window allows.

- Click the Expand/Collapse button in the Files panel's toolbar. It's the button farthest to the right. The expanded, window-sized Files panel window shows the Local Files in the right pane and the server information in the Remote Site pane in the left (see the following illustration).

- To collapse the Files panel window, click the Expand/Collapse button in the window's toolbar.

Expanded Files panel window

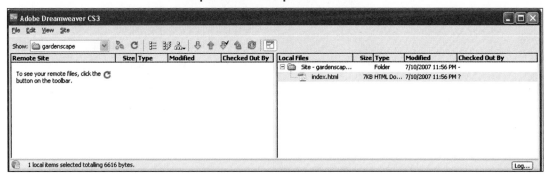

Web Design Guidelines

- Dreamweaver is an application that encourages creativity, and it gives you considerable support and assistance as you work to bring your ideas to life. Before jumping in and starting your site design, however, you may want to consider some design guidelines that can help you turn out professional-quality pages.

  ✔ *This book assumes that you are using Dreamweaver for business and informational sites, but the following design rules apply equally well to less formal content or to personal Web sites.*

- **Know your audience.** Who will be visiting your site? Thinking through what they expect to see—and then surpassing their expectations—will ensure a successful browsing experience for users.

- **Name your pages well.** Search engines pick up the titles you use—the title of your site as well as page titles. Make your titles clear and easy to understand.

- **Be consistent.** Consistency in color, graphics, and placement helps your visitor understand your site.

- **Make your site easy to navigate.** When visitors come to your Web site, they should be able to tell from your home page how to get around your site and find the features they need.

- **Pay attention to connection speed.** If it takes too long to download your Web site, your visitors will not return. Time is valuable, both theirs *and* yours.

- **Keep it simple.** Clean lines and clear, easy-to-read content are features you always should keep in mind when building your site.

- **Be unique.** When you copy another designer's site ideas, you are not only plagiarizing but also limiting your own ideas and site potential.

- **Take it easy.** Resist the temptation to overdo your site by loading it up with large image files or media objects. The more you add, the more you may affect your site download times. And visitors love fast-loading sites.

- **Respect your visitors.** Make sure your site looks professional from the very first moment it is online. Don't fall into the habit of posting a "construction guy" graphic or similar icon to notify your visitors that your site is under construction. If your visitors are visiting your site for information, when they don't find what they are looking for, they likely will look elsewhere.

Web Design Connection

The Importance of Design

A Web site's design can have a huge impact on a visitor's impression of the professionalism and reliability of a business. A well-designed site encourages visitors to stay in the site and use the site's services. A poorly designed site can drive visitors away, resulting in loss of potential sales.

Evaluate Web Page Design

Before you begin creating your site, answering three key questions can help you make choices about the look, feel, and content of your site:

- **Who**: Know who will be visiting your site.
- **What**: Know what the purpose of your site is.
- **How**: Determine how you'll know when you reach the site goals you have set.

Look through some of your favorite Web sites and see whether you can answer these questions. Also, explore some sites that you feel are not designed well to see what they are lacking.

PROCEDURES

Create a Web Site

✔ *Note that the options available in the Site Definition dialog box depend on your system setup and the choices you make related to server technology and remote server options.*

1. Click [⊞ Dreamweaver Site...] on the Start page.

   OR

   a. Click **Site** ....[Alt]+[S]

   b. Click **New Site**..............[N]

2. Click the **Basic** tab if necessary.

3. Type the site name in the *What would you like to name your site?* text box.

4. Type the HTTP address (URL) of the site if you know it.

5. Click [Next >].

6. Select the desired server technology option:

   ■ **No, I do not want to use a server technology** ....[Alt]+[O]

   OR

   ■ **Yes, I want to use a server technology** ....[Alt]+[Y]

   ■ **Which server technology?** ....[Alt]+[W]

   Select the desired server technology from the drop-down list.

7. Click [Next >].

8. Select the desired option for *How do you want to work with your files during development?*

   ✔ *Depending on the option you choose, you may, after clicking Next, skip some or all of the screens used in steps 11–15*

9. Type the path to the root folder in the *Where on your computer do you want to store your files?* text box.

✔ *The server software on your computer may already be recognized (such as Microsoft IIS Web server software), in which case the path will be entered by default and the name of your Web site will be the name of its storage folder.*

OR

Click [📁] to browse to the Web site folder, and click [Select].

10. Click [Next >].

11. Type the URL of your site in the **What URL would you use to browse to the root of your site?** text box ....[Alt]+[W]

    ✔ *If you are using the Microsoft IIS Web server, the URL will be entered by default.*

12. Click [Test URL] to test the URL.

13. Click [Next >].

14. Select the desired remote server option:

    ■ **Yes, I want to use a remote server**...................[Alt]+[Y]

    OR

    ■ **No**..........................[Alt]+[N]

15. Click [Next >].

    ✔ *If you select No, skip to step 18.*

16. Select, configure, and test the desired remote server type if you have that option. Consult Dreamweaver Help for additional information using the remote server type as the index or search keyword(s).

17. Click [Next >].

18. Select the desired check in and check out option:

    ■ **Yes, enable check in and check out**..............[Alt]+[Y]

    OR

    ■ **No, do not enable check in and check out** ....[Alt]+[N]

✔ *If you select Yes, click the desired options and type a name and e-mail address (optional).*

19. Click [Next >].

20. Review the information in the Summary tab and click [Done].

Add a New Web Page (Ctrl + N)

■ On the Dreamweaver Start page, click the type of page you want to create.

   OR

1. Click **File** ....[Alt]+[F]

2. Click **New**............................[N]

3. Click the item that reflects the way you want to start the page.

4. Click a page type in the first column.

5. Click a page option in the Page Type list.

6. Click [Create].

Save a Web Page (Ctrl + S)

1. Click **File** ....[Alt]+[F]

2. Click **Save** ....[Alt]+[S]

   OR

   Click **Save As**.......................[A]

   OR

   a. Right-click the Web page's document tab.

   b. Click **Save** or **Save As**.

3. Type the file name in the **File name** text box ....[Alt]+[N]

4. Click [Site Root] if necessary to go to the current Web site's root folder.

5. Click [Save].

Set a Page Title (Ctrl + J)

- Click in the **Title** box in the Document toolbar and type the page title.

  OR

1. Click **Modify** .... [Alt] + [M]
2. Click **Page Properties** .... [P]

   OR

   Click [Page Properties...] in the expanded Property inspector.
3. Click **Title/Encoding** in the list at the left side of the dialog box.
4. Type the page title in the **Title** text box .... [Alt] + [T]
5. Click [OK].

Select an Open Web Document

1. Click **Window** .... [Alt] + [W]
2. Select the Web document's file name.

   OR

   Click the desired Web document tab in the Document window.

View the Files Panel (F8)

1. Click **Window** .... [Alt] + [W]
2. Click **Files** .... [F]

Expand/Collapse the Files Panel Window

- Click [▣] in the Files panel toolbar.

Set a Home Page

1. Display the Files panel, if necessary.
2. Right-click the file name and select **Set as Home Page**.

EXERCISE DIRECTIONS

✔ *Instructions in this and subsequent exercises assume you will be using the IIS local Web server available for Windows 2000, XP, and Vista. If you are using a different server type, your instructor will supply the necessary instructions for setting up the site.*

1. Start Dreamweaver.
2. Create a new Web site and name it gardenscape using the Site Definition wizard, as follows:

   - Verify that the Web site's local root folder is also named *gardenscape*.
   - Choose not to use a server technology.
   - Choose to edit local copies on your machine and then upload when ready. You should see a path similar to C:\Inetpub\wwwroot\gardenscape\ in the *Where on your computer do you want to store your files?* box.
   - Choose to connect by Local/Network, and store files on the server in the C:\Inetpub\wwwroot\gardenscape\ folder.

   ✔ *Note that the folder in which your files are stored is likely to be different from the one shown here.*

   - Do not enable check in and check out.
3. Use the Start page to create a new HTML page. Save it as index.html in the gardenscape folder.

   ✔ *Make sure that your Web page is saved as an HTML document with an .html extension.*

4. Give the page the title **Home Page**.
5. Create a new blank page of HTML type and name it services.html. Give it the page title **GardenScape Services**.
6. Create a new blank HTML page and name it contactus.html. Give it the page title **Contact Us**.
7. Close the services.html and contactus.html documents and click Yes when prompted to save.
8. View the Web site's files in the Files panel. If you do not see any files in the site, choose **Local view** from the drop-down list to the right of the site name.
9. Expand the Files panel.
10. Set the index.html file as the site's home page.
11. Collapse the expanded Files panel window.
12. Close the index.html page, saving changes if prompted, and exit Dreamweaver.
13. **Optional.** Read the Web Design Guidelines in the Notes section again.

    - Either on your own or with other classmates, use a search engine to locate Web design criteria used by Web design firms.
    - Use appropriate keywords and search engine techniques such as Boolean search strategies to narrow your search.
    - Use the design criteria document that you create for creating your Web sites.
    - Share your results with others via your network or as an e-mail attachment.

ON YOUR OWN

✔ *You will create a new Web site for a local coffee shop. The site is similar to the example pages you reviewed in Exercise 1.*

1. Start Dreamweaver.

2. Create a new site and name it java2go using the Site Definition wizard. Use the same settings you used to set up the gardenscape site.

3. Create a new blank page of HTML type and save it as index.html with the page title **Java 2 Go Home**.

4. Create another new blank HTML page and save it as contact.html with the page title **Contact Information**.

5. View the files in the Files panel.

6. Make the index.html page the site's home page.

7. Save changes to all pages and close them.

8. Exit Dreamweaver.

Skills Covered

- About HTML and XHTML
- HTML Document Structure
- HTML Tags
- Add Keywords to a Web Site
- Enter Text on a Web Page
- Use Paragraph and Heading Tags
- Use Code and Design Views
- Open a Different Web Site

Software Skills If you choose, you can create a Web site in Dreamweaver without ever having to work directly in HTML at all. But any person interested in learning Web design really needs a basic understanding of HTML. HTML skills help you understand what's going on behind the scenes on your pages and give you the ability to better control the styles and attributes of page elements. What's more, with HTML you can add keywords to your pages, which enables people searching on the Web to find your site.

Design Skills Learning HTML basics is essential for a Web designer because it provides the structure on which the rest of your design experience will be based. When you have a working knowledge of HTML, you can confidently (and carefully) work in the code to tweak text, images, and other objects; you can add special effects to elements on your page, and do much more. Understanding HTML gives you flexibility as you create, modify, and enhance the items on your page.

Application Skills In this exercise, you enter text on several pages in the GardenScape site, add keywords to the site, view HTML content, and display pages in different views in Dreamweaver.

TERMS

Attribute A characteristic that is applied to an HTML tag (for example, **align** is one example of an attribute).

Cascading Style Sheet (CSS) A group of formatting instructions that enable you to easily apply formats to specific items on your Web pages.

Closing switch The / character used in a closing HTML tag (such as </strong>).

Closing tag An HTML tag used to indicate the end of an element. For example, </h1> is the closing tag placed at the end of Heading 1.

Code view This is the view that shows HTML code. Dreamweaver can show an entire page of code or show both Code view and Design view on a split page.

Design view This is the default Document window view that shows page content similar to the way it will appear in the browser.

Element The name of an HTML tag.

Head An important section of code on your Web page that contains information browsers need in order to display the document, such as the page title and the character set used to create the page.

HTML (Hypertext Markup Language) The code used to create all Web pages.

HTML tag Formal name for an HTML markup element. HTML tags appear inside angle brackets (<tag>).

Insertion point The blinking vertical line that shows you where text will appear when you begin typing or an object will appear when you create or insert one.

Keywords Words or phrases that describe the site content. Keywords are important because search engines scan and index them, creating the links that bring visitors to your site.

Line break A HTML tag, <br>, that starts a new line but not a new paragraph.

Nest To place one object inside another. HTML tags are often nested.

One-sided tag A type of HTML tag that does not require a closing tag. The
 line break tag is a one-sided tag.

Opening tag An HTML tag that identifies the start of a new element. The opening tag for a paragraph is <p>.

Styles Saved formatting specifications that you can apply to items on your page.

Syntax Rules that govern the use of HTML code and create a connected, orderly system.

Value The precise instruction for the way in which an attribute should function. (For example, the value for the **align** attribute might be **center.**)

Wicket The angle brackets (< >) that surround the HTML tag.

XHTML (Extensible Hypertext Markup Language) The current version of HTML that combines HTML structure with XML power and flexibility.

NOTES

About HTML and XHTML

- **HTML (Hypertext Markup Language)** is a scripting language—or code—you use to create pages that can be viewed with a Web browser. Nearly every item on a Web page—including text, formatting, pictures, and other page elements—is controlled by HTML coding.

  ✔ *In addition to HTML coding, Web pages may also incorporate Java scripts, ColdFusion's CFML code, ActiveX, and other specialized Web page coding designed for different kinds of dynamic or interactive application and content. These codes, too, can be applied and edited in Dreamweaver.*

- Unlike some programming languages, HTML is text-based and easy to read and follow. Even developers with little programming experience can read and generally understand what's happening in HTML code.

- Dreamweaver CS3 supports **XHTML (Extensible Hypertext Markup Language)**. XHTML is a reformulation of the most current version of HTML (HTML 4.0) that uses *XML (Extensible Markup Language)*. XML is a language that uses tags to structure information, similar to HTML. Unlike HTML, however, XML allows you to create your own tags to fit your information more specifically.

- XHTML was developed to answer a need for a stricter version of HTML that could be used to deliver content across a wide variety of devices: not merely computer browsers, but also mobile phones, laptops, PDAs, and so on. XHTML combines the standard HTML structure with the power and flexibility of XML.

- By default, Dreamweaver saves new Web pages as XHTML Transitional documents and applies any code necessary to meet XHTML requirements, such as including an XHTML DOCTYPE declaration in the Head section of the document. You can convert HTML documents to XHTML documents if you choose by using the File>Convert menu command. Converting HTML documents to XHTML Transitional format ensures that the document meets current Web coding standards.

  ✔ *If you are interested in learning more about how Dreamweaver supports XHTML standards, consult the Dreamweaver Help files.*

- The value of using a program such as Dreamweaver is that you do not have to work with HTML, XHTML, or XML in order to create Web content. Dreamweaver automatically applies the correct coding (also known as *markup*) as you select features from its menus and panels.

- As you become more proficient with Dreamweaver, however, you may find that you need to "tweak" the code for a specific page element. Knowing the basics of HTML coding can help you to troubleshoot page display problems and easily modify page elements. The following information gives you a brief tutorial in HTML basics.

HTML Document Structure

- HTML documents have a standard structure that consists of two sections: a Head section and a Body section.

- The **Head** section contains information that browsers need to display the Web page, such as the page title and the character set used to create the page (see the following illustration). None of the information in the Head section appears in the browser except the page title, which displays in the browser's title bar.

- The Body section contains the actual Web page content, such as the page's headings (see the following illustration), paragraphs, and pictures.

Head and Body sections in Dreamweaver Code and Design views

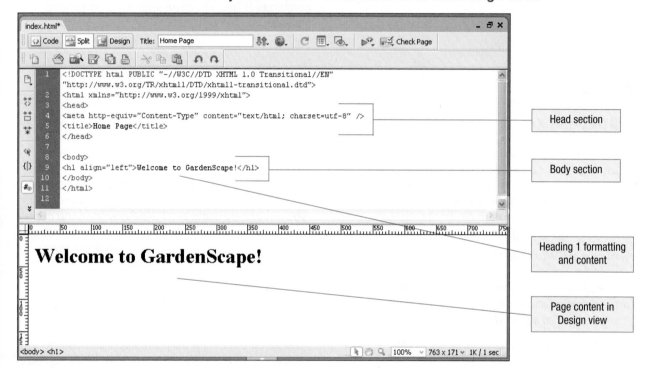

HTML Tags

- HTML coding instructions are delivered to the browser by means of **HTML tags**. As you can see in the preceding illustration, HTML tags have a specific structure, or **syntax**:

  - The first part of an HTML tag is the left **wicket** (<).

  - Next is the tag **element**, or name, such as title or h2.

  - Tag **attributes** may follow the tag element. For example, the align="left" information that follows the h1 tag in the preceding illustration is the attribute that controls the alignment of the text.

  - Last is the right wicket (>).

  - ✓ *HTML tags may be written with all capital letters or all lowercase letters, but lowercase letters are recommended to conform with the latest Web standards. Dreamweaver's tags are all lowercase, so that convention will be used in this book.*

- Most HTML codes require both an **opening tag** and a **closing tag**. The opening tag instructs the browser to begin displaying a format or feature (for example, <title>).

- The closing tag usually has the same syntax as an opening tag, but also contains a **closing switch** (/) before the tag element (for example, </title>).

- Text that appears between an opening tag and a closing tag is affected by that tag. For example, in the following HTML code, the (Heading 1) formatting is applied to a heading:

  ```
  <h1>Welcome to GardenScape!</h1>
  ```

- Tags may be **nested** to supply additional formatting to text. For example, in the following HTML code, the word *three* will appear in italics in the paragraph:

  ```
  <p>We also have <i>three</i> award-
  winning landscape designers on staff!</p>
  ```

  - ✓ *Don't forget the closing switch when nesting tags, or applied formats will not be "turned off."*

- Some HTML tags are **one-sided tags** (also called *standalone* or *empty tags*). One-sided tags do not require a closing tag. The
 (line break) tag is a one-sided tag.

- XHTML coding handles one-sided tags in a special way, by adding the closing switch after the element in the opening tag. To make sure the tag will not cause problems in older browsers that are not XML compliant, a space is inserted before the closing switch. If you create a line break in your text and view the code in Code view, the break tag looks like this: <br />.

Attributes and Values

- Tag attributes modify a tag element by supplying additional instructions to the browser about how to display an element.

- Attributes appear within HTML tags, usually between the tag element and the right wicket. Attributes often include **values** that give specific instructions to the browser. Attribute values are usually enclosed in quotation marks.

- Typically, attributes are not repeated in the closing tag.

- In the following HTML code, for example, the tag element is font. The size attribute tells the browser to display a specific size. The value is "4", and this is the exact size the browser will display.

```
<font size="4">
```

Common HTML Tags

- You can use dozens of HTML tags and attributes to create sophisticated effects on Web pages. The following table lists some of the most common tags.

Tag(s):	Result:
<html> </html>	Sets the page as an HTML document so that its code can be interpreted by the browser software.
<head> </head>	Begins and ends the section that contains information on content, language, and keywords for the page.
<title> </title>	Encloses the Web page's page title. In a browser, the page's title appears in the browser's title bar.
<meta>	Records information about the current page and supplies information such as keywords that search engines use to identify your page. (Does not require a closing tag and appears in XHTML coding as <meta />.)
<body> </body>	Defines the section of the Web page that displays in a browser.
<p> </p>	Begins and ends a paragraph on the Web page.
 	Inserts a line break. (Does not require a closing tag and appears in XHTML coding as .)
<h1> </h1>	Defines the first heading level (Heading 1). Use the same syntax for other heading levels, such as <h2> </h2>, <h3> </h3>, etc.
<b> </b>	Turns on and off bold formatting. Use the same syntax for font styles such as italics: <i> </i>, etc. You may also use the <strong> </strong> tag to apply bold formatting.
<font> </font>	Changes the font of text between the tags; requires an attribute to identify the new font.
<align> </align>	Changes the alignment of text between the tags; requires an attribute (for example, "right") to specify exact alignment.
<ol> </ol>	Begins and ends an ordered (numbered) list.
<ul> </ul>	Begins and ends an unordered (bulleted) list.
<li> </li>	Identifies each item in an ordered or unordered list.
<dl> </dl>	Begins and ends a definition list.
<a> </a>	Identifies a hyperlink; requires the href attribute and a value to specify target of link.
<img> </img>	Indicates location of a picture in a Web page.

HTML vs. CSS

- Today **cascading style sheets (CSS)** are considered the standard for formatting Web pages. Using CSS, a designer can format a page precisely using styles. **Styles** are saved instructions that tell the Web browser how to display the styled element. Styles can be used to format text and headings, tables, blocks of type on a page, and images, and even change the default formats of HTML tags.

- As a result of the widespread use of CSS, many standard HTML tags have been *deprecated* in recent versions of HTML. This means that, although they are still supported by most browsers, they may not be supported for much longer. The <font> tag is one of these tags. In later exercises, when you learn how to validate the markup language in your site, you may be warned that <font> is deprecated and you should instead consider using CSS styles to format text.

- By default, Dreamweaver is set up to create CSS styles for you when you apply formats to text. This means that if you check the code after applying formats to a page, you will not see HTML tags, attributes, and values such as those discussed in previous sections of this exercise. You will instead see CSS style definitions.

- You can change this default setting in the Preferences dialog box so that Dreamweaver will display HTML tags rather than create CSS styles.

- Because it is important for new Dreamweaver users to gain an understanding of HTML tags, you will be directed in Lesson 2 to change the default to display HTML tags rather than CSS styles. You will restore the default setting later in the book, once you are a bit more familiar with Dreamweaver, so you can create and apply CSS styles.

Add Keywords to a Web Site

- To make sure others can find and visit your site, you can supply **keywords** on your pages that search engines use to index a site in their databases. You add keywords to the Head section of a site using a <meta> tag.

- To add a <meta> tag containing keywords to your home page, use the Insert>HTML>Head Tags>Keywords menu command to open the Keywords dialog box (see the following illustration). Here you can type the keywords that summarize your site's subject.

Keywords dialog box

✔ You can also display this dialog box by displaying the Common tab on the Insert bar, clicking the Head button's list arrow, and then selecting Keywords.

- Separate groups of keywords with commas, and use care when selecting them. Some search engines accept only a specific number of keywords and ignore keywords altogether if too many are supplied.

- Clicking the OK button in the Keywords dialog box inserts the keywords as a value for a new <meta> tag in the Head section of the Web page.

Web Design Connection

Use Effective Keywords

One of the most important aspects of creating a new Web site is to identify keywords that will help potential visitors find your site using a search engine. Keyword research is an important strategy for creating a new Web site.

Learn about Keywords

Think about your goals in creating your site. Use the answers you created in the last Web Design Connection to identify five or six words that you think will bring visitors to your site. Use the Internet to search for information using those keywords. What kind of sites do you find? Are the words you identified the ones that will be most effective in bringing people to your site? Revise your list and create a summary report of the top five sites in your topic area. Share your list with others in your group to find out how they might search for your site differently.

Enter Text on a Web Page

■ After you have set up your site and created pages, you are ready to add content. Your pages should contain a balance of text and graphics to make the pages both informative and attractive. You can display rulers on the pages (see the following illustration) so you can easily position content on the page.

■ By default, Dreamweaver displays the rules in pixels (the standard display measurement for on-screen work). If you want to change the measurement to Inches or Centimeters, right-click the ruler and select your choice from the list.

■ A newly opened Dreamweaver document displays a blinking **insertion point** at the top left of the Document window. To enter text on a page, simply begin typing at the location of the insertion point (see the following illustration).

Type text at the insertion point

■ Simply type the text as you would in a word-processing document; there's no need to press Enter at the end of each line. Dreamweaver wraps the text automatically at the right side of the page. Press the Enter key only when you want to start a new paragraph.

> ✔ As a general rule, Web page paragraphs do not have a first-line indent. Dreamweaver does not recognize tabs or spaces at the beginnings of paragraphs.

■ Dreamweaver automatically inserts a line space after a paragraph, so you do not have to double-space between paragraphs as you might do in a word-processing document.

■ If you do not want the default space to appear after a paragraph, you can insert a **line break** rather than a paragraph break.

■ For easy access to the break tag (and other special characters), display the Text tab on the Insert bar, as shown in the following illustration. Clicking the [BR] ▾ button on the Text tab inserts the HTML
 (Break) tag, which creates a new line but not a new paragraph. You can also insert this tag as you type by pressing the [⇧ Shift] + [Enter] key combination.

Tools on the Text tab

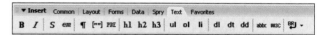

Use Paragraph and Heading Tags

■ You can format the text in a Dreamweaver document with standard HTML paragraph and heading tags that control font style and size.

■ By default, all new text is formatted with the Paragraph format. This format equates to the HTML <p> (Paragraph) tag.

■ You can use the Property inspector or the Text tab on the Insert bar to apply other formats, including six levels of headings and the preformatted font that can be used to display program code (see the following illustration).

Apply text formats with the Property inspector

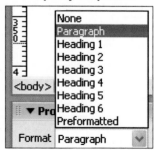

■ Click anywhere in the paragraph you want to format and click the Format list arrow on the Property inspector to display the list of paragraph and heading formats. Or, you can choose the format and then begin typing. The format is applied automatically to the new text.

- Heading levels are ordered from largest (Heading 1) to smallest (Heading 6) (see the following illustration).

HTML heading levels

Heading 1

Heading 2

Heading 3

Heading 4

Heading 5

Heading 6

- The Property inspector does not show font sizes or styles for headings because these formats are specified by the HTML tag for that heading.

Use Code and Design Views

- By default, the Document window displays page content in **Design view**. In Design view, content looks almost identical to the way it will appear in a browser.

- When you switch to **Code view**, the page content's HTML coding appears (see the following illustration). You can write or edit HTML code while working in Code view.

Page shown in Code view

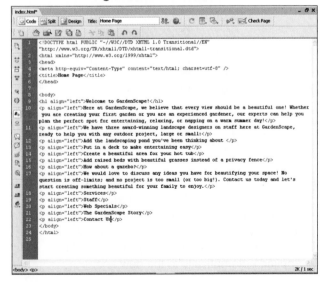

- Switch to Code view using the View>Code menu command, or simply click the ⟨⟩ Code Show Code view button at the far left of the Document toolbar. (The button is labeled Code, but if you hover the mouse pointer over it, you will see a tooltip identifying the button as Show Code view.)

- When you have finished working in Code view, use the View>Design menu command or the Design Show Design view button to restore Design view. (The Show Design view button is labeled Design.)

- Dreamweaver also allows you to display both views in the Document window at the same time so you can see immediately the results of your coding. Use the View>Code and Design menu command or the Split Show Code and Design views button to turn on a display like the one shown in the following illustration. (The Show Code and Design views button is labeled Split.)

Display both Code and Design views

- By default, Code view appears at the top of the window. You can move Design view to the top by clicking the View options button on the right side of the Document toolbar and selecting Design View on Top.

Open a Different Web Site

■ As you work with Dreamweaver, you will probably create a number of Web sites in various folders on your local drive. When you start Dreamweaver, the program opens the last Web site you worked on.

■ You can open a different Web site from the Files panel. Click the drop-down list in the Files panel's toolbar—either in its expanded window or collapsed panel form—and select the desired Web site (see the following illustration).

Click a Web site in Files panel toolbar to open it

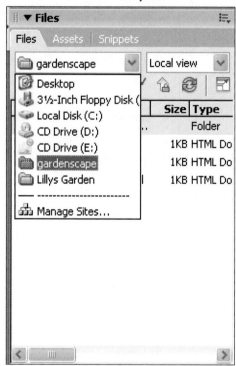

■ When you open a Web site using this method, the Files panel's contents change to the selected site. You can then open pages or other objects directly from the Files panel.

■ You can also use the Manage Sites dialog box, shown in the following illustration, to switch from one site to another. Display this dialog box using the Site>Manage Sites menu command or Manage Sites at the bottom of the Files panel menu.

Choose site to work with

■ You can also use this dialog box to create a new site, edit a site, duplicate a site, remove a site, or export or import a site. You can duplicate a site to create a backup or to save yourself creation time and effort when you are creating a site with a similar layout or identical content.

PROCEDURES

Add Keywords to a Web Site

1. Click **Insert** .... Alt + I
2. Click **HTML** .... H
3. Point to **Head Tags** .... H
4. Click **Keywords** .... K
5. Type keywords in the Keywords dialog box, separating keywords with commas.
6. Click **OK** to save the keywords.

   OR

1. Click the Common tab on the Insert bar.
2. Click the **Head** button ▢ ▾ list arrow and click **Keywords**.
3. Type keywords in the Keywords dialog box, separating keywords with commas.
4. Click **OK** to save the keywords.

Insert a Line Break

- Press ⇧ Shift + Enter at end of a line of text.

   OR

- Click ▢ ▾ on the Text tab of the Insert bar.

Apply a Paragraph or Heading Tag

> ✔ *Click in the paragraph to format the entire paragraph or click to place the insertion point where the new format should begin.*

1. Click the **Format** arrow in the Property inspector.
2. Select a heading level or paragraph format.

   OR

1. Click **Text** .... Alt + T
2. Point to **Paragraph Format** .... F
3. Select a heading level or paragraph format on the submenu.

   OR

1. Click the Text tab on the Insert bar.
2. Click the buttons for the desired heading level or paragraph format.

Display Code and Design Views (Ctrl+`)

To display Design view:

1. Click **View** .... Alt + V
2. Click **Design** .... D

   OR

- Click **Show Design view** button ▢ Design on the Document toolbar.

To display both Code and Design view:

1. Click **View** .... Alt + V
2. Click **Code and Design** .... A

   OR

- Click **Show Code and Design views** button ▢ Split on the Document toolbar.

Open Different Web Sites

In Files panel toolbar:

- Click the drop-down list in the Files panel toolbar and select a site to open.

   OR

1. Click **Site** .... Alt + S
2. Click **Manage Sites** .... M
3. Select a site to open.
4. Click Done .

EXERCISE DIRECTIONS

1. Start Dreamweaver.
2. Switch to the gardenscape site if necessary.
3. Open index.html.
4. Add the following keywords for this site: **landscaping services, garden design**.
5. Display Code view and locate the new <meta> tag in the page's Head section. Also take this opportunity to locate the DOCTYPE declaration at the top of the page that identifies this document as an XHTML 1.0 transitional document.
6. Switch back to Design view and enter the text shown in Illustration A. After you type *Add the landscaping pond you've been thinking about*, insert a line break rather than a new paragraph, and repeat this process after the next four items in the list.

    ✔ *If you prefer not to type the text in the example, open the file gardenscape_text.txt using a text editor (like Windows Notepad) and then copy and paste the text onto the web page. Be sure to add the line break, if needed, after you paste the text.*

7. Display Code and Design view. (Click the Split button.)

8. Apply heading and paragraph formats as follows:

    ▪ On the Property inspector, click the Style list arrow and select None. (This prevents Dreamweaver from creating CSS styles as you format the text.)

    ✔ *You will learn about creating CSS styles later in this course.*

    ▪ Apply the Heading 1 tag to *Welcome to GardenScape!*

    ▪ Apply the Heading 4 tag to *A Few Project Ideas…*

9. In the Code view region of the split document, locate the HTML tags that have been applied to the text you just formatted.
10. Open contactus.html and type **Contact GardenScape** at the top of the page.
11. Apply the Heading 2 tag to the new text.
12. Switch to Design view.
13. Save and close all open pages and exit Dreamweaver.

Illustration A

Welcome to GardenScape!

Here at GardenScape, we believe that every view should be a beautiful one! Whether you are creating your first garden or you are an experienced gardener, our experts can help you plan the perfect spot for entertaining, relaxing, or napping on a warm summer day!

We have three award-winning landscape designers on staff here at GardenScape, ready to help you with any outdoor project, large or small.

A Few Project Ideas…

Add the landscaping pond you've been thinking about
Put in a deck to make entertaining easy
Create a beautiful area for your hot tub
Add raised beds with beautiful grasses instead of a privacy fence
How about a gazebo?

We would love to discuss any ideas you have for beautifying your space! No question is off-limits, and no project is too small (or too big!). Contact us today and let's start creating something beautiful for your family to enjoy.

Services
Staff
Web Specials
The GardenScape Story
Contact Us

ON YOUR OWN

1. Start Dreamweaver.

2. Create a new site using the same settings as the java2go site you created in the On Your Own section of Exercise 2. Name the new site yardart.

3. Create a new page and save it as index.html. Give the page the title **YardArt Home Page**.

4. Type the heading **YardArt Summer Specials!**.

5. Apply the Heading 1 tag to the heading.

6. Create contact.html and save it. Add the page title **Contact Information**.

7. Type the heading **Contact Us**.

8. Apply the Heading 2 tag to the heading.

9. Insert the following text below the heading. Use line breaks when typing the last five items (the artists' contact list).

   We want to hear from you! If you want to place a new order, check on the status of an existing order, or just say hello, contact Julie by clicking here.

If you want to know more about a piece of yard art you've seen on this site, feel free to contact the artists directly, using the links below:

Contact John for sundials
Contact Jo for natural benches
Contact Wendy for wind chimes
Contact Bill for ornamental rock
Contact Lou for waterfalls

10. Add the following keywords on the index.html page: **yard art**, **lawn ornaments**, **landscaping**, **artists**.

11. Use Code view or Code and Design view to locate the new keywords in the Head section of the page.

12. Save and close all pages and exit Dreamweaver.

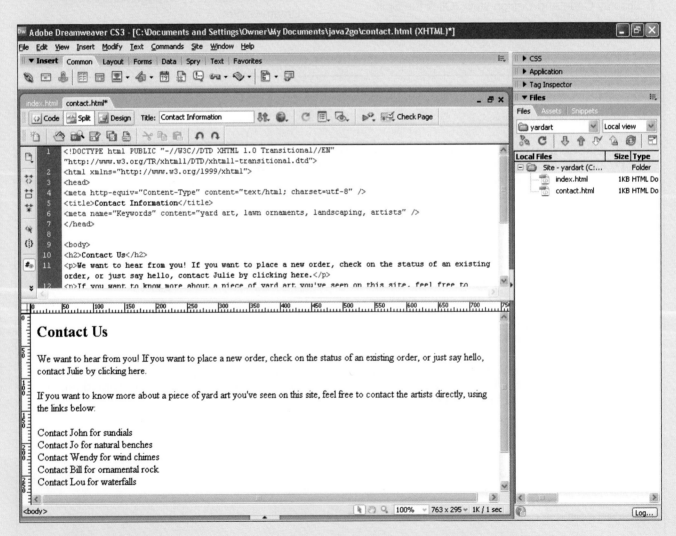

Summary Exercise

Application Skills The director of the Tierra Verde Summer Camp has asked you to design a Web site for campers, parents, and camp counselors. The site will provide information about the camp, including the summer schedule, contact information, camp fees, and permission and health forms. In this exercise, you create the site and add text and keywords for the home page.

DIRECTIONS

1. Start Dreamweaver.
2. Use the Site Definition wizard to create a site using the following settings:
   - Name the site tierraverde.
   - Choose not to use a server technology.
   - Choose to edit and test the site locally using the Windows IIS, if available. Make sure the folder in which to store files is the same as the site name.
   - Test the URL if you are storing your site on the http://localhost site. If you receive a warning about the site URL not matching the HTTP address, you can click OK to dismiss the warning.
   - Choose not to use a remote server.

3. Create a new Web page and save it as index.html. Give the page the title **Tierra Verde Summer Camp**.
4. Make this page the site's home page.
5. Insert the text shown in Illustration A on the next page. Use line breaks when creating the list of camp features.
6. Format the first heading with the Heading 1 format. Format the heading *Camp Features* with the Heading 2 tag.
7. Add the following keywords to the site: **Tierra Verde**, **summer camp**, **camping**, **Tierra Verde Summer Camp**.
8. Check in Code view to make sure you entered the keywords correctly.
9. Save your changes to index.html.
10. Close the document and exit Dreamweaver.

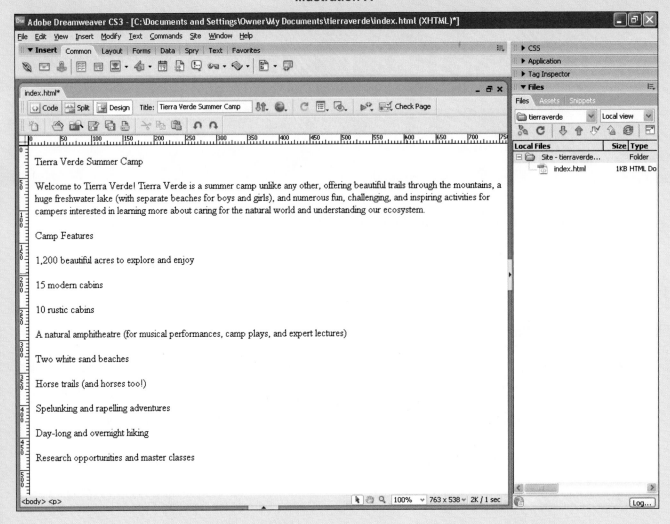

Application Exercise

Application Skills Your Technology instructor has asked you to create a Web site that will serve as a hub to link all your classmates' blogs, Myspace, and Facebook pages. In this exercise, you define a new site called Classmate Connections and create content for the home page and contact page.

DIRECTIONS

1. Start Dreamweaver.
2. Define the new site. Use the site name classmate_connections and use your own judgment about site settings.
3. Create a home page for the site and save it as index.html. Give the page the title **Get Connected!** .
4. Enter the following text on the index.html page:

   Get Connected!

   Lots of your friends are posting text and pictures daily on their favorite blog sites. Find out what's going on and connect with your classmates by using the links on this site.

   Where Do I Start?

   To add your own contact information, click the Add Me link. You can add all sorts of online contact information (no home addresses or phone numbers, please):

   Blog addresses
   MySpace page
   Facebook page
   Flickr page
   AOL IM contact name
   Windows Live Messenger or MSN contact name

   Note: This site is hosted on the school's secure server and can be viewed only by Technology students with the appropriate permissions. Please do not share your user ID and password with anyone. This is for our private use only.

5. Format the two headings (*Get Connected!* and *Where Do I Start?*) with the Heading 2 tag.
6. Create another new blank HTML page and save it as addme.html. Give it the page title **Add Your Contact Info**.
7. Enter the following text on the addme.html page:

   Add Me!

   Adding your online contact information is simple. Here's the process:

8. Type the following, adding a line break at the end of each item in the numbered list:

   First, be sure the instructor has your parent's signature on file, giving you permission to participate in this activity.

   Click the Add My Info button below to display the contact information form.

   In the Name field, add your first name.

   Click the Class Period arrow and choose your class from the list.

   In the Description field, type a brief (25 word) intro, telling us about your interests in technology.

   In the space provided, add the name of each site and the related URL.

   When you're finished, click the I'm Done button.

You will receive notification by e-mail when your information has been added to the site.

8. Format the heading with the Heading 2 format.

9. Add keywords to the index.html page. Use your own judgment about what kinds of keywords would help others find this site.

10. Save and close all open pages.

11. Exit Dreamweaver.

Illustration A

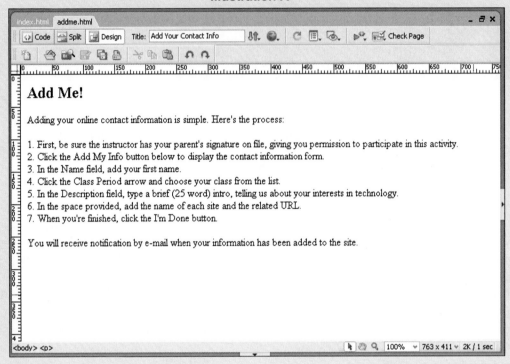

Exercise | 6

Curriculum Integration

Application Skills The English Department at your school is developing a Web site that gives students a way to earn extra credit by practicing their writing skills. You have been asked to design a page that lists and defines the four basic writing styles. Before you begin this exercise, refresh your memory about these terms:

- Descriptive Writing
- Narrative Writing
- Expository Writing
- Persuasive Writing

DIRECTIONS

You can define a new site if desired, or simply create the page in any site and then save it in your Lesson 1 solutions folder.

If you create a site, use your own judgment about what to name the site and what settings to apply to it. Name the page writingstyles.html and give it an appropriate page title.

Add a heading for the page and format it in a style you like.

Type the phrases listed above on the page. Then add a definition for each phrase below the item.

Add a sentence at the end of each definition that gives an example of each writing style.

> ✔ **Extra:** Search for Web pages that reflect the different writing styles and copy and paste the URLs after the definitions. You will learn how to turn the URLs into links later in this course.

Format the phrases with a heading of your choice to make them stand out on the page. View the page in Code view to see the HTML tags applied for the term headings.

Save changes to the page and close it. Exit Dreamweaver.

Critical Thinking

Application Skills In this exercise, you create a Web site for a nonprofit organization in your town. After sketching out the site and getting feedback from your classmates, you define the site and add pages for content.

DIRECTIONS

- First determine the subject of your new Web site. You might want to create a site for any group or organization that focuses on a topic you care about—housing, environmental issues, job training, animal rights, or another kind of advocacy group.

- Next, make a list of the information you want to include in your site.

- Sketch a quick diagram showing the pages that will be required to present that information.

- Before you create the site, trade your diagram with a classmate and ask him or her to critique your Web page design using the guidelines for effective page design you developed in Exercise 1. Incorporate any suggestions you think are important.

- Create the new site with an appropriate site name and site settings.

- Create a basic HTML page that will be the home page of the site. Name it index.html and give the page an appropriate page title.

- Come up with a list of keywords that will help visitors find your site. Add those keywords to the page.

- Enter text on the index.html page that introduces the organization and gives some information about it. Insert headings as necessary to separate areas of text and format them with appropriate heading tags.

- Add another page to the site from your site diagram and save it with an appropriate name and title.

- Enter text on the new page and format any headings with heading tags.

- Save all open documents and close them.

- Exit Dreamweaver.

Lesson | 2

Work with Web Page Text and Links

Skills Covered

- Insert Text from Office Documents
- Modify Font Formats
- Insert Special Characters
- Check Spelling
- Find and Replace Text
- Save Edits

Software Skills Depending on the type of site you are creating, text is likely to be the most important aspect of your Web page content. You can type your site content directly onto the page, or you can import or copy text from other documents. Once you enter the text, you use formatting to ensure that your text is both easy to read and attractive. Be sure to use the spelling checker and find and replace features to make sure text is correct and accurate.

Design Skills Text plays an important role in the overall design of your site. The look of the text—including the font, style, and size you select—all help to convey a certain tone to your site visitors. Further, the spacing you use around text elements helps contribute to the readability of your site.

Application Skills In this exercise, you will add site content to the GardenScape site by importing and copying text, modifying font formats on several pages, inserting special characters, checking the spelling, and using Find and Replace to locate and change text on a page.

TERMS

Font A specific design of type (also referred to as a *typeface*) .

Font combination Also referred to as a *font family,* a collection of fonts that can be applied to text on a Web page. The browser will display the first font listed in the collection, and if the user's system doesn't have that particular font, the second font is substituted, and so on.

Font style A format applied to a font to change its appearance, such as **bold** or *italic.*

Points A common measurement used for fonts. There are 72 points in one inch.

Sans-serif A type of font in which strokes do not appear at the end of the characters.

Serif A kind of font in which strokes appear at the end of the characters.

Typeface A specific family of type that includes alphabetic characters, numerals, and punctuation marks.

NOTES

Insert Text from Office Documents

■ Although you can type all the text you need for your Web site's pages, you have another option for adding text to pages: You can insert text from Microsoft Office Word or Excel.

■ The Word or Excel document you use can be in its native format—.doc or .docx for Word, .xls or .xlsx for Excel—or saved in HTML format.

■ The method you use to insert the text depends on the format in which the document is saved. The sections that follow explain more about that.

Importing or Copying Office Text

■ The easiest way to insert Office text in a Dreamweaver page is to use the File>Import>Word Document or File>Import>Excel Document menu command. This command displays the Import Word Document or Import Excel Document dialog box, where you can navigate to the location of the Word or Excel document you want to insert.

■ Word text inserted this way is imported into the current page, and its text is converted to HTML text indistinguishable from other HTML text on the page.

■ Excel spreadsheet text inserted this way displays on the Dreamweaver page in tabular format that can be edited just like any other tabular material you might create using Dreamweaver's table tools.

■ You can also insert Office document text using the Copy and Paste commands. Copy the Word text or Excel spreadsheet data and then use one of the following Paste options:

  ■ Use Edit>Paste to convert the pasted text to HTML format, the same as when importing a Word or Excel file.

  ■ Use Edit>Paste Special to open the Paste Special dialog box shown in the following illustration.

Paste Special dialog box

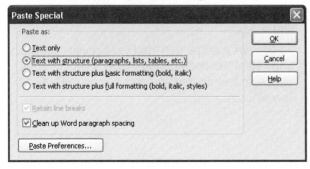

■ Use the options in this dialog box as follows:

  ■ Text only pastes the copied material as basic text. Excel data pastes as a block of text without any tabular organization.

  ■ Text with structure pastes the copied material with its basic paragraph or spreadsheet structure in place.

  ■ Text with structure plus basic formatting pastes the copied material with structure plus any bold or italic formatting that has been applied.

  ■ Text with structure plus full formatting pastes the copied material with structure and all applied formatting, such as font color or cell fill color.

■ If both the Office document and the Dreamweaver page are open on the screen at the same time, you can simply select the content you want to use and drag it from the Office document onto the Dreamweaver page. This moves the content from the Word document to the Dreamweaver page and gives you the same result as using the Text with structure plus full formatting option.

  ✓ *If you want to copy the content (instead of moving it), press and hold Ctrl while dragging the Word or Excel information to the Dreamweaver page.*

Create a Link to an Office Document

■ Another method of inserting Office information into a Dreamweaver page is to drag the file itself from an application such as Windows Explorer or the Dreamweaver Files panel onto the Dreamweaver page.

■ After you drag file icon to the page and release the mouse button, Dreamweaver displays the Insert Document dialog box, shown in the following illustration.

Insert Document dialog box

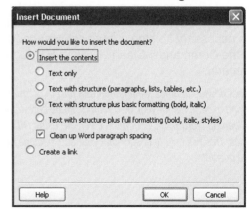

- The Insert Document dialog box gives you two ways to add the file to your page. You can choose to insert the contents of the file and select one of the four options (the same ones you saw in the Paste Special dialog box).

- You can choose instead to create a link to the Office document. This choice places a link on the page where you "dropped" the file. The link text is the same as the file name.

- If the Office document is not already stored in the site folder along with the other site files, Dreamweaver will let you know and ask whether you want the program to copy the file there.

- It's important that all files associated with the site be in the site folder; otherwise, the file will not be available when a visitor clicks the link.

- Being able to link other files to your Web pages means that you can easily include on your Web site information in formats other than HTML. For example, you could include a Word or PDF version of a form for people who prefer to print and mail a form rather than complete it online.

Opening Office HTML Files

- All Microsoft Office applications include the capability to save documents in HTML format. A user can, for example, create a Word document or Excel workbook and save it as an HTML file that will display in a browser the same as any page created in Dreamweaver.

- Office files that are saved in HTML format can be opened in the same way as any Dreamweaver page, using the File>Open menu command. Office HTML files are opened as complete pages, rather than being inserted on an existing page, as is the case with importing or copying.

- The pages you open this way take their file names (and page titles, for Word files) from the original HTML page, but you must still save the new page as part of the site.

- Word HTML pages may contain coding that is not necessary in Dreamweaver, making the files larger than necessary. To strip out unnecessary codes, use the Commands>Clean Up Word HTML menu command.

  ✓ *Fast download times are an important part of creating a good experience for your Web visitors, so be sure to use the Clean Up Word HTML command if you are using Office HTML files. This will help to ensure that your site loads as quickly as possible.*

- The Clean Up Word HTML dialog box (see the following illustration) shows the steps Dreamweaver takes to streamline the Word code.

Clean Up Word HTML dialog box

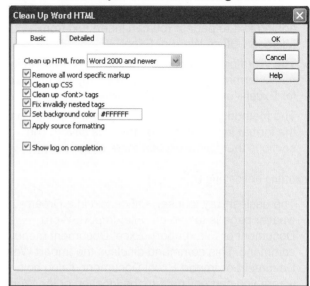

- After the cleanup has been completed, Dreamweaver displays another dialog box to show you what cleanup operations it has undertaken (see the following illustration).

Results of cleanup operations

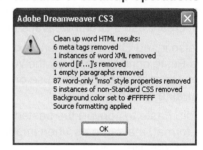

- When you add a page that has been created in another program, such as a Word HTML page, it is a good idea to convert the code to the version of XHTML being used in the site. This ensures that all the pages in your site meet the current coding standards.

- To convert a page, use the File>Convert command and select the code option you're using for other pages. In this course, the standard is XHTML 1.0 Transitional.

Modify Font Formats

- Text you type in a Dreamweaver document is formatted with a default appearance, including the **typeface**, size, and color (black). A typeface is a set of alphabetic, characters, numbers, and punctuation marks in a specific design. Dreamweaver also applies a default style (Paragraph). You can change text typeface, size, style, and color using tools in the Property inspector.

- Text that you drag and drop from an Office document onto your Dreamweaver page will retain the format it has in the Office document if Dreamweaver uses the same fonts. If the font used in the Office document is not used in Dreamweaver, the program will substitute a default font.

  ✔ *The Property inspector provides you with a fast way of changing font settings, but you can also use commands on the Text menu to apply formats. Keyboard shortcuts are also available for some settings.*

- Changing a font format involves selecting the text you want to change, clicking the arrow of the item in the Property inspector, and clicking a new setting. For example, you might select text on your page, click the Format arrow in the Property inspector and click Heading 1. A new set of font formats is applied to the selected text.

- Each time you apply font formats to text, Dreamweaver creates new cascading style sheet (CSS) styles by default. This feature gives you a list of CSS styles that you can then easily apply elsewhere in your site, but it can be confusing for first-time Dreamweaver users. If you would prefer to use regular HTML formatting instead of CSS styles, click Edit>Preferences and click the Use CSS instead of HTML tags option to clear the checkbox. Click OK to save your change.

Select New Font Combination

- A **font** is one particular design of type. When you first enter text in a Dreamweaver document, it is formatted with the current default font, usually Times New Roman.

  ✔ *You can change the default font using the Edit>Preferences command.*

- You can specify a new **font combination** using the Property inspector's font list (see the following illustration). The first font in each combination is the font that will be displayed first. If the user's browser does not support that font, the browser will substitute the next font in the combination, and so on.

Apply new font combination

✔ *At the end of each font combination in the list, you see the term **serif** or **sans-serif**. A serif font is one in which small strokes appear at the ends of the character. Times New Roman is one example of a serif font. A sans-serif font does not have the strokes. Serif fonts are typically used in print publications, and sans-serif fonts are often used online. Designers feel that sans-serif fonts (such as Verdana or Arial) are easier to read on low-resolution displays.*

- To apply a new font combination to an existing text, select the text and then click the Font arrow on the Property inspector to display the available font combinations. Click a combination to apply it to the selected text.

- You can also apply a font combination before typing text. After the new combination is selected, all text you type will use that combination.

Add Fonts to the Font List

- By default, the Dreamweaver font list offers only a few popular fonts that display well in most browsers. You can, however, add fonts to the list using the Edit Font List option at the bottom of the Property inspector's font list (or click Text>Font>Edit Font List).

- When you select this command, the Edit Font List dialog box opens (see the following illustration), showing the current font list and the fonts available in your system's Font folder.

Edit Font List dialog box

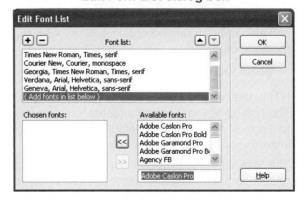

- Select a font from the Available fonts list and click the ⎣<<⎦ button to add it to the Chosen fonts list. It will then be available in the font list of the Text menu and in the Property inspector.

Apply Font Styles

- Font styles apply text effects to change the appearance of a font. Font styles add emphasis to text so that it stands out from surrounding text.

- The font styles used most often are **bold** and *italics*. You can easily apply bold or italic formatting (or both formats) to selected text using the ⎣B⎦ Bold or ⎣I⎦ Italic button on the Property inspector. These styles can also be applied from the Text category on the Insert bar.

- These font styles can also be turned on before you type text. Click the appropriate button on the Property inspector and begin typing. The font style will be applied to the text you type.

Change Font Size

- Font sizes are measured in points when they are used in a regular text document (such as a word processing document). There are 72 points to a vertical inch. This means that if you want to create a heading on your Web page with characters that are one inch tall, you would use 72-point text.

- You can choose a different font size for selected text by highlighting it and clicking the Size arrow in the Property inspector to display the list of available font sizes. Click the size you want to apply. Alternatively, you can change the size first and then start typing. The text you enter will appear in the size you selected.

- By default, Dreamweaver displays the font size options used in CSS formatting, shown at left in the illustration in the next column. If you have chosen to display HTML tags rather than CSS tags, you will see the font size options shown at the right.

- CSS font sizes look more like those available in a word processing program, and you can specify units of measurement such as pixels or points. You can also select a relative option such as x-small, medium, or large.

  ✔ *You will learn more about CSS font options in Lesson 5.*

- HTML tags use font sizes that range from 1 to 7. The default size is 3, which equates to a regular font size of 12 points. The default font size is shown in the Property inspector as None.

- The Size list in the Property inspector also includes relative font size measurements you can apply to selected text to increase or decrease the text size.

Choose new font size

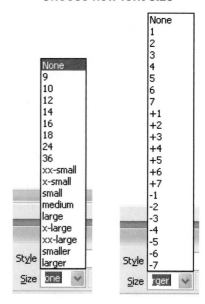

- Sizes marked with a + sign (such as +3) increase the font size by increments from the base font size (default is 3), no matter what size the text is currently. Sizes marked with a - sign (such as -2) decrease the font size by increments.

- If text is size 2, for example, applying the +2 relative font size increases the text size to 5 (not size 4), because the +2 is "added" to the default font size of 3.

- You can also select HTML font sizes by using the Text>Size menu command. Select a size from the list to apply it. To apply relative font sizes by using the menu commands, select Text>Size Change.

  ✔ *Many of the text formatting commands you use may also be available when you select and right-click the text you want to change. To apply a formatting command, click the one you want in the displayed list.*

Apply Font Color

- Black is the default text color in Dreamweaver. Black text provides the greatest contrast to most light-colored backgrounds and thus is easiest for visitors to read.

- To add visual interest to a Web page, you can select a new color for text using the Text Color selector in the Property inspector.

- Click the ⎣▾⎦ Text Color button on the Property inspector to open a palette of colors that will display properly in a browser (see the illustration on the next page). Click on the desired color.

Select new font color in Dreamweaver

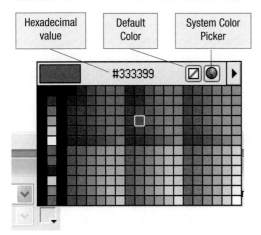

Hexadecimal value | Default Color | System Color Picker

- Click the ☑ Default Color button to restore the page's default text color (usually black). You can change color palettes by clicking the right-pointing arrow in the palette and selecting a palette such as Continuous Tone.

  ✔ Only the default Color Cubes and Continuous Tone palettes are considered Web-safe; that is, colors selected from these palettes will display correctly in any browser.

- Each color in the Text Color palette has a hexadecimal—six-digit number—value. If you know the hexadecimal value of a color, you can type it directly in the text box to the right of the Text Color button on the Property inspector.

- To create a custom color, click the ⊙ System Color Picker button to open the Color dialog box. However, it is best to use only Web-safe colors for creating your Web site, even though the latest browsers can support a vast array of color ranges.

Insert Special Characters

- As you create your Web page text, you may need to use special characters such as em dashes (—), copyright symbols (©), currency symbols (£), or foreign language characters (¿).

- Common special characters are listed on the drop-down menu that appears when you click the 🔲 ▾ Line Break button in the Text category of the Insert bar. If you don't see the character you need, click Other Characters at the bottom of this list to display the Insert Other Character dialog box.

  ✔ The button on the Insert bar will change to show the last character you used, so you may see a button other than the Line Break button in this position on the Insert bar.

Insert a special character

BRJ ▾
BRJ Line Break (Shift + Enter)
⬇ Non-Breaking Space
" Left Quote
" Right Quote
— Em Dash
£ Pound
€ Euro
¥ Yen
© Copyright
® Registered Trademark
™ Trademark
⟦⟧ Other Characters

Web Design Connection

Choosing Text Color

The color of text you display on your pages has a lot to do with how readable your text will be for site visitors. For best results, choose a color that contrasts well with the background color. For example, choose a light text color such as yellow if it will appear on a dark background such as blue.

Experiment with Text Color Contrast

Use the Internet to search for information on how to find the right mix of text and background colors for your site.

Hint: A free online utility for contrasting text and background colors can be found at http://markup.co.nz/colorPicker/back_to_font.htm

Check Spelling

■ After you type a paragraph or a small section of text on your Web page, check your spelling. Even though you may be certain that you haven't misspelled anything, it is easy to miss typos in text you've typed. Running the spelling checker enables you to be sure that your text is as accurate as possible.

■ Use the Text>Check Spelling command to launch the spelling checker. If the spelling checker finds spelling errors on the page, it lists alternatives you can choose to correct spelling (see the following illustration).

Check document spelling

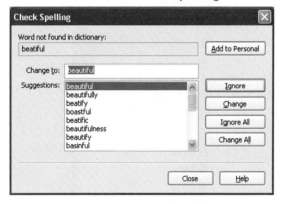

■ Use the Add to Personal button to add proper names or other terms from your site to the dictionary so they will not be flagged as errors in the future. Choose Ignore or Ignore All to skip words you know are not misspelled.

■ To correct a misspelling, click the word in the Suggestions list that reflects the accurate spelling of the word. Click Change to change only that occurrence of the word or click Change All to replace all occurrences of that word with the word you selected.

■ You can quickly check the spelling of a specific word or phrase by highlighting the text you want to check and pressing ⟨⇧ Shift⟩ + ⟨F7⟩.

Find and Replace Text

■ You can use the Find and Replace feature to locate and change text and tags on the current page or throughout your site. For example, you could use Find and Replace to change all occurrences of a product name on your site. When used to find and replace text, this feature works much the same way as it does in a word processing program.

■ In the Find and Replace dialog box (see the illustration at the bottom of the page), first choose where you want to search, and then choose to search for text, type the text to find, and type the replacement text. Click Find Next to locate the first occurrence of the text you've entered. When Dreamweaver finds the text, click Replace to insert the new text.

■ If you know you want to find and replace all instances of a text phrase in your site, you can do it all at once by clicking Replace All. Dreamweaver finds all occurrences and replaces them without any further action from you.

■ The options at the bottom of the Find and Replace dialog box enable you to fine-tune the search process. Match case will find only those phrases with the same capitalization as the Find text; Ignore whitespace (selected by default) finds a phrase whether it includes spaces or not; Match whole word locates only those phrases that are complete words; and Use regular expression enables you to use search operators (for example, ? or *) in the Find text.

■ This dialog box also offers a Text (advanced) setting that enables you to search for text that is either inside a specified tag or not inside a tag. This gives you some additional control over which instances of text to find and replace.

■ In addition to finding and replacing text, this feature gives you the option of finding and replacing specific tags and their attributes. You will learn more about this option later in the course.

Find and replace text

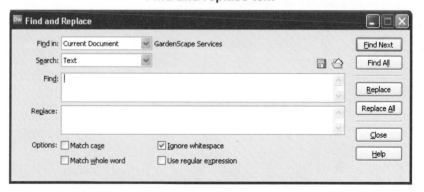

Save Edits

■ Remember to save your work regularly as you enter and format text. This guards against computer or power failures, and just might save you from losing hours of work. Use the File>Save command on the menu bar, press the shortcut [Ctrl]+[S], right-click the document tab and click Save, or click the [icon] Save button on the Standard toolbar to save the page. Make a habit of using one of these methods frequently.

   ✔ *Display the Standard toolbar by right-clicking the Document toolbar and selecting Standard, or by clicking View>Toolbars>Standard.*

■ Use the Save All command—in the File menu, document tab shortcut menu, and Standard toolbar—to save all the pages open in Dreamweaver at once when you have made a series of changes to multiple pages.

■ Dreamweaver displays an asterisk after a page name in the Dreamweaver (or Document) window title bar if changes have been made since the last save. An asterisk will also be visible in the document tab.

PROCEDURES

Import Office Text

1. Click **File** .... [Alt]+[F]
2. Click **Import** .... [I]
3. Click **Word Document** .... [W]
   OR
   Click **Excel Document** .... [E]

   ✔ *Note that you must be in Design view in order for the Word Document and Excel Document commands to be available.*

4. Navigate in the Open dialog box to the location where the file is stored.
5. Click the file name and click [Open].

Copy Office Text
(Ctrl + C, Ctrl + V)

1. Open an Office document, such as a Word document or an Excel worksheet.
2. Select desired information.
3. Click **Edit** .... [Alt]+[E]
4. Click **Copy** .... [C]
5. Switch to Dreamweaver and position the cursor where the copied information should appear.
6. Click **Edit** .... [Alt]+[E]
7. Click **Paste** .... [P]
   OR
   a. Click **Paste Special** .... [S]
   b. Choose an option to paste **Text only**, **Text with struc-ture**, **Text with structure**

plus **basic formatting**, or **Text with structure plus full formatting**.
   c. Select **Retain line breaks** when using the **Text only** option to maintain separate rows of data.
   d. Select **Clean up Word para-graph spacing** to remove extra spaces between Word paragraphs.
   e. Click [OK].

Create a Link to an Office Document

1. Display the file you want to link in a program such as Windows Explorer, and if necessary, arrange the screen so that Windows Explorer and Dreamweaver are both in view.
2. Drag the Office file icon from the file list to the Dreamweaver page.
3. In the Insert Document dialog box, choose **Create a link**.

   ✔ *Click **Insert the contents** in this dialog box to copy file contents at the insertion point. You can then select one of the pasting options described for Paste Special in the previous set of instructions.*

4. If the current page has not been saved, Dreamweaver prompts you to save the file. Click [OK] and save the file.

5. A message box lets you know the file is outside the root folder of your site. Click Yes to copy the file to the root folder.
6. In the Copy File As dialog box, choose the folder for the file and click [Save].

Open Office HTML Files

1. Click **File** .... [Alt]+[F]
2. Click **Open** .... [O]
3. Click the **Look in** arrow .... [Alt]+[I], [↓]
4. Select the drive or folder where the file is stored.

   ✔ *If necessary, double-click folder name.*

5. Click the file name to select it.
6. Click [Open].

Clean Up Word HTML

1. Click **Commands** .... [Alt]+[C]
2. Click **Clean Up Word HTML** .... [U]
3. Click [OK] to run the clean-up operation.
4. Click [OK] to close the information dialog box.

Convert HTML to XHTML Code

1. Click **File** .... [Alt]+[F]
2. Click **Convert** .... [V]
3. Click the code option you want to convert the file to, such as XHTML 1.0 Transitional.

Display HTML Formatting Tags (Ctrl + U)

1. Click **Edit** .... Alt +E
2. Click **Preferences** .... P
3. In the General settings, deselect **Use CSS instead of HTML tags**.
4. Click OK .

Select New Font Combination

Select the text or position the cursor.

1. Click the **Default Font** list arrow in the Property inspector.
2. Select a new font combination.

OR

1. Click **Text** .... Alt +T
2. Click **Font** .... N
3. Select a new font combination on the submenu.

Add Fonts to the Fonts List

1. Click **Text** .... Alt +T
2. Click **Font** .... N
3. Click **Edit Font List** .... E

OR

Click **Edit Font List** on the Property inspector's font list.

4. Choose a font from **Available fonts** list.
5. Click `<<`.
6. Click OK .

Apply Font Style

Select the text or position the cursor.

- Click **Bold** button **B** on the Property inspector to apply bold formatting.
- Click **Italic** button *I* on the Property inspector to apply italic formatting.

OR

1. Click **Text** .... Alt +T
2. Click **Style** .... S
   Click **Bold** .... B
   Click **Italic** I

   ✔ *Or click another font style on the submenu.*

OR

- Press Ctrl +B for **bold**.
- Press Ctrl +I for *italic*.

Change Font Size

Select the text or position the cursor.

1. Click the **Size** list arrow in the Property inspector.
2. Select a new size.

OR

1. Click **Text** .... Alt +T
2. Click **Size** .... Z
3. Select the size on the submenu.

OR

1. Click **Text** .... Alt +T
2. Click **Size Change** .... H
3. Select the size on the submenu.

Apply Font Color

Select the text or position the cursor. where the new font color should take effect.

1. Click **Text Color** button in the Property inspector to display the Web-safe color palette.
2. Click the color you want in the color palette.

OR

- Type the exact hexadecimal value for the color you want in the text box to right of the Text Color button.

OR

1. Click **Text** .... Alt +T
2. Click **Color** .... R
3. Select the color you want or create it in the Color dialog box.
4. Click OK .

Insert Special Characters

1. Position the cursor where you want the character to appear.
2. Display the Text Insert bar.
3. Click list arrow to right of  Characters.
4. Select the desired character on the drop-down list.

OR

a. Click **Other Characters** on the drop-down list to display the Insert Other Character dialog box.
b. Click the desired character.
c. Click OK .

Check Spelling (Shift + F7)

1. Click **Text** .... Alt +T
2. Click **Check Spelling** .... K
3. Review each flagged word:
   - Click Ignore or Ignore All to skip words.
   - Click Change or Change All to replace incorrect words with correct ones.
   - Click Add to Personal to add terms to your personal dictionary.
4. Click OK to end spelling check.

Find and Replace Text (Ctrl + F)

1. Click **Edit** .... Alt +E
2. Click **Find and Replace** .... F , Enter
3. Select the location you want to search: **Selected Text**, **Current Document**, **Open Documents**, **Folder**, **Selected Files in Site**, or **Entire Current Local Site**.
4. Select what to search for: **Source Code**, **Text**, **Text (Advanced)**, or **Specific Tag**.
5. Type the text to search for in the **Find** box.
6. Type the replacement text in the **Replace** box.
7. Click Find Next to find the first instance.
8. Click Replace to replace the text with replacement text.

OR

a. Click Find All to display all instances in a panel below the Property inspector.
b. Click Replace All to replace all instances at once.

EXERCISE DIRECTIONS

1. Start Dreamweaver and open the Preferences dialog box from the Edit menu. In the General settings, deselect *Use CSS instead of HTML tags.* Click OK.

2. Open the gardenscape site and then open services.html. You need to add some text to this page:
   - Position the cursor at the beginning of page.
   - Import the ⊙newtext.doc Word document in the Lesson 2 Data files folder.
   - Insert the em dash special character after *in the city* in the *You won't find a team like this anywhere in the city* sentence. (See Illustration A, which shows the top portion of the completed page.)
   - Delete the extra character space that follows the em dash you inserted.

3. Make the following formatting changes to index.html:
   - Change the color of the *Welcome to GardenScape!* heading to the green with the hexadecimal number #339933.
   - Change the font of the *A Few Project Ideas…* heading to the combination that begins with Georgia. Change its color to the dark blue with the hexadecimal number #000099.
   - Change the size of the first paragraph on the page to Heading 4.
   - Italicize the word *three* in the second paragraph.

4. Open contactus.html. Change the font combination for the heading to the one that begins with Georgia and change its color to the dark teal with the hexadecimal number #009999.

Illustration A

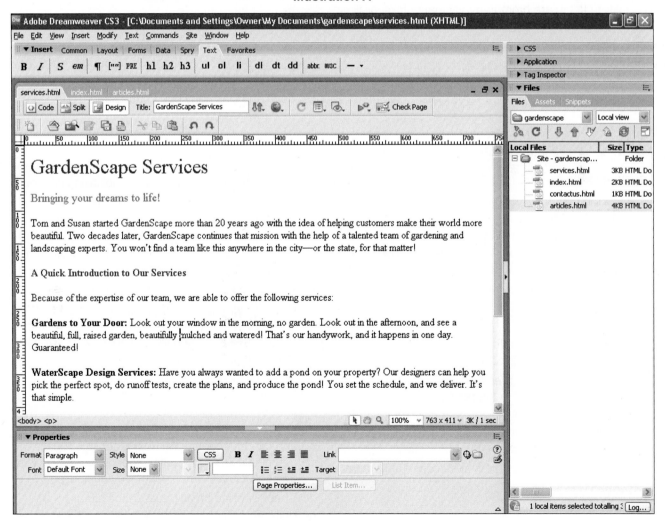

5. Return to services.html. Make the following formatting changes:

- Change the size of the *GardenScape Services* heading to +3. Give it the color #000099.
- Apply the size of +1 to *Bringing your dreams to life!* Change its color to the green #339933.
- Make the heading *A Quick Introduction to Our Services* bold. Color it #000099.
- Boldface each of the following phrases: *Gardens to Your Door:, WaterScape Design Services:, GardenScape Lawn Care:*, and *GardenScape TLC Packages.*
- Adjust the line spacing between paragraphs so your page resembles Illustration A.

6. Open ⊙ articles.html from the data files folder.

   ✔ This is an HTML document created in Microsoft Office Word.

7. Save the articles.html page to your gardenscape folder as articles.html with the page title **Expert Articles**. (Be sure to use Save As to save the page, or you will overwrite the page in the data folder.) If you are prompted to Update Links, click Yes.

   ✔ Click the Site Root button in the Save As dialog box to quickly open the gardenscape folder.

8. Clean up the Word HTML tags (accept default settings).

   ✔ After you clean up the page, you will still see a dotted line border around the text that indicates it is enclosed in <div> tags. You will remove the unnecessary tags in a later exercise.

9. Convert the page to XHTML 1.0 Transitional code. Click OK in the message about not being able to fix the Style tags. You will remove these tags in a later exercise.

10. Format the articles.html page as follows:

- Format the *Articles!* heading the same way as the contactus.html heading.
- Scroll down and select the word *Note:*.
- Boldface the word.
- Select the three lines listing the landscaping associations (beginning with *American Nursery…*).
- Italicize the associations.

11. Check your spelling on all pages of the site and correct any errors you find.

   ✔ You can add GardenScape to your personal dictionary.

12. Use Find and Replace to replace the word *Discouraging* with the phrase **Dealing with**. If the Results panel opens during this operation, close it.

13. Save and close any open pages and exit Dreamweaver.

ON YOUR OWN

1. Start Dreamweaver.
2. Open the yardart site and then open the index.html page.
3. Position the insertion point below the heading and import or copy the text from ⊙ indextext.doc from the Lesson 2 Data folder.
4. Format the index.html page as follows:

- Click at the end of the second sentence and press Enter.
- Click at the end of *Today's Web Specials* and press Enter a second time.
- Highlight *Today's Web* Specials and assign the Heading 3 format to the heading.
- Change the heading color to a dark green and choose a different font combination for the heading, if desired.
- Change the size of the first sentence of paragraph text to 4.

5. Open contact.html and make the following changes:

- Change the heading color to one of your choice.
- Apply italic to product names in the contact list (*sundials, natural benches, wind chimes, ornamental rock, waterfalls*).
- Boldface the artists' names in the contact list.

6. Open ⊙ aboutus.html from the Lesson 2 Data folder. Save the file in the yardart folder with the same name and the page title **About Us**. Update links when prompted.

7. Clean up the Word HTML in this document. Format the heading the same way as the heading on the contact.html page.

8. Find all instances of *YardArt* throughout the site and change them to **Yard Art,** adding a space in the middle. (If the Results panel opens during this process, close it when you have finished.)

9. Check spelling on all pages in the site.

10. Save and close all open pages and exit Dreamweaver.

Skills Covered

- Adjust Paragraph Alignment
- Change Paragraph Indentation
- Create Lists
- Insert a Date
- Use the History Panel

Software Skills Alignment, indentation, and lists help to organize areas of a Web page to make text easier to read and understand. Add a date to one or more pages in a site to let visitors know when pages were last updated. The Dreamweaver History panel makes it easy to perform repetitive tasks.

Design Skills The alignment and spacing of the content on your site is an important part of overall design because it makes the content easier for visitors to read and navigate. Similarly, lists can give visitors important information quickly, which adds to the usefulness of your site.

Application Skills In this exercise, you will continue working on the GardenScape Web site. You will format page text in list format, adjust text alignment and indentation, and use the History panel to insert dates on site pages.

TERMS

Alignment Horizontal placement relative to the left and right edges of a page.

Bullet An indicator or simple graphic file used to denote individual points or items in an unordered (bulleted) list.

Definition list An HTML list type that includes a term set on one line and its description indented below.

History panel A Dreamweaver feature providing visual maps of past work on Web pages.

Line length The width of the text line as it appears on your web page.

Ordered list A list—also called a *numbered list*—whose items must be in a certain order.

Unordered list A list that does not have to be in order. Also called a *bulleted list*.

Adjust Paragraph Alignment

- Text in a Dreamweaver document is left aligned by default. This means that the text lines up at the left margin of the page and the text along the right margin is ragged.

- You can change the alignment to center text or right-align text using the ☰ Align Center or ☷ Align Right button on the Property inspector. Return text to left alignment using the ☰ Align Left button.

- Dreamweaver also supports justified text using the ☰ Justify button, although some browsers may not support justified text.

  ✔ *Justified text is the term used when the text is lined up along both the left and right margins. This alignment is achieved by adding space between words in the selected text.*

- Text that has been center aligned is spaced an equal distance from the left and right edges of the page. Right-aligned text lines up evenly at the right margin of the page.

Change Paragraph Indentation

- You can indent text from the left and right margins (see the illustration below) using the ☲ Text Indent button on the Property inspector. You can also select text to indent or apply the indent and then start typing. The text you type will be indented according to your selection.

  ✔ *You can use Text Indent more than once, if you choose, to include the amount of space used for the indent.*

- Use the ☲ Text Outdent button on the Property inspector to move the cursor or the selected text toward the left margin. If you have indented the text or cursor only once, the selection is returned to the left margin. If you have clicked Text Indent multiple times, the selected text or cursor is moved one indent to the left.

  ✔ *Use Text Indent to help reduce the **line length** of your text paragraphs. Web sites that include text that stretches from margin to margin are usually considered difficult for visitors to read. To make it easy on the reader, use Text Indent to shorten the lines.*

Indent text from both edges of page

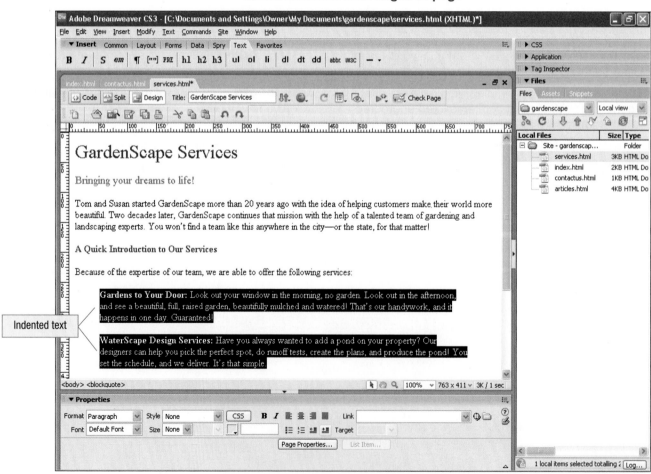

Create Lists

- Web pages often include lists to emphasize text items and enable readers to find information quickly and easily. You can create two types of lists using buttons on the Property inspector: **unordered lists** and **ordered lists** (see the illustration below).

- Use the ▤ Unordered List button to create a list whose items do not have to be listed in a specific order. Each item begins with a small character called a **bullet**, so this type of list is often called a list.

- Use the ▤ Ordered List button to create a list whose items must be in a specific order. Each item begins with a number, so this list is often called a numbered list.

- To apply either list format, click the appropriate button on the Property inspector. Dreamweaver automatically supplies the bullet or number.

- The unordered list is formatted using the HTML <ul> (unordered list) tag. The ordered list is formatted using the HTML <ol> (ordered list) tag. Each individual line is formatted using the <li> (list item) tag.

  ✔ *Remember, you can see—and select—the HTML tags for text you are working on by checking the left side of the Document window's status bar.*

- You can also apply HTML list tags directly by clicking the tag you want to insert in the Text category of the Insert bar.

- You can change the properties of ordered lists by clicking on a list item and using the Text>List> Properties command on the menu bar or clicking the ⬚ List Item... button on the expanded Property inspector.

Unordered and ordered list in Web page

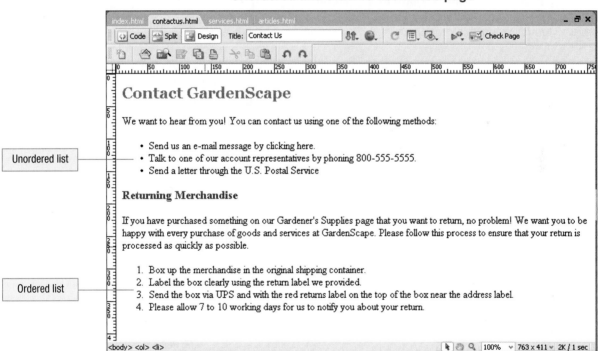

- Dreamweaver displays the List Properties dialog box (see the following illustration). In this dialog box, you can change the number of the first list item (to start a list with the number 3, for example). You can also change the format of the list from the default numeric order to roman numerals or alphabetic order.

Change properties for ordered (numbered) list

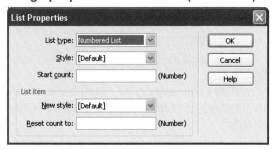

- Dreamweaver offers a third type of list called a **definition list** that you can create using the Text>List>Definition List command on the menu bar. A definition list consists of a term that is set on one line, and its description that is set on the next line (see the following illustration).

Definition list

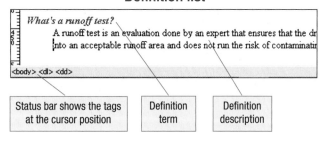

| Status bar shows the tags at the cursor position | Definition term | Definition description |

- When you select the Definition List command, Dreamweaver applies the <dl> and <dt> (definition term) HTML tags.

- After you have finished typing the term, press the Enter key. Dreamweaver automatically formats the next line with the <dd> (definition description) HTML tag, which indents the description below the term.

- Definition lists can be used for text other than strict terms and definitions. You can use this type of list to quickly create headings and indented text, a site map or table of contents, and so on.

- You can format the definition text as needed, adding bold or italic to the definition term or using color to make the definition stand out.

Insert a Date

- You can insert the current date on any page in your site using Dreamweaver's Date feature. If you choose, the inserted date updates each time you save the page. This is a good way to keep track of modifications made to a Web site.

- Use the Insert>Date command or the 🗓 Date button on the Common category of the Insert bar to open the Insert Date dialog box (see the following illustration).

Insert and format day, date, and/or time

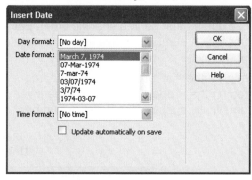

- You can insert a day, a date, and/or a time. Dreamweaver supplies a number of formats to choose from for each item.

- If you want the date/time information to update each time you save the page, select the Update automatically on save checkbox. Otherwise, the inserted date will stay the same as when it was inserted.

Use the History Panel

- Dreamweaver's History panel is a useful tool for tracking tasks. The **History** panel (see the following illustration) shows a list of tasks that have been performed since the current page was created or opened.

History panel shows recent tasks

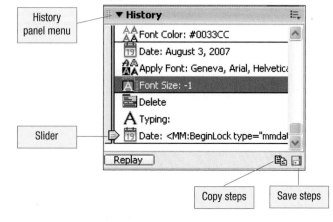

- Not only can you keep track of the tasks you have performed in the History panel, but you also can use the History panel to repeat a series of steps or undo a number of recent tasks quickly and easily.

- Display the History panel using the Window>History command.

- As you perform each task, the History panel displays the task, along with an identifying icon. The icon for a text entry, for example, is a capital A.

- Select a step by clicking it in the panel. Select more than one step by clicking the first, holding down the Shift or Ctrl key, and clicking additional steps.

- To save time in performing repetitive tasks, you can repeat steps. Select the steps you want to repeat, position the insertion point where you want to begin the steps, and click ⌷ Replay ⌷.

- To reverse a series of steps, drag the slider upward to "gray out" the steps you want to undo. You can redo those steps by dragging the slider back down to activate the steps again.

- The History panel tracks steps on the current page only. If you open another page, the History panel will not show the tasks you performed on the previous page.

- You can, however, copy steps from one page to use on another. Select the series of steps and click the 📋 Copy selected steps to the clipboard button on the History panel.

- Switch to the page you want to copy the steps to and use the Dreamweaver window's Edit>Paste menu command to paste the steps. The copied steps are replayed as soon as they are pasted.

- If you find that you repeat a series of steps often, you can save them as a command by using the 💾 Save selected steps as a command button on the History panel.

  ✔ *If you need to later delete the command, use the Commands> Edit Command List menu command, select the desired command, and click Delete.*

- Select the steps, click 💾 and provide a name for the command. Your new command displays at the bottom of the Commands menu so that you can choose it at any time on any page.

- When copying or saving steps, you might want to start with an empty History panel. You can clear the History panel of all entries by clicking the History panel menu and choosing Clear History from the menu.

- Dreamweaver will warn you that this step cannot be undone. Click Yes in the warning box to clear the History panel.

PROCEDURES

Change Paragraph Alignment

Click in the paragraph to align or position the cursor where the new alignment should begin.

1. Click the **Align Left** button ▤ on the Property inspector to left-align text .... Ctrl + Alt + ⇧ Shift + L

2. Click the **Align Center** button ▤ on the Property inspector to center text .... Ctrl + Alt + ⇧ Shift + C

3. Click the **Align Right** button ▤ on the Property inspector to right-align text .... Ctrl + Alt + ⇧ Shift + R

4. Click the **Justify** button ▤ on the Property inspector to justify text .... Ctrl + Alt + ⇧ Shift + J

   OR

1. Click **Text** .... Alt + T

2. Click **Align** .... A
   - Click **Left** L
   - Click **Center** C
   - Click **Right** .... R
   - Click **Justify** .... J

Indent Paragraphs

Click in the paragraph to indent or position the cursor where the new indentation should begin.

1. Click the **Text Indent** button ⊒ on the Property inspector to indent .... Ctrl + Alt + ⟩

2. Click the **Text Outdent** button ⊏ on the Property inspector to remove indent .... Ctrl + Alt + ⟨

   OR

1. Click **Text** .... Alt + T

2. Click **Indent** I

   OR

   Click **Outdent** .... O

Create Ordered and Unordered Lists

Select text to format or position the cursor where the new format should begin.

1. Click **Text** .... Alt + T
2. Click **List** .... I, →
3. Click **Ordered List** .... O

   OR

   Click **Unordered List** .... U

   OR

- Click the **Unordered List** button ▤ on the Property inspector.

- Click the **Ordered List** button ▤ on the Property inspector.

  ✔ *To remove unordered list or ordered list formatting, follow the same steps.*

Change List Properties

1. Place the cursor in the desired list.
   a. Click **Text**.................⌥`Alt`+`T`
   b. Click **List**..................`I`, `→`
   c. Click **Properties**.............`P`
   OR
   - Click `List Item...` on the expanded Property inspector.
2. Make the desired changes in the List Properties dialog box.
3. Click `OK`.

Create a Definition List

1. Click **Text**.....................`Alt`+`T`
2. Click **List**.......................`I`, `→`
3. Click **Definition List**.............`D`
4. Type the definition term.
5. Press `Enter`.
6. Type the definition description.

Insert a Date

1. Click **Insert**...................`Alt`+`I`
2. Click **Date**...........................`D`
   OR
   - Click the Date button 🗓 in the Common category of the Insert bar.
3. Select the format for Day, Date, and/or Time.
4. Select **Update automatically on save** checkbox to update date/time information each time the page is saved.

Use the History Panel (Shift + F10)

To display the History panel:

1. Click **Window**...............`Alt`+`W`
2. Click **History**........................`H`

To work with steps in the panel:

- Click a step to select it.
- Click the step, hold down `Ctrl` or `⇧ Shift`, and click additional steps to select more than one step at a time.
- Select the steps and click `Replay` to repeat steps.
- Drag the slider up to undo steps or down to redo steps.
- Select the steps and click 🖫 to save steps as a command.
- Click the History panel menu arrow and select **Clear History** to empty History panel.

To copy steps from one page to another:

1. Select the steps to copy and click 📑 on the History panel.
2. Open the page where the steps are to be copied.
3. Click **Edit**......................`Alt`+`E`
4. Click **Paste**..........................`P`

EXERCISE DIRECTIONS

1. Start Dreamweaver and open the gardenscape site.
2. Open contactus.html.
3. Position the insertion point below the heading and import or copy the text from ⊙ returntext.doc from the Lesson 2 Data folder.
4. Create an unordered list as follows:
   - Highlight the three lines following the opening sentence.
   - Apply the Unordered List format. Notice that the bullets are applied automatically and the spacing is changed.
   - Click at the end of the last item in the list and press Enter. Notice that a new bullet appears.
5. Create an ordered list as follows:
   - Click in the line beginning with *Box up...*
   - Apply the Ordered List format. The sentence is now numbered 1.
   - Apply the Ordered List format to the next three lines. Your page should look similar to Illustration A on the next page.
6. Make the following alignment and format changes:
   - Center the heading *Returning Merchandise*.
   - Indent the paragraph beneath *Returning Merchandise*.
   - Indent the four steps in the ordered list.
   - Apply the color #009999 to *Contact GardenScape*.
   - Apply the Heading 2 format to *Returning Merchandise* and color it #0033CC.
7. Open the articles.html page. Highlight the items from *Design basics* to *The ins and outs of composting* and apply the Unordered List format.
8. Display index.html. Format the list following the heading *A Few Project Ideas* as an unordered list.
9. Display the History panel and clear the contents of the panel.
   ✔ *Dreamweaver may warn you that you will not be able to undo steps if you clear the list. Click* **Yes**.
10. Click to the right of the last sentence on the page. Press Enter.
11. Type **Last update:** and press the Spacebar. Apply the center alignment.
12. Insert the date and time using the format of your choice. Choose to update the date and time automatically.

13. Deselect the date you just entered on the index.html page.

14. In the History task panel, select and replay the last four steps.

15. Use the History panel slider to undo the repeated steps.

16. Copy the last two steps (the last two steps are typing *Last update* and inserting the date and time) in the History panel.

17. Activate articles.html and insert a new blank paragraph below the last line. Paste the copied steps. If you need to adjust the alignment of the *Last update* text, remove any indent and apply the center alignment.

18. Save and close any open pages. Note that the time updates on the pages where you inserted the date and time.

19. Exit Dreamweaver.

Illustration A

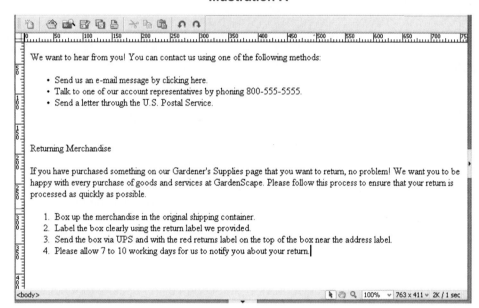

ON YOUR OWN

✔ *In this activity, you indent and align text and work with the History panel in the sample site you created in Lesson 1.*

1. Start Dreamweaver and open the java2go site.

2. Open index.html. Add the following text:

Welcome to Java2 Go!

For the best cup of java on the north side, visit us at

1010 Maple Street
Minneapolis, MN 55402

Call ahead for special orders: 555-1212

Click to see whether you're on our delivery route!

3. Indent the mailing address on this page.

4. Open contact.html. Add a heading on the page and apply any format you choose.

5. Insert a new paragraph below the heading and add the following text and list. (Find the en dash used in the day and time ranges in the last row of the Insert Other Characters dialog box.)

Java2 Go hours:

Monday – Friday, 6:00 a.m. – 3:00 p.m.
Saturday, 7:00 a.m. – 3:00 p.m.
Sunday, 7:00 a.m. – 12:00 p.m.

6. Return to index.html. Display the History palette.

7. Insert a new paragraph below the last text paragraph. Change the alignment to center and the text size to 2. Insert the following text. (Insert the copyright symbol from the Text Insert bar, and use your choice of date format.)

Copyright © Java2 Go. Site updated

8. Add the date in any format you choose following the *Site updated* text.

9. Copy the steps, or save them as a command, and insert the copyright notice on the contact.html page as well.

10. Save and close all pages and exit Dreamweaver.

Skills Covered

- About Dreamweaver's HTML Code Features
- Use the Code Inspector
- Display Head Content
- Use Code Hints and the Tag Chooser

- Use the Tag Inspector
- Insert Snippets
- Use the Reference Panel
- Clean Up XHTML Code
- Find and Replace Code

Software Skills Dreamweaver's Web design tools make it unnecessary for you to work directly with HTML and other Web page programming code. However, you should know how to use Dreamweaver's Code view tools so that you can modify, change, replace, or troubleshoot the tags that make up your site.

Design Skills By working in Design view, you can easily see the effects of your changes as you add to and enhance your site. However, knowing how to work with HTML in Code view gives you the added benefit of knowing how to tweak and troubleshoot the code when things on your site don't look or act the way you want them to.

Application Skills In this exercise, you will continue to work with the GardenScape site. You will use Code view and code editing options to modify code on several pages in the site.

TERMS

Code inspector A Dreamweaver feature that displays the HTML code used to create page elements.

Reference panel A Dreamweaver panel that supplies reference material about HTML tags, CSS, and JavaScript.

Snippets Predefined HTML forms, tables, menus, and other Web page scripts that you can insert on your page by using the Snippets panel in the Files panel group.

Tag inspector A Dreamweaver panel that maps and shows the properties of the tags used in a Web page's code.

NOTES

About Dreamweaver's HTML Code Features

- As you have already learned, you do not need to know a lot about HTML coding to create Web pages. Dreamweaver takes care of the coding "behind the scenes" so that you don't have to.

- Many designers, however, prefer to work directly with HTML code to create page elements. Dreamweaver offers a great deal of support for such designers, making it easy to view code, insert code, and troubleshoot code problems.

- It's a good idea to have a working knowledge of HTML—to be able to recognize common tags, know what they do, and know how to change them—so that you will know your way around the code in case you ever need it.

- This exercise introduces some of the most common methods of working with HTML code in Dreamweaver. Dreamweaver's Help files include additional options for customizing the code interface.

Use the Code Inspector

- Even if you prefer to work in Design view, you can keep an eye on a page's HTML code by using the **Code inspector**. The Code inspector displays the page's code in a floating window, as shown in the illustration below.

- Use the Window>Code Inspector command to open the Code inspector, or press F10.

- To work directly in the Code inspector, click in it.

- You can drag the lower-right corner to increase the Code inspector's window size.

- Click the 🔲 View Options button in the Code inspector to display a menu of options for displaying the code. Selecting the Word Wrap option from this menu causes code to wrap within the window so that you can see the line endings without scrolling to the right.

- The Line Numbers view, selected by default, displays a number to the left of each line of code. Line numbers help you find your position in the code. You can make the view more readable by selecting the Auto Indent view option to automatically indent the lines of code.

Code inspector

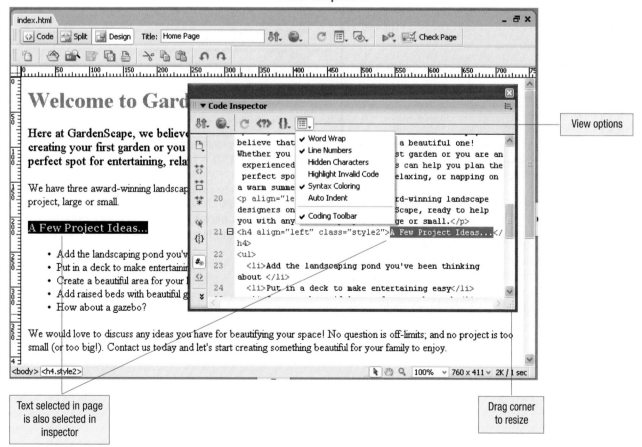

Text selected in page is also selected in inspector

Drag corner to resize

- The Syntax Coloring view option displays HTML tags and attributes in dark blue so that you can easily distinguish them from text. This option, too, is selected by default in the other code views.

  ✔ *You can adjust Code inspector display settings by using the Edit>Preferences command to open the Preferences dialog box and then selecting the Code Coloring category.*

- You can type directly in the Code inspector just as you do in the Document window; the only difference is that you enter HTML codes and text in the Code inspector. You can also edit text and code by inserting, deleting, and copying and pasting items as needed.

- The changes you make to tags in the Code inspector do not appear in the Document window until you activate the Document window by clicking in it.

- The Highlight Invalid Code view option helps you identify mistakes in your HTML code. If you make a coding mistake in the Code inspector, the error is highlighted in the code. In the following illustration, for example, Dreamweaver has detected that there is no closing tag for the <font> tag used to apply color to the heading.

Dreamweaver highlights error in code

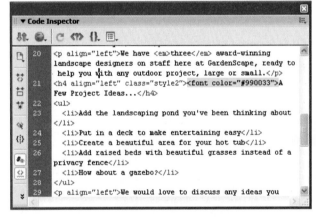

  ✔ *Dreamweaver provides a brief explanation of why the markup code is invalid in the Property inspector.*

- If you want errors in the code highlighted in the Document window when you are in Code view, select the Highlight Invalid Code option in the View options button menu on the Document toolbar. You can then easily find and fix errors in code.

Display Head Content

- Another way to display HTML information for a page without leaving Design view is to display the contents of its Head section in the Document window.

- Use the View>Head Content command to open a pane at the top of the current page with icons representing each HTML tag in the Head section (see the following illustration). Click an icon to see information about that tag in the Property inspector.

Display Head content in page

Information about selected tag (Keywords) appears in Property inspector

Head content pane

- You can also display Head content by clicking the View options button on the Document toolbar and selecting Head Content from the resulting menu.

Use Code Hints and the Tag Chooser

- Dreamweaver offers several features that can make the process of entering code faster and more accurate.

- The code hints feature helps you insert a specific HTML tag or attribute. When you type an opening wicket, the code hints list appears in the code view that you are using (see the following illustration). You can scroll down this list to find the tag you want, highlight it, and press Enter to insert it following the wicket you typed.

Insert a tag using the code hints list

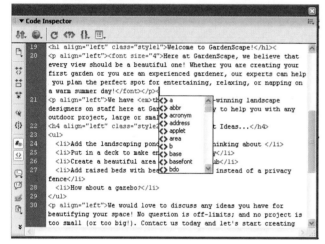

- After you type the closing wicket, you can enter the tag content, such as text or a heading. To insert the proper closing tag, type </. Dreamweaver automatically supplies the tag that needs to be closed along with the final wicket.

- Code hints can also help you find an attribute for a tag. If you type a space after entering the h2 tag in the previous illustration, for example, another list displays, containing the attributes that can be used with that tag.

- Another way to find a specific HTML tag and insert it is to right-click at the desired location and select Insert Tag from the shortcut menu (or click the Insert>Tag menu command) to open the Tag Chooser (see the illustration in the next column).

- The Tag Chooser displays a list of tag libraries at the left, including HTML tags, the CFML tags used with ColdFusion files, and ASP and JSP tags used for active server pages and JavaScript.

- The libraries may have subcategories, such as the ones shown for HTML tags in the following illustration. Click the + to display any subcategories.

Tag Chooser dialog box

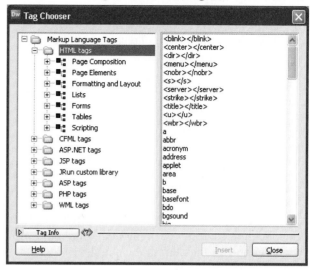

- When you click a category, the list on the right contains the tags available for that category.

- The Tag Info pane at the bottom of the Tag Chooser gives information about the selected tag. You can display what the tag is for and whether it requires an end tag.

- Clicking the [Insert] button opens the Tag Editor dialog box for that tag (see the following illustration). You can further define the tag in this editor by providing information for the categories listed at the left side of the dialog box. After you have finished with the Tag Editor, click OK, and the tag is inserted in the page code.

Tag Editor for tag

- You can display a Tag Editor for any code that has already been entered in a page by right-clicking the code and selecting Edit Tag from the shortcut menu.

Use the Tag Inspector

■ The **Tag inspector** is in some ways similar to the Property inspector, in that it displays attributes applied to a currently selected tag. Also like the Property inspector, the Tag inspector can be used to select and modify attributes for a tag. Unlike the Property inspector, the Tag inspector can display a list of every attribute available for a tag, allowing you to easily fine-tune a tag.

■ The following illustration shows a small portion of the attributes list for a table. If you compare this list with the options on the Property inspector, you will see that many—such as bgcolor, border, cell padding—are the same. Scrolling down in the Tag inspector list shows you many more attributes you can change for the current table tag.

Tag inspector for a table tag

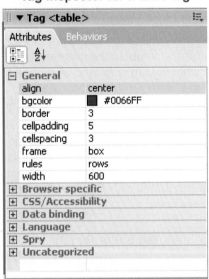

■ If an attribute has a value, it appears in the right column of the list. You can apply values for an attribute by clicking in the right column to see a list of available options. As you make changes in the Tag inspector, the HTML code is immediately applied and the appearance of the object changes in Design view.

■ The previous illustration shows the attributes displayed in an alphabetical list. Display this list by clicking the [AZ] Show list view button in the panel. You can also display attributes organized in categories by clicking the [≣] Show category view button.

Insert Snippets

■ **Snippets** are predefined HTML elements you can add to your pages. You will find snippets for forms, tables, menus for selecting month and year (handy for credit card order forms), Javascript tools for computing the area of a circle and other shapes, headers, footers, navigation bars, and other complex and/or commonly used code . You can select and insert snippets using the [Insert] button or drag them directly onto your Web page (see the following illustration).

Snippets panel

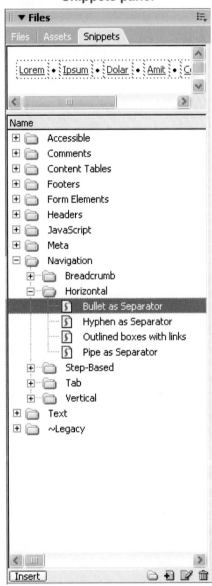

■ The Snippets panel is divided into two panes. When you select a snippet in the Snippets panel file tree in the lower pane, the upper pane reveals the snippet's content or code.

Use the Reference Panel

■ You use the **Reference panel** (see the illustration at the bottom of this page) to find information on HTML tags, CSS (cascading style sheets) tags, and JavaScript objects. The Reference panel is one of the panels in the Results panel group that can be displayed below the Property inspector. The panels in the Results panel group show information about a number of different site elements. You will use it more extensively in Lesson 7.

■ To get help on a specific HTML tag (or other object), select the tag or object and use the Window>Reference command or click the [<?>] Reference button on the Code inspector toolbar.

✔ *The Reference panel's content is provided by O'Reilly & Associates.*

■ Use the two list boxes in the Reference panel to locate the tag or object and its properties and methods for which you want information. The Reference panel provides proper syntax and other important information about the item.

■ You can also right-click in any HTML tag in Code view and select Reference on the shortcut menu to see information on that tag.

Clean Up XHTML Code

■ One of Dreamweaver's most useful HTML tools is the Clean Up XHTML command, which you can find on the Commands menu. Use this command on your own files, for pages created by other authors that you want to incorporate in your Web site, or for text you have pasted from another source.

✔ *If your document is an HTML file created in a previous version of Dreamweaver or in another application, this menu command is Clean Up HTML. You can convert older HTML documents to XHTML using the File>Convert>XHTML 1.0 Transitional menu command if you want all documents in your Web site to meet the latest standards for XHTML.*

■ The Clean Up XHTML command removes empty tags, combines nested font tags, and otherwise improves messy HTML coding on a page. This process is similar to cleaning up Word HTML codes, which you learned how to do in Exercise 8.

✔ *The Commands>Clean Up Word HTML command is used when you insert text copied from a Word HTML page or if a Word HTML page has been copied into your Web folder.*

■ When you issue the command, you can select specific items to clean up in the Clean Up HTML/XHTML dialog box (see the following illustration). Use the Specific tag(s) box to type specific tag names you want Dreamweaver to clean up.

✔ *Do not type wickets when entering specific codes. Type only the tag name.*

Specify codes to clean up

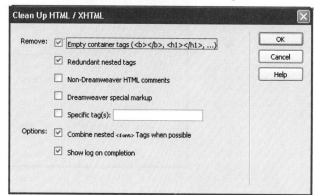

■ You can issue the Clean Up XHTML command at any time while working on page content to make sure your code is always correct and up to date.

Reference panel

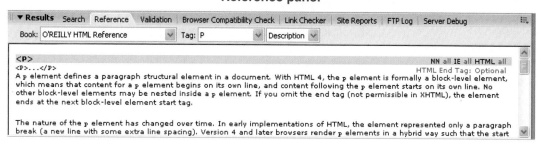

Find and Replace Code

- In Exercise 8, you learned how to use the Find and Replace feature to locate and change text on a page or throughout a Web site. You can also use this feature to locate and modify code in a site.

- The illustration below shows how the Find and Replace dialog box looks to replace one code (strong) with another (b).

- To the right of the Search box is a list box you use to specify the tag you want to find or change. The Action box contains a list of actions that can be performed when the tag is found. You can replace the tag itself, replace the tag and its contents, change the tag, add a tag before or after the start

tag, strip (remove) the tag, and so on. Depending on the action you choose, you may need to specify additional information, such as what information to use as a replacement or what attribute to substitute for a specified attribute.

- To refine the search, click the ⊕ button to add another search box containing options such as With Attribute, Containing, or Inside Tag. These options allow you to be very specific about the text or tags you want to find. You can continue to click the button to add search fields, or click the ⊖ button to remove search fields.

- Use the Find Next and Replace buttons just as when finding text to locate instances of code and replace them.

Find and replace codes in Web site

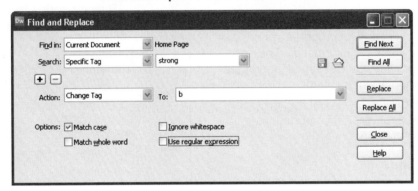

PROCEDURES

Open Code Inspector (F10)

1. Click **Window** ....[Alt]+[W]
2. Click **Code Inspector**..............[D], [D], [Enter]

Adjust Code Inspector Display

1. Resize the Code inspector window by dragging the lower-right corner.
2. Click **View options** button [▤] in the Code inspector toolbar and select options:
   - Select **Word Wrap** to force code to wrap within the inspector window.
   - Select **Line Numbers** to display numbers to the left of each line of code.
   - Select **Hidden Characters** to show space and paragraph markers in the code.

- Select **Highlight Invalid Code** to highlight coding errors.
- Select **Syntax Coloring** to display tags and text in different colors.
- Select **Auto Indent** to enable automatic indenting of code lines.

Enter Text and Codes Using Code Inspector

1. Click in the Code inspector window to activate window.
2. Position the insertion point as desired and type or edit text or codes.
3. Click in the Document window to record and display changes.

Display Head Content (Ctrl + Shift + H)

1. Click **View** ....[Alt]+[V]
2. Click **Head Content**.............[H]
3. Click icon in the Head content pane to see information in Property inspector.

   ✔ Follow the same procedure to close the Head content pane.

Enter Tags and Attributes Using Code Hints

In Code view:

1. Position the insertion point where the new tag is to be entered.
2. Type < to begin the tag. The code hints list displays.
3. Scroll down the list to locate the tag to enter.

4. Click the tag to select it and press {Enter} to insert it.

5. Type > to complete the opening tag.

6. After typing content, type </ to automatically complete the closing tag.

To use code hints to insert an attribute:

1. After entering the tag (step 4 above), press the Spacebar. The code hints list of attributes appears.

2. Scroll down the list to locate the desired attribute.

3. Click the attribute to select it and press {Enter}.

Use the Tag Chooser (Ctrl + E)

In Code view:

1. Position the insertion point where a new tag is to be entered.

2. Click **Insert** ....{Alt}+{I}

3. Click **Tag**.

   OR

   a. Right-click the location where you want to enter a new tag.

   b. Click **Insert Tag** on the shortcut menu.

4. Select the library that contains the tag you want in the Tag Chooser dialog box.

5. Select the desired tag from the list of tags at the right of the Tag Chooser dialog box.

6. Click [Insert].

7. In the Tag Editor, choose additional attributes for the tag if desired.

8. Click [OK] to insert the code.

9. Click Close.

Use the Snippets Panel (Shift + F9)

1. Click **Window** ....{Alt}+{W}

2. Click **Snippets**.....................{N}

   OR

   ■ Click the **Snippets** panel tab in the Files panel group.

3. Open categories in the Snippets panel to see the available snippets.

4. Click a snippet to display its code in the upper pane of the panel.

5. Click [Insert] to insert the snippet at the cursor position.

   OR

   ■ Drag the snippet to the Document window and drop it where you want it to appear.

Use the Reference Panel (Shift + F1)

1. Select the tag or object you want to know more about.

2. Click **Window** ....{Alt}+{W}

3. Click **Reference**...................{F}

   OR

   ■ Click the **Reference** button {<?>} on the Code inspector toolbar.

   OR

   ■ Click the **Reference** panel tab in the Results panel group.

Use the Tag Inspector Panel (F9)

To display the Tag Inspector panel:

1. Position the cursor in the tag you want to inspect.

2. Click **Window** ....{Alt}+{W}

3. Click **Tag Inspector**.............{T}

To work with Tag inspector options:

■ Click {A↓Z} to display an alphabetical list of attributes for the current tag.

■ Click {▤} to see attributes organized in categories.

■ Click to the right of an attribute to see the values you can set for that attribute.

Clean Up XHTML Code

1. Click **Commands**..........{Alt}+{C}

2. Click **Clean Up XHTML** ....{L}

   ✔ This command may appear as Clean Up HTML for some pages.

3. Select the specific items you want to clean up.

4. Select the **Show log on completion** checkbox to see a report on the items that have been fixed.

Find and Replace Code (Ctrl + F)

1. Click **Edit** ....{Alt}+{E}

2. Click **Find and Replace** ....{F}

3. Click {Enter}.

4. Select location to search: **Selected Text**, **Current Document**, **Open Documents**, **Folder**, **Selected Files in Site**, **Entire Current Local Site**.

5. Select **Specific Tag** in the **Search** box.

6. In the list box on the right, type the tag you want to search for, or click the list arrow and select the tag from the drop-down list.

7. Click **Action** and select the appropriate action for the identified tag.

8. Supply additional information for the action if necessary, such as the tag that will replace the specified tag.

9. Click [Find Next] to find the first instance of the tag.

10. Click [Replace] to change the tag as indicated by the action.

    OR

    a. Click [Find All] to display all instances in the Results panel below the Property inspector.

    b. Click [Replace All] to change all instances at once.

EXERCISE DIRECTIONS

1. Start Dreamweaver and open the gardenscape site.

2. Open index.html.

3. Display the Head content pane and click the Keywords icon to see the keywords in the Property inspector.

4. Click the Meta icon to see the information on this tag in the Property inspector.

5. Look up information in the Reference panel on the <meta> tag.

6. Close the Head content pane and the Results panel group.

7. Open articles.html. Edit the page in the Code inspector as follows:

   ■ Select and delete all text between the <style> </style> tags and the tags themselves in the Head section of the page. Use the Tag inspector if you cannot locate it quickly.

   ■ Delete the blank line 4 of the code.

   ■ Delete the lang attribute and its value following the opening body tag. (You should select and delete lang=EN-US".)

   ✔ Do NOT delete the bgcolor="#FFFFFF" attribute and value.

   ■ Scroll up to display the Head section and locate the <meta> tag.

   ■ Find the <meta> tag and make sure the character set information is set to charset=iso-8859-1.

8. Click in the Document window to record your changes.

9. Now use Find and Replace to clean up the code of the page as follows:

   ■ Change the strong tag to b.

   ■ Strip the div tag from the page. (This will eliminate the dotted line border around the page content.)

   ■ Strip the span tag from the page.

   ■ Change the h1 tags to h3. (This reduces the size of the article titles in the lower half of the page.)

   ■ Format the Articles! page title as h1.

10. Use the Clean Up HTML command to check coding on this page. (Use the default options; the clean-up process may find no mistakes to fix.) Then save and close the page.

11. Open the ⊙ glossary.html page from the Lesson 2 Data folder and save it in the current site. Choose to update links when prompted.

   ✔ The definitions on this page could be displayed better as a definition list.

12. Make the following formatting changes in the Code inspector or any Code view option:

   ■ Type < to begin the definition list. The code hints list displays. Scroll down to locate the dl tag and double-click it. Type >.

   ■ Press Enter. Type <dt><b> to start and bold the first term, using the code hints list if desired.

   ■ Move the cursor to the end of the line and delete the <br> tag.

   ■ Type </ to close the <b> tag, and then type </ to close the <dt> tag.

   ■ Move the cursor to the beginning of the next line. Type <dd>.

   ■ Click at the end of the definition, to the left of the <br> tag and type </ to close the <dd> tag.

   ✔ Delete the <br> tag at the end of <dt> items, but leave them following the <dd> lines. The <br> tag inserts a line break on the page.

13. Format the next term (biennial) the same way you formatted bare root roses and provide the proper codes for its definition.

14. Repeat the process for all terms and definitions in the list.

15. Following the last definition, create a new line and type </ to end the list.

16. Click in the Document window or switch to Design view to inspect your changes. Your page should look similar to Illustration A on the next page.

17. Use the Clean Up XHTML command to check your coding.

18. Save and close all open pages and exit Dreamweaver.

Illustration A

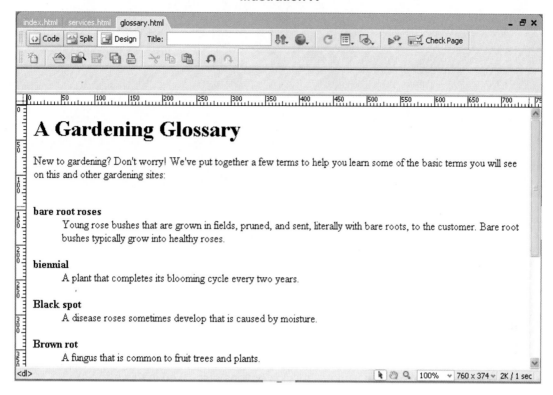

ON YOUR OWN

1. Start Dreamweaver and open the Java2Go site.

2. Open ⊙ recipe.html in the Lesson 2 Data folder and save it to the root folder of your site. Update links when prompted.

3. This page was created from a Word HTML page and needs the same kind of code fixes that the articles.htm page needed in the Exercise Directions. Use cleanup instructions for that page to make the following changes. You can use the Code inspector or any Code view:

   ■ Delete the unnecessary <style> </style> tags and all information between them.

   ■ Delete the lang attribute and its value following the opening <body> tag.

   ■ Change the charset attribute to **charset=iso-8859-1**.

   ■ Remove the <div> tags.

   ■ If necessary, apply the h1 format to the *Banana Muffins* heading.

   ■ Change the format for *(Our secret recipe!)* to h2.

   ■ Convert the page to an XHTML 1.0 Transitional page.

4. Open index.html and display the Snippets panel in the Files panel group.

5. Position the insertion point to the left of the word *Welcome* in the heading.

6. In the Snippets panel, open the Navigation folder, open the Horizontal folder, and select the *Outlined boxes with links* snippet.

7. Click ⌊Insert⌋ in the Snippets panel to insert the navigation bar above the main heading.

   ✔ *You will edit the links in this navigation bar in the next exercise.*

8. Open contact.html and select the main heading *Contact Us*.

9. Display the Tag inspector and use it to change the color of the heading to #CC3300.

   ✔ *Hint: Click to the right of the color attribute to display the Text Color box. Deselect the text to see the color change.*

10. Display index.html and change the heading color as you did in step 9.

11. Use the Clean Up XHTML command to check code on all pages.

12. Save and close all open pages and exit Dreamweaver.

Skills Covered

- **About Links**
- **Create Text Links**
- **Link to Named Anchor**
- **Link to E-Mail Address**
- **Other Ways to Link**

Software Skills Links provide connections between Web pages that allow visitors to navigate your site. You can set links within a Web page, from page to page in a site, to an e-mail address, and from your site to other Web sites.

Design Skills The design of your site should help visitors find and navigate the links easily. Links usually appear in a second color with an underline, or with some other kind of effect that enables people visiting your site to find and click the links.

Application Skills In this exercise, you will create links among the pages in the GardenScape Web site using all the link options discussed in this exercise.

TERMS

Absolute link A link that includes the complete path name in the URL (for example, http://www.yoursite.com). Used for linking to Web sites that are external to your site.

Link A connection between pages in the same file or different files.

Named anchor A named location in a Web page that is used for links on the same page. Sometimes also referred to as a **bookmark**.

Relative link A link set within a specific site that does not include the domain name (for example, ../yoursite/file.html.

URL (Uniform Resource Locator) Another name for a Web page address, this is the server and path information used to locate documents on the Internet.

NOTES

About Links

- Web sites rely heavily on **links**. Links are the means by which visitors "jump" and "browse" among Web pages and sites on the Internet.

- Links work by directing a browser to open a page at a specific World Wide Web address called a **URL (uniform resource locator)**. The URL www.gardenscape.com/, for example, tells the browser to find the site and open its home page on the GardenScape server on the World Wide Web (www). Alternately, this URL could tell the browser to find the server that hosts Gardenscape, which may be one of many sites on the server (a Web server can host more than one Web site).

- Links are usually formatted in such a way that they stand out from surrounding text so visitors can easily recognize them. They are usually in a different color and underlined.

- You can create several types of links in Dreamweaver:

  - *Text links*—links created using a word or phrase.
  - *Named anchor links*—links from one location on a page to another location on the same page.
  - *E-mail links*—links that open an e-mail program so a visitor can send a message to a Web site's e-mail address.
  - *Graphic links*—links created using an image or icon on a page.

  ✔ *You will learn about the first three types of links in this exercise. Graphic links are covered in Lesson 3.*

- Links can be either *relative* or *absolute*.

  - A **relative link** is a link to a page within your Web site. As you know, all Web site pages are stored together in a single folder. These pages remain in the same locations relative to each other even after a Web site is published to a Web server.

  - An **absolute link** takes a visitor from a page within your site to a different Web site. Because the browser must open a new Web site, it needs the full URL for the page it is to open.

Create Text Links

- To create a text link, select the text you want to use as the link and then use the Property inspector's Link text box to set up the link.

- To create a relative link to a page in your site, you type the address of the page you want to link to directly in the Link text box (see the illustration below) or use the 🗀 Browse for File button to the right of the Link text box to open the Select File dialog box for a list of your Web site pages from which to select.

- As soon as you complete the page name, Dreamweaver underlines and changes the color of the selected text to indicate it is a link.

- For Relative links, you do not need to include the entire URL in the link address. Instead, you can include simply the actual page name. Note in the following illustration, for example, that the Link text bar shows simply contactus.html.

Select text and type the link in the Link text box

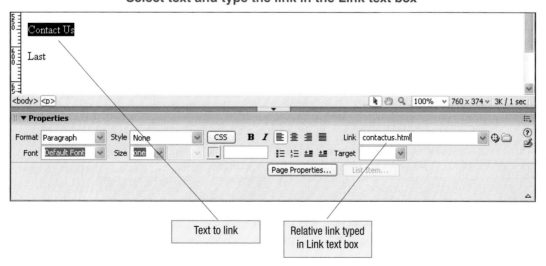

Text to link

Relative link typed in Link text box

- Another way to create a relative link to a page in your site is to use the ⊕ Point to File icon on the Property inspector to point directly to a page you want to link to:
  - Select the text for the link and then click the ⊕ Point to File icon on the Property inspector.
  - Drag the icon to an open page or to the file name in the Files panel (see the illustration below).
- The Link box updates with the name of the page you point to. Release the mouse button to complete the operation.
- Another easy way to create a link is to select the text and right-click it. Then click Make Link from the shortcut menu and choose the desired file in the Select File dialog box.
  - ✔ Yet another method is to select the text for the link and then press and hold Shift while dragging the mouse to the file name in the Files panel or to an open page that is not maximized.

- If you want to create an absolute link, you must use the Property inspector. Type the complete URL in the Link text box, including the proper protocol, such as http:// or ftp://.
- Remove a link by selecting the text used as the link and clicking the Link list arrow on the Property inspector. On the list that appears, click in the blank area at the bottom of the list.
- You can also right-click a link and select Remove Link from the shortcut menu.

Link to Named Anchor

- A **named anchor**—also called a *bookmark*—is a specific location in a Web page (such as the top of the page). After you create a named anchor, you can create a link to help visitors navigate to that point on the page.

Use Point to File to point to file name to link to

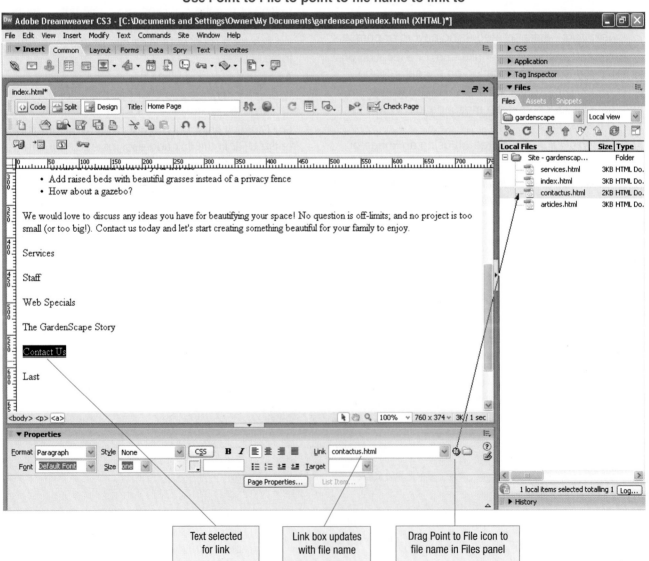

Text selected for link

Link box updates with file name

Drag Point to File icon to file name in Files panel

- Create a named anchor by positioning the insertion point at the location for the anchor (or select text to use as the anchor). Then use the Insert>Named Anchor command to open the Insert Named Anchor dialog box.

- You can also insert a named anchor by clicking the Named Anchor button from the Common category of the Insert bar.

- You can enter any name for the anchor (see the following illustration). If you have selected text as the anchor, that text appears in the Anchor name text box. You can change the displayed text if desired, however.

Insert name for anchor

- Dreamweaver inserts an anchor marker at the location where you created the named anchor and the Property inspector changes to show the name of the anchor when it's selected.

- Create the link to the named anchor by selecting the text that will form the link and then typing a pound sign (#) followed by the anchor name in the Property inspector's Link box (see the following illustration).

  ✔ *When you select text for the link, the Property inspector changes back to its default view.*

Named anchor link in Link box

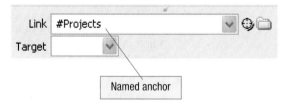

Link to E-Mail Address

- One of the most helpful items to place on your site is a link to an e-mail address where your site visitors can send you questions, feedback, comments—even complaints.

- When creating an e-mail link, you type the e-mail link directly in the Property inspector. Select the text you want to use as the link and then type **mailto:** followed by the designated e-mail address in the Property inspector's Link box (see the following illustration).

Link to e-mail address

- You can also insert an e-mail link using the Insert>Email Link command or the Email Link button from the Insert bar's Common category.

- When you use one of these options, Dreamweaver opens the Email Link dialog box (see the following illustration). Here you can type the text for the link and the e-mail address to link to.

Email Link dialog box

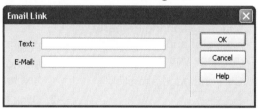

- When a visitor clicks an e-mail link in a Web page, the default e-mail program opens with the designated e-mail address already displayed in the To box.

Other Ways to Link

- The links you have learned about in this exercise are not the only ways to link pages in Dreamweaver. In the next lesson, you will learn about the following link options:

  - Graphic links—Use a graphic as the link so that when a site visitor clicks the graphic, a new page opens. The graphic may be a button or any other image, including photos.

  - Image maps—Also called *hotspots*, image maps are portions of an image used as links.

  - Navigation bars—A navigation bar is a collection of links often organized using a table. You can specify images to accompany each link.

Linking Pages in a Site

One of the most important parts of planning a site is determining how pages will be linked within the site and what links will be created to other Web sites. Search programs such as Google often evaluate links among sites as a way of weighting search results. Your site visitors need to be able to understand easily how to navigate on your Web pages.

Create a Site Map

Use the Internet to search for information on what a site map is and how it can be used to plan a site. You can sketch out a site map by hand to work out how you want all the links to connect. After you create your site, you may want to create a site map page to show visitors how all the pages in your site connect.

PROCEDURES

Create Text Links (Ctrl + L)

To create a relative link:

1. Select the text or graphic you want to use for the link.
2. Type the page address in Link text box on the Property inspector.

   OR

   a. Click the **Browse for File** button 🗀 on the Property inspector and navigate to the page you want to use.
   b. Click the page and click [OK].

   OR

   a. Click the **Point to File** button ⊕ on the Property inspector.
   b. Drag the Point to File icon to open the page or drag it to the file name in Files panel.

To create an absolute link:

1. Select the text or graphic you want to act as link.
2. Type a complete URL in Link text box on the Property inspector.

   ✔ *You must include a protocol such as http:// or ftp://.*

Create a Named Anchor (Ctrl + Alt + A)

1. Position the cursor at the anchor location, or select the text for the anchor.
2. Click **Insert** .... Alt + I
3. Click **Named Anchor** .... N

   OR

   ■ Click or drag the **Named Anchor** button 🔖 from the Common category in the Insert bar.
4. Type a name for the anchor in Named Anchor dialog box.
5. Click [OK].

Link to Anchor

1. Select the text or graphic you want to act as link.
2. Type # followed by the anchor name in the Link text box on the Property inspector.

Link to E-Mail Address

1. Select the text or graphic you want to act as link.
2. Type **mailto:** followed by the e-mail address in the Link text box on the Property inspector.

   OR

1. Click **Insert** .... Alt + I
2. Click **Email Link** L

   OR

   ■ Click or drag the **Email Link** button ▣ from the Common category in the Insert bar.
3. Type the text you want to act as a link in the Text box of the Email Link dialog box.
4. Type the e-mail address in the E-Mail box.
5. Click [OK].

EXERCISE DIRECTIONS

1. Start Dreamweaver and open the gardenscape site.
2. Open articles.html.
3. Create an anchor named **Top** to the left of the main heading on this page.
4. Scroll to the bottom of the page, and, just above the *Last update* line, type **Back to Top**.
5. Link the *Back to Top* text at the bottom of this page to the *Top* named anchor.
6. Save and close the page.
7. Open the index.html page.

8. Create relative links from the *Contact Us* paragraph to contactus.html and from *Services* to services.html.
9. Add the phrase **National Garden Association** just below *Services* and create an absolute link to the site (http://www.garden.org/).
10. Select the words *Contact us* in the last line above the Last update line and use them to create an e-mail link to the e-mail address **lisa@gardenscape.com**. The bottom of the page should look similar to Illustration A.
11. Save and close any open pages and exit Dreamweaver.

Illustration A

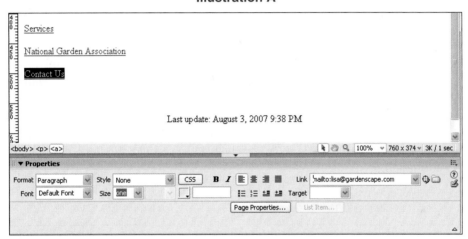

ON YOUR OWN

1. Start Dreamweaver and open the tierraverde site.
2. Open the ☉ index.html page. Scroll to the bottom of the page, highlight *Contact Us*, and create an e-mail link to the e-mail address **director@tierraverde.com**.
3. Open ☉ events.html, ☉ schedule.html, and ☉ for_parents.html from the Lesson 2 Data folder and save the pages in the current site. Update links if prompted.
4. Insert a named anchor to the left of the main heading and to the left of each of the season headings (*Spring, Summer, Autumn, Winter*).
5. Link the references to the four seasons in the last sentence of the first text paragraph to the named anchors.
6. Insert a new paragraph following the last text paragraph (and before the centered copyright notice) and insert the text **Top of page**. Link this text to the named anchor you inserted in the first text paragraph.

7. Open index.html. Modify the default links in the navigation bar as follows:
   - Select the word *Lorem* in the first table cell and type **Home**. You will not create a link for this text, because you are already on the home page.
   - Select the word *Ipsum* in the second table cell, and change the text to **Schedule**. Link the page to schedule.html.
   - Select the word *Dolar* in the third table cell, change the text to **For Parents**, and link to for_parents.html.
   - Select the words *Sic Amet* in the fourth table cell, change the text to **Events**, and link to events.html.
   - Delete the last entry, *Consetetur*.
8. Save and close any open pages and exit Dreamweaver.

Exercise | 12

Skills Covered

- Preview a Site in a Browser
- Preview a Site in Device Central
- Work in the Files Panel

Software Skills You can use the Preview in Browser feature at any time to see how your Web page will look when viewed by a site visitor. Once you have set up links, you can move from page to page in the browser to make sure the links are correct. Adobe Device Central makes it easy to view Web content as it will appear on a mobile device. Use the Files panel—collapsed and expanded—for site maintenance and to display the site map that shows how your pages are linked.

Design Skills All the greatest design techniques in the world won't help you much if your links don't work or your pages get jumbled by the Web browser. Use the techniques in this exercise to make sure your site looks just the way you want it to before you begin inviting visitors to your site.

Application Skills In this exercise, you will preview your GardenScape site in a browser and on a mobile device to check how the pages look and test the links you created in the last exercise. You will also work with the Files panel to view site information.

TERMS

Broken link A link to a page that is not available in the site because it has been deleted, renamed, or not yet created.

Child Page A subordinate page that is an off-shoot of a first-level page (for example, the home page of your site).

Device Central A feature that allows you to preview various types of content on simulated mobile devices.

Parent Page A first-level page (for example, your home page) to which other subordinate pages are linked.

Site Map A diagram that shows you the file structure of your site and enables you to identify any broken links

NOTES

Preview a Site in a Browser

■ Links are not active in Dreamweaver's Document window. To test a link, you must preview a Web page in a browser.

■ To preview a Web page, use the File>Preview in Browser command. You can select a browser from the submenu.

■ You can also click the 🌐 Preview/Debug in Browser button on the Document toolbar. Click the button to display a short menu of options for previewing or debugging the page in a browser.

> ✔ *You can use the Preferences dialog box to add browsers to the preview list. It is a good idea to test your pages on several popular browsers to avoid display problems. You learn more about checking browser compatibility in Lesson 8.*

■ The latest versions of browsers such as Internet Explorer and Mozilla Firefox support tabbed browsing, which allows you to display a whole series of visited pages as tabs at the top of the browser window, making it easy to move from page to page. Dreamweaver pages will preview correctly in a tabbed environment, so you can easily review all pages in a site by simply opening them as new tabs.

> ✔ *Check your browser's Help files to find out whether you have tabbed browsing capability, or try right-clicking a link to see whether you have the option of opening the page as a new tab.*

Preview a Site in Device Central

■ Increasingly, Web visitors are viewing Web content on mobile devices such as PDAs and cell phones. As a Web designer, you need to consider how their Web pages will appear when viewed on a mobile device.

■ Adobe **Device Central**, new in Dreamweaver CS3 (and other CS3 suite applications), allows a designer to preview content for mobile devices. To open Device Central, click Preview in Device Central on the Preview/Debug in browser list, or use the File>Preview in Browser>Device Central command.

■ The Device Central window, shown in the illustration below, shows how Web content looks on sample mobile devices. Choose a manufacturer to see a list of devices available for testing. Double-click a device and then open the file you want to view to see how content looks in the device's screen.

■ The Emulator panel shows the simulated device and allows you to view content and also interact with the device using its buttons and keypad.

■ Use the Device Profiles tab to view specifications for the selected device and see the kind of content it supports.

■ Device Central adjusts the Content Type list in the right pane according to what you are previewing. When previewing a Web page, for example, the Content Type list contains only the Browser option.

Device Central displays a simulated device in the Emulator panel

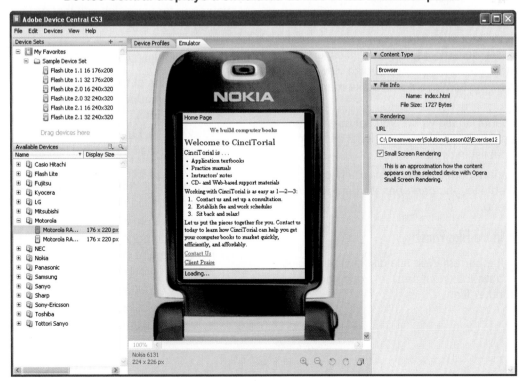

- If your page contains links, you can click them in the device's screen just as you would in a browser to verify that they work correctly.

- An in-depth exploration of designing for mobile devices is beyond the scope of this book, but there are some general guidelines that you should keep in mind when creating content that might be viewed on a mobile device:
    - Opera Small-Screen Rendering, used to display content in the mobile devices, does not support some standard Web features such as frames and pop-up menus, and some font features such as underlining, strikethrough, and blink effects.
    - The simpler the Web page, the better it will look on a mobile device. Fonts and colors should be kept to a minimum.
    - Images should be sized to exact dimensions using CSS or HTML tags to ensure that they will appear in a size appropriate for the mobile screen. Previewing in Device Central can help you select the best sizes for graphics.

Work in the Files Panel

- You've already seen and worked with the Files panel. The Files panel is one of three panels in the Files panel group that is docked by default on the right side of the Dreamweaver window.

    ✔ *You have already been introduced to the Snippets panel, one of the other Files panels. The remaining panel, the Assets panel, can contain image files, URLs, Flash movies, and other "assets" you might use throughout your site. You will use the Assets panel later in this course.*

- The Files panel is designed to make it easy for you to perform maintenance operations such as creating new HTML documents, renaming files, creating folders, and deleting files. You can also view the Web site's navigation layout with a site map in the left pane.

- The Files panel is also where you set up and control the transfer of files between a local and remote site when publishing your site.

- If the Files panel does not automatically open with the Web site, you can open it from the Window menu.

Displaying Files in the Files Panel

- All files for the current Web site display in the Files panel's window, making it easy for you to access pages and other files.

- You already know that you can switch to a different Dreamweaver site by selecting the site name on the Files panel's Site menu. This menu also gives you access to the computer's desktop and all drives on your system (see the following illustration).

Use the Site menu to access files on all drives

- Clicking a drive (such as Local Disk (C:) in the preceding illustration displays all files on that drive in the Files panel window. You can open folders to view their contents just as you can do in Windows Explorer.

- Using this feature, you can easily locate materials you need for your Web site that are not currently stored in your site.

Basic Files Panel Operations

- When the files of the current Web site are displayed in the Files window, you can perform a number of basic operations:
    - Click the ⊞ button to display subfolders within a specific folder. Expanded folders show the ⊟ button.
    - Open a page from the list of site files by double-clicking the file name.
    - Add a new page to the site by right-clicking an existing page and selecting New File. Dreamweaver creates a blank page with a selected placeholder name that you can change by simply typing a new name.

        ✔ *If you are using an application server, the new page will be created with its particular file extension.*

- Rename a file by clicking on its name twice, slowly, to select the name, or right-click the file, select Edit, and then select Rename on the pop-out menu. Once the file name is selected (see the following illustration), type the new name.

- Delete a file by clicking its icon to select all information about the file and pressing the Delete key (or right-click and select Edit>Delete).

✔ *You cannot undo actions in the Files panel. However, if you delete a file you didn't intend to, you can restore it from the Windows Recycle Bin.*

Selected file name

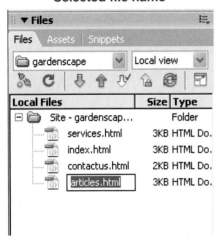

- When you rename a file, you can also change the file extension, but use caution when you do so. Specific types of pages, such as ASP pages, contain code that is required in order for that page to function properly. Simply renaming an .html page as an .asp page will not apply that code.

- If you rename a file that is linked to other pages in a Web site, Dreamweaver will ask whether you want to update links with the new page name (see the following illustration).

Update links when renaming pages

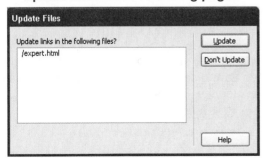

- Click the [Update] button and let Dreamweaver update the links for you.

- Dreamweaver will caution you if you delete a page that is linked to other pages in the site (see the following illustration).

Dreamweaver warns about deleting a linked page

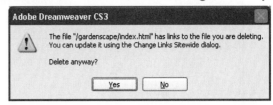

- Deleting a linked page results in a **broken link**; that is, a link that doesn't take the user to a destination. You can find any broken links easily by using the site map, which is discussed in the next section.

View the Site Map

- The **site map** enables you to view a diagram of the file structure of your site (see the following illustration at the top of the next page).

- You can view the site map in either the collapsed or expanded Files panel. In the collapsed Files panel, click Map View on the Site View pop-up menu. In the expanded Files panel, click the 🔳 Site Map button on the toolbar and select either Map and Files (as shown in the preceding illustration) or Map Only (to display only the map).

- Each page in the site is represented by a page icon with the page's name (or title) shown below the icon. The site's home page appears at the top of the map structure. The site map structure also shows absolute and e-mail links on the home page, if used.

- Organization chart–type lines show the relative links between the home page and its subordinate, or *child,* pages.

- A **child page** is a second-level page that is linked from a first-level page, also called a **parent page**. In the illustration on the next page, index.html is a parent page and services.html is a child page.

- Child pages that contain links display a ⊞ plus sign. Click this symbol to expand the site map and show links from the child page. After you click the plus sign, it becomes a ⊟ minus sign you can click to collapse the portion of the site map under the current page.

- The site map makes it easy for you to see the absolute links to pages outside the site. This helps you keep track of these links. External links are shown in blue, with the 🌐 Web symbol above the link.

The site map in the expanded Files panel

Site Map   Site Map Button   Expand/Collapse Button

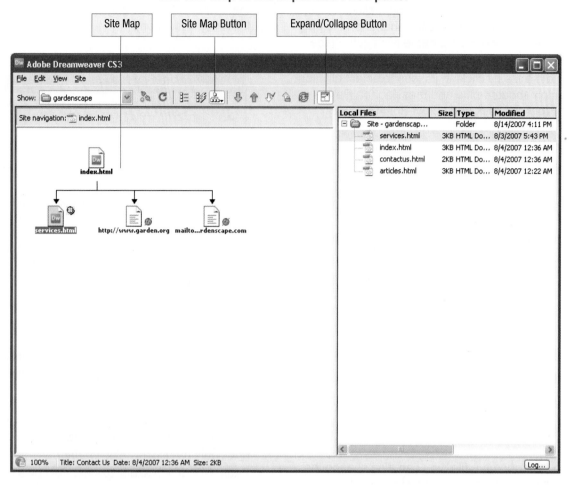

■ The site map can help you identify and resolve problems in your Web site (for example, broken links). The page name or title of a page with a broken link appears in red, with a broken link symbol above the name (see the following illustration).

Page with broken link

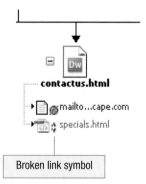

Broken link symbol

■ If you delete a linked page from the Local Files pane of the Files panel, the page remains in the site map, displaying the broken link symbol, until you remove it by selecting it and choosing the Site>Remove Link command on the Files panel menu bar.

■ You can easily modify the site map layout. Choose the Site>Manage Sites command on the Dreamweaver menu bar or at the bottom of the Files menu in the Files panel menu bar. This opens the Manage Sites dialog box. Select the desired site to edit and click the Edit button.

■ The first screen of the Site Definition wizard appears. Click the Advanced tab and select the Site Map Layout category in the Site Definition dialog box (see the illustration on the next page).

   ✔ *You may get an error message if you try to click the Basic tab when you are in the edit site mode.*

Change the site map layout

- You can make the following adjustments to the layout:
  - Change the number of columns from the default value of 200. Columns equate to the number of pages displayed below the home page.
  - Change the column width from the default value of 125. Column width is the amount of space in pixels taken up by each page displayed in the site map. You must enter a value between 70 and 1000 for this option.

- Change the way labels are displayed for the pages by changing the Icon Labels default to Page Titles. This would change, for example, the label of the top-level page from index.html to Home Page.
- Choose to display in the site map files that are normally hidden or dependent files, such as a page's images.

Web Design Connection

Checking Site Flow

Viewing your Web site through the site map gives you a great opportunity to ask yourself whether the pages in your site flow logically from one to another. Are your pages arranged in an order your site visitors will understand? Visitors should be able to move from your home page to child pages easily.

Take a Look at Site Maps

Get a sense of how other Web designers are using site maps on their sites by doing some research online. Save to your Favorites folder five or six Web sites that you think use site maps effectively.

PROCEDURES

Preview a Site in a Browser (F12)

1. Click **File** .... `Alt` + `F`
2. Point to **Preview in Browser** .... `P`, `P`, `Enter`
3. Select a browser from the submenu.

   OR

   Click **Preview/Debug in Browser** button 🌐 on the Document toolbar and select a browser from the menu.

Preview a Site in Device Central (Ctrl + Alt + F12)

1. Click **File** .... `Alt` + `F`
2. Point to **Preview in Browser** .... `P`, `P`, `Enter`
3. Click **Device Central** .... `D`

   OR

   Click **Preview/Debug in Browser** button 🌐 on the Document toolbar and then click **Preview in Device Central**.

4. Click a Manufacturer name in the Available Devices list, and then double-click a specific device from that manufacturer.
5. Click **File** .... `Alt` + `F`
6. Click **Open** .... `O`
7. Navigate to the location of the file you want to display in the selected device.
8. Select the file. Click `Open`.

   ✔ *The page opens in the Emulator tab.*

9. To see the page in a different device, double-click the new device name.

Display Files in the Files Panel

■ In the Files panel, click the Site menu and select a drive or Web site.

Files Panel Operations

To open a page from the current Web site:

■ Double-click the file name in the Files panel window to open a page in the Document window.

To add a new page to the site:

1. Right-click any existing page to display a shortcut menu.
2. Click **New File**.
3. Type a name for the new file.

To rename a page:

1. Click the file name twice, slowly, in the Files panel window to open the file name for editing.

   OR

   a. Right-click the file name to display a shortcut menu.
   b. Point to **Edit**.
   c. Click **Rename** from the shortcut menu.

2. Type the new name (and file extension if necessary).
3. Press `Enter`.
4. If the renamed page is linked to other pages, click `Update` to update links.

To delete a file:

1. Click the file name once to select and press `Delete`.

   OR

   a. Right-click the file name to display a shortcut menu.
   b. Point to **Edit**.
   c. Click **Delete**.

2. If the deleted page is linked to other pages, click `Yes` to delete.
3. Click the deleted page icon in expanded site map.
4. Click **Site**.
5. Click **Remove Link**.

Modify Site Map Layout

1. Click **Site** .... `Alt` + `S`
2. Click **Manage Sites** .... `M`
3. Select the site name in Manage Sites dialog box and click `Edit...`.
4. Click the **Advanced** tab.
5. Click **Site Map Layout** category.
6. Change **Number of columns** or **Column width** value.
7. Specify **File names** or **Page titles**.
8. Choose to display hidden files and/or dependent files.
9. Click `OK`.
10. Click `Done`.

EXERCISE DIRECTIONS

1. Start Dreamweaver and open the gardenscape site.

2. Open index.html and display this page in your default browser.

3. Test the links on the Home Page. Use the browser's Back button as necessary to return to the Home Page.

4. Click the e-mail link on the Contact Us page to see how it opens your e-mail program, but do not send a message.

5. Test the link to the named anchor on the Articles page.

6. Close the browser.

7. Open ⊙ webspecials.html and save it to your gardenscape site.

8. Preview the home page in Device Central:
   - Expand the Nokia list in the Available Devices list.
   - Double-click Nokia 6300.
   - Use the File menu to open the index.html page from the current site.
   - Change the device to another (try your own mobile phone if you have one).

9. Click the *Contact Us* link on the displayed Web page to see how the linked page displays.

10. Close Device Central.

11. Open the Files panel, if necessary.

12. Rename the articles.html file to experts.html. Update links when Dreamweaver prompts you to do so.

13. You have decided you do not need a Web Specials page in the Web site. Delete the webspecials.html page in the Local Files pane and answer *Yes* when asked if you really want to delete it.

14. Expand the Files panel and select to display the entire site map.

15. Modify the site map layout to set 15 columns and a column width of 90. Choose to show page titles rather than file names.

16. Show both the site files and the site map in the Expanded files panel.

17. Collapse the Files panel.

18. Open the index.html page from the Files panel. Scroll down and remove the History link text from the text on this page. Notice that it is no longer underlined.

19. Save and close any open pages and exit Dreamweaver.

ON YOUR OWN

1. Start Dreamweaver and open the most current version of your tierraverde Web site.

2. Open index.html and change the *Schedule* link text in the navigation bar to **Information**.

3. Point to the outside border of the navigation bar table and click to select it. You will know it is properly selected when a heavy black border displays around the outside of the table.

4. Copy the navigation bar table and paste it below the main heading on the events.html page.

5. Copy this revised navigation bar and paste it below the main heading on the other two pages in the site.

6. In the Files panel, change the name of the location.html file to info.html and update links.

7. On the info.html page, change the page heading from *Schedule* to **Information and Schedule**, and make the same change to the page title.

8. View the site map in expanded view, and click the plus signs for the pages that have them to see the links on each page.

9. Collapse the site map.

10. Save changes to all pages, and preview index.html in the browser.

11. Test each link on the home page, using the *Home* link on each page to return to the home page. When you reach the events.html page, test all links to named anchors.

12. Close the browser.

13. Preview the site in Device Central, choosing several of the sample devices to check pages. Try the page links in the Emulator screen.

14. Close Device Central.

15. Close all open pages and exit Dreamweaver.

Summary Exercise

Application Skills In this exercise, you will continue your work on the Tierra Verde site. You will add a new page, create a link to a Word registration form, and format the pages.

DIRECTIONS

1. Start Dreamweaver and open the tierraverde site.
2. Open the ⊙ registration.html file from the Lesson 2 Data files. Save it in your tierraverde site and change the page name to **Registration**.
3. Clean up the code on this page:
   - Use the Clean Up Word HTML command to remove unnecessary Word HTML code.
   - Use the Code inspector to remove unnecessary codes such as the <style> tags, change the charset attribute to **iso-8859-1**, and remove unnecessary attributes in the opening body tag.
   - Use Find and Replace to strip any <div> tags.
   - Clean up HTML to make sure the page code is up to date.
4. In the Files panel, display the drive that contains your data files.
5. Copy the ⊙ registrationform.doc file from the Lesson 2 Data files to the tierraverde site folder.

   ✔ Select the file, right-click and choose Edit, and then choose Copy. Open the tierraverde site again, right-click in the Files panel, choose Edit, and choose Paste.

6. On the registration.html page, link the text *click here to download our registration form* to the registrationform.doc file.
7. Under the *Camp Fees* heading, boldface the types of fees.
8. Increase the indent of the three specialty classes and boldface the class names.
9. Under the *Registration Steps* heading, replace the numbered steps with an ordered list in Dreamweaver by deleting the numbers and applying the Ordered List format.
10. Apply text formats on the page as follows:
    - Apply the same color to the page heading that you used for the heading on index.html.
    - Apply the Heading 2 format to *Camp Fees* and *Registration Steps*.
11. Open info.html and copy the navigation bar. Paste it just below the heading on registration.html.
12. Return to index.html and type the following text:
    Registration for the upcoming camping season is now open! Click here for more info.
13. Create a link from *Click here for more info* to **registration.html**.
14. Copy the text and link you added to info.html and paste it after the first paragraph on index.html.
15. Add the word **NEW!** preceding the new text. Boldface it and apply a red color.
16. Center the new text you added to index.html. Your page should look like the one shown in Illustration A on the next page.
17. Display an expanded view of the site map of the Tierra Verde site. Check all links to all pages to make sure no broken links exist in the site.
18. Return to Local View and save and preview the index.html page in the browser. Test the link to the Registration page.

19. On the Registration page, test the link to the membership form. A File Download box should display asking if you want to open or save the file. Choose to open it to see the form linked to your site.

20. Close the form, and close the browser.

21. Close all open pages and exit Dreamweaver.

Illustration A

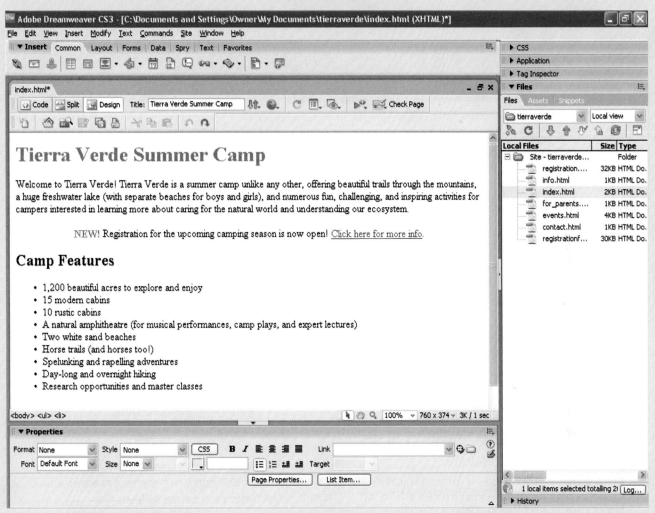

Application Exercise

Application Skills In this exercise, you will continue to work on the Classmate Connections Web site that you began in Exercise 5. You will add page content, format pages, and create links to start setting up site navigation.

DIRECTIONS

1. Start Dreamweaver and open the classmate_connections Web site.

2. Use the Files panel to create a new file and name it groups.html. Give it the page title **Classmate Groups**.

3. Enter the following text on the groups.html page.

   ✔ If you prefer, you can copy and paste text from the file ⊙ groupstxt.doc in the Lesson 2 Data folder.

   Welcome to the Groups Page!

   Talk to others who are interested in the same things you are!

   This page lists six basic interest categories (oh come on—you have to like at least one thing here). Check out the favorite links provided by your classmates. Click here to submit your own favorite links.

   Music
   Movies
   Web stuff
   Shopping
   Books
   Nature

   Back to Top

   Back to Top

4. Apply a heading tag of your choice to the page heading.

5. Format the list items (from *Music* to *Nature*) as Heading 2.

6. Add a navigation bar beneath the page heading that includes the following items: *Home*, *Add Me!*, *Groups*, *Pages*, and *Links*.

7. Create the following links for the navigation bar:
   - Link Home to index.html.
   - Link Add Me! to addme.html.
   - Leave Groups, Pages, and Links unlinked for now.

8. Under each category, insert several links to popular sites. You can use links that are well-known or insert your own personal favorites.

9. Format the links in each category as unordered lists.

10. Insert a named anchor to the left of the first item on the page, and then link to it using the *Back to Top* text at the bottom of the page.

11. Use Clean Up XHTML to check coding on the page.

12. Open the index.html page. Make the following changes:
    - Format the page heading as Heading 1.
    - Copy the navigation bar from **groups.html** to **index.html**.
    - Link the Groups item on the navigation bar to **groups.html**.

13. Create an unordered list from the *Where Do I Start?* list.
14. Format all three pages of the site:
    - Select a new font combination if desired.
    - Create a color scheme for the headings throughout the site.
    - Adjust font sizes if desired.
15. Display an expanded site map of the site and check for any broken links.

16. Display head content on the index.html page and check your keywords for this site.
17. Check spelling on all three pages.
18. Save all pages and then display the home page in the browser and check links in the site.
19. Close all open pages.
20. Exit Dreamweaver.

Curriculum Integration

Application Skills Your Math class is studying various math forms and applications and has decided to create a Web site that will include brief descriptions and examples of various mathematical approaches. Your group has been assigned the topic *Discrete Mathematics*.

Before you begin work on the site, you need to gather information about the following things:

- A definition of discrete mathematics (in your own words)
- Examples of the ways discrete math is used in the world today
- Samples of mathematical problems using discrete math

DIRECTIONS

Define a new site with the name discrete_math. Create a new page for the site and name it discrete.html. Give it a page title of your choosing.

If you have Microsoft Office Word available, open it and type your definition of discrete mathematics. (This gives you the advantage of instant spell checking.) Import the Word document to the discrete.html page.

Format the definition as desired. For example, boldface the title and italicize any sources you used. Make any other adjustments to the layout of the definition you think are necessary.

Create a new Web page and give it a name such as uses.html. Add an appropriate page title and a heading. On this page, you will add a list of ways in which discrete math is used in the work world today.

Create an unordered list of examples. After each item, include a description in your own words of the way discrete math is used for that application.

Create a list of resources giving any Web links or print resources you used to find the information.

Add the heading **Resources** above the resources list.

Create a third page and name it samples.html. Add a heading and provide two or more samples of discrete math problems that might be included on a test. Be sure to provide any resource used for the equations.

Return to discrete.html and add links to the uses.html and samples.html pages.

At the bottom of the page, add your name, the current date, and your class information. Also include the names of the other members of your team. Format the information as needed.

Use the History panel to record this information and copy it to the other two pages.

View the site in the expanded site map and check all page links.

Save your pages and then preview the pages in the browser. Make any final changes necessary and save all pages.

Exit Dreamweaver.

Exercise | 16

Critical Thinking

Application Skills   In this exercise, you will continue to work on the non-profit Web site you started in Exercise 7. You will format existing page content, add new content to the site, use a snippet to create a navigation bar, and insert other links to improve site navigation.

DIRECTIONS

■ Review the pages you have already created for your Web site and modify them as desired. For example, you might want to create ordered or unordered lists from some of the page text, change text formats (font combination, font size, font style, font color), modify paragraph alignments and indentations to improve the look of the pages, insert special characters if needed, and so on.

■ Create additional text for the site in Microsoft Office Word. You may save the new material in default Word format and then import it, or save it as a Word Web page and open it directly in the site. (Don't forget to save the page in the site if you use the second option.)

■ Clean up XHTML coding as needed for the new material you added.

■ Insert a navigation bar snippet on the home page and modify it to link to the pages currently in your site. Copy the navigation bar to other pages in the site and make sure all links are correct.

■ Create other links from page to page in the site as desired. You may want to add links to named anchors or links from text to other pages. You may also want to insert links to pages outside the site.

■ Add an e-mail link somewhere in the site using your school or personal e-mail address so that site visitors can contact you with questions or comments.

■ Check spelling on all pages.

■ Save all pages and preview the site in the browser.

■ Preview the site in Device Central using several devices of your choice.

■ Save all open documents and close them.

■ Exit Dreamweaver.

Lesson | 3

Work with Graphic Elements and Templates

Skills Covered

- **Change the Page Background Color**
- **Use Web-Safe and Custom Colors**
- **Insert Horizontal Rules**

Software Skills The color and style you choose for your Web page background can liven up your page or make it stand out among other pages in a site. You can also add horizontal rules to divide pages so that certain parts of the page are emphasized. When selecting colors for a Web site, you can use Dreamweaver's palette of Web-safe colors or create your own colors.

Design Skills Creating an appealing background for your page helps ensure that your site visitors will like your overall page design. Adding rules on your pages helps group information so that readers can clearly understand how your page content is organized.

Application Skills In this exercise, you add some visual interest to the GardenScape Web site by applying a background color to a page and inserting horizontal rules.

TERMS

Rules Horizontal lines added as a design element to a page to help organize the content and add a design element.

Web-safe colors A palette of 216 colors that will display the same in any browser, regardless of the operating system.

NOTES

Change the Page Background Color

- A simple way to add graphic interest to a Web page is to change its background color. By default, the Web pages you create in Dreamweaver have a white background. You don't have to leave them white, however; you can use any of the colors in the Dreamweaver color palette as a page background color—but Web-safe colors are recommended.

- To change page background color, use the Modify>Page Properties command to open the Page Properties dialog box (see the illustration below). If you have the Property inspector expanded, you can also click [Page Properties...] to open the Page Properties dialog box.

Page Properties dialog box

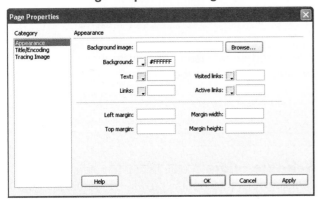

- Click the [ ] Background color button to display the color palette and use the eyedropper to select a color.

- You can use the [Apply] Apply button to apply your color choice without closing the Page Properties dialog box. If you do not like the applied color, you can open the color palette and choose a different color.

- Notice the other color buttons in this dialog box. You can use them to change the color of all text and links on the page. You can also change the colors of visited links and links in the process of being clicked (called *active links*).

- You can also apply margin settings from this dialog box. You will learn more about setting page margins in a later exercise.

Insert Horizontal Rules

- You can insert horizontal rules on your Web pages to separate sections of text. Position the cursor at the beginning or end of a paragraph and use the Insert>HTML>Horizontal Rule command.

  - ✔ *If you position the cursor at the end of a paragraph, the horizontal rule is inserted below the paragraph. If you position the cursor at the beginning of a paragraph, the horizontal rule is inserted above the paragraph.*

- You can change horizontal rule formats by selecting the horizontal rule and changing settings in the Property inspector (see the illustration below).

- By default, the rule runs the full width of the Web page. You can specify a width in the W text box using either a pixel measurement or a percentage of the page width. If you specify a width less than the full page, you can choose an alignment option of left, center, or right to tell Dreamweaver how you want the rule positioned on the page.

- Use the H box to specify a height for the rule in pixels. Select the Shading checkbox to add shading to the rule that makes it look three-dimensional. Deselect this checkbox to make the rule a solid color.

- The Properties panel does not have a feature to change the horizontal rule's color. However, you can change the color of the horizontal rule by editing the HTML <hr> tag in the Tag inspector's property sheet or in Code view, as follows:

<hr color="009999">

- The rule color does not display in Design view. You must preview the page in the browser to see the color.

  - ✔ *If you specify a color for the rule, you cannot also display shading. Regardless of whether Shading is selected, the rule will display as a solid color.*

- The color attribute for horizontal rules may not display correctly in all browsers. To make sure the rule displays as you want it to, you can modify the HTML tag using a CSS style. (You will learn how to do this later in the course.)

- Although horizontal rules are easy to insert, you may want to consider using CSS styles to apply them because you have many more options about where to position rules and how to format them. CSS styles make it easy for you to apply the same settings to rules you add at other points in your Web site.

Change horizontal rule formats

▼ Properties						
Horizontal rule	W		pixels	Align	Default	Class	None
	H				☑ Shading		

Use Web-Safe and Custom Colors

■ As you learned earlier in this course, the color palette that appears when you click a color box in a panel or dialog box displays **Web-safe colors**. The 216 color blocks in this palette display the same way, regardless of the browser or operating system you (or your site visitors) are using. This means that if you choose color #990000 for a heading, you can be sure that the color will appear as the same dark red in Internet Explorer, Netscape, Firefox, or Opera, running on a Windows, Macintosh, or Linux operating system.

■ When the Web-safe color palette was developed, most computers could display a maximum of 256 colors. Now that many systems are capable of 16-bit and 32-bit display, which enables them to display millions of colors, it is not as important to stick to the Web-safe color palette as it once was.

■ One exception to free expression of color occurs when you are designing for Web devices such as cell phones or PDAs. Adobe's Device Central makes it easy for you to check how colors will display on other mobile devices.

■ To choose a color outside the Web-safe palette, click the 🔘 System Color Picker icon at the upper-right corner of the color palette to open the Color dialog box (see the illustration in the next column).

Color dialog box

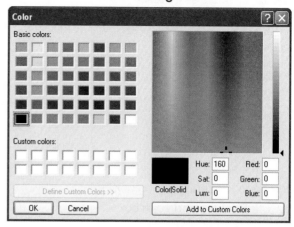

■ Select one of the basic color blocks or create a custom color as follows:
- Enter values for Hue, Saturation, and Luminescence or for Red, Green, and Blue.
- Drag the pointer in the continuous color palette and then adjust intensity in the vertical slider.

■ You can add the custom color you create to the Custom colors palette so it will be available for future use.

■ The Web-safe color palette that appears when you click a color box offers an options arrow at the upper-right corner of the palette. Click this arrow to display additional options. You can choose to display the Continuous Tone palette or palettes especially for Windows or Macintosh systems. A grayscale palette is also available on this menu.

Web Design Connection

Color and Site Effectiveness

By now you're accustomed to viewing Web sites with a designer's eye. The background color on the pages you visit has a significant, but subtle impact. The background color should support the font, pictures, and other design elements on the page but not overwhelm any of the other items.

Evaluate Color Backgrounds

Open some of the Web sites you've saved in your Favorites folder and take a look at the background colors that are used. Which ones look great with the text on the page? Which ones are too loud? Which ones could use some livening up?

PROCEDURES

Change Background Color (Ctrl + J)

1. Click **Modify**.................. Alt + M
2. Click **Page Properties**.......... P

   OR

   - Click [Page Properties...] on the expanded Property inspector.

In the Page Properties dialog box:

3. Click **Background** color box ⬜ to display color palette.
4. Use the eyedropper to pick a color.
5. Click [Apply] to apply color without closing the dialog box.
6. Click [OK] when finished in the dialog box.

Insert a Horizontal Rule

Position the cursor at beginning or end of a paragraph.

1. Click **Insert** .... Alt + I
2. Point to **HTML**.................. H
3. Click **Horizontal Rule**.......... Z

To modify rule properties:

In the Property inspector or Tag inspector:

- Specify the width you want in pixels or percent measurement.
- Specify the height in pixels.
- Select the alignment if the rule is less than 100% of the page width.
- Turn shading on or off.
- Specify color in one of the code views or in the Tag inspector using the color attribute and a hexadecimal value.

  ✔ *The Tag inspector enables you to use a color palette if you prefer that method of picking a color.*

To copy rule to new location:

1. Right-click the rule and select **Copy**.
2. Right-click at the point you want the role to be inserted and select **Paste**.

Create a Custom Color

1. Click any color box ⬜ in any panel to display the Web-safe color palette.
2. Click **System Color Picker** 🔘 to display the Color dialog box.
3. Specify values for **Hue**, **Sat**, and **Lum** or **Red**, **Green**, and **Blue**.

   OR

   - Drag the pointers in the continuous tone palette and vertical intensity slider.
4. Choose to add the color to the Custom colors palette, if desired.
5. Click [OK].

EXERCISE DIRECTIONS

1. Start Dreamweaver and open the gardenscape site.
2. Emphasize the experts.html page by applying a green background color to the page (#66FF99).
3. Open the ⊙ designers.html page and save it in the current Web site. Update links if prompted.
4. Change the page title to **Meet Your Designers**.
5. Change the background color of the page to match experts.html.
6. Insert a horizontal rule above the heading *All-Natural Gardening*.
7. Remove the rule's shading and change its height to 3.
8. Use the Tag inspector to modify the horizontal rule's color to #990033.
9. Save the page and preview it in the browser to see the color applied to the rule. Close the browser.

10. You would like the rule color to be a little darker. Create a custom color:
    - Click the color box for the rule in the Tag inspector, and then click the System Color Picker icon to open the Color dialog box.
    - Change the Lum setting to 60.
    - Add the color as a custom color.
11. Copy the rule and paste it above the *Garden Pest Expert* heading.
12. Copy and paste the rule above *Create a Living Habitat*.
13. Save the page and view it in the browser again. The top of your GardenScape page should look similar to Illustration A on the next page.
14. Save and close any open pages and the browser, and exit Dreamweaver.

Illustration A

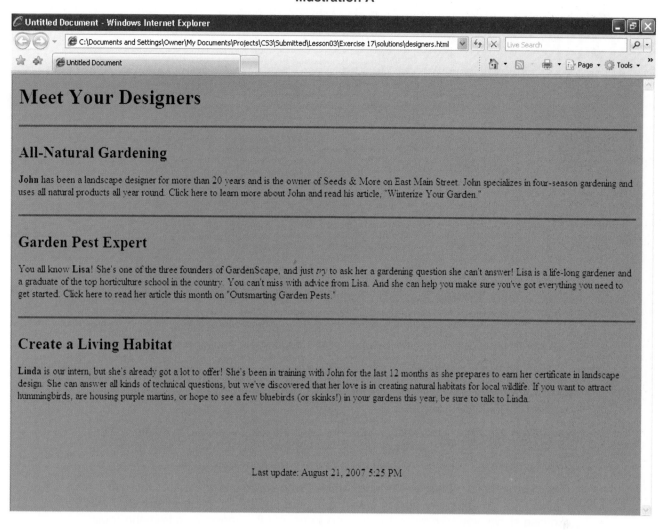

ON YOUR OWN

1. Start Dreamweaver and open the java2go Web site.

2. Open index.html.

3. Choose a new background color for this page. Choose a color that contrasts well with the main heading color.

   ✔ You can either choose a Web-safe color or mix your own custom color.

   ✔ Notice that the table cells that create the navigation bar do not fill with color. You will learn how to change table background color in a later exercise.

4. Open recipe.html.

5. Insert a horizontal rule above *The Ingredients* heading. Format the rule as follows:

   ■ Specify that the rule is 95% of the page width.

   ■ Center the rule.

   ■ Use your judgment about the height, shading, and color of the rule.

6. Copy and paste the rule just above the heading *The Steps*.

7. Save and close all open pages and exit Dreamweaver.

Skills Covered

- **About Adobe Fireworks**
- **About Bitmap and Vector Images**
- **Start Fireworks and Create a New Document**
- **Learn the Fireworks Window and Tools**

- **Understand the Select Tools**
- **Learn the Bitmap Tools**
- **Understand Vector Tools**
- **Change the View**
- **Fit the Canvas**

Software Skills Adobe Fireworks is a software program that enables you to create and edit both **vector** graphics and **bitmap** graphics. Fireworks makes it easy for you to create objects for your Web pages, such as interactive buttons and rollovers. You can also optimize the images you add to your pages so that they download more quickly on the Web. When you start a new Fireworks document, you choose the size, resolution, and background color. You can arrange the Fireworks work area and tools in a way that fits the way you want to work. When you are finished working in Fireworks, save your files.

Design Skills Fireworks provides you with the tools you need to create quality, interactive graphics for your Web pages. In this exercise, you learn how to start a graphic image in Fireworks and get to know the Fireworks tools.

Application Skills Getting familiar with the basic tools you will use in Fireworks is an important part of knowing how to use the program effectively. This exercise shows you how to start a Fireworks document, choose tools from the Tools panel, and learn about the bitmap and vector tools.

TERMS

Bitmap graphics A type of image made up of individual dots (also known as *pixels*).

Canvas color The color used as the background color for the image you create in Fireworks.

Crop Changing the size of an object by removing unneeded parts of the image.

Interactive buttons Objects you create and place on your Web site that enable users to interact with your site.

Optimize Reducing the size of images so that your Web pages will load quickly while displaying the highest possible quality.

Path The line that defines the outer edge of a vector object.

Pixels The individual dots that make up a bitmapped image.

Resolution The number of dots or pixels per linear unit of measurement. For example, a computer monitor typically displays about 72 pixels per inch.

Rollovers Areas on a Web page that change in appearance when the mouse pointer passes over them.

Scalable Type of object that can be resized easily without any loss of quality or proportion.

Slices Areas in an image that react to the mouse pointer.

Vector graphics A type of image that is defined mathematically and drawn as an object on the screen (as opposed to the dots that comprise bitmap images).

NOTES

About Adobe Fireworks

- Adobe Fireworks is a professional-level software program you can use to create and modify images and objects for your Web sites.
- Adobe Fireworks is part of the Adobe CS3 Web Design suite.
- Adobe Fireworks runs on both Windows and Macintosh computers. The keys you use to perform specific tasks may differ slightly between the two systems.

  ✔ *This text covers the techniques you use on Windows computers. You can use this book with the Macintosh version, however, by using the [CMD] key instead of Ctrl, and the [OPTION] key instead of Alt. Some other menu commands or mouse options may also differ slightly.*

- You can create both vector graphics and bitmap graphics in Fireworks.
- Fireworks enables you to easily resize vector images without any loss of quality.
- You can use Fireworks to add interactive elements to your graphics. You might create an interactive button, for example, or add a rollover effect to an object on the page.

About Bitmap and Vector Images

- Bitmap images are made up of colored dots called **pixels**. Digital photographs and images created in paint programs like Windows Paint are bitmap images.
- When you enlarge a bitmap images, the dots become visible, resulting in a jagged quality.
- Large bitmap images (or large images that have been scaled down to a smaller size) can significantly increase the amount of time it takes your page to download.
- Vector images are created by mathematical calculations that draw the object on the screen. For example, when you use a vector tool to draw a polygon, the program uses a calculation to produce the shape as you draw it.
- You can resize vector images without any loss of quality because vector images are **scalable**.

Start Fireworks and Create a New Document

- Start Fireworks by using the Start>All Programs>Adobe Web Standard CS3>Adobe Fireworks CS3 menu command in Windows.

  ✔ *If you are using the standalone version of Fireworks, the program name you select to launch the program may be slightly different.*

- On the Fireworks start page, in the Create New area, click Fireworks Document. The New Document dialog box appears.
- You can also create a new document by choosing the File>New menu command. This action also displays the New Document dialog box.

New Document dialog box

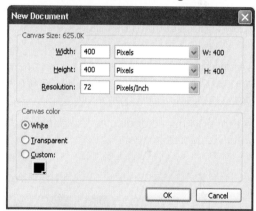

- Enter the width, height, and resolution you want to use for the new document.

  ✔ *You can choose pixels, inches, or centimeters for the width and height of your document. Always use pixels for Web documents. You can also choose to show pixels per inch or per centimeter.*

- The settings you enter in the New Document dialog box determine the canvas size of your Fireworks document. You can change the canvas size later by clicking anyplace on the work area (make sure no objects are selected). The Property inspector displays the Canvas Size, Image Size, and Fit Canvas buttons and you can click the one you want to resize the work area as needed.
- Choose the **canvas color** for your document. This color acts as the background for your document.

- If you click the Custom option in the Canvas Color choices, click the selector box to choose the color you want to use.

  - ✔ *If you want your Web page to show through the background of the image you create, click the Transparent option in the Canvas Color options, which appears as a white object with a red line through it.*

- Click OK to save your selections in the New Document dialog box and create the new document.

Learn the Fireworks Window and Tools

- The Fireworks window displays a work area, the tools panel, the Property inspector, and command panels.

- You work on the document in the work area.

- The tools panel contains all the tools you need to work with vector and bitmap images in a variety of ways.

- The command panels on the right of the Fireworks window contain commands related to specific tasks in Fireworks.

  - ✔ *The command panels on your screen may be different from the ones shown in the illustration. You can choose other command panels in the Window menu.*

- The Property inspector displays settings for the currently selected image.

Understand the Select Tools

- The Select tools are found at the top of the Tools panel.

- You use the Select tools to select objects in your Fireworks documents so that you can work with them.

- The tools shown by default in the Select area are the Pointer tool, the Subselection tool, the Scale tool and the Crop tool, as shown in the following illustration.

The tool in the Select tools area

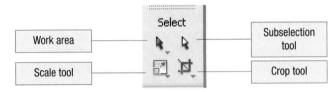

- You use the Pointer tool to select most objects by clicking or by dragging.

- Use the Subselection tool to select the end of a **path** so that you can join it to another path.

  - ✔ *You can also use the Subselection tool to select part of an object without selecting the entire object.*

The Fireworks window and tools

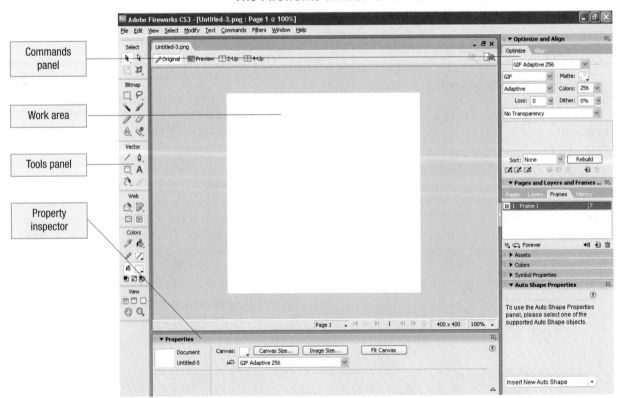

- The Scale tool enables you to change the size of objects by dragging a handle on the corner or side of the selected object, increasing or reducing their size, as the illustration at the bottom of this page shows.

- The Crop tool enables you to change the size of objects by cropping out the parts of the image you don't want to use.

- Three of the tools show small arrows in the lower-right corner of the tool. This lets you know that there are hidden tools available for that tool. Click the triangle to display the additional tools and click the one you want to use.

- The Select Behind tool, hidden behind the Pointer tool, enables you to select objects that are hidden behind other objects.

- The Skew tool, hidden behind the Scale tool, changes the shape of objects when you drag their edges. The opposite edge of the object remains parallel to the edge you drag, changing both sides of the object proportionally.

- The Distort tool, also behind the Scale tool, enables you to change the shape of objects by dragging any corner or edge.

  ✔ *You must select an object with the Pointer tool before you can use Scale, Skew, or Distort to modify it.*

- The Export Area tool, hidden behind the Crop tool, enables you to export a rectangular area of an object to another file.

Learn the Bitmap Tools

- Bitmap images are made of individual pixels. Digital photos are one example of bitmap images.

- The Bitmap section of the Tools panel, shown in the following illustration, provides you with the tools you need to work with bitmap images.

The tools in the Bitmap area of the Tools panel

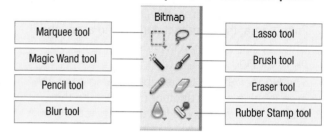

- You use the Marquee tool to select a rectangular area of an object. The Oval Marquee tool is hidden behind the Marquee tool. This tool enables you to select an oval area.

- The Lasso tool enables you to select an irregular, freeform area. Behind the Lasso tool is the Polygon Lasso tool, enabling you to create a selection area by clicking a series of points on the object, which connect to form a polygon.

- You use the Magic Wand tool to choose a color in a specific area of an object.

Resize a bitmap object

- The Brush tool enables you to paint a brush stroke on the image.

- The Pencil tool gives you the means to draw lines on the document.

- The Eraser tool enables you to remove pixels from an image.

- The Blur tool reduces the sharpness of an area of your image. Several tools are hidden behind the Blur tool: The Sharpen tool increases the sharpness of the image area, the Dodge tool lightens an image area; the Burn tool darkens an area; and the Smudge tool pushes a colored area in the displayed image.

- The Rubber Stamp tool enables you to copy an area in an image to another area. Behind the Rubber Stamp tool, you find the Replace Color tool, which enables you to replace one color in the image with another. Finally, the Red Eye Removal tool is also behind the Rubber Stamp tool. You use this tool to reduce the red eye effect in a digital photo.

Understand Vector Tools

- Vector images are based on mathematical calculations, so they can be resized without any loss of quality.

- Fireworks includes a set of Vector tools in the Tools panel, as shown in the following illustration.

The tools in the Vector area of the Tools panel

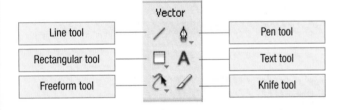

- You use the Line tool to draw straight lines on your image.

  ✔ To draw perfectly straight horizontal or vertical lines, or lines at a 45-degree angle, press and hold Shift as you draw using the Line tool.

- The Pen tool enables you to draw smooth curves. Behind the Pen tool is the Vector Path tool. You use the Vector Path tool to draw **paths** using a variety of brush strokes. The Redraw Path tool is another tool hidden behind the Pen tool. This tool extends or redraws an existing path using the same settings as the current path.

- You use the Rectangle tool to draw rectangles. Behind the Rectangle tool is the Ellipse tool, which you use to draw ovals or circles. The Polygon tool is also hidden behind the Rectangle tool. This tool enables you to multi-sided objects.

  ✔ To draw perfect squares or circles, press and hold Shift as you draw using the Rectangle or Ellipse tool.

  ✔ Behind the Rectangle tool you will find a number of shape-specific tools: the Arrow, Beveled Rectangle, Chamfer Rectangle, Connector Line, Doughnut, L-Shape, Pie, Rounded Rectangle, Smart Polygon, Spiral, and Star tools.

- The Text tool enables you to add text to your object.

- You use the Freeform tool to bend and reshape objects. Behind the Freeform tool is the Reshape Area tool, which you use to adjust the shape of a path that appears inside the circle of the Reshape Area tool pointer. Two other tools behind the Freeform tool, Path Scrubber tool–additive and Path Scrubber tool–subtractive, enable you to change a path's stroke by adding or reducing characteristics, respectively.

- The Knife tool enables you to slice a path into more than one path.

Change the View

- Fireworks gives you several tools for changing the way you view your work, as the following illustration shows.

Use View tools to change the display

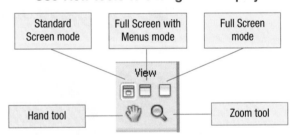

- The top row of the View tools includes tools that enable you to display normal view (the default), hide the Fireworks title bar, or hide both the title bar and the menus.

- Use the Hand tool to drag the workspace so you can view a specific area of the object.

- Use the Zoom tool to magnify an area of your object. The Zoom tool centers the new view at the point you click.

  ✔ To zoom out, press and hold Alt while you click with the Zoom tool.

Fit the Canvas

- You can easily change the size of the canvas to fit the image you are working with.

- Fitting the canvas to the object enables you to cut out any background surrounding the image that you don't want to import into Dreamweaver or another application.

- If you want to adjust the size of the canvas but not shrink it to fit exactly the size of the image, you can use the [Canvas Size...] Canvas Size button and enter values for the width and height of the canvas as you want it to appear.

- Use the [Fit Canvas] Fit Canvas button in the Property inspector to reduce the size of the canvas to fit the image.

  ✔ *You can use Fit Canvas only to reduce the size of the canvas to match the size of the image; you cannot use Fit Canvas to enlarge the canvas to accommodate an image that may extend beyond the visible edges of the canvas.*

PROCEDURES

Start Fireworks

1. Click [start] / [ ] on the Windows taskbar.................................[⊞]
2. Click **All Programs**.
3. Click **Adobe Web Standard CS3** (if applicable).
4. Click **Adobe Fireworks CS3**.

Create a New Document (Ctrl + N)

1. Click [Fireworks Document (PNG)] **Fireworks Document** in the Create New area.

   OR

   - Click the **File>New** menu command ....[Ctrl]+[N]

2. Type a **Width** setting for the new document...............[Alt]+[W]
3. Enter a **height** setting for the new document...............[Alt]+[H]

   ✔ *These settings determine the canvas size for your image.*

4. Enter a **Resolution**.......[Alt]+[R]
5. Choose a Canvas color from the following:
   - Leave **White** selected for a blank background.....[Alt]+[I]
   - Click **Transparent** for no background color .....[Alt]+[T]
   - Click **Custom** and choose a color ....[Alt]+[C]
6. Click [OK] OK.

Open a Fireworks Document (Ctrl + O)

1. Click **File** ....[Alt]+[F]
2. Click **Open** ....[O]
3. Click the **Look in** arrow.
4. Select the drive or folder.
5. Click the file name to select it.
6. Click [Open] Open.

Show/Hide Panel

Alternately display or hide command panels in Fireworks:

1. Click **Window** ....[Alt]+[W]
2. Click to select or deselect a panel name.

Save a Fireworks File (Ctrl + S, Shift + Ctrl + S)

To save a file for the first time:

1. Click **File** ....[Alt]+[F]
2. Click **Save**...........................[S]
3. Click the **Save in** arrow.
4. In the Save As dialog box, select the drive or folder where the file should be stored.
5. Type the file name in the File name box, if necessary.
6. Select the file format in the Save as type box, if necessary.
7. Click [Save] **Save**.

To save a file with a new name or to a new location:

1. Click **File** ....[Alt]+[F]
2. Click **Save As**........[A], [A], [Enter]
3. Follow steps 3–7 above.

Display Tools Panel Tool Names

- Move the mouse pointer over a tool.
- View the tool name and short-cut key in the pop-up tip.

Select an Object

1. Click the [ ] **Pointer** tool to activate it.
2. Click the object you want to select.

Select a Group of Objects by Dragging

1. Click the [ ] **Pointer** tool to activate it.
2. Drag a marquee that encloses each object you want to select.

Select a Group of Objects by Clicking

1. Click the [ ] **Pointer** tool.
2. Press and hold **Shift** as you click each object you want to add.................................[⇧ Shift]

Pan the View

1. Click the 🖐 **Hand** tool to activate it.
2. Position the mouse pointer on the document where you want to drag.
3. Press and hold the mouse button and drag the document.

Zoom the View In

1. Click the 🔍 **Zoom** tool.
2. Position the pointer where you want to zoom in.
3. Click the mouse button.

Zoom the View Out

1. Click the 🔍 **Zoom** tool.
2. Move the mouse pointer to the place in the document you want to zoom out.
3. Press and hold Alt and click .... [Alt]

Fit to Canvas

1. Save the image.
2. Click the [Fit Canvas] **Fit Canvas** button in the Property inspector.

EXERCISE DIRECTIONS

1. Start Adobe Fireworks.
2. Open ⊙ 18_gslogo.png.
3. In the Tools panel, click the 🔧 Pointer tool.
4. Click the rectangular-shaped object in the lower-right corner of the document.
5. Click the 🔧 Scale tool.
6. Click and drag the left edge of the rectangle to make it larger.
7. Click the 🔧 Pointer tool and hold down the mouse button until the hidden tools appears.
8. Click the 🔧 Select Behind tool to select it.
9. Move the mouse pointer over the rectangle until the outline of the hidden object appears and then press [Ctrl] and click the hidden object to select it.

10. Drag the hidden object up until it is sitting above the rectangle.
11. Select the 🔧 Pointer tool.
12. Click to select the flower.
13. Drag the flower so that it is on top of the rectangle, as shown in Illustration A.
14. Save the file in your solutions folder as S_18_gslogo_xx.png.

   ✔ When you see _xx in any instructions in this book, it means that you should type an underscore followed by your own initials—not the actual text "_xx". This will help your instructor identify your work.

15. Leave the file open for the On Your Own exercise. Or, close the file and exit Fireworks.

Illustration A

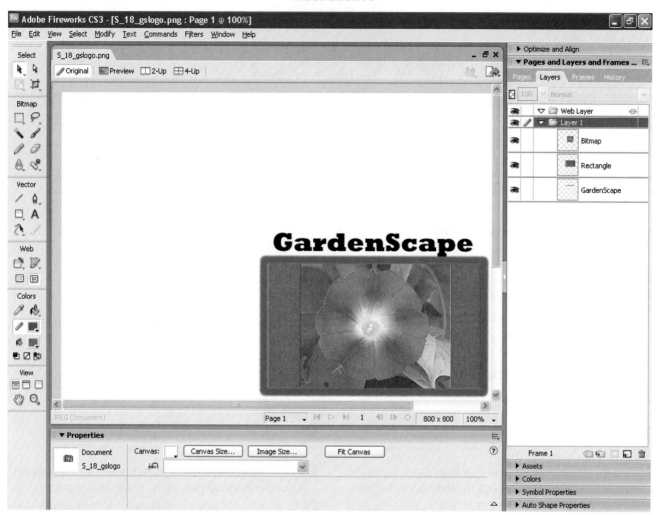

ON YOUR OWN

1. In S_18_gslogo_xx.png, select the text object at the top of the image.
2. Select the remaining two items and move the group to the upper-left corner of the work area.
3. Fit the canvas size to the image.
4. Save the file in your solutions folder as SO_18_gslogo_xx.png.
5. Close the file and exit Fireworks.

Skills Covered

- **Learn about Bitmap Objects**
- **Select the Drawing Colors**
- **Draw with the Brush Tool**
- **Draw with the Pencil Tool**
- **Select Bitmap Objects**
- **Copy and Paste Bitmap Objects**

Software Skills Fireworks provides a full set of professional tools you can use to create, modify, and enhance bitmap objects for your Web pages. The Brush tool, Pencil tool, and the bitmap selection tools are important tools you will use often as you work with bitmap images. Learning how to work with bitmap image tools will give you the ability to edit and enhance photos and other images on your Web pages.

Design Skills Being able to open, work with, and enhance bitmap images for your Web pages is a specialized skill that can help you create a professional look for your Web pages.

Application Skills In this exercise, you use the bitmap tools to select and modify objects in a digital image.

TERMS

Anti-aliasing A technique that smooths the rough edges of a bitmapped image by adding transitional colors to the pixels along the edges.

Fill The color, pattern, or texture used in the interior of a shape, arc, or text.

Opacity The transparency level of the selected object. An object that is 100% opaque is completely solid, and one that is 0% is transparent.

Stroke The outline of an object, including characteristics such as weight, color, style, and more.

RGB A common color model that uses a hexadecimal value (for example, #C7C7C7) to communicate a color by the amount of Red, Green, and Blue used to create the color.

NOTES

Learn about Bitmap Objects

■ Bitmap images are made up of colored dots called pixels. When you enlarge a bitmap image, you can see the individual pixels.

■ The digital photos you create, as well as designs or pictures you create in a paint program like Windows Paint, are all bitmap images.

■ Fireworks includes a full set of Bitmap tools you can use to edit bitmap images. Each of the tools enable you to work with the individual pixels in a different way.

Select the Drawing Colors

■ Because you use Fireworks to create and modify objects for the Web, the program uses the RGB color model, a common color model used in Web design. **RGB** stands for Red, Green, and Blue.

■ Two different tools in the Tools panel enable you to select colors easily for both bitmap and vector images. Use the ⬛ Stroke Color tool to choose the color you want to use for the color of the line you draw with the Pencil, Pen, Brush, or shape tools. You will use the ⬛ Fill Color tool when you draw shapes that are filled with color.

■ When you click either the ⬛ Stroke Color tool or the ⬛ Fill Color tool, a selection palette appears as shown in the following illustration.

The color selection palette

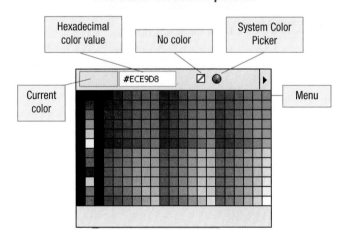

■ You can click the System Color Picker to choose your own custom color if the one you want doesn't appear in the selection palette. The Color dialog box opens so that you can click the color you want and use the color slider to set the intensity. Click Add to Custom Colors to save the color to the Custom Colors palette.

✔ *You will recognize the Color dialog box from the color discussion in Exercise 17. The color tools in Fireworks work the same way they function in Dreamweaver.*

Draw with the Brush Tool

■ The ✏ Brush tool paints a **stroke** onto an image. The stroke consists of individual pixels that are placed in specific locations in the image, according to where you drag the mouse.

■ You use the Property inspector to adjust the settings of the ✏ Brush tool. As you change the properties, the Tip preview box in the Property inspector shows the current appearance of the brush.

✔ *The Brush tool can be challenging to use correctly at first, so take some time to practice using the tool before you need to use it in a project.*

✔ *Press and hold the Shift key as you draw to paint a line that is horizontal, vertical, or at a 45-degree angle.*

■ You can create many different effects with the ✏ Brush tool, as shown in the illustration on the top of the following page. You can change the width of the brush to create a wider or thinner line; you can change the type of stroke that is painted on the image; and you can even add a texture to the stroke.

Draw with the Pencil Tool

■ The ✏ Pencil tool draws a line that is one-pixel wide, using the selected stroke color.

■ The Pencil tool offers fewer options than the Brush tool because it cannot use a texture or an adjustable size.

■ You can use the **anti-aliasing** option to make your pencil lines look smoother.

Choosing Brush settings in the Property inspector

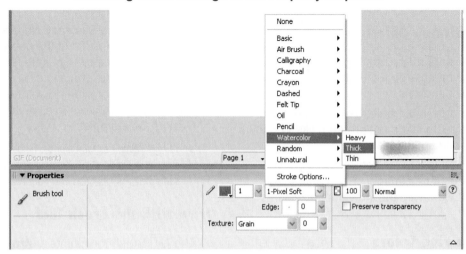

Select Bitmap Objects

- Because bitmap images are actually collections of pixels, you need to use a bitmap selection tool to select items you want to copy, cut, or move.

  ✔ *You can select your bitmap object using one of the tools in the Select area, but Fireworks will treat the object as a single item and won't allow you to work with individual pixels.*

- The three bitmap selection tools are the ⬚ Marquee tool the 🔎 Lasso tool and the 🪄 Magic Wand tool. You find the tools in the Bitmap section of the Tools panel.

- Use the ⬚ Marquee tool when you want to select a rectangular area of a bitmap image.

- Use the 🔎 Lasso tool when you need to select an irregularly shaped area. You use the Lasso to draw around the edges of the area you want to select.

- Use the 🪄 Magic Wand tool when you want to select all contiguous pixels in a specific color. For example, in the image shown in the following illustration, the Magic Wand tool has been used to select the magenta color on the petals of the flowers.

Selecting a portion of a bitmap image with the Magic Wand tool

- To use one of the selection tools, click the one you want and drag the area on the image you want to select.

- After you use the bitmap selection tools to select the portion of the bitmap image you want to work with, you can click a tool in the Select area if needed.

  ✓ *To add another item (or selection) to the current selection, press and hold ⇧ Shift while you click the item.*

Copy and Paste Bitmap Objects

- When you copy a bitmap object, an exact duplicate of the selected item is placed on the clipboard. The original is left intact on the page.

- The clipboard holds only one object at a time, so the next time you copy an item, the existing item is replaced on the clipboard.

- You can copy a selected item by right-clicking it and choosing Copy, by choosing the Edit>Copy menu command, or by pressing Ctrl+C.

- When you paste a selected object, Fireworks places on the page the copied selection that was saved to the clipboard.

- After you paste an object, you can drag it to the place you want it to appear on the image. Click outside the selection to position the item in place.

- You can paste the same object as many times as needed. The selected item remains on the clipboard until you replace it by copying another selection.

  ✓ *You can also cut a bitmap object to remove it from the Fireworks document. This places the cut item on the clipboard. You can then paste the item onto another layer, into another document, or simply discard the item by leaving it on the clipboard until you overwrite it the next time you copy a selection.*

PROCEDURES

Select a Drawing Color

1. Click the color selector of of either the ✏️ ■▼ **Stroke Color** tool or the 🖌 ▢ **Fill Color** tool.
2. Click the color in the palette you want to use.

Select a Color Using the System Color Picker

1. Click the color selector you want to set.
2. Click the 🔘 **System Color Picker** tool in the upper-right corner of the palette.
3. Drag the intensity slider until you see the color you want.
4. Click the [OK] **OK** button.

Draw a Line with the Pencil Tool

1. Click the ✏️ **Pencil** tool.
2. Choose the stroke color you want to use.
3. To smooth jagged lines, click the **Anti-aliased** checkbox in the Property inspector.
4. Drag to draw the line.

   ✓ *Press and hold the Shift key to draw straight lines.*

Draw a Stroke with the Brush Tool

1. Click the ✏️ **Brush** tool.
2. n the Property inspector, select the tip size.
3. Click the Stroke color and category you want to use.
4. Choose the edge softness.
5. Set the texture, if desired.
6. Click on the document and drag to draw the stroke.

Select an Area Using the Marquee Tool

1. Click the ▢ **Marquee** tool to select it.
2. Drag the ▢ **Marquee** tool to select the bitmap area.

   ✓ *You may need to use the Layers panel to select the layer containing the object you want to select. Exercise 23 shows you how to work with layers in your Fireworks document.*

3. Release the mouse button.

Select an Area Using the Lasso Tool

1. Click the 🔍 **Lasso** tool.
2. Drag the 🔍 **Lasso** tool to select the bitmap area you want to select.

Select an Area Using the Magic Wand Tool

1. Click the 🪄 **Magic Wand** tool.
2. Set properties for the tool in the Property inspector. You may want to change the Tolerance level (the higher the tolerance, the larger the area selected) and the Edge settings.
3. Be sure Live Marquee is checked in the Property inspector before you begin using the Magic Wand tool. The Live Marquee makes it easy for you to see which areas on the image are selected.
4. Click in the area of color you want the Magic Wand to select. Add other areas by pressing and holding ⇧ Shift while you click.

Copy a Bitmap Object (Ctrl + C)

1. Select the bitmap object.
2. Click **Edit** .... [Alt] + [E]
3. Select **Copy** .... [C]

Cut a Bitmap Object (Ctrl + X)

1. Select the bitmap object.
2. Click **Edit** .... [Alt] + [E]
3. Select **Cut** .... [T]

Paste a Bitmap Object (Ctrl + V)

1. Select the bitmap object.
2. Click **Edit** .... [Alt] + [E]
3. Select **Paste** .... [P]

EXERCISE DIRECTIONS

1. Open ⊙ 19_tree.png. If necessary zoom out so the whole tree is visible in the canvas by clicking the Set Magnification arrow in the bottom-right corner of the Fireworks window and choosing a smaller display percentage.

2. Click the 🖌 Magic Wand tool.

3. Set the Tolerance to 120 in the Property inspector.

   ✔ If you have trouble getting the value 120 using the slider, simply click in the box and type the value.

   ✔ If the whole top of the tree isn't selected the first time you click the Magic Wand tool, press Esc to cancel the selection and try again.

4. Click the leaves of the tree to select the top of the tree. A flashing outline shows you the area that is selected.

5. Next you need to select the trunk and base of the tree. Press and hold [⇧ Shift] through the following two steps. (Holding the [⇧ Shift] key keeps the top of the tree selected.)

6. Click and hold the 🔎 Lasso tool until the hidden tools appear.

7. Click the 🏳 Polygon Lasso tool.

8. Click the Set Magnification control in the lower right corner of the work area and zoom the display to 66%.

9. Using the Polygon tool (still holding [⇧ Shift]), click at the top of the tree trunk on the left side of the tree.

10. Drag the pointer down the tree trunk and click to anchor a selection point.

11. Continue selecting the trunk and the base of the tree; then continue up the right side of the tree, as shown in Illustration A on the next page.

12. Double-click the starting point at the top of the tree trunk.

13. Choose the Edit>Copy menu command.

14. Create a new Fireworks document. Leave the Width and Height values as they are and choose a transparent canvas color. Click OK to create the document.

15. Choose the Edit>Paste menu command.

16. Click the Set Magnification tool and change the display to 50%.

17. If necessary, click the tree object and reposition it in the canvas so the entire tree appears.

18. Click the 🖉 Eraser tool.

19. In the Property inspector, choose the size, edge, and brush shape you want to use.

20. Erase the extra branch on the upper right side of the tree top (from another tree) that the Magic Wand added. Clean up and additional areas as needed. Your tree should look something like the one shown in Illustration B on the next page.

21. Save the image as S_19_tree_xx.png.

22. Exit Fireworks.

Illustration A

Illustration B

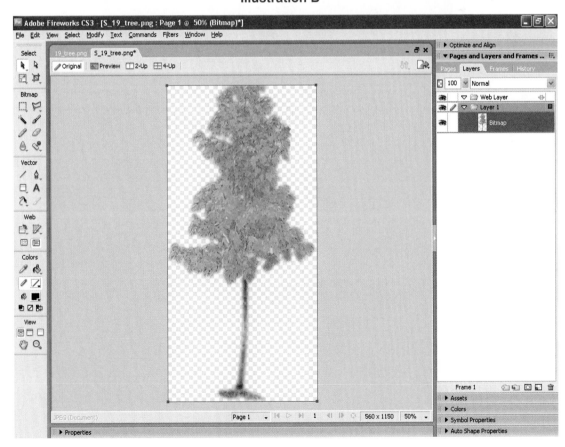

ON YOUR OWN

1. Open the **SO_18_gslogo_xx.png** file you created in the last On Your Own exercise.

2. Click the Brush tool.

3. Click the Stroke Color tool and choose a shade of green that will go along with the logo.

   ✔ *You can use the*  *Eye Dropper tool to choose the green border around the image.*

4. In the Property inspector, select a stroke category and brush size for the tool.

5. Click the Edge softness slider and set the type of edge you want to create.

6. Add a texture if you want to.

7. Draw a climbing vine in the pink area on the left side of the flower.

8. Select the vine and duplicate it.

9. Flip the copied vine by selecting it as choosing the Modify>Transform>Flip Horizontal menu command.

10. Place the flipped vine on the other side of the image.

11. Save your file as **SO_19_gslogo_xx.png**.

12. Exit Fireworks.

Exercise | 20

Skills Covered

- **Adjust Brightness and Contrast**
- **Apply Filters**
- **Sharpen and Blur an Image**
- **Use the Burn and Dodge Tools**
- **Use the Rubber Stamp Tool**
- **Use the Smudge Tool**

Software Skills Knowing basic image editing techniques for bitmap images, such as adjusting brightness and contrast and applying filters, gives you a foundation of skills for your Web graphics work. Additionally, you can add a few special techniques to your skill set by learning to modify images with the Burn, Dodge, Smudge, and Rubber Stamp tools.

Design Skills Fireworks includes tools that enable you to easily apply professional effects to your images. By learning to adjust the brightness and contrast in your images and apply filters, you can make dramatic enhancements to your graphics with just a few clicks of the mouse.

Application Skills In this exercise, you use the adjustment controls and filters to enhance images for your site.

TERMS

Brightness The amount of light in an image.

Contrast The difference between the light and dark areas of an image.

Filters Enhancements you can add to objects in a Fireworks document.

NOTES

Adjust Brightness and Contrast

■ Digital photos often need some adjustment in order to look their best. The type of adjusting you are likely to do involves changing the **brightness** and **contrast** of the image.

■ Brightness and contrast are related, so you will often make slight changes to both settings.

■ You make changes to the brightness and contrast of your bitmap images by choosing Adjust Color and then Brightness/Contrast from the Filters menu.

> ✔ If you make changes to the brightness or contrast and decide that you don't like the change, you can undo your changes by pressing Ctrl+Z.

■ In the Brightness/Contrast dialog box, drag the sliders to adjust the color and brightness. You can also type a specific value in the boxes if you choose. See the illustration below.

■ Make sure you leave the Preview checkbox selected so that you can immediately see the effect of your changes.

Apply Filters

■ Fireworks includes a number of **filters** you can apply to objects in your document.

■ A filter enables you to add a ready-made enhancement to the selection. For example, you might want to add a shadow to an image or sharpen the appearance of the object.

■ You can apply filters to bitmap objects, vector objects, or text objects.

■ When you apply a filter by using the Filters menu, the filter is destructive, meaning the change is made to the object instantly and you cannot modify the properties of the filter.

> ✔ Use Ctrl+Z or the Edit>Undo menu command to reverse a filter effect you don't like.

■ You can also apply live filters by using the Property inspector, as the illustration at the top of the next page shows. When you use a live filter, you can continue to work with and modify the settings of the filter.

> ✔ Click the [▸] Pointer tool, select the object, and the live filter selection will appear in the right side of the Property inspector.

> ✔ When you are first learning about filters in Fireworks, it's a good idea to experiment with live filters because you can see the effects of the changes easily and make any changes you want.

The Brightness/Contrast dialog box

Live filters in the Property inspector

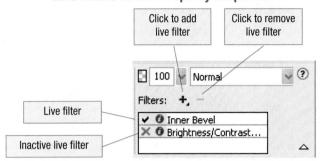

Click to add live filter

Click to remove live filter

Live filter

Inactive live filter

Sharpen and Blur an Image

■ Sharpening an image helps bring a fuzzy object into focus. The filter creates this effect by increasing the contrast between adjacent pixels in an image.

■ The Sharpen tool is one of the hidden tools found behind the Blur tool in the Bitmap section of the Tools panel.

■ Blurring an image is the opposite of sharpening; adjacent pixels are blended so the boundary is less distinguishable.

■ Fireworks includes six different blur filters: Blur, Blur More, Gaussian Blur, Motion Blur, Radial Blur, and Zoom Blur.

Use the Burn and Dodge Tools

■ The Burn tool and the Dodge tool are hidden tools behind the Blur tool.

■ The Burn tool darkens a part of an image; the Dodge tool lightens a part of an image.

■ Use Burn and Dodge tools to adjust selected areas of an image.

Use the Rubber Stamp Tool

■ The Rubber Stamp tool enables you to create a kind of "rubber stamp" of a selected area of your image so that you can apply the same effect to other areas of the document. For example, suppose you want to remove the hand from the pile of leaves shown in the illustration below.

■ You begin by selecting the Rubber Stamp tool. Choose the brush size and edge softness in the Property inspector. Then press Alt as you click the place you want to copy. A blue crosshair appears at the point you clicked.

■ Click and drag to make the copy. The copy destination appears marked with a blue circle, and you can paint the image with the selected portion of the object.

Rubber Stamp tool indicators

Rubber Stamp tool selected

Select Size and Edge

Copy destination

Copy origin

Use the Smudge Tool

- The [icon] Smudge tool blends nearby objects by pushing colors together at the pointer position.

- You might want to use the [icon] Smudge tool, for example, when you want to cover up or hide an unwanted object in your image.

- Use the Property inspector to set options for the [icon] Smudge tool, as the illustration below shows. The changes you can make include these:
  - Change the size of the tool
  - Set the softness of the tool's edges
  - Choose a round or square shape
  - Set the pressure to determine the tool's strength
  - Choose a smudge color
  - Select Use entire document to smudge using colors from all layers

Smudge settings in the Property inspector

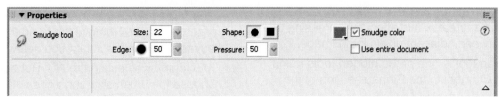

PROCEDURES

Adjust Brightness and Contrast

1. Select the bitmap object.
2. Click **Filters** .... [Alt]+[I]
3. Select **Adjust Color**.
4. Select **Brightness/Contrast**.
5. Drag the Brightness slider to the level you want.
6. Drag the Contrast slider as needed.
7. Click **OK**.

Apply a Filter

1. Select the object you want to filter.
2. Click **Filters** .... [Alt]+[I]
3. Click the filter you want to apply.
4. Click **OK**.
5. In the Property inspector, choose the options for the selected filter.

Use a Live Filter

1. Select the object you want to apply the filter to.
2. In the Property inspector, click the + in the Filters area.
3. Click the filter you want to apply.
4. Choose options for the filter.
5. Click outside the filter's options box to apply the settings.

Sharpen an Object

1. Click and hold the [icon] **Blur** tool in the Tools panel to display the hidden tools.
2. ..Choose the [icon] **Sharpen** tool.
3. In the Property inspector, click the brush tip size and shape.
4. Select the edge softness and intensity.
5. Drag the [icon] **Sharpen** tool over the area you want to sharpen.

Blur Parts of an Image

1. Click the [icon] **Blur** tool.
2. Set the tip size and shape.
3. Select edge softness and intensity.
4. Drag the [icon] **Blur** tool over the area you want to blur.

Use the Burn and Dodge Tools

1. Click and hold the [icon] **Blur** tool to reveal the hidden tools.
2. Click either the [icon] **Burn** tool or the [icon] **Dodge** tool.

   ✔ *Choose Burn if you want to darken an area; choose Dodge if you want to lighten the image.*

3. Set tool options in the Property inspector.
4. Drag the tool over the areas of the image you want to change.

Use the Rubber Stamp Tool

1. Click the  **Rubber Stamp** tool.
2. Choose settings in the Property inspector to set stamp size and edge softness.
3. Press and hold `Alt` and click at the point you want to create the origin point.

4. Move the pointer to the place you want to begin adding the copies.
5. Press and hold the mouse button and drag to copy.

OR

- Click multiple times and press Esc when you're done using the tool.

Apply the Smudge Tool

1. Click and hold the **Blur** tool to display the hidden tools.
2. Click the **Smudge** tool.
3. Set tool options, including tool size, shape, pressure, and edge softness in the Property inspector.
4. Drag the Smudge tool over the areas you want to smudge.

EXERCISE DIRECTIONS

1. Open the file sitka_spruce.png.
2. Choose the Filters>Adjust Color> Brightness/Contrast menu command.
3. Set the Brightness to -15.
4. Set Contrast to 14.
5. Click OK.
6. Reverse the setting by pressing Ctrl+Z.
7. Click the Pointer tool.
8. Click the Add Live Filters tool in the Property inspector.
9. Choose Adjust Color>Brightness/Contrast.
10. Leave Brightness set at -15, but increase Contrast to 22.
11. Click OK.
12. Click the Rubber Stamp tool.

13. In the Property inspector, set Size to 50 and Edge to 47.
14. You are going to cover up the white spots in the trees (use Illustration A as a guide to locate the spots). Click a green area of a tree close to the first spot on the left.
15. Press `Alt` and click to choose the area to copy.
16. Move the pointer to the white spot and click.
17. Repeat steps 13 through 15 for each of the white spots in the image.

    ✔ It may be tempting to use the same sample for each spot in the image, but you'll get a better result if you choose colors and patterns from the immediate area surrounding the spots.

18. Save the file as S_20_sitka_spruce_xx.png.
19. If you are continuing with the On Your Own exercise, leave the file open on your screen. Or, close the file and exit Fireworks.

Illustration A

ON YOUR OWN

1. Continue using S_20_sitka_spruce_xx.png from the last exercise.

2. Use the ⬎ Magic Wand tool to select the sky area in the upper-left corner of the photo.

3. Click the ⬎ Paint Bucket tool.

4. Use the Property inspector to set options to make the sky a soft blue that looks natural with the photograph.

   ✔ *Hint: Leave the Preserve Transparency checkbox clear, but click the Fill Selection checkbox.*

5. Position the pointer over the selection and click the mouse button to fill the sky with the new color.

6. Save your work as SO_20_sitka_spruce_xx.png.

7. Exit Fireworks.

Skills Covered

- **Learn about Vector Objects**
- **Draw Lines**
- **Draw Rectangles**
- **Draw Ellipses**
- **Create Polygons**
- **Scale Vector Objects**

- **Draw Using the Vector Path Tool**
- **Use the Pen Tool to Create Paths**
- **Add, Change, and Delete Points**
- **Apply a Stroke to a Vector Path**
- **Add a Fill to a Path**

Software Skills Vector tools enable you to create perfectly formed shapes and lines of all sorts. What's more, the vector objects keep their shape—and their quality—no matter how many times you may change them.

Design Skills As a designer, you will spend a lot of time and energy working with vector objects. Knowing how to create, modify, and enhance vector objects is a key skill in any designer's skill set.

Application Skills This exercise shows you how to draw, change, and enhance a vector object in Fireworks.

TERMS

Bounding box A rectangular shape that completely encloses a shape and defines the total height and width of the shape.

Group Joining two or more objects so they function as a single object.

Points Places where vector paths change direction.

Transform To modify by scaling, skewing, rotating, or distorting.

NOTES

Learn about Vector Objects

- Vector images are created by mathematical calculations that draw the object on the screen. For example, when you use a vector tool to draw a polygon, the program uses a calculation to produce the shape as you draw it.

- You can resize vector images without any loss of quality because vector images are scalable.

- Vector images include one or more objects that you can select and resize, drag, scale, skew, rotate, copy, and paste.

- When you select a vector image in the document, handles appear on the outer edges of the object.

- You can resize the object by dragging a handle. You can move the vector object by positioning the pointer on the object and, when the pointer changes to a four-sided arrow, click and drag the object to a new location on the page.

- Vector objects are different from bitmap objects in that you cannot edit the individual pixels when you are working with a vector image.

Draw Lines

- The ☐ Line tool draws straight vector-based lines between the first point you click and begin dragging and the point where you release the mouse button.

- You can use any type of stroke available in Fireworks to draw a line using the ☐ Line tool.

  ✔ *One important difference between lines drawn using the Line tool and one of the bitmap tools is that you cannot erase any part of a vector-based line using the Eraser tool.*

Draw Rectangles

- A rectangle is any four-sided, closed shape where each of the four corners forms a 90-degree angle.

- Rectangles can have both a stroke and a fill. Use the Property inspector to specify the settings you want.

- Press and hold ☐ Shift ☐ while using the ☐ Rectangle tool to draw a perfect square.

Draw Ellipses

- The ☐ Ellipse tool is hidden behind the ☐ Rectangle tool. Click and hold the Rectangle tool to display other vector shape drawing tools.

- A circle is a special type of ellipse where all points along the edge of the circle are exactly the same distance from the center point of the circle.

  ✔ *Hold down* ☐ Shift ☐ *as you draw with the Ellipse tool to draw a circle.*

- An ellipse can have both a stroke and a fill color.

- Drawing ellipses can seem a little confusing because you drag from one corner to the **bounding box** of the diagonal corner. The resulting ellipse touches the edges but never touches the corners of the bounding box.

Create Polygons

- You can use the ☐ Polygon tool or ☐ Smart Polygon tool to draw polygons with between 3 and 25 sides.

- When you finish drawing a polygon using the ☐ Polygon tool, the number of sides is fixed at the value you specified in the Property inspector.

- When you use the ☐ Smart Polygon tool to draw a polygon, you can continue to make changes and add sides by using special handles on the edges of the polygon, as the illustration on the top of the next page shows.

Scale Vector Objects

- The ☐ Scale tool enables you to quickly change the size of any object regardless of its type.

- You can use the ☐ Scale tool to rotate an object.

- You can also use the ☐ Skew tool and the ☐ Distort tool to change the shape of an object by dragging the handles that appear around the edges of a selected vector object, as the illustration on the bottom of the next page shows. These tools are called **transform** tools.

Special handles on smart polygons

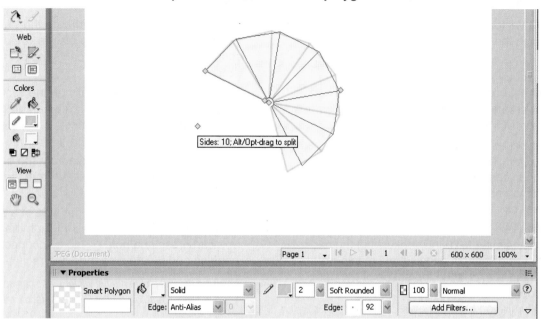

Transform tools

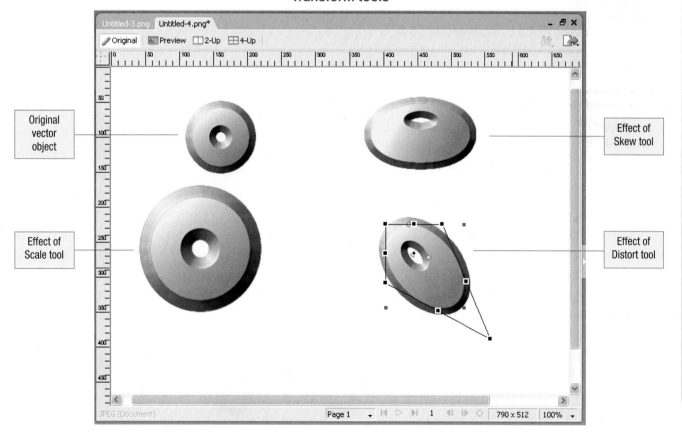

Original vector object

Effect of Skew tool

Effect of Scale tool

Effect of Distort tool

Draw Using the Vector Path Tool

- The 🖊 Vector Path tool is hidden behind the 🖊 Pen tool in the Vector area of the Tools panel.

- Vector paths are valuable because vector images take up much less space (which means faster download times for your Web site) and you can use paths to create bitmap-like lines, arcs, and curves in your drawings.

- Another benefit of vector paths is that vector paths can be changed at any time; you can continue to add points, change colors or effects, or modify them as you need to. Bitmap lines, on the other hand, are pixels that are set to the page as soon as you paint them.

- Paths look similar to brush strokes, but they are actually vector-based objects that contain **points** you can move to change the shape of the path. Once you create the path, you can fill it with color, as the illustration below shows.

- You can use the precision option in the Property inspector to specify the number of points you want to add (the greater the number of points, the more jagged the line).

- You can set any of the stroke properties before drawing the vector path and they will be applied to the path you draw.

Use the Pen Tool to Create Paths

- When you draw a vector path with the 🖊 Pen tool, points are added only at the places you click the mouse button. The tool connects the points smoothly as you draw.

- Handles appear automatically on the vector path you create with the Pen tool. You can drag the handles to control the distance, arc, and direction of the path.

- The farther you drag a handle from the point, the farther away the path will extend from the opposite side of the point.

- Normally the handles on either side of a point are on a straight line that passes through the point. You can press and hold Alt to disconnect two handles and create a change of direction.

  ✔ *Using the Pen tool to modify vector paths can seem a bit confusing at first, but a little experimentation will help you get the hang of it.*

A vector path

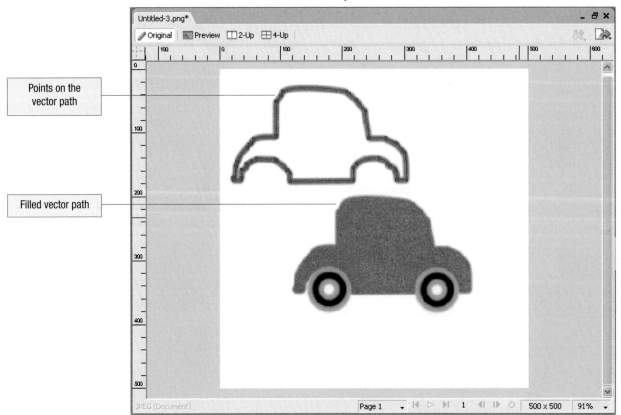

Points on the vector path

Filled vector path

Add, Change, and Delete Points

- You can easily add new points on a line by using the [✒] Pen tool. When you position the pointer in a place where you can add a point, the [✒] Pen tool displays a plus sign (+) in the lower-right edge of the pointer. Simply click to add a point.

- Move points on a line by choosing the [▸] Subselection tool and dragging the points where you want them on the line.

- To delete a point using the [▸] Subselection tool, choose the point and press Del.

- To delete a point using the [✒] Pen tool, position the tool on a point, and when the [✒] Pen tool pointer shows a minus sign (-), click the point to delete it.

Apply a Stroke to a Vector Path

- You can easily add or change the stroke of a vector path at any time.

- You can create dramatically different looks for a single vector path by selecting different strokes, as the following illustration shows.

- Select a path and change the stroke properties by changing them in the Property inspector. The changes you make are applied to all selected vector paths.

  ✔ *You can easily make changes to several different paths at once by selecting them and choosing the settings you want in the Property inspector.*

Add a Fill to a Path

- Paths can have fills even if the path is not closed.

- You can add a fill to a vector path at any time, either while you draw the path or after the path has been drawn.

- If the path is open, Fireworks adds the fill between the starting point of the path and the last point that was drawn.

- If the path crosses itself, the results of the fill may be unpredictable.

Same path, different strokes

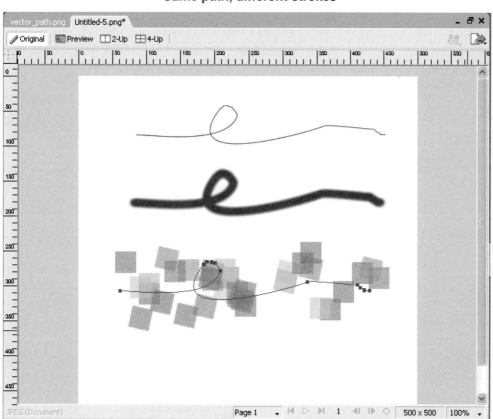

PROCEDURES

Draw a Line

1. Click the ✏ **Line** tool.
2. Select the stroke color you want to use.
3. Drag the tip slider to set the size of the tip.
4. Choose the stroke category and the edge softness.
5. If desired, set the texture, opacity, and blend mode.
6. Move the point where you want to begin the line.
7. Hold down the mouse button and drag to draw.

Draw a Rectangle

1. Click the ▢ **Rectangle** tool.
2. Choose the fill color and edge properties.
3. Select the stroke color and the tip size.
4. Select any additional settings you want to apply to the rectangle.
5. Click and drag to draw the rectangle on the screen.

Draw an Ellipse

1. Click the ◯ **Ellipse** tool.
2. Choose the stroke color and fill color or texture, if desired.
3. Choose the tip size and select the stroke category.
4. Set any additional options you want to apply to the Ellipse.
5. Click and drag to draw the ellipse.

Draw a Polygon

1. Click and hold the ▢ **Rectangle** tool.
2. Select the ◯ **Polygon** tool.
3. Choose the stroke and fill settings you want.
4. Click the shape drop-down list in the Property inspector and choose the shape you want.
5. Choose the number of sides.
6. Press and hold the mouse button and drag to draw the polygon.

   ✔ *You can also use the Smart Polygon tool to create a polygon that is easy to modify.*

Scale Vector Objects

1. Click the ▸ **Pointer** tool.
2. Click the object you want to scale.
3. Click the ▣ **Scale** tool.
4. Position the pointer on a handle.
5. Drag to resize the object.

Draw a Vector Path with the Pen Tool

1. Click and hold the ✒ **Pen** tool to display the pop-up menu.
2. Select the ✏ **Vector Path** tool.
3. Select the level of precision you want.
4. Select the stroke characteristics you want to use.
5. Press and hold the mouse button to draw the path.

Add Points

1. Click the ✒ **Pen** tool.
2. Move the ✒ **Pen** tool over the path until the pointer shows a plus sign.
3. Click to add the point.
4. Drag it to the point on the path where you want it to appear.

Delete Points

1. Click the ▸ **Subsection** tool.
2. Click the path to select it.
3. Click the point you want to remove.
4. Press **Delete** ....[Delete]

Apply a Stroke to a Path

1. Click the ▸ **Pointer** tool.
2. Click the path to select it.
3. Select the stroke properties you want to use.

Add a Fill to a Path

1. Click the ▸ **Pointer** tool.
2. Click the path to select it.
3. Select the fill properties you want to use.

EXERCISE DIRECTIONS

1. Create a new document in Fireworks.
2. Set the canvas size to at least 500 by 500 pixels.
3. Set the canvas to white.
4. Click the ✏ Line tool.
5. In the Property inspector, select a stroke color of #663333.
6. Set a tip size of 7.
7. Display the Stroke Category list, point to Random, and click Fur.
8. Click to draw the line near the bottom of the document.
9. Click the Ellipse tool.
10. Set the stroke category to Soft Rounded (in the Basic category).

11. Set a fill color of #FFFF99 and a stroke color of #FFCC66.

12. Set the tip size to 9.

13. Draw an ellipse that is wider than it is tall. (This will be the saucer for the coffee cup for the Java 2 Go logo.)

14. Click the ✏ Vector Path tool.

15. Select a stroke color of #FFCC66.

16. Draw an outline of a coffee cup, using Illustration A as a guide.

17. If you need to adjust the points on the path, click the ▶ Subselection tool to move and delete points if needed.

18. When the cup is the shape you want, choose a fill color of #FFFF99.

19. Finish the cup by adding an ellipse with a fill color and stroke color of #FFCC66 at the top of the cup.

20. If you used two strokes to create the arc on the inside of the handle, click both strokes and right-click your selection. Choose Group.

21. Set the fill color of the group to #FFFFFF.

22. Save the file as S_21_javalogo_xx.png.

23. If you are continuing with the On Your Own exercise, leave the file open on the screen. Or, close the file and exit Fireworks.

Illustration A

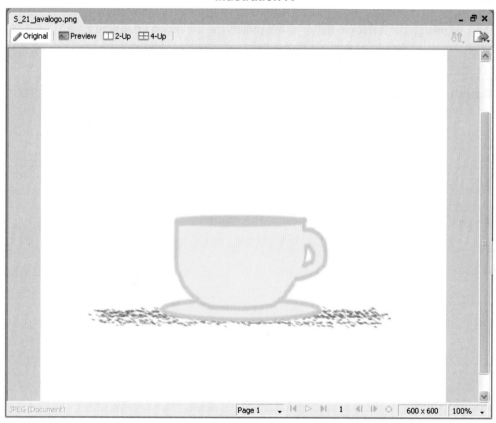

ON YOUR OWN

1. In the file S_21_javalogo_xx.png, group all the objects that make up the cup.

2. Add an ellipse at the top to make it appear as though there is coffee in the cup.

3. Modify the canvas size to fit the logo.

4. Enhance the image by adding shadow and light reflections if you like.

5. Increase the point size of the line at the bottom to 11.

6. Add steam rising above the cup.

   ✔ The stroke category you choose will help you create an "airy" effect for the steam.

7. Save your work as SO_21_javalogo_xx.png.

8. Close the file and exit Fireworks.

Skills Covered

- **Create a Text Block**
- **Add Text**
- **Choose a Font**
- **Set Text Size**

- **Add Strokes to Text**
- **Add Fills to Text**
- **Make Text Follow a Path**

Software Skills The text tools in Fireworks enable you to add special graphic touches to your designs. You might want to include a company name on your logo, or design professional buttons that match the styles on your site.

Design Skills Knowing how to work with the text tools in Fireworks will give you the ability to create unique, professional text effects for your Web pages.

Application Skills In this exercise, you learn how to use the Fireworks text tools and add a stylized logo to an image for your Web site.

TERMS

RTF Rich Text Format, a text file format that includes formatting information such as font name, size, and attributes like bold.

Text blocks Groups of editable text used in Fireworks documents.

NOTES

Create a Text Block

- In a Fireworks document, all text is contained in text blocks. You use the [A] Text tool to create text blocks.

- You can edit the text in a text block at any time.

- You can change the properties of text blocks in much the same way you change the properties of vector objects. You can, for example, change the fill and stroke colors. You can also apply filters to text blocks to create special effects.

- You can create a text block two ways:
  - Click once with the [A] Text tool to create an auto-sizing text block that expands as you type, or
  - Drag the [A] Text tool to create a fixed-width text block that expands vertically as you type.

- You can use text blocks to add text to buttons so that users will know the purpose of a button.

Add Text

- The most common way to add text to a text block is simply to type the text directly into the text block.

- You can also use text from another application in a Fireworks text block by following one of three methods:
  - Drag and drop text from another open program into Fireworks.
  - Use Edit>Copy and Edit>Paste to copy text from one application to another.

- Use the File>Import menu command to import plain text or **RTF** text into Fireworks.

  ✔ *When you import text, Fireworks creates a new text block to hold the imported text.*

Choose a Font

- Most computers have a variety of different fonts installed and available for use in your documents. The particular fonts vary on different PCs, but you can usually find several to choose from.

- To choose a font, click the font list box in the Property inspector. As the illustration at the bottom of this page shows, the text box on the page displays a sample of the way the font will look if selected.

- You can use more than one font in a text block if needed, but be careful not to overdo it. Using too many fonts or selecting novelty fonts can make your content hard to read.

Set Text Size

- In the Property inspector, click the size box to choose the point size for text.

- You can use the size slider to choose a value between 8 points and 96 points. 72 points equals 1 inch.

- You can type point sizes directly into the size box.

- For most text blocks, a size between 10 and 14 points is adequate. Smaller sizes may be hard to read, and larger sizes can take up too much room.

Text font samples

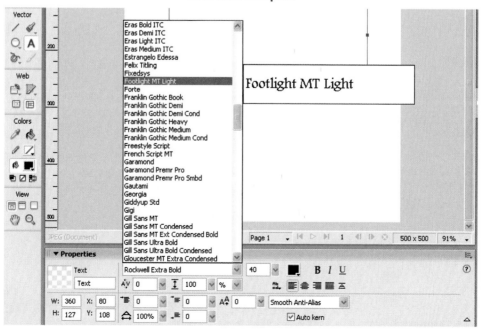

Add Fills to Text

- Fireworks automatically applies a solid, single color fill to text.
- When you click the Fill Options button in the Fill Color Selector, the fill options pop-up, as the illustration below shows.

Fill Options for text

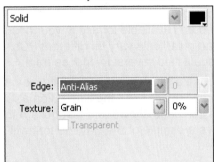

- You can choose none, solid, Web dither, gradient, or pattern files.
- The fill options pop-up displays additional choices related to the type of fill you selected. For example, the illustration at the bottom of this page shows the text for the GardenScape logo after the gradient fill option has been selected. You can make additional choices about the style of the fill in this pop-up.
- You can apply strokes and fills together or individually.
- You can change text at any time after you apply fills.

Make Text Follow a Path

- Normal text by default follows a straight horizontal line. You can attach text to a path to make the text twist and curve in interesting ways.
- When you attach text to a path, any stroke, fill, or filter properties that have been applied to the path are hidden.
- If you want the path to be visible after the text has been attached to the path, you can use the Edit> Clone menu command to create an exact duplicate of the path.
- For best results, keep the text on a single line; that is, don't press Enter when you are entering the text.

  ✔ *To change the direction of the text on a path, use the Text> Reverse Direction command.*

Text following a path

Setting additional fill options

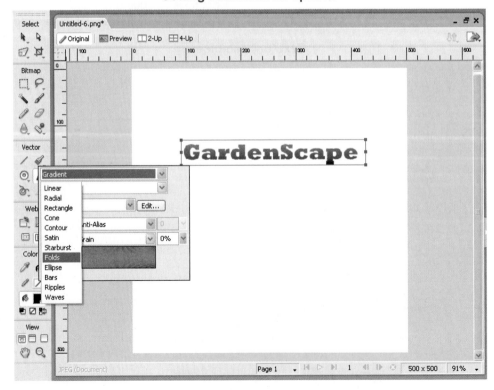

PROCEDURES

Create a Text Block and Add Text

1. Click the **A** **Text** tool.
2. Click the point on the work area where you want to create the text block.
3. Choose any necessary settings in the Property inspector you want.
4. Type your text.

Choose a Font

1. Click the **A** **Text** tool.
2. Create the text block.

   OR

   Select the text you want to change.
3. Click the font arrow in the Property inspector.
4. Click the font you want to use.

Set Text Size

1. Select the text block you want to change.
2. Click the size box in the Property inspector to display the list.
3. Click the size you want to apply.

Add Fills to Text

1. Create the text block.
2. Click the **Pointer** tool.
3. Click the text block you want to change.
4. Click the **Fill Color Selector** in the Tools panel or in the Property inspector.
5. Click the **Fill Options** button.
6. Choose the fill category.
7. Select any additional settings you want to apply.
8. Click outside the fill options pop-up to close it.

Make Text Follow a Path

1. Create the text block.
2. Create the vector path object.
3. Click the **Pointer** tool.
4. Press ⇧ Shift and click the text block and the path.
5. Click **Text** .... Alt + T
6. Select **Attach to Path** .... P

EXERCISE DIRECTIONS

1. Open the file ⊙ 22_gslogo.png.
2. Select the **Pointer** tool.
3. Click the text block to select it.
4. Click the **Fill Color** tool.
5. Click Fill Options... Fill Options.
6. Click the fill category and choose Pattern.
7. Click the Pattern Name arrow and scroll to the bottom of the list and click Other.

   ✔ *Hint: You may need to click the arrow at the bottom of the list to get to Other.*

8. Navigate to ⊙ flower.png and select it.
9. The flower image fills the text object.
10. Two black handles appear that control the horizontal and vertical position of fill image. Drag the handles to adjust the image position as desired.

11. Save the image as S_22_gslogo_xx.png.
12. Close the file.

Illustration A

ON YOUR OWN

1. Open the file ⊙ 22_javalogo.png.
2. Add two types of dashed borders surrounding the logo.
3. Leave room for a text logo above the cup of coffee.
4. Add **Java 2 Go!** in a text box.
5. Apply text properties that fit the color and style of the logo.
6. Create a rectangle that encloses the entire logo.

7. Use the [A] Text tool to add a slogan for the company.
8. Attach the Text so that it follows the edge of the rectangle. See Illustration A for ideas.

   Have fun with this! Vector tools and text objects enable you to add all sorts of creative things to your sites.

9. Save the file as SO_22_javalogo_xx.png and then close the file.

Illustration A

Exercise | 23

Skills Covered

■ Add Layers

■ Place Objects on Layers

■ Hide and Display Layers

■ Create a Vector Mask

■ Create a Bitmap Mask

■ Convert an Object to a Mask

■ Add a Blend

■ Set Opacity

■ Set a Blending Mode

Software Skills Fireworks uses layers to help you organize and work with the various elements in your drawings. You can use layers to keep objects independent of each other and to make it appear as though your document has depth. Masks and blends add further design options by enabling you to change the overall appearance of the object.

Design Skills Mastering the concept of layers is a great benefit for any serious Web designer, because in order to put objects together professionally on the page, you need to be able to position, overlap, and work with them as objects in their own right. A good designer knows how to use layers, masks, and blends to create the best possible effect in a drawing.

Application Skills In this exercise, you learn how to use layers, masks, and blends to enhance objects on various layers in your document.

TERMS

Mask An object that influences the display of other objects by applying a form or shape through which the object is viewed.

Thumbnail A small picture that represents the contents of each layer in the Layers panel.

NOTES

Add Layers

■ You use the Layers panel to add, remove, move, hide, or lock layers in Fireworks.

■ Each vector or path object you create is automatically placed on its own layer.

■ You can add layers to add to the level of control you have over the way objects are organized in your document.

■ Fireworks automatically creates a layer called *Layer 1*. When you add layers, they will be numbered sequentially. You can rename a layer by double-clicking its name in the Layers panel and entering a new name.

■ The Layers panel shows you the content of each layer and provides information about each object, as the following illustration shows.

The Layers panel

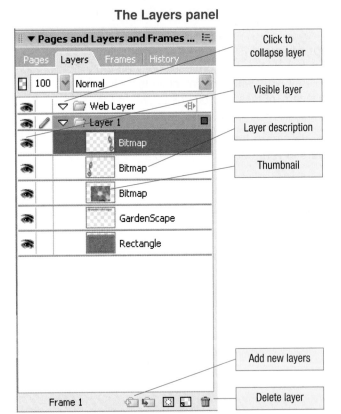

■ The Web Layer is a special layer that sits above all other layers in a Fireworks document. The Web layer is used to create interactivity on a Web page.

  ✔ *See Lesson 6 for more information on creating interactivity on your Web pages.*

■ You can add a layer using several different methods:

  ● Select the Edit>Insert>Layer menu command.
  ● Click Options in the upper-right corner of the Layers panel to display the menu, and click New Layer.
  ● Click the New/Duplicate Layer button at the bottom of the Layers panel.

■ When you add a new layer, the layer is inserted above the currently selected layer.

  ✔ *You can easily change the layer order in the Layers panel by dragging the layer you want to move to a new position in the list. Note, however, that the order in which the layers appear reflect the order they appear on the page—layers at the top of the list appear in front of objects lower on the list. So when you drag a layer from a lower position up the list, you are at the same time making it more visible on the page.*

Place Objects on Layers

■ Fireworks handles bitmap and vector objects differently, as you've already seen in other exercises. The Layers panel is no exception. When a bitmap object layer is selected and you draw another bitmap object, the new object is added to the same layer the existing object occupies. When a vector layer is selected and you add a bitmap object, a new bitmap object layer is automatically corrected and the new bitmap object is added to that layer. The vector remains on its own layer, alone.

■ You can tell whether a layer is a vector or a bitmap layer by looking for the identifier to the right of the layer's **thumbnail**.

  ✔ *It's a good idea to pay careful attention to the way you organize your layers when you're just getting started. Suppose you're creating an image of a tree. You could create layers for each of the major areas of the tree—trunk, branches, leaves, fruit—and then create sublayers within each of those main layers to manage each of the vector and bitmap objects used to create the main elements.*

Hide and Display Layers

■ You can hide a layer completely to see how your drawing will look without it. This is helpful when you are trying to decide between two ways to show something in a drawing; you can alternately show and then hide each item so that you can easily choose between them.

■ To hide a layer, click the eye for that layer in the first column of the Layers panel, as you see in the illustration at the top of the next page. To display the layer, click the first column again.

Hiding layers

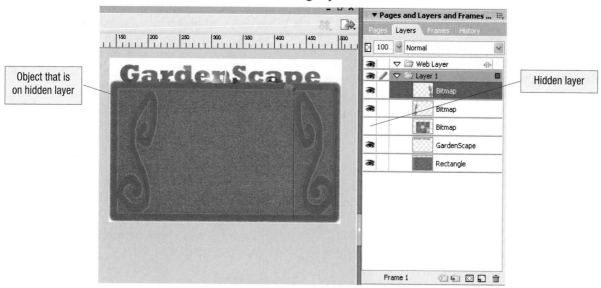

Object that is on hidden layer

Hidden layer

- Hiding a layer does not affect objects on any of the other layers in your Fireworks document.

- Once a layer is hidden, the objects on that layer cannot be selected. Similarly, when you print or export your Fireworks document, any hidden layers will not be included in the print or export procedure.

  ✔ *When you get your layers just the way you want them, protect them from being inadvertently changed by locking them. To lock a layer, click in the second column of the Layers panel. A little lock symbol appears. All sublayers included within a layer are locked automatically when you lock a main layer.*

Create a Vector Mask

- You can use a **mask** to change how much of an object is visible in a Fireworks document.

- Masking an object is similar to cropping, but you are not limited to a rectangular area as you are when you crop an image.

- You can use any vector object to create a mask in Fireworks. The following illustration shows an object that uses an ellipse mask.

  ✔ *You can also use text as a mask. You learn to do this later in this exercise.*

A photo with an ellipse mask

- It is easiest to create the object you want to mask first and then create the mask.

- Creating a mask is as simple as creating the shape you want, choosing the Edit>Cut menu command to place the shape on the clipboard, and choosing Modify>Mask>Paste as Mask.

- Masks and the objects they mask are grouped together on the same layer after you apply the mask.

Create a Bitmap Mask

- A bitmap mask is similar in that it influences the display of the object to which it is applied, but as you might expect, it goes about the process differently. A bitmap mask in effect masks every pixel instead of applying an object mask to the drawing.

- The bitmap mask overlays the object you want to mask, and the underlying object shows through. For this reason, dark areas on the bitmap mask will appear as the lightest areas on the masked object (because not as much of the object can show through the dark area).

- To create a new bitmap mask from scratch, select the object you want to mask and then click the Add Mask button along the bottom of the Layers panel. Then select the Brush tool to draw the mask and use the Property Inspector to set the attributes.

  ✔ *Masks may seem like a difficult concept at first, but they are really fun to do. Take some time to experiment with both vector and bitmap masks and create a few of your own.*

Convert an Object to a Mask

- To convert an object into a mask, place the mask object over the object you want to mask and then group the objects. This places both objects onto the same sublayer in the Layers panel and links them so they function as a single unit.

- If you've previously placed an object on the clipboard and want to turn it into a mask, you can choose the Modify>Mask>Paste as Mask menu command.

  ✔ *To turn off a mask, choose the Modify>Mask>Disable Mask menu command. A red X appears across the mask's thumbnail to show it is not in use.*

  ✔ *To delete a mask, choose the Modify>Mask>Delete Mask command, and click Discard.*

Add a Blend

- A blend is created when you overlap two objects and join the two colors to produce a mixture of both.

- Fireworks includes more than 30 different blending modes, as the illustration below shows.

- You choose a blend using the blend mode list box in the Property inspector or in the Layers panel.

- You can apply a blend that adds, subtracts, multiplies, or otherwise combines the colors and brightness levels of the two images. Each blending mode combines these elements in different ways to produce a variety of effects.

Blend modes

- In the default Normal mode, no blending occurs; when objects are overlapped, one object appears in front, and then other, behind.

Set Opacity

- The opacity of an image is the degree to which the object is transparent. When an object is transparent, the opacity is set to 0%. When an object is solid and you cannot see through it, the opacity is set to 100%.

- You will often work with opacity while you're creating blends because the two are related. When you change opacity, you change the strength of a blend.

Set a Blending Mode

- After you have added the objects you want to blend, select the top object and then choose the blending mode in the Property inspector or the Layers panel.

- To set the blending mode before you create an object, choose the blending mode in the Property inspector before you draw.

- Only one blending mode can be active at any one time. When you choose a new blending mode, any existing blends are removed from the object and the new mode is applied.

Set Opacity

PROCEDURES

Open the Layers Panel (F2)

1. Click **Window** .... [Alt]+[W]
2. Select **Layers** .... [L]

Add a New Layer (Shift + L)

1. Click **Edit** .... [Alt]+[E]
2. Select **Insert** .... [I]
3. Select **Layer** .... [L]

Hide and Display a Layer

- **To hide:** In the Layers panel, click the eye icon in the first column of the selected layer.

- **To display:** In the Layers panel, click the first column of the layer to make it visible.

Create a Mask by Copy and Paste

1. Create the object you want to mask.
2. Create the object you want to use as a mask.
3. Move the mask object over the first object.
4. Click the **Pointer** tool.
5. Select the mask object.
6. Click **Edit** .... [Alt]+[E]
7. Select **Cut** .... [T]
8. Select the object you want to mask.
9. Click **Modify** .... [Alt]+[M]
10. Select **Mask** .... [M]
11. Select **Paste as Mask** .... [P]

Create a Mask by Drawing

1. Create the object you want to mask.
2. In the Layers panel, click the **Add Mask** button.
3. Click the **Brush** tool.
4. In the Property inspector, choose the properties for the mask.
5. Drag the **Brush** tool to draw the mask.

Delete a Mask

1. Click the ⬉ **Pointer** tool.
2. Click the mask or masked object.
3. Click **Modify**.................. ⟨Alt⟩+⟨M⟩
4. Select **Mask**........................ ⟨M⟩
5. Select **Delete Mask**............. ⟨L⟩
6. Click [Discard] **Discard** to delete the mask.

   ✔ *If you change your mind and don't want to delete the mask, click Cancel. To apply the mask one more time before deleting it, click Apply.*

Add a Blend to Existing Objects

1. Click the ⬉ **Pointer** tool.
2. Click the object in front.
3. In the Property inspector or Layers panel, click the blend mode list arrow.
4. Click the blend mode you want to apply.

   ✔ *To use a blend mode for new objects you create, set the blend mode before you draw.*

Set Opacity

1. Click the ⬉ **Pointer** tool.
2. Click the object you want to change.
3. In the Property inspector or Layers panel, drag the opacity slider to the setting you want.

EXERCISE DIRECTIONS

1. Open the file 🔘 **23_treeline.png**.
2. Open the file 🔘 **23_tierraverde.png**.
3. Click the ⬉ Pointer tool.
4. Click the text object to select it.
5. Click the 🔳 Scale tool.
6. Drag the top of the text object up to make it larger.
7. With the text object selected, choose the Edit>Cut menu command.
8. Click the **23_treeline.png** tab.
9. Click the picture to select it.
10. Choose the Modify>Mask>Paste as Mask menu command.
11. Click outside the text object, and click the canvas close to the text. A large blue rectangle appears around the masked object.
12. Click the small blue crosshair on the mask (see Illustration A on the next page) and drag it to move the image that shows through the mask. Position the image so that the water and the treeline shows through the text.
13. Click the 🔲 New/Duplicate Layer tool and make sure the new layer is selected in the Layers panel.
14. Click the 🔳 Rectangle tool and draw a rectangle on the canvas large enough to completely cover the text object.
15. Set the rectangle's fill color to #99CCCC.
16. In the Layers panel, drag the new layer down to a position below the Background layer.

17. Right-click the new rectangle, point to Arrange, and click Send to Back.
18. Add another new layer by clicking 🔲 New/Duplicate Layer and select the layer in the Layers panel.
19. Click and hold the 🔳 Rectangle tool to display the hidden tools. Click the 🔳 Beveled Rectangle tool. Choose a fill color of #666666.
20. Draw a rectangle along the top edge, but overlapping, the background rectangle. Use Illustration B for reference.
21. With the new rectangle selected, click to display the Fill category list, point to Gradient, and click Bars.
22. Click Fill Color and click the Preset arrow. Choose White, Black.
23. On the rectangle, click the gradient handle (the black square on the right side of the shape) and drag it to the top center of the square. This changes the light reflection on the shape. Arrange the light reflection so that it runs horizontally the length of the bar.
24. Click the ➕ Add Filters button, point to Shadow and Glow, and click Drop Shadow.
25. Set the Opacity for the shadow to 50%.
26. Click the Edit>Duplicate menu command.
27. Drag the shape to the bottom edge of the logo.
28. Save your work as **S_23_tierralogo_xx.png** and then close the file.

Illustration A

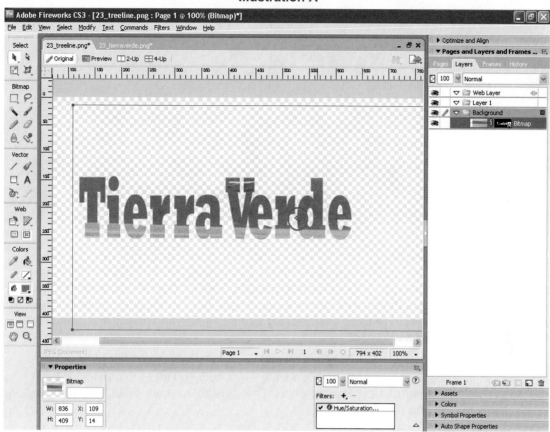

Illustration B

ON YOUR OWN

1. Open a new Fireworks document.

2. Set the canvas size and color to anything you want.

3. Create a logo for the Classroom Connections Web site.

    ✔ *Hint: You may want to start with an image you already have, design a text logo, or draw something yourself using the tools in Fireworks.*

4. Add a new layer, and add background color and a border to the logo.

5. Apply a filter to the logo to give it a sense of depth.

6. Save your work in your solutions folder.

> **NOTE**
>
> **In the next exercise, you return to Dreamweaver so that you can add your Fireworks images to your Web site.**

Exercise | 24

Skills Covered

- About Adobe Bridge
- Insert an Image on a Page in Dreamweaver
- Modify Image Properties

- Position an Image on a Page
- Edit Graphics within Dreamweaver
- Insert and Edit a Fireworks Image
- Manage Graphic Files

Software Skills Adobe Bridge enables you to view and organize images on your computer and import them easily into Dreamweaver. You can place images on your page to illustrate or emphasize text, position them so that the text wraps to the left or right. Adobe Bridge also enables you to use Fireworks tools to modify and enhance your images without ever leaving Dreamweaver and insert and optimize Fireworks images.

Design Skills Learning how to use programs seamlessly together—and determining when to use each independently—will help you learn to create the best possible pages without duplicating effort. That gives you more time and creative energy to pour into your site design!

Application Skills In this exercise, you add images to the GardenScape Web site, modify their properties and position, and edit a graphic in Dreamweaver. You will also create a folder in the site to hold all graphic files.

TERMS

Adobe Bridge A file management application included with the applications that are part of Adobe Web Design, enabling you to view and manage image files.

GIF (Graphics Interchange Format) A bitmapped image format designed for on-screen viewing of images.

JPEG (Joint Photographic Experts Group) A file format particularly suited for Web graphics, such as photos.

PNG (Portable Network Graphic) A bitmapped image format designed for easy use of images on the Internet.

NOTES

About Adobe Bridge

- You can access **Adobe Bridge** from within Dreamweaver to import your Fireworks images and other media files you plan to use on your Web pages.

- To open Adobe Bridge while you're working in Dreamweaver, use the File>Browse in Bridge command or click the 🖼️ Browse in Bridge button on the Standard toolbar. Adobe Bridge opens and displays the contents of the current folder, as shown in the illustration below.

- The Bridge window is divided into three areas. The left panel provides tabs that enable you to display your Favorites, work with Folders, and Filter the files displayed in the center area.

- The Content area in the center of the Bridge window displays thumbnails of each of the files in the current folder.

- The right panel displays a Preview tab where you can see a preview of the selected file(s).

  ✔ *Web pages display only as HTML thumbnails, but photos will appear showing their actual content in the Preview panel.*

- You can easily insert an image from Bridge to a Dreamweaver Web site. As the illustration at the top of the next page shows, you can use the File>Copy to command in Adobe Bridge and then select the current Web site's root folder, or click Choose Folder and navigate to the folder into which you want to copy the image.

- For more information on how you can use Adobe Bridge to manage your files, consult the Adobe Bridge Help files.

Adobe Bridge

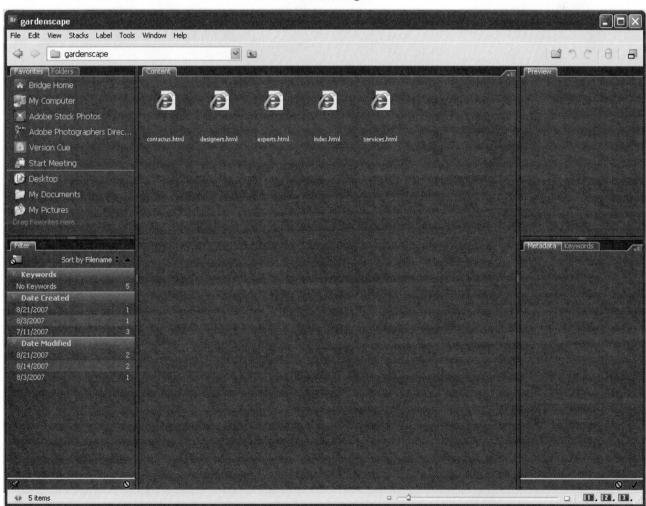

Copying files in Adobe Bridge

Choose destination folder

Previewed images

Selected images

Insert an Image on a Page in Dreamweaver

- The images you add to your Web sites are an important part of the overall design. Images illustrate ideas in your text, welcome the visitor to the page, or simply provide something beautiful or interesting that connects to your site content in some way.

- Put some energy into making sure your images— photos you capture with a digital camera, objects you create in an image editor like Fireworks, or other designs you create or purchase—are as good as they can be before you place them on your Web page. You can do some image editing within Dreamweaver, but doing most of your fine-tuning before you import the files is a good practice.

- To make sure others will be able to see the images you place on your pages, save the files in one of three formats: **JPG**, **GIF**, or **PNG**.

- Dreamweaver will not automatically convert image files in other formats such as BMP or TIFF, so you will need to convert the files before you can add them to your pages.

- To add an image to your page, you can use the Insert>Image menu command to open the Select Image Source dialog box, or you can click the Images button from the Common tab of the Insert bar and then select Image from the drop-down list to open the Select Image Source dialog box, as the illustration on the next page shows.

  ✓ You can also simply drag the Image button to the desired location on the page to open the Select Image Source dialog box.

■ In the Select Image Source dialog box, select the image you want to insert and then save the image file in your Web site.

> ✔ The Manage Graphic Files *section in this exercise gives you more information about organizing graphic files in your Web site.*

Select Image Source dialog box

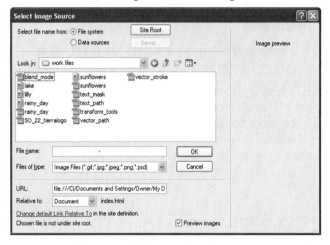

■ If the file you select is not currently saved in the current site, Dreamweaver will prompt you to save the file in the root directory of the site. Click Yes, and the Copy File As dialog box appears. Here you can enter a name for the file and click ⬚ Save ⬚ Save.

■ After you tell Dreamweaver where to store the image, the Image Tag Accessibility Attributes dialog box opens to allow you to specify alternate text or a long description for the image (see the following illustration). This dialog box encourages a designer to include accessibility information when an image is first inserted, rather than wait and supply this information later when fine-tuning the site using accessibility reports.

> ✔ You will work with accessibility reports in Lesson 8.

Image Tag Accessibility Attributes dialog box

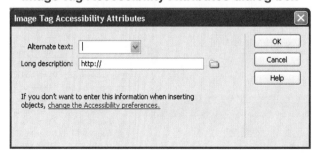

■ Alternate text displays in place of the image in text-only browsers. If a site visitor is using a screen reader, the alternate text is read aloud so the visitor knows the content of the image.

■ Some browsers display alternate text as a ScreenTip when you rest the mouse pointer over the image, while other browsers, such as Firefox and Mozilla, do not.

> ✔ To create text that will display as a ScreenTip in all browsers, use the title attribute. You can find information about using this attribute by searching for it online.

■ Alternate text should be kept fairly short; Dreamweaver suggests no more than 50 characters. If an image is especially complex or meaningful to the site and needs more description, you can create a document to describe the image and store the document in the Web site. Use the Long description box to type the path to the explanatory document, or use the ⬚ Browse icon to navigate to the location of the document.

■ Search engines do pick up the alternate tags on your images, so if the keywords of your site fit the image you're displaying, feel free to include them as part of the alternate text. Don't load your alternate text with keywords, though, because that is considered bad form and could cause search engines to skip your site altogether.

■ Some images that you insert, such as those used to create a navigation bar, may not require alternate text. However, you should still specify a value for the Alt attribute to satisfy accessibility standards. If you don't want to enter a phrase, you can add a null value by clicking the Alternate text list arrow and selecting <empty>.

■ After the picture has been inserted, you can modify its appearance and position it on the page using the Property inspector.

> ✔ You learn how to do that later in this exercise.

■ As you add images to a page, keep an eye on the page size/download time measurements 143K / 21 sec shown in the right side of the status bar at the bottom of the Document window.

■ Images can significantly increase the size of a page and, even if a visitor is using a broadband connection, increase its download time. (This is especially true with digital photographs, which can produce very large files.) A page that loads too slowly is an inconvenience to your site visitors, so you should try to keep download times low by eliminating or reducing large image files.

■ The download time is based by default on a connection speed of 56.0kbps. You can set a different connection speed for this measurement in the Preferences dialog box in the Status Bar category.

Modify Image Properties

- Click an image and its properties appear in the Property inspector, as the illustration below shows.

- Notice that a thumbnail-size version of the image appears at the left side of the Property inspector. On pages that have more than one image or where images may be layered, this thumbnail helps you make sure that you are editing properties for the correct image.

- Next to the thumbnail is the Name text box, which by default is empty. You can supply a name for the image if you need to refer to the image in a script.

- You can use an image to link to other pages or sites in the same way you use text. Select the image and then type the link address in the Link text box, or use the 🚫 Point to File icon or 🗀 Browse for File button to specify the link target.

- If you don't supply alternate text when you insert an image, you can use the Alt box on the Property inspector to supply the text or the <empty> value.

Resize Image

- You can use the sizing handles on the picture to adjust its size. Click on a handle and drag it in the direction you want to resize the image. Dragging a corner handle adjusts both width and height at the same time.

  ✔ If you need to resize proportionately, press and hold the ⇧ Shift key as you drag the corner handle.

- To resize an image to exact measurements, use the W and H text boxes on the Property inspector. You must supply both a width and a height— Dreamweaver does not automatically resize proportionally if you supply only one dimension.

Image properties in Property inspector

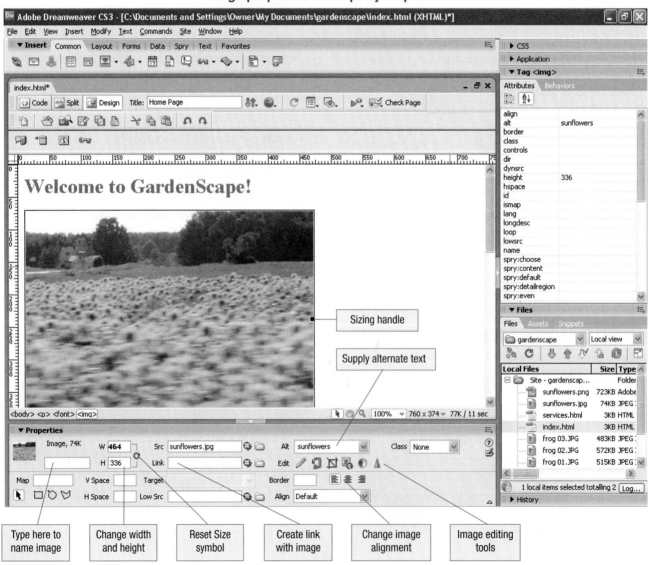

138

- If you need to go back to the original proportions, click the [C] Reset Size symbol to the right of the W and H text boxes.

    ✔ *The Reset Size symbol appears only after you have resized an image. If you're working with an image in its original size, the symbol won't appear.*

- The Width and Height boxes show the size of the image in pixels. Use pixel measurements when you need to display the image in a precise size. Pixel measurement is also a Web design standard.

About Image Borders

- By default, an image does not display a border. Use the Border text box on the expanded area of the Property inspector to specify a border width such as 1 or 2. Border measurements are in pixels.

- An image border is always black, unless the image is being used as a link. When used as a link, the image's border becomes the default link color.

    ✔ *If you want to apply a colored border to an image, you can use the CSS Border property, which allows you to specify width as well as color for each side of an image. You learn about CSS in Exercise 44.*

Position an Image on a Page

- You have several options for positioning an image on a page. You can use alignment buttons or settings in the Align list.

Position a Standalone Image

- If the image appears on a line by itself (not on the same line with text), you can use the Align Left, Align Center, or Align Right text alignment options to position like you would a text paragraph.

- Select the image and use the alignment buttons that appear in the expanded area of the Property inspector to left align, center, or right align the image.

    ✔ *You can also use keyboard shortcuts such as Ctrl + Alt + Shift + C or Ctrl + Alt + Shift + R to center or right align an image.*

Wrap Text around an Image

- When an image is inserted in the same line as text, you use the options on the Align list in the Property inspector to position the image. Options on this list allow you to wrap text around the image or position it precisely, relative to the text on the same line.

- Dreamweaver selects the Default position for a new image. This setting puts the image at the left edge of the page with the bottom of the picture aligned with the baseline of text (see the following illustration).

Default image alignment

- The Align list offers nine other alignment options, but be careful when you make your choice. Some of the alignment options Dreamweaver offers are supported by only a few browsers, and others do not meet some XHTML standards.

- Valid XHTML alignments include Top, Bottom, Middle, Left, and Right.
  - Top aligns the top of the image with the top of the text's tallest letters. If the text is a paragraph of several lines, only the first line aligns at the top; the remaining lines of the paragraph display below the image.
  - Bottom aligns the image and text the same way as Default.
  - Middle aligns the middle of the image with the text baseline. Only the first line of text is aligned at the middle; remaining lines display below the image.
  - Left positions the image at the left margin and wraps text around it on the right.
  - Right positions the image at the right margin and wraps text around it on the left.

- The Align list also includes Text Top, Baseline, Absolute Middle, and Absolute Bottom, but you will probably find that you can achieve the desired alignment effect using one of the options above, with the added security of knowing these alignments will display correctly in all browsers.

- When you apply the Left or Right alignment option, Dreamweaver places an anchor at the location where the image was inserted. Selecting this anchor is the same as selecting the image itself.

  ✔ To make sure the anchor will be displayed, click the Edit> Preferences menu command and select the Invisible Elements category. If necessary, click to add a checkmark to the Anchor Points for Aligned Elements checkbox. Click OK to save your changes.

- You can drag and drop the anchor to pinpoint the image file's position in the text and change the way text wraps around the image (see the following illustration).

Drag anchor to adjust right alignment

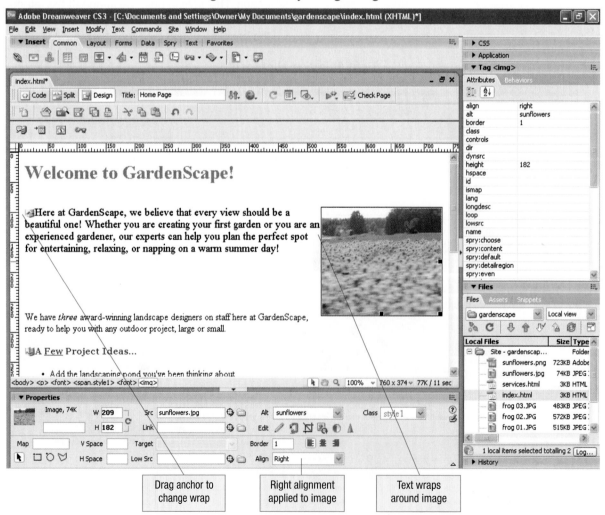

Drag anchor to change wrap

Right alignment applied to image

Text wraps around image

About Spacing around Images

■ When you wrap text around an image, Dreamweaver doesn't apply any standoff spacing between the image and the text, so text may run right to the edge of an image, especially if Left alignment has been applied.

■ The V Space and H Space text boxes on the Property inspector allow you to add space around an image, but the options in the Property inspector do not provide very flexible control of the space.

■ For example, the H Space box adds space to both the left and right sides of an image, but you may want to add space on only one side, to provide a buffer between text and an image. Likewise, the V Space option adds space both above and below an image even if you only want space below the image.

■ For best appearance, you are advised to use CSS properties to adjust spacing around an image. The CSS padding property, for example, allows you to specify space as desired on each side of an image.

✔ *You learn about working with CSS in Exercise 44.*

Use Rulers and Guides to Help Position Graphics

■ As you arrange objects on a page, you may want to display rulers and guides to help you position the page content.

■ If the rulers are not already displaying, you can show them using the View>Rulers menu command. Rulers appear at the top and left sides of the Document window. You have the option of setting the unit of measurement for the rulers.

■ You can add guides to the display by dragging down from the horizontal ruler or to the right from the vertical ruler. As you drag, a ToolTip displays the current vertical or horizontal position in pixels, as shown in the following illustration.

✔ *You can add both horizontal and vertical guides at the same time by clicking in the upper-left corner of the rulers (where the rulers meet) and dragging a guide from that point.*

Display a guide to help position page content

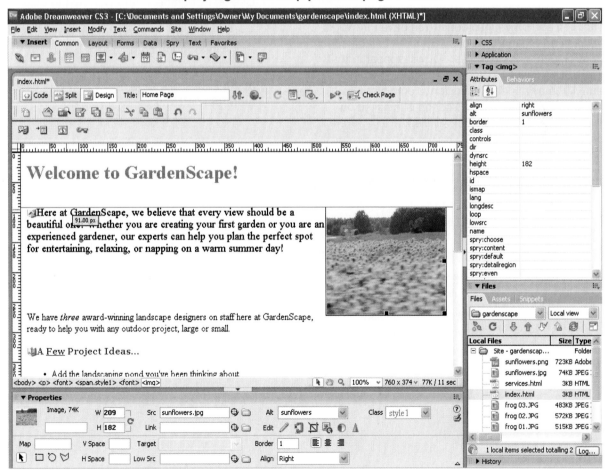

- Use the View>Guides pop-out menu commands to control guides on the page. This pop-out menu allows you to hide, lock, edit, and clear guides, as well as adjust snapping options for the guides. You can also select the browser window size if you want to display guides that show you where the "fold" appears for different screen resolutions.

  ✔ *The "fold" of your Web page is the point at which users have to scroll down to see additional content. By adding a guide at that point, you can remind yourself where the most important content on your page needs to go if you want the majority of your visitors to see it.*

Edit Graphics within Dreamweaver

- As part of Adobe's studio of Web design applications, Dreamweaver has built-in graphics-editing capabilities that rely on other Adobe programs such as Photoshop and Fireworks. You can use these editing tools to modify graphics right in Dreamweaver, which can save a great deal of formatting time in a complex Web site.

- The graphic editing tools are located on the Property inspector, as shown in the illustration below.

- The first tool in the Edit row may look different from what you see on your screen. If you have Fireworks installed and that program is set as the default editor for JPG, GIF, and PNG files, Fw will appear in that space. If you have Photoshop installed on your system, Ps may appear in addition to or in place of Fw. If neither Fireworks nor Photoshop is installed on your computer, the Edit tool will display a 🖉 Pencil tool.

  ✔ *The Pencil tool will also appear if you have the graphics programs installed but do not have either of them set as the default graphics editor.*

- You can use the tools as follows to edit a selected image.

  - Click Fw or Ps to open the image in the respective program.

    ✔ *You can adjust settings to specify which application opens which type of graphics. Click Edit>Preferences and click the File Types/Editors category to display your choices. Click OK to save any changes you make.*

  - Use 🔳 Optimize to open an Image Preview dialog box such as the one shown in the illustration at the top of the next page, where you can modify settings for the best appearance on the Web page. The settings available in the Image Preview dialog box differ depending on the file type of the selected image.

  - Use 🔳 Crop to remove portions of the image you don't need. Be careful, though—you can't reverse this operation unless you choose the Edit>Undo menu command.

  - Use 🔳 Resample after you resize an image to make sure the pixel size matches the display size. Resampling keeps the image looking sharp and can reduce image file size.

  - Use 🔳 Brightness and Contrast to adjust these attributes for the selected image. This is another action you can't reverse unless you choose the Edit>Undo menu command.

  - Use ▲ Sharpen to adjust the contrast of pixels at the edges of image areas to give a clearer, more defined look.

Graphic editing tools on the Property inspector

Image Preview

Set options for the Fireworks file in Image Preview

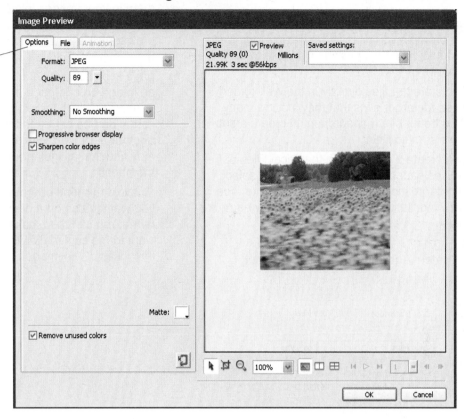

Insert and Edit a Fireworks Image

- Adobe has built another attractive graphic-handling feature into Dreamweaver CS3: You can add a file you created in Fireworks directly onto a Dreamweaver page and then use Fireworks to edit that image.

- Use the Insert>Image or Images button on the Common tab of the Insert bar to insert the Fireworks file.

- You can also copy and paste an image from Fireworks directly into Dreamweaver. Dreamweaver then displays the Image Preview dialog box. In this dialog box, you can specify the file format and settings to optimize the image for Web use.

- Select a format from the Format list, such as JPEG, GIF, or PNG. The dialog box options change to allow you to adjust settings specific to the chosen format type. The Saved settings list offers some common settings predefined for you so that you merely have to click one of the list options to optimize the image.

- Tools below the preview let you crop or magnify the image. You can also display several versions of the image and change optimization settings for each view to compare how the images look with different settings applied.

- The File tab allows you to specify exact dimensions for the image or scale it to a percentage of its original size.

- If you have Fireworks CS3 available, you can edit the image in Fireworks using the Modify>Image> Fireworks command, or by clicking the ▨ Edit button in the Property inspector. The image opens in Fireworks, where it can be modified using any of Firework's tools.

- You can paste the edited image back into Dreamweaver to update the image on the Web page.

- You can also insert Fireworks images by copying and pasting them. You can copy all or part of an image in Fireworks and then paste that copy directly on a Dreamweaver page. This process opens the Image Preview dialog box for optimization.

  ✔ *If you have Photoshop CS3 installed instead of (or in addition to) Fireworks CS3, you can use all the preceding operations with that program as well.*

Manage Graphic Files

- As you add image files to your Web site, Dreamweaver prompts you to save the files to your Web site's root folder so they will be available to display in the browser.

- You can store the files directly in the Web folder. However, for larger sites that may include many files, it is better site management to create a sub-folder for graphic files.

- You can create a subfolder in the Local Files pane of the Files panel. Right-click any file and select New Folder to insert a new folder in the site (see the following illustration). Then type a new name for the folder, such as **images**.

Create a subfolder in the Files panel

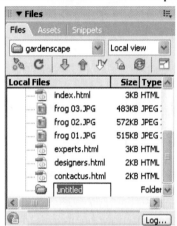

- When you are prompted to save graphic files, save them in your images folder. Be sure to include this folder when copying files for publication so the browser will be able to locate them.

- If you intend to use an image on more than one page in a site, you should be aware that modifying an image on one page may change it on other pages as well. If, for example, you insert a full-size image on one page, and then insert it again on another page and resize it to thumbnail size, you may find that all instances of the image are now thumbnails.

- To avoid this kind of problem, copy the image file you want to use on a new page and give it a unique name. You can then make any modification you want to the copied file without affecting other instances of the image.

Web Design Connection

Using Graphics Applications

You have a number of options to choose from if you want to create your own graphic images for a Web site. You can scan an image, import it from a digital camera, or use an application such as Photoshop, Illustrator, or Fireworks. You can even use Windows' Paint program to create simple graphic or text images.

Learn about Web Graphics

Successful Web designers are careful to create a site that visitors want to visit—and that means creating a visually appealing site that loads quickly. The different types of images you use on your Web page will have differing impacts on the page download speed. Research online to discover which file formats are best—JPG, GIF, or PNG—and learn how to optimize the files you scan and import.

PROCEDURES

Use Adobe Bridge (Ctrl + Alt + O)

To open Adobe Bridge:

1. Click **File** .... Alt + F
2. Click **Browse in Bridge** .... B

   OR

- Click the **Browse in Bridge** button 🖼 on the Standard toolbar.

To display images in a folder:

1. Click the **Folders** tab in the upper-left corner of the left pane.
2. Navigate to the desired folder and click it to display its images in the Content pane.
3. Click an image in the Content pane to preview it in the Preview panel.

To insert an image into Dreamweaver:

1. Click the image to select it.
2. Click **File** .... Alt + F
3. Click **Copy to** .... C, C, Enter
4. Select the current root folder on the pop-out list.

   OR

   a. Click **Choose Folder** C
   b. Browse to the desired folder to select it.
   c. Click OK .

Insert an Image on a Page (Ctrl + Alt + I)

1. Click **Insert** .... Alt + I
2. Click **Image** I

   OR

   a. Click the drop-down arrow on **Image** button 🖼▾ from the Common tab of the Insert bar.
   b. Select **Image**.

   OR

- Drag the **Image** button 🖼▾ to the page to open the Select Image Source dialog box.

3. Locate and select the image file.
4. Click OK .
5. Click Yes to copy the file to the root folder.
6. Open the folder in which the images will be stored and rename the file if necessary.
7. Click Save .
8. Type a short description of the image in the **Alternate text** box.

   OR

   Type a path to a document that contains a more lengthy description of the image in the **Long description** box, or click 📁 and navigate to the document.

9. Click OK .

Modify Image Properties

To name an image:

1. Click the image to select it.
2. Click in the **Name** box and type a name for the image.

To use an image as a link:

1. Click an image to select it.
2. Type the page or site address in the **Link** text box in the Property inspector.

   OR

- Use **Point to File** 🎯 or **Browse for Folder** 📁 to locate the link page.

To add alternate text for image:

1. Click the image to select it.
2. In the Property inspector, click in the **Alt** text box and type the alternate text.

   OR

- Click the **Alt** box list arrow and select **<empty>**.

To resize an image:

1. Click the image to select it.
2. Click a sizing handle and drag it to expand or reduce the image.

   ✔ *If you want to keep the original proportions of the image, press and hold* ⇧ Shift *while dragging.*

   OR

   a. Click in the **W** text box on the Property inspector and type the pixel size for width.
   b. Click in the **H** text box on the Property inspector and type the pixel size for height.

To reset image size:

- Click the **Reset Size** button 🔄 .

Align a Standalone Image

Click the image to select it and expand the Property inspector if necessary.

- Click the **Align Left** button ▤ in the Property inspector to left align the image.
- Click the **Align Center** button ▤ in the Property inspector to center it.
- Click the **Align Right** button ▤ in the Property inspector to right align it.

Wrap Text Around an Image

Click the image to select it.

1. Click the **Align** list arrow on the Property inspector.
2. Select one of the following alignment options:

Default	Bottom
Top	Left
Middle	Right

   ✔ *The above options all display correctly in any browser. You can also choose the other options, but they may not be supported by all browsers or XHTML standards.*

To adjust wrap alignment:

- Click the anchor 🔲 and drag it to a new location in the text.

Display "Visible Area" Guides

1. Click **View** .... Alt + V
2. Click **Guides** .... U
3. Select the browser size from the pop-out list.

Clear Guides

1. Click **View** .... Alt + V
2. Point to **Guides** .... U
3. Click **Clear Guides** C

Edit Graphics within Dreamweaver

With the image selected:

- Click the **Edit** button (🔲 or 🔲) to open the image in Fireworks or Photoshop.

  ✔ *Fireworks and/or Photoshop must be installed to use this command.*

- Click the **Optimize** button 🔲 to open the Image Preview dialog box and change settings.

- Click the **Crop** button 🔲 and then drag the crop outline to select the portion of the image you want to keep; click outside the image, or press Enter, to complete the crop.

- Click the **Resample** button 🔲 after resizing an image to adjust the pixel size to match the new image size.

- Click the **Brightness and Contrast** button 🔲 and drag the sliders to adjust the brightness and/or contrast of image.

- Click the **Sharpen** button 🔲 and drag the slider to adjust the contrast of edge pixels in image objects.

Insert and Edit a Fireworks Image

To insert a Fireworks image:

1. Click **Insert** .... Alt + I
2. Click **Image** I

   OR

   a. Click the drop-down arrow on the **Image** button 🔲 from the Common tab of the Insert bar.

   b. Select **Image**.

   OR

   - Drag the **Image** button 🔲 to page to open the Select Image Source dialog box.

3. Locate and select image file.
4. Click OK .

In Image Preview dialog box:

5. Click the **Format** list arrow and select a format type.
6. Change the settings for the image:

   - For a JPEG image, click the Quality slider arrow and drag to set the quality of the imported image, or click the **Saved settings** list arrow and select a quality option.

   - For a GIF image, select the desired palette and the desired number of colors.

7. Make any other adjustments you'd like to make:

   - Click the **Crop** button and drag the crop borders to set the import image area.

   - Click the **File** tab in the dialog box and specify a **Scale** percentage or type the exact measurements for the imported image.

8. Click OK .
9. Type a new name for the imported image, and then click Save .

10. Type a short description of the image in the **Alternate text** box.

    OR

    - Type a path to a document that contains a more lengthy description of the image in the **Long description** box, or click 🔲 and navigate to the document.

11. Click OK .

To edit a Fireworks image in Fireworks:

1. Click the image to select it.
2. Click the **Edit** button 🔲 in the Property inspector to open Fireworks.
3. Modify the image as desired using Fireworks tools.

To reinsert an edited Fireworks image:

1. In Fireworks, use a selection tool to select the area you want to reinsert.
2. Click **Edit** .... Alt + E
3. Click **Copy** C
4. In Dreamweaver, click **Edit** .... Alt + E
5. Click **Paste** .... P

   ✔ *The pasted image replaces the original image in the Files panel.*

Create a Folder in Site Window

In Local Files pane of Files panel:

1. Right-click any file name.
2. Click **New Folder**.
3. Type name for new folder.

EXERCISE DIRECTIONS

1. Start Dreamweaver and open the gardenscape site.

2. Right-click in the Files tab of the Files panel and click *New Folder*.

3. Name the folder images.

4. Choose the File>Browse in Bridge menu command.

5. In Adobe Bridge, navigate to the file S_22_gslogo_xx.png you created in Exercise 22.

   ✔ If you do not have that file, open ⊙ gslogo.png.

6. Right-click the file and click Copy To. Click *Choose Folder*.

7. In the Browse for Folder dialog box, navigate to the gardenscape folder and expand the subfolders by clicking the triangle. Click the images subfolder and click OK.

8. Display Dreamweaver and the gardenscape site.

9. Display the Files panel, if necessary. Verify that the file is listed in the images folder.

10. In the Files panel, rename experts.html to articles.html.

11. Open index.html.

12. Position the insertion point to the left of the first heading on the page (*Welcome to GardenScape!*) and press Enter to create a new line.

13. Move the insertion point up into the new line.

14. Drag the S_22_gslogo_xx.png image from the Files panel to the location of the insertion point. When prompted, supply the alternate text **GardenScape logo**. Click OK.

15. Center the alignment of the image.

16. Create a copy of the logo image to use on other pages in the site as follows:

    ■ Open the images folder if necessary, right-click the S_22_gslogo_xx.png file, point to Edit, and then select Copy to create a copy of the image file.

    ■ Right-click on the images folder, point to Edit, and select Paste.

    ■ Rename the copied image S_22_small_logo_xx.png.

17. Open services.html and insert the S_22_small_logo_xx.png file from the images folder to the left of the first heading. Supply the alternate text **link logo**.

    ■ Reduce its size to 150 pixels wide by 110 pixels high.

■ Link the image to index.html. (If a blue border surrounds the image, click in the Border box on the expanded Property inspector and type **0** to eliminate the border.)

■ Click to the right of the picture and press Enter to move the heading to a new line.

18. Select and copy the image, then save and close the page.

19. Open experts.html and paste the copied image between the named anchor and the first heading. Move the heading to the next line. Save and close the page.

20. Open designers.html and paste the copied image to the left of the first heading. Move the heading to the next line.

21. Position the insertion point to the left of the paragraph under the *All-Natural Gardening* heading. Use the Image button on the Insert bar to insert the ⊙ terrace.jpg image from the Data folder. Save the image in your images folder. Supply the alternate text **Photo of terrace design**.

22. Insert the ⊙ lotus.jpg image to the left of the second paragraph. Accept the default JPEG settings and save the image in the images folder. Supply the alternate text **Picture of water garden**.

23. Insert the ⊙ butterfly.jpg image to the left of the Tyler Meadows paragraph. Save the image in the images folder and supply the alternate text **Photo of butterfly garden**.

    ✔ In both cases, "paragraph" means the body copy under the name headings.

24. Format the pictures as follows:

    ■ Change the size of the first two photos to 250 by 180 pixels.

    ■ Resample the images after resizing.

    ■ Crop the third photo to remove the corner of the house from the image. Accept the default crop value suggested by Dreamweaver.

    ■ Change the size of the third picture to 250 by 180 pixels and then resample.

    ■ Increase the contrast of the third picture to 20.

    ■ Apply Left alignment to the first and third photos. Apply Right alignment to the second photo.

    ■ If necessary, drag the anchor for each picture up and to the left of the headings, so the anchor is just to the left of the heading.

    ✔ If you don't see anchors, use Edit>Preferences and select Invisible Elements from the list at left. Select Anchor points for aligned elements. You can adjust Caitlin's picture by simply dragging the image to the left of the heading.

25. Add space around the images to add a little padding for the text. Click each photo and then click in the H Space box and type **10**.

26. Add line spaces as needed to create a balanced looking page.

27. Save and close the page.

28. On the index.html page, insert a blank paragraph above the *Services* link and type **Meet Our Designers!** in the blank paragraph. Link this text to the designers.html page.

29. Display guides to show how the page will break using a browser size of 800 by 600.

30. Clear the guides.

31. Preview the index.html page in the browser and test the link to the designers.html page. The top of your Meet Your Designers page should look similar to Illustration A.

32. Close the browser.

33. Save and close any open pages and exit Dreamweaver and Adobe Bridge.

Illustration A

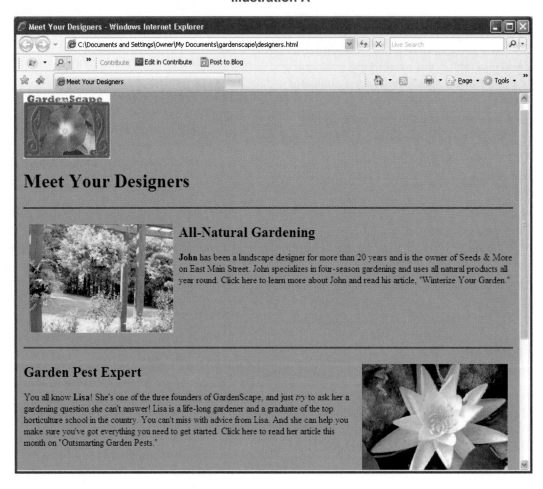

ON YOUR OWN

1. Start Dreamweaver and open the java2go Web site.

2. Create a new subfolder in the site named images to hold all image files.

3. Open index.html.

4. Use Adobe Bridge to copy the ⊙ javalogo.jpg image from the Lesson 3 Data files to the java2go images folder.

5. In Dreamweaver, drag the image to a point just beneath the navigation bar. Supply appropriate alternate text. Resize the image to a size you think appropriate. Be sure to resample after resizing. Center the image on the page.

6. Modify the image as you think necessary. You may want to crop it or adjust its brightness and contrast.

7. Open recipe.html.

8. Insert the ⊙ muffins.jpg image from the Lesson 3 Data files and save it in your images folder. Drag the image to the left of the first paragraph on the page. Supply appropriate alternate text. Resize the image to 280 W and 210 H and then resample it. Position it to the right of the first text paragraph and wrap text around it.

9. Create a copy of the threeberry.jpg image in the images folder and rename the copy SO_22_link_threeberry_xx.jpg.

10. Drag the SO_22_link_threeberry_xx.jpg image from the images folder and position it above the first heading on the contact.html page. Provide appropriate alternate text. Resize to a small size, such as about 63 pixels wide by 49 pixels high. Create a link from this image to the index.html page. Copy the link image.

11. Return to the recipe.html and paste the link image above the first heading.

12. Save all open pages and preview the Web site in the browser. Don't worry that your navigation bar isn't functional yet. You will fix it in a later exercise.

13. Close the browser and all open pages and exit Dreamweaver.

Skills Covered

- Insert a Background Picture
- Create Image Maps
- About Rollover Images
- Use the Assets Panel

Software Skills Another way to add visual impact to your Web page is to add a background picture behind the text. You can also make your pictures functional by creating image maps and navigation bars that enable visitors to get around on your Web site. Rollover images also add a dynamic touch to a Web page. You use the Assets panel to view and access all these objects in a Web site.

Design Skills Your pictures can (and in some cases, should) be more than just a pretty face. The best sites use images creatively, not only for illustration, but also for function. You can create professional navigation bars, page backgrounds, and more by using the images you add to your site.

Application Skills In this exercise, you will continue to work with graphic images in the GardenScape Web site. You will add a page background, create image maps and navigation bars, and view the site's assets in the Assets panel.

TERMS

Assets panel In Dreamweaver, a panel in the Files panel group that displays the "assets" of the site: images, colors, URLs, library items, templates, and other objects used in a Web site.

Element An item in a Dreamweaver navigation bar.

Hotspot A region on an image map that provides a link to another Web page.

Image map An image on your Web site that has been linked to other documents or areas of the Web site. An image map can have one or many regions linking to one or many other pages or documents.

Navigation bar A set of links to pages in a Web site.

Rollover image An interactive effect created by specifying two images, one of which loads with the page and the other that displays when the mouse rolls over the image.

NOTES

Insert a Background Picture

- You can use an image as a background. Background images can create an attractive and unobtrusive appearance that gives a Web site an identity while keeping the Web file size small and download times minimal.

- Insert the background image from the Page Properties dialog box (see the following illustration). You can use the Browse... button to the right of the Background image text box to open the Select Image Source dialog box and locate the file you want to use for the background image.

Locate graphic image file

```
Page Properties                                    [X]

Category        Appearance
Appearance      Background image: [_____] Browse...
Title/Encoding
Tracing Image   Background: [_][_____]

                Text: [_][_____]      Visited links: [_][_____]

                Links: [_][_____]     Active links: [_][_____]


                Left margin: [_____]  Margin width: [_____]

                Top margin: [_____]   Margin height: [_____]


                [ Help ]              [ OK ] [ Cancel ] [ Apply ]
```

- If the Preview images checkbox is selected in the Select Image Source dialog box and you choose Thumbnails in the View menu (to the right of the Look In box), you can see a preview of the image at the right side of the dialog box when you click the image's file name.

  ✔ *If you are using Windows Vista, the Thumbnails open in the View menu won't be available.*

- After you choose the file, Dreamweaver prompts you to save the image in your root folder. When you click Yes, Dreamweaver displays the Copy File As dialog box, where you can rename the file and specify a folder to store the image if desired.

- You can then apply the background image from the Page Properties dialog box to see the effect without having to close the dialog box, or you can close the dialog box to see the background image in place on the page.

- If the image is not large enough to cover the entire page area, Dreamweaver *tiles* the image—repeats it across and down the page to fill the entire page area.

- The background image information appears as an attribute of the <body> opening tag in the HTML code.

Create Image Maps

- As you know from the last exercise, you can use an entire image to create a link. You can also use an image to create an **image map,** which contains a **hotspot** that links the current page to another location. Image maps are creative ways to add both visual appeal and functionality to your Web site.

- To create image maps, you use the hotspot tools (see the following illustration) on the expanded portion of the Property inspector to draw an area on the image.

Hotspot tools on the Property inspector

- Use the ▭ Rectangular Hotspot tool to create a square or rectangular area on the image.
- Use the ○ Oval Hotspot tool to create a circular area.
- Use the ♈ Polygon Hotspot tool to create an irregular-shaped area.

  ✔ *The Polygon Hotspot tool will not work on an image that has been absolutely positioned either at the left or right with text wrapped around it.*

- After you click the appropriate tool, the insertion point changes to a crosshair you use to draw the area on the image. Drawing a hotspot is the same as drawing an object in a program such as Paint or Word. Dreamweaver reminds you to supply alternate text for the image map.

- The area you draw fills with blue shading to show the location of the hotspot and the Property inspector changes to display settings for the hotspot (see the following illustration at the top of the next page).

  ✔ *The blue shading will not appear when the image map is viewed in the browser.*

- Type the link address in the Link box, or use the 🌀 Point to File icon or 📁 Browse for File button to select the page or site to which you want to link.

- Dreamweaver automatically inserts a pound sign (#) in the Link box. Delete the # sign in the Link box before typing a file name to create a link to another page or another Web site, or use the 📁 Browse for File button to locate the page.

  ✔ *An interesting use for an image map is to reduce an image to thumbnail size and link it to a larger version of the image.*

Hotspot

Alt text box

- You can type a name in the text box next to Map on the Property inspector to name each image map on a page. This is helpful if you create more than one hotspot on an image.

- As for any image, you can use the Alt box to supply text for text-only browsers to inform a site visitor of the link. Some browsers, such as Internet Explorer, will display this text as a ScreenTip when a visitor rests the mouse on the hotspot.

- Adjust a hotspot's size by selecting it with the Pointer Hotspot tool. Drag any sizing handle on the hotspot to change its size.

   ✔ *You cannot adjust the size of a hotspot on an image that has been positioned absolutely with text wrapped around it.*

- Click on a hotspot and hold down the mouse button while dragging the shape to move it to another position.

- To delete a hotspot, select it and press the Delete key.

- If you do not like the look of the blue-shaded hotspot on your image, you can hide the hotspot. Use the View>Visual Aids>Image Maps menu command or click the Visual Aids button on the Document toolbar and deselect Image Maps.

About Rollover Images

- The Images list on the Insert bar offers two options that you can use to add interactivity to a Web page: Rollover Image and Navigation Bar.

- Both of these are designed to replace one image with another when the visitor moves the mouse pointer over the original image in a browser or clicks on an image.

- The process you follow to insert rollover images and navigation bars is quite similar, as you will discover in the following sections.

Insert a Rollover Image

■ A **rollover image** is composed of two images that are controlled by JavaScript. The original image loads with the page. When a site visitor hovers the mouse over the image, the original image is replaced by another.

■ The illustration below shows how one image replaces another in the browser. The original image, at left, is an overexposed version of a photo to give a dreamy effect. When the mouse pointer rolls over the image, it changes to a brightly colored version of the photo.

A rollover image in a browser

■ Rollover images can be used in a number of ways on a Web site. Use them to show two different versions of an image, as shown above, or to display related images. Rollover images can also be used to create navigation buttons.

■ To create a new rollover image, click the 🖳▾ Images list arrow from the Common category of the Insert bar and select 🔳▾ Rollover Image from the list of image options. Or use the Insert>Image Objects>Rollover Image menu command.

■ The Insert Rollover Image dialog box displays, as shown in the following illustration.

Insert Rollover Image dialog box

Insert Rollover Image			
Image name:	spring_dreams		OK
Original image:	images/hyacinths_dream.jpg	Browse...	Cancel
Rollover image:	images/hyacinths_spring.jpg	Browse...	Help
	☑ Preload rollover image		
Alternate text:			
When clicked, Go to URL:		Browse...	

■ Supply a name for the rollover image and then specify the original image and the rollover image. Use the ⬚Browse...⬚ button to locate the images, and then save the images with the other images in your site.

■ Note that you can also create a link from the rollover image so that when you click the image in the browser, a new page displays.

■ When you are creating images for rollovers, be sure to make the original and rollover images the same size so that one will completely replace the other.

Insert a Navigation Bar

■ A **navigation bar** is a set of links to pages in a Web site. Navigation bars display text or image links horizontally or vertically in a group to make it easy for visitors to get to other pages in the site. The links in a navigation bar are often included inside a table structure to make it easy to position the links.

   ✔ *You have already worked with text navigation bars available as snippets in previous exercises.*

■ The Navigation Bar option on the Images list allows you to create a visual, interactive navigation bar that, as for rollover images, uses JavaScript to replace original navigation images with other images depending on the action of the mouse pointer in the browser.

■ You can provide up to four images for each element in a navigation bar:

   ● *Up*—This image is the one that appears when the page opens.

   ● *Over*—This image appears when the visitor moves the mouse pointer over the element.

   ● *Down*—This image appears when the navigation bar element is clicked.

   ● *Over While Down*—This image appears when the visitor moves the pointer over the element after it has been clicked.

■ To create a new navigation bar, click the 🖳▾ Images list arrow from the Common category of the Insert bar and select 🔳▾ Navigation Bar from the list of image options. Or use the Insert>Image Objects>Navigation Bar menu command.

■ The Insert Navigation Bar dialog box opens (see the following illustration at the top of the next page) with a default unnamed element displayed in the *Nav bar elements* list.

■ A navigation bar **element** is the image that will appear in the navigation bar. Each element must have a unique name.

■ To add the first navigation bar element, replace the *unnamed1* default element with your first navigation bar element. When creating a navigation bar to link pages in a Web site, the elements should reflect the names of the site's pages.

Insert Navigation Bar dialog box

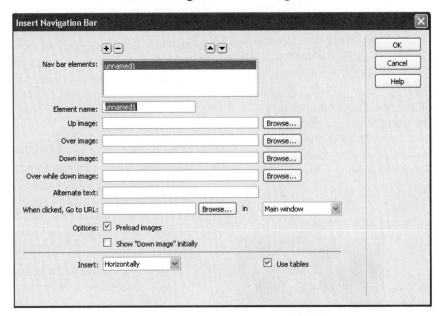

- Add other elements by clicking the ⊞ button and typing new element names. Remove an element from the Nav bar elements list by selecting it and clicking the ⊟ button. Move an element in the list by selecting it and clicking either ▲ or ▼.

- As you add each element, you specify images for the various appearances of the element. Use the `Browse...` button for each image to locate the image, and then save the images with the other images in your site.

  ✓ A navigation bar image can be a PNG, GIF, or JPEG file of a button or bullet—although virtually any kind of Web-compatible image file can be used.

  ✓ You can easily create buttons for the various rollover effects using Fireworks. Refer to exercises earlier in this lesson to find out how.

- You can choose a graphic for each selection—Up, Over, Down, and Over While Down. A common option is to use the same image in a different color for each state.

- You do not have to use all four states when you are creating a button. You may choose only to use Up and Over states, if you want the buttons you add to your site to have a consistent look whether they have been clicked or not.

- For each element, type a relative or absolute address in the *When clicked, Go to URL* text box, or use the `Browse...` button to locate the page or site that should open when the element is clicked.

- By default, Dreamweaver will preload the images with the page so they are available immediately. You can also choose to have the "down" image displayed initially rather than the "up" image.

- You can choose to insert the navigation bar horizontally (the default) or vertically on the page, and in a table or freestanding.

- After you click OK to finish the navigation bar, the images you selected display on the page, as shown in the following illustration.

Completed navigation bar

- If you have created the navigation bar in a table, you can make some adjustments to the table, such as changing column widths, but you cannot format the table in the same ways you format other tables. You cannot, for example, add cell borders, although you can change the background color of cells or the entire table.

- Images used to create navigation bars generally include labels, as shown in the previous illustration, to let visitors know what page will open when the navigation button is clicked. If the image used for the navigation element is merely decorative, such as a button or arrow, you will have to supply a text label beside the image to identify the link. To create a label with the same link properties as the image, select the image, press the right arrow key, and begin typing. The label is automatically formatted as a link to the same page the image is linked to.

- To modify a navigation bar after creating it, click anywhere in the navigation bar and use the Modify>Navigation Bar menu command.

■ Creating a navigation bar in a Web site with a number of pages can take time. Fortunately, after you create the navigation bar you can select it, copy it, and paste it on other pages in the site. You can also make it part of a template so that it appears whenever a document is created with the template.

✔ *You will learn about creating templates in the next exercise.*

■ You can also copy the navigation bar and then create a new library item. The copied navigation bar is automatically "pasted" in the Library when you name the new library item.

✔ *You will learn about the Library in Exercise 27.*

■ There are several advantages to making a navigation bar a library item: It easy to insert on other pages, and it cannot be changed accidentally on a page.

■ Most important, when new pages are added or old pages deleted, the navigation bar can be modified in the Library and then updated easily on all pages.

Use the Assets Panel

■ The **Assets panel** is a tab in the Files panel group that also includes the Files panel. It is divided into two panes. The lower pane is a list of asset files available for your site. The upper pane is a viewing window in which to inspect a selected asset (see the following illustration).

Assets panel

■ To display the Assets panel, use the Window> Assets menu command, or click the Assets tab of the Files panel group.

■ As you work with a Web site, the Assets panel collects information that makes it easy for you to keep track of objects and other elements. For example, all graphic files you add to a site display in the Images category of the Assets panel. Each color you apply in the Web site displays in the Colors category of the Assets panel.

■ The Assets panel's vertical toolbar lets you choose the different categories of objects and style elements available to your Web site.

■ Click a category button to see assets of that type listed in the bottom pane of the panel. Further information about or a representation of the asset may be displayed in the top pane when you click an asset listed in the bottom pane.

■ The Assets panel collects and displays the following items:

  ● Images (▨) stored in the site.
  ● Colors (▦) used in the site.
  ● External URLs (✎) that pages in the site link to.
  ● Flash (⬚) and Shockwave (▥) movie files present in the site.
  ● Other movie files (▤), such as QuickTime or MPEG movies, used in the site.
  ● Scripts (✎) used in the site.
  ● Templates (▤) present in the site.
  ● Library items (▥) stored in the site.

■ The Assets panel makes it easy to insert objects and format pages throughout a site. For example, to insert an image that you have already saved in the site, simply position the insertion point, click the image file in the Assets panel, and click the [Insert] button on the Assets panel. To format text in a color you have already used in the site, select the text, select the color in the Assets panel, and click the [Apply] button.

■ By default, the Assets panel displays objects for the current site (the Site option is selected just below the Assets tab at the top of the panel). However, you also can add assets to a Favorites list to make it easy to locate specific assets.

✔ *The Site and Favorites options are not available in the Templates and Library categories.*

■ Click the asset you want to make a favorite and then click the [+▨] Add to Favorites button on the Assets panel. To view your favorites, select the Favorites option at the top of the Assets panel. You can right-click any item in the Assets panel to access a shortcut menu with commands that allow you to add the item to the Favorites panel, edit the item, or insert it in a document.

■ If desired you can create folders within the Favorites list to store items that you want to group. With Favorites displayed, click the [▨] New Favorites Folder button and name the new folder. You can then drag assets into the folder to store them.

PROCEDURES

Insert a Background Picture (Ctrl + J)

1. Click **Modify**.................[Alt]+[M]
2. Click **Page Properties**.........[P]

   OR

   - Click [Page Properties...] in the expanded Property inspector.

In the Page Properties dialog box:

1. Click [Browse...] to open the Select Image Source dialog box.
2. Locate the image file you want to use for the background.
3. Click [OK].
4. Click [Yes] to copy the file to the root folder.
5. Open the folder in which images will be stored and rename the file if necessary.
6. Click [Save].
7. Click [OK].

Create an Image Map

Click the image to select it and expand the Property inspector.

1. Click the desired hotspot tool on the Property inspector:
   - **Rectangular Hotspot** tool [▢]
   - **Oval Hotspot** tool [◯]
   - **Polygon Hotspot** tool [▽]
2. Click [OK] when prompted to add alternate text.
3. Draw a hotspot:
   - For a rectangle or circle, position the pointer above and to the left or right of area you want to map. Hold down the mouse button and drag to create a hotspot.
   - For a polygon, click to start and click to change direction.
     - ✔ *Drag a blue handle to adjust the polygon's shape.*

4. Type a page or site address in the **Link** box on the Property inspector.
   - ✔ *Remember to delete the pound sign (#) that Dreamweaver automatically puts in the Link box if you are typing the page or site address.*

   OR

   - Use **Point to File** icon [⊕] or **Browse for Folder** [📁] to locate link page.

To modify a hotspot:

- Modify the size or location of the hotspot by clicking outside the picture and then using the **Select Hotspot** pointer [▶] to drag the hotspot or one of its handles.

To hide a hotspot:

1. Click **View**....................[Alt]+[V]
2. Point to **Visual Aids**.............[V]
3. Click **Image Maps**...............[I]

   OR

1. Click [👁] on the Document toolbar.
2. Click **Image Maps**.

Insert a Rollover Image

1. Position the cursor at the location you want to insert the rollover image.
2. Click **Insert**...................[Alt]+[I]
3. Point to **Image Objects** ....[G], [Enter]
4. Click **Rollover Image** ....[R]

   OR

   - Click the **Rollover Image** tool [▣▾] from [▣▾] Images button list.

In the Insert Rollover Image dialog box:

1. Type a name for rollover image.
2. Type the path to the image for the original image, or click [Browse...] and navigate to the image.

3. If necessary, save the image in current site.
4. Type a path or browse to the image for the Rollover image, and save the image in the current site.
5. Type the path for the page to link to in **When clicked, Go to URL** box, or click [Browse...] and navigate to the page.
6. Click [OK].

Insert a Navigation Bar

1. Position the cursor at the location you want to insert the navigation bar.
2. Click **Insert** ....[Alt]+[I]
3. Point to **Image Objects** ....[G], [Enter]
4. Click **Navigation Bar**............[G]

   OR

   - Click **Navigation Bar** tool [▤▾] from [▣▾] Images list.

In the Insert Navigation Bar dialog box:

1. Type the name of the first element for the navigation bar.
2. Type the path to the image you want to use for the Up image, or click [Browse...] and navigate to the image.
3. If necessary, save the image in the current site.
4. Select another or the same image for Over, Down, and/or Over While Down images.
5. Type the path for the page to link to in **When clicked, Go to URL** box, or click [Browse...] and navigate to the page.
6. Click [+] to add the elements or [−] to remove the elements.
7. Use [▲] or [▼] to move elements in the list.
8. Click [OK].

Modify a Navigation Bar

1. Click **Modify**................[Alt]+[M]
2. Click **Navigation Bar**...........[B]

Display the Assets Panel (F11)

1. Click **Window** ....[Alt]+[W]
2. Click **Assets** ....[A]

   OR

- Click the Assets tab on the Files panel group.

Manage Assets

- Click the category button in the Assets panel to see assets for that category.
- Apply or insert an asset on any page by selecting the asset and clicking [Insert] or [Apply].

Work with Favorites

- Display Favorites by clicking the **Favorites** option in the Assets panel.

To add an asset to Favorites:

1. Click the asset to select it.
2. Click [+] in the Assets panel.

   OR

- Right-click an asset's name and then choose **Add to Favorites** from the shortcut menu.

To create folder in Favorites:

1. Display Favorites in the Assets panel.
2. Click [] in the Assets panel.
3. Type a name for the new folder.
4. Drag your favorite assets into the folder to organize them.

EXERCISE DIRECTIONS

1. Start Dreamweaver and open the gardenscape site.
2. Open index.html.
3. Apply the ⊙ wildflowers.png image from the Lesson 3 Data folder as a background picture on this page. Save the image in the images folder.
4. Open designers.html. Select the first picture on this page and use the Oval Hotspot tool to create a hotspot area on the hanging basket. Cancel the dialog box that asks you to enter alternate text (you will enter it in the next step).
5. Link the hotspot to services.html and type the following text in the Alt box: **Click here to find out more about our services!**.
6. Create rectangular hotspots on the second and third pictures on the page.
7. If desired, hide the hotspots on the image maps.
8. Click to the left of the first text paragraph on this page and create a navigation bar as follows:
   - For the first element, type the name **Home**.
   - For the Up Image, browse to the Lesson 3 Data folder and select ⊙ gshome_up.png. For the Over image, select ⊙ gshome_ovr.png. When prompted to copy each image to the root folder, click *Yes* and navigate to the images folder, then save the image there.
   - Link the element to index.html. (Use the *When clicked, Go to URL* box to set up the link.)
   - Add additional elements named **Designers**, **Services**, **Contact**, and **Articles**. Use the appropriate images for each element. For example, use gsdesigners_up.png and gsdesigners_ovr.png for the Designers element

and gsservices_up.png and gsservices_ovr.png for the Services element.
   - Link the elements to designers.html, services.html, contactus.html and articles.html, respectively.
   - Move the Articles element up in the list until it is below the Designers element.
   - Choose to create a horizontal navigation bar, and deselect the Use tables checkbox.
   - Click OK to create the navigation bar.
9. Click to the right of the navigation bar on the page and press Enter to go to the next line if necessary.
10. Save the page and open it in the browser. Check the links in the navigation bar and the image map links on this page. The top of your page should look like Illustration A on the next page.

   ✔ *If Internet Explorer displays the Information bar to tell you it has blocked some content on the page, click the bar and select Allow Blocked Content. If you are using a browser other than Internet Explorer, you may not see the ScreenTip when you rest your pointer on a picture.*

11. Close the browser.
12. Open the Assets panel. View the images that have been added to the site. Then view the site's colors.

   ✔ *Click the Refresh button in the Assets panel toolbar if necessary to see the images that you have added to the site in the Assets list.*

13. Add the S_22_small_logo_xx.png file to your Favorites.
14. Save and close any open pages and exit Dreamweaver.

Illustration A

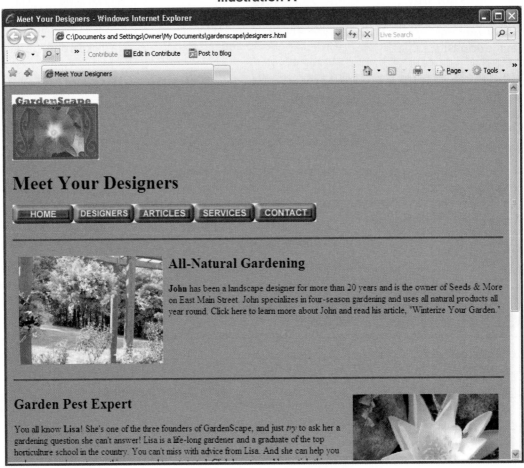

ON YOUR OWN

1. Start Dreamweaver and open the java2go site.

2. Open index.html. Replace the existing navigation bar with a new one:

   - Click in the first cell of the navigation bar table (the Home cell).

   - In the status bar at the bottom of the Document window, click the first <table> tag to select the entire table. Press Delete to remove the navigation bar.

   - Create a new navigation bar at the same location with the following elements: **Home**, **Recipes**, **History**, **Locations**, and **Contact**.

   - Use the following images in the Lesson 3 Data folder to associate with the elements listed above: jhome_up.png, jhome_ovr.png, jrecipes_up.png, jrecipes_ovr.png, jhistory_up.png, jhistory_ovr.png, jlocations_up.png, jlocations_ovr.png, jcontact_up.png, and jcontact_ovr.png. Save all images in your images folder.

   - Associate each element with the correct page in the site.

     - ✔ You will have two more buttons than you have pages! Simply leave the When clicked, Go to URL box empty at this point and you will add the links later in this exercise, after you add the new pages to the site.

3. Create two new pages: history.html and locations.html.

4. Modify the navigation bar to link the appropriate elements to those pages. Select and center the navigation bar.

5. Copy and paste the navigation bar to the top of each page in the site.

6. Save all open pages. Preview index.html in the browser and test links in the new navigation bar.

7. Close the browser and all open pages and exit Dreamweaver.

Skills Covered

Software Skills Templates can help you easily maintain a uniform look and feel throughout your entire Web site. Dreamweaver provides flexible template design features. You can control individual sections of your page without affecting the basic design.

Design Skill Creating a great template helps you showcase all the best element of your design and also saves you considerable time and effort because you can create a template once and use it an infinite number of times.

Application Skills In this exercise, you create a template for the GardenScape site, apply the template to several pages, and then modify and update the template.

TERMS

Editable region In a template, an area that an author can change in a page to which the template is applied.

Noneditable region In a template, an area that is locked so that the designer cannot change its content.

Template A collection of formats and page elements that can be used to give pages in a Web site a consistent look.

NOTES

About Templates

- A **template** is a collection of formats and page elements that you can use to give pages in your Web site a consistent look.

- For example, a template could include a background image or color, images, headings, and text styles and formats. Using a template can save you considerable development time.

- When you create a template, you can specify **noneditable** and **editable regions**:

  - Noneditable regions contain items that you want to include on each page, such as a copyright notice or a logo.

  - Editable regions contain items such as text or headings that can change on a page.

- The value of creating and using templates is that you can easily adjust formats over an entire Web site. When you modify a template, you can update all pages at once that use that template.

Create a New Template

- You can create a template from a new, blank page or from an existing page that contains text and other page elements. If your pages contain complex layouts, it makes sense to use a page you have already formatted as the basis for the template.

- You have several options for creating a new template:

  - In an open document, use the File>Save As Template menu command. Dreamweaver opens the Save As Template dialog box (see the following illustration) where you can name the template. This option creates a template of the same page type as the page you are saving. If you are saving an ASP page, for example, your template will also be an ASP page.

Save As Template dialog box

- Click the  Templates button from the Common tab of the Insert bar and then click Make Template on the drop-down list. This option will create a template of the same page type as the currently active page.

- In the Assets panel, click the Templates button. Then click the New Template button at the bottom of the panel and provide a name for the template.

- Dreamweaver stores templates automatically in the Templates folder in the current site. If no templates have been created, Dreamweaver will create the Templates folder as well.

- If you used the File>Save as Template method, the new template opens automatically after you save the template. If you have created the template in the Assets panel, you must click the Edit Template button to open the template.

- A Dreamweaver template looks like any other Web page. The title bar, however, shows the page title <<Template>> so that you know you are working in a template page.

- If you are creating a template from scratch, add and modify page elements as you would on any Web page.

- You can use the objects and style elements in your Assets panel or insert or format new ones.

- You can specify a background color or picture, format levels of headings, format paragraph text, add a logo, and so on.

  ✔ You can also create a layout with frames or absolutely positioned elements or attach cascading style sheets (CSS). You will learn about these features in Lesson 5.

- As you create the template, you must give some thought to editable and noneditable regions. Noneditable regions are locked on any page created using the template. That is, an author will not be able to change anything in a noneditable region. This helps to protect items such as logos, official photographs, and the like from being changed without authorization, no matter who may work on your page.

- All items on a template are noneditable unless you specify that they be editable. To create an editable region, select the item such as a heading or text paragraph. For best results, select while in Code and Design view so that you select the tags around the text as well. Not doing so may result in error messages requesting that you edit your code.

- Click the Templates button list arrow on the Common tab of the Insert bar. Then click the 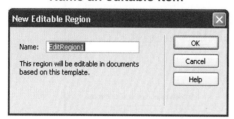 Editable Region button on the drop-down list. Dreamweaver opens the New Editable Region dialog box (see the following illustration), where you can supply a name in place of the default name for the editable item.

Name an editable item

- You can also create an editable region using the Insert>Template Objects>Editable Region command.
- The editable region name displays on the template page surrounded by a light blue box that has a tab containing the editable item name.
- In pages based on templates, the entire page is bordered in yellow with the template name in the upper-right corner (see the following illustration).

- A person adding content can click on an editable region placeholder in a page based on the template to add new content to the page. If you move the mouse over any other region, the mouse pointer turns to a ⊘ "not permitted" symbol to inform you that the region cannot be edited.

Apply a Template

- Apply a Dreamweaver template to existing pages or to new pages. Dreamweaver supplies several options for applying a template.
- To apply a template at the time you create a new page, use the File>New menu command, and click Page from Template in the New Document dialog box.
- Dreamweaver displays templates available for sites on your server so you can select the template to use on the new page from a list of templates available for your site (see the illustration at the top of the next page).

  ✔ *The New Document dialog box offers the* Update page when template changes *checkbox. This checkbox is selected by default and allows you to automatically update the page if changes are made to the template.*

Editable items in a template document

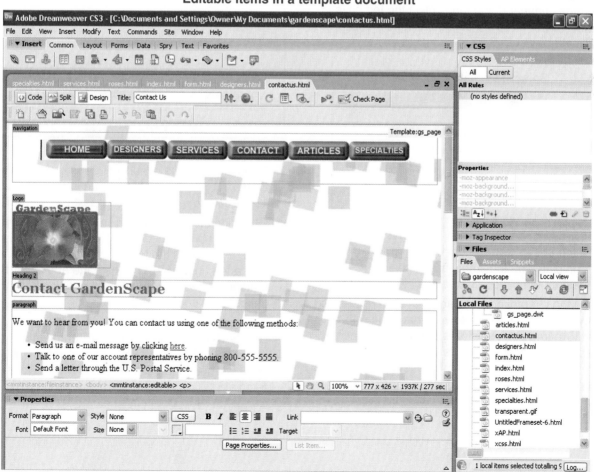

Apply a template to a new page

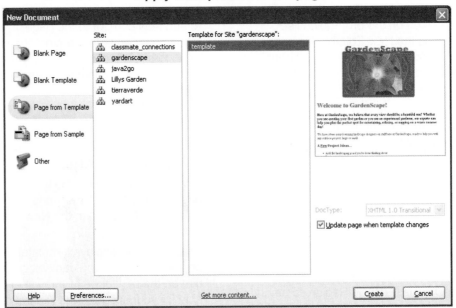

- After you select the desired template, click the
  Create button to open the new page in
  the Document window.

- You have two options for applying a template to an
  existing page:

  - Use the Modify>Templates>Apply Template to
    Page command and then select the template in
    the Select Template dialog box (see the following
    illustration).

Select Template dialog box

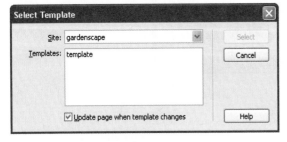

  - If the Assets panel is open, click the 🗐
    Templates button if necessary, select the
    desired template, and drag it onto the page.

- Applying a template to a page that already has text
  may require that you "resolve" what to do with that
  text. Dreamweaver analyzes the page and then
  displays the Inconsistent Region Names dialog box
  similar to the one shown in the illustration at right to
  alert you to the fact that it does not know what
  editable region to use for the preexisting text.

Applying editable regions to existing text

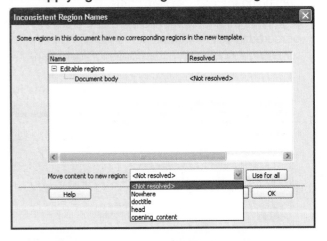

- Choose one of the editable regions in the *Move
  content to new region* list, shown in the previous
  illustration, to relocate existing text.

- Choosing the Nowhere option in the *Move content
  to new region* list throws away all content on the
  page and inserts the template's content. If you have
  only a few lines of text on the page and its format
  matches an editable region in the dialog box,
  choose that editable region.

- You can detach a page from a template using the
  Modify>Templates>Detach from Template menu
  command. All template formatting remains, but the
  page will not update if changes are made to the
  template.

Edit a Template and Update Pages

■ After you have created a template, you can edit it at any time by opening it from the Assets panel. You can make changes to both editable and non-editable regions—and remove them, too.

    ✔ *To open a template to edit it, double-click on the template file name in the Assets panel. Make sure the page title <<Template>> appears in the title bar.*

■ When you save revisions to a template that has been applied to pages in a Web site, Dreamweaver asks if you want to update the pages that use the template (see the following illustration).

Dreamweaver prompts you to update pages

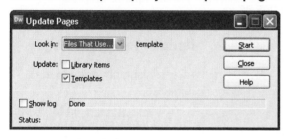

■ If you click ⟨ Update ⟩, Dreamweaver performs the updates for you and displays a report to tell you what pages have been updated (see the illustration at right).

Update Pages report

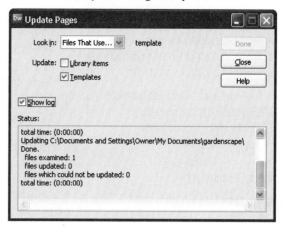

■ If you deselected the *Update page when template changes* option in the New Document or Select Template dialog box, pages attached to a template will not be changed automatically when changes to the template are saved and you will not see either dialog box prompting you to update.

■ If you choose ⟨Don't Update⟩ Don't Update button, you can update pages individually using the Modify>Templates>Update Current Page command. This command essentially reapplies the template to the current page only.

■ If you have chosen not to update pages immediately after saving changes to the template, you can at a later time update all pages using the Modify>Templates>Update Pages command. When you do so, Dreamweaver displays an empty Update Pages dialog box. Click the ⟨ Start ⟩ Start button to begin the update process.

PROCEDURES

Create a New Template

Using existing page:

1. Open the page you want to base the template on, and click **File**................[Alt]+[F]
2. Click **Save as Template**.......[M]

    ✔ *This will create a template of the same page type as the page you are saving.*

    OR

■ Click the **Templates** button ▣▾ from the Common tab of the Insert bar and select **Make Template**.

    OR

1. Display the Assets panel.
2. Click the **Templates** button ▣.
3. Click the **New Template** button ▣.

For templates created with any of the above options:

1. Type the name for template.
2. Click ⟨ Save ⟩ if necessary.
3. Edit and modify the formats as desired.
4. Save the template after editing.

Create an Editable Region (Ctrl + Alt + V)

1. Select any text or graphic you want to make editable or position the cursor in an area of the page you want to make editable.
2. Click the **Templates** list arrow from the Common tab of the Insert bar and click the **Editable Region** button ▧ on the drop-down list.

    OR

    a. Click **Insert** ....[Alt]+[I]
    b. Point to **Template Objects**.........................[O]
    c. Click **Editable Region** .....[E]

3. Type a name for editable area.

4. Click [OK].

✔ *To remove an editable region, select the region by right-clicking its tab and then clicking Remove Tag.*

✔ *Make an editable area noneditable by selecting it and clicking Modify>Templates>Remove Template Markup.*

Apply a Template

To apply a template when creating a page:

1. Click **File** ....[Alt]+[F]

2. Click **New** ....[N]

3. Click **Page from Template**.

4. Select the site, if necessary.

5. Select the desired template.

6. Click [Start].

✔ *Update page when template changes is selected by default. If you want to control when to update pages, deselect this check box.*

To apply a template to an existing page:

1. Click **Modify**..................[Alt]+[M]

2. Point to **Templates**..............[E], [E], [Enter]

3. Click **Apply Template to Page**...................[A], [A], [Enter]

4. Select the desired template.

5. Click [Select].

OR

■ Drag the template name from the Assets panel to the page.

Detach a Page from a Template

1. Click **Modify**..................[Alt]+[M]

2. Point to **Templates**..............[E], [E], [Enter]

3. Click **Detach from Template** ....[D]

Edit a Template

From Files panel:

1. Open the **Templates** folder.

2. Double-click the template file.

3. Make changes to the editable and noneditable regions as desired.

4. Save the template file and update any attached files, if desired.

From Assets panel:

1. Click **Templates** button [▦] in the toolbar.

2. Double-click the template file.

OR

a. Select the template.

b. Click **Edit** button [✎].

3. Make changes to editable and noneditable regions as desired.

4. Save the template file and update attached files, if desired.

Delete a Template

From the Files panel:

1. Open the **Templates** folder.

2. Right-click the template file.

3. Click **Delete**.

From the Assets panel:

1. Click **Templates** button [▦] in the toolbar.

2. Right-click the template file.

3. Click **Delete**.

OR

1. Select the template.

2. Click the **Delete** button [🗑].

Update Template Pages

After making changes to the template:

■ Click [Update], in the Update Template Files dialog box to update all files that use the template.

OR

If files have not been updated after changes:

1. Click **Modify**..................[Alt]+[M]

2. Point to **Templates**..............[E], [E], [Enter]

3. Click **Update Current Page** ....[C]

OR

Click **Update Pages** .....[U], [Enter]

4. Click [Start].

EXERCISE DIRECTIONS

1. Start Dreamweaver and open the gardenscape site.

2. To save time, you want to create a template that contains a space for the logo link to the home page, a formatted Heading 2, and a placeholder for a navigation bar. Create the template as follows:

   ■ Use the Assets panel to make a new template named gs_page.dwt. Open the template page for editing. (You may need to open one of the site pages before the Assets panel's tools become available to create the new template.)

   ■ Click [✎] to open the template for editing.

   ■ Click the Files tab and open contactus.html. Click in the heading, then select the <h2> tag in the status bar to select the heading and its tags. Copy the heading.

   ■ Paste the heading in the template page.

   ■ Apply the [◉] squares.jpg image as a page background.

   ■ Copy the navigation bar from designers.html.

- Click the gs_page.dwt tab and click to position the insertion point to the left of the heading. Press Enter to create a new line.

- Position the insertion point at the end of the *Contact GardenScape* heading, press Enter, and type **logo**. On the next line, type **Heading 2**; and on the next line, type **paragraph**. These will be your editable regions on the template.

  ✔ *Don't worry about the formats of the paragraphs you have just typed. You will change these formats later.*

- Create editable regions from each of the three lines in the template, using the names **logo**, **Heading 2**, and **paragraph**.

  ✔ *To avoid error messages, work in Code and Design view (Split view) so that you can select the <p> and <h2> tags as well as the text between them when you create the editable regions.*

3. Format the editable regions as follows.

  ✔ *Try this shortcut. Right-click anywhere in the text and click Paragraph Format from the shortcut menu and select the desired format.*

- Format the Heading 2 editable region with the formats you used for Heading 2 on other pages, if necessary.

- Format the paragraph, subhead, and subsection regions with Paragraph formatting. If necessary, change the font to Default Font and the font color to black.

4. Save and close the <<Template>> page. If you are asked to update, do so. (No pages will be changed.)

5. Apply the gs_page template to the contactus.html page.

6. The Inconsistent Region Names dialog box opens because the page already has content. Click Document body, and then choose paragraph to receive the existing content on the page.

7. Enter the page title **Contact Us** for this page. Illustration A shows your work thus far.

  ✔ *The previous page title disappeared when you applied the template, because the template does not have a page title.*

8. Create a new page that uses the gs_page template. Name the page specialties.html and give it the page title **Our Specialties**.

9. Replace the Heading 2 placeholder with **Our Specialties**.

10. Now that you have basic formatting in place for contactus.html and specialties.html, detach these pages from the template.

11. Save and close any open pages and exit Dreamweaver.

Illustration A

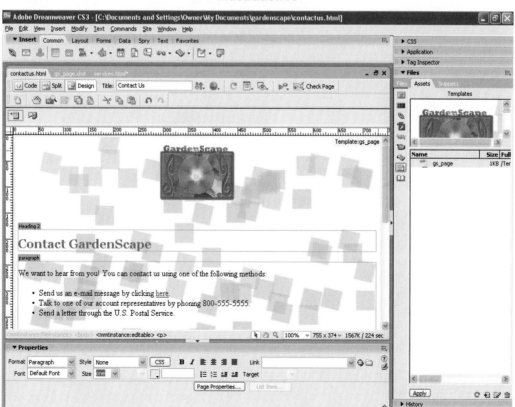

ON YOUR OWN

1. Start Dreamweaver and open the yardart site.

2. Create a new template for the site using the Assets panel. Name the template appropriately.

3. Add a navigation bar at the top of the page. (Use the ⊙ ya buttons in the data folder.)

   ✔ *Notice that there are no text labels on these buttons. Make sure the Alt text you enter tells visitors what these buttons do.*

4. Add a main heading.

5. Add a text paragraph below the navigation bar.

6. Insert a second level heading.

7. Add copyright information at the bottom of the page.

8. Apply the ⊙ splatter.jpg image as a page background.

9. Make the main heading, the text paragraph, and the second-level heading editable areas. (You may want to combine the text paragraph and the second-level heading into one editable area to make it easy to insert new content.) Save and close the template.

10. Create a new page using the template and save it as favorites.html with the page title **Favorite Artists**.

11. Change the main heading to **Favorite Artists**.

12. Insert the following text paragraph:

    This page introduces you to some of our favorite local artists. Some of these talented people showed up at our art show last summer, others got in touch over the Internet, and still others were part of the art workshops we hosted in the spring. We hope you enjoy their work.

13. Save and close the new page.

14. Reopen yardart.dwt and add a new button named **Favorites**, using two states, ⊙ ya_favorites_ovr.png and ⊙ ya_favorites_up.png, to the navigation bar. Save and close the template.

15. Attach the template to all pages in the site.

16. Adjust the content of the pages as necessary so that the right type of content is in the right type of editable region. (For example, cut and paste the paragraph content on index.html into the Paragraph region.)

    ✔ *Notice that the About Us page still has the dotted border it displayed when you imported the original Word HTML file. Do you remember how to remove the border? (Hint: See Exercise 10 for details.)*

17. Save your changes.

18. Preview the site in your Web browser and test all links.

19. Close any open pages and exit Dreamweaver.

Skills Covered

Software Skills The Assets panel's Library feature enables you to insert and change elements automatically on multiple pages in your site. You can use the Design Notes feature to track your project.

Design Skills Saving time really is a design skill, because the time you save by using the library to add and modify items automatically gives you more time to create new pages. Design Notes help you keep track of design decisions you've made so that other designers or authors who work on your site will be able to be consistent with your style.

Application Skills In this exercise, you will work with library items and add design notes to the GardenScape Web site.

TERMS

Key In the Design Notes feature, an identifier for a set of information, such as *status*.

Library A Dreamweaver feature that stores text, images, or other objects so that you can add them easily on any page in the Web site.

Library items Objects and page elements stored in the Library.

NOTES

Use the Library

- The **Library** feature in the Assets panel is a wonderful tool that saves you time and enables you to use the same elements repeatedly—while still being able to update and change them in every Web page that uses the element in a Web site. This tremendously reduces creation time, especially when you are working with a team that has a variety of skills.

- When you place a library item on a page, Dreamweaver inserts a copy of the HTML source code for that item into the document and adds an HTML comment containing a reference to the original, external item—a link from the page item to the library item.

- You can modify that library item wherever it appears in the Web site by modifying the item in the Library. In this way, a library item differs from an item inserted from the other Assets panels.

- A proficient designer can create a logo and save it to the Library, for example, allowing a less experienced team member to go to the Library and use the element. This assures consistency and eliminates the need for redevelopment.

- You can store images, text, or other elements in the Library and then use these **library items** on any page in a Web site.

Add Items to the Library

- To view the Library, click the 📖 Library button in the Assets panel toolbar.

- Library items display in the upper pane of the palette. Click the library item's name in the lower pane to display it in the upper pane, as shown in the following illustration. You can use the scroll bars if necessary to display the entire item.

Library pane in Assets panel

- Dreamweaver automatically creates a Library subfolder in the site's root folder to contain the library items.

- You can create library items from existing text or images by selecting the object in the document and clicking Modify>Library>Add Object to Library.

- When selecting items, it can be helpful to view the status bar in the Document window to make sure you are selecting a complete item, such as the complete paragraph or table in which a navigation bar is contained.

- You can also create new library items. Click the 🔳 New Library Item button and then the 📝 Edit button on the Library pane of the Assets panel to open a new <<Library Item>> in the Document window.

- Use this Document window to type text or insert images or other elements to create the library item. When you are finished, click on File>Save As to save the library item, and then close the <<Library Item>> window.

- You can remove an item from the library at any time by right-clicking its name in the Library pane and then clicking Delete—or selecting it and clicking the 🗑 Delete button on the Library pane.

Insert Library Item on Page

- Inserting library items on a page is even easier than adding them to the Library. Position the insertion point where you want the library item to appear in the Document window, select its name in the Library pane of the Assets panel, and click the Insert button.

- You can also simply drag a library item or its name from the Library pane of the Assets panel to the desired position on the Web page.

- Inserted images are initially shaded but will look normal as soon as you click in the Document window. Inserted text retains a yellow shading to remind you it is a library item.

- You cannot edit a library item once it has been inserted on a page unless you break the link between the item on the page and the Library. You can detach an item from the Library by clicking it on the page and then clicking the Detach from Original button in the Property inspector.

Modify Library Item and Update Pages

- Similar to templates, the value of using library items is that all library items inserted throughout a Web site can be modified at once by modifying the item stored in the Library.

- Edit a library item by double-clicking either the item itself or its name in the Library pane of the Assets panel. Or, select the item name and click the ▨ Edit button.

- The library item opens in a <<Library Item>> window. You can then edit or modify it using Dreamweaver's editing tools.

  - ✔ *Once the item is open in the <<Library Item>> window, you can select the item and click Edit in the Property inspector to open the object in Fireworks and make your changes there.*

- After you save the modified item, Dreamweaver will ask if you want to update all pages on which that library item appears (see the following illustration). You can choose to update all pages or not update.

Choose to update library items

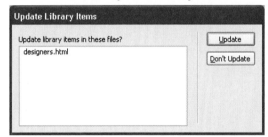

- If you choose not to update, you can use the Modify>Library>Update Current Page or Update Pages commands to update a single page or all pages with Library changes.

- Dreamweaver displays an Update Pages dialog box similar to that displayed when a template is updated to show you which pages have had a library item updated.

Use Design Notes

- Design notes work much like comments in Word, but you have much more control over who sees your notes.

- This is especially helpful when designing your site with sensitive data that must be shared only with your team members. Design notes are never displayed in a browser but they do travel with your files.

- Add design notes to a page using the File>Design Notes command. Or click the ⬆⬇ File management button on the Document toolbar and select Design Notes from the menu.

- On the Design Notes dialog box's Basic info tab, you can specify the page's status, insert the current date, and add comments (see the following illustration).

  - Click the Status list arrow to display a list of status options, including draft, revision1, and final.

  - Click the 🗓 date icon to insert the current date in the Notes box.

  - Type comments or insert other necessary information in the Notes text box.

Add basic design notes information

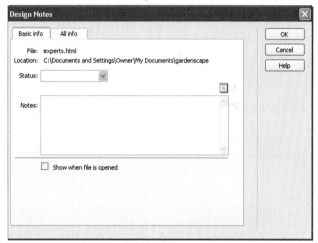

- If you want the design notes to appear each time the page opens, select the *Show when file is opened* checkbox.

- To see more design note information, click the All info tab. This tab shows information as sets of **keys** (identifiers) and values. In the illustration at the top of the next page, status and notes keys display in the Info list. The = sign separates a key from its value.

Add new keys on All info tab

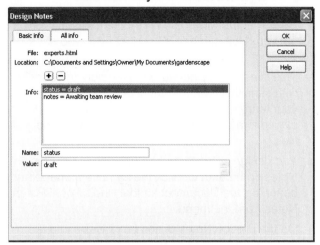

- Add new keys (such as *author*) by clicking the ⊕ button. The Name and Value boxes at the bottom of the tab empty so you can type the name of the new key and its value.

- Select a key/value combination in the Info list and click ⊖ to remove the key/value.
- In addition to Web pages, design notes can also be added to objects such as image files.

View Design Notes

- The same steps used to create a design note can be used to view a design note. However, to easily see that a page has a design note attached to it, expand the Files panel.
- Design notes that are attached to a Web page or object are shown with a 💬 note icon in the Notes column in the Local Files pane of the expanded Files panel window. The Notes column is hidden by default. To display it, click the View>File View Columns command in the expanded Files panel, choose the Notes column, and select the Show checkbox. Click OK.
- To open the note, double-click the 💬 icon.

PROCEDURES

Add Items to the Library

1. Select the object you want to add to the library.
2. Click **Modify**.................[Alt]+[M]
3. Point to **Library** ......[l], [l], [Enter]
4. Click **Add Object to Library**................................[O]
5. Type a name for the new item.

   OR

1. Select the object.
2. Click **Window** ....[Alt]+[W]
3. Click **Assets** ....[A]
4. Click **Library** button [📖] on the Assets toolbar.
5. Select and drag the item from the Document window to the lower pane in the Library.
6. Type a name for the new item.

Insert Library Item on Page

1. Position the cursor where the library item should appear.
2. Select the library item in the Library pane.
3. Click [Insert].

   OR

- Drag the library item from the Library pane to the desired location on the page.

Modify Library Item

From the Assets panel:

1. Click the **Library** button [📖] on the Assets toolbar.
2. Double-click the library item.

   OR

   a. Select the library item.
   b. Click the **Edit** button [✏️].
3. Make changes to the library item as desired.

Delete Library Item

From the Assets panel:

1. Click the **Library** button [📖].
2. Right-click the library item.
3. Click **Delete**.

   OR

1. Select the library item.
2. Click the **Delete** button [🗑️].

Update Library Items on Pages

After making changes to the library item:

- Click [Update], in the Update Library Items dialog box to update all files that use the library item.

   OR

If items have not been updated after changes:

1. Click **Modify**.................[Alt]+[M]
2. Point to **Library** ......[l], [l], [Enter]
3. Click **Update Current Page** ....[C]

   OR

- Click **Update Pages** ....[P]

Enable Design Notes

If the Design Notes command does not appear on the File menu:

1. Click **Site**......................[Alt]+[S]
2. Click **Manage Sites** ....[M]
3. Click the name of the site to edit.
4. Click [Edit...].
5. Click the **Advanced** tab and then click **Design Notes** in the Category list.
6. Select the **Maintain Design Notes** checkbox if necessary.
7. Select **Upload Design Notes for sharing**, if desired.
8. Click [OK].
9. Click [Done] to close the Manage Sites dialog box.

Add Design Notes to Page

1. Select the desired Web page or object.
2. Click **File** ....[Alt]+[F]
3. Click **Design Notes** ....[G]
4. Click the **Status** list arrow and choose the status for page.
5. Click [📅] to add the current date to the Notes box.
6. Type your comments in the **Notes** box.
7. Select the **Show when file is opened** checkbox if you want to see the design notes each time the file opens.
8. Click [OK].

To add a new key:

In the Design Notes dialog box:

1. Click the **All info** tab.
2. Click [+].
3. Type a name for the key in the **Name** box.
4. Type a value for the key in the **Value** box.
5. Click [OK].

To remove a key:

In the Design Notes dialog box:

- Select a key and click [−] to delete it, if desired.

View Design Notes

To display the Notes field:

1. Expand the Files panel.
2. Click **View** ....[Alt]+[V]
3. Click **File View Columns**......[F]
4. Click **Notes** in the File View Columns list.
5. Click the **Show** option to select it....................[Alt]+[S]
6. Click [OK].

To view a design note:

- Double-click the Note icon [💬] in the Notes column of the Local Files pane in the expanded Files panel.

EXERCISE DIRECTIONS

1. Start Dreamweaver and open the gardenscape site.

2. Display the Library pane in the Assets panel and add—and update—items to the Library as follows:

   - Open index.html and drag the logo image to the Library. Name it **Logo**.

   - Open designers.html and drag the small logo that links to the home page to the Library. Name it **Home link**.

   - Still on designers.html, select the navigation bar by clicking on the first button and then selecting the <p> tag in the tag selector to make sure you have selected the entire paragraph. Add the navigation bar to the Library. Name the item **Navigation bar**.

     ✔ If your navigation bar is created within an <h2> tag, you may want to replace that tag and any attributes and values with the <p> tag to eliminate unnecessary code around the navigation bar.

     ✔ If you are asked to update library items, do so.

3. Create a new library item named **Copyright** that contains the text **Copyright © GardenScape. All rights reserved.** Apply a center alignment for the item.

4. Insert library items as follows:

   - Insert the Home link library item in place of the Logo placeholder on contactus.html and specialties.html. Delete the place marker *logo* before you drag the image.

   - Insert the Copyright library item below the last paragraph of type on all pages in the site.

     ✔ Make sure the Copyright library item is centered on all pages. You may need to adjust HTML code in the Code view or Code inspector.

     ✔ In the contactus.html and specialties.html documents, the Copyright library item should go at the bottom of the paragraph region.

   - Insert the navigation bar library item at the top of the page on contactus.html, services.html, articles.html, and specialties.html.

     ✔ Note: If you get an error message when you try to add the navigation bar to the page, detach the template from the page and try again.

   - The navigation bar does not look good on the designers.html page with its green page background. Remove the background on this page and apply the squares.png background that is used on other pages in the site.

5. Cut the *Last update* paragraph on index.html and delete it on services.html, designers.html, and

articles.html. You will add this information to the Copyright library item. Remove the blank paragraph that remains after you delete the *Last update* text.

6. Modify the Copyright library item by pasting the cut *Last update* information following the *All rights reserved* sentence. Change the font color of the text to #990033.

7. Don't update pages automatically. Instead, view each page in the site and update it to see the change to the library item.

8. Save and close each page after you update it.

9. Open contactus.html and create the following design notes:

   - Set the status as draft.

   - Insert the following comment: **Create form on this page**.

   - Add a new key named **author** and assign the value **Ellen**.

10. Open specialties.html and create the following design notes:

    - Set the status as draft.

    - Insert the following comment: **Create table on this page.**

11. Expand the Files panel and view the design notes. (Display the Notes field if necessary to see the design note icons.) Collapse the view to the File panel.

    ✔ If you don't see the Design Note icons in the Notes column, choose the View>File View Columns command and make sure the Notes column is set to Show. If Hide is currently selected, click Notes, click the Show checkbox, and click OK.

12. Open index.html and add the words **Our Specialties** at the end of the list of links. Use these words to create a link to specialties.html.

    ✔ You realize you do not have a link in the navigation bar to the specialities.html page.

13. Open the Navigation bar library item. Choose to modify the navigation bar and add the specialties element using the ⊙ gsspecialties_up.png and ⊙ gsspecialties_ovr.png images in the Lesson 3 Data folder. Save the new images in your site's images folder. Link to the specialties.html page.

14. Update all pages with the new navigation bar.

15. Preview index.html in the browser. Check navigation to and from all pages in the site. Your Contact Us page should look like Illustration A on the next page. (The date on your page will be different.)

16. Close the browser.

17. Close any open pages and exit Dreamweaver.

Illustration A

ON YOUR OWN

1. Start Dreamweaver and open the yardart site.
2. Add a new subfolder and name it images.
3. Move all the site images into the new folder. Update links.
4. Open index.html. Drag daffodils.jpg from the images folder to the left of the *Today's Web Specials* heading. Resize the image. Press Enter to move the heading to the next line.
5. Add a hotspot to the image with a link to contact.html. In alternative text, let visitor know the link will take them to the Contact page. Save the page.
6. Select the flower image and add it to the Library. Give it an appropriate name.
7. Open the yardart.dwt template. Select the navigation bar. (Click Split so that you can ensure you've selected all tags that go along with the bar.)
8. Cut the navigation bar out of the template. Create a new editable region at the top of the page and name it nav bar. In Code view, change the <h2></h2> tags to <p></p>. Refresh the page. Save and close the template. Update links.
9. Create a new library item called **navigation bar**. Click to edit the item. Paste the navigation bar into the library item. Save and close the item. Update links.
10. Open contact.html and detach it from the yardart.dwt template.
11. Insert the navigation bar library item in place of *nav bar* at the top of the page.
12. Repeat steps 10–11 for each page in the site.
13. Open the navigation bar library item, select the Contact button, and copy it.
14. Create a new library item and name it **small_contact**. You want an e-mail message window to appear whenever a visitor clicks the small_contact item, so add **mailto: info@yardart.aaa** in the Link box in the Property inspector. Change the Alt text to say **Click here to send a message**.

    ✔ *Note that this e-mail address is for demonstration purposes only. To test out the link on your own system, use a live e-mail address given to you by your instructor.*

15. Close the navigation bar library item without saving it.
16. Edit the small_contact library item to resize it to W 31, H 32. Save and close the item.
17. Drag the small_contact library item to the beginning of each of the five contact lines on contact.html. Add a space between the image and the beginning of the text on each line.
18. Save your work and close contact.html. Test the site in the browser, clicking each link to make sure the navigation bars work and look correct on each page. Also test out the small_contact items on the Contact page.
19. Close the browser and exit Dreamweaver.

Summary Exercise

Application Skills In this exercise, you will continue to work on the Tierra Verde site. You will add and modify images, create a template and a navigation bar, and add items to the Library.

DIRECTIONS

1. Start Dreamweaver and open the tierraverde site.
2. Create a new folder in the site named graphics to store the graphic images you will add to the site.
3. Open index.html. Position the cursor to the left of the first heading and insert ⊙ cabin.jpg from the Lesson 3 Data files. Optimize the image as a JPEG using default settings. Save the file in the graphics folder and add the alternate text **A quiet cabin in the woods**.
4. Modify the image as follows:
   - Resize the image to 320 by 240 and resample the image after resizing.
   - Change the contrast to 10.
   - Apply right alignment to the picture.
5. Open registration.html. Apply the ⊙ background.jpg image as a background picture on this page. Save the page.

   ✔ You are ready to add more pages to the site. Create a template to make this process easier.

6. Create a new template based on the registration.html page and save it as tierra_page. Update links if prompted. Format the template as follows:
   - Create an editable region for the main head with an appropriate name.
   - Create another editable region that includes paragraph text and the second-level heading.
   - Below the last editable region, insert a horizontal rule and then the following text:

Copyright © Tierra Verde. For more information, contact manager@tierraverde.net.

- Format the text as desired and create an e-mail link from the e-mail address. Save the page.

   ✔ If you use the E-mail Link tool in the Common tab of the Insert toolbar to add the e-mail link, take a look at the way it appears in the Link box in the Property inspector. If the mailto: link shows a period (.) at the end, delete it before saving the page.

7. Save the horizontal rule and copyright information as a library item with an appropriate name, and then insert it on the index.html and registration.html pages.
8. Work with the site pages to make the following changes:
   - Create a new page and name it news.html. Give it the page title **Camp News**. Change the main heading to **News and Events** and the page text to **Text in progress.**
   - Create a second page and name it beachtime.html with the page title **Water Fun**. Change the main heading to **Swimming & Boating** and the page text to **Text in progress.**
   - Open info.html. Apply the tierra_page.dwt template. Delete the existing title and navigation bar that is placed in the Paragraph region. (Leave the last line with the registration form link.) Change the page title to **Camp Info**. Change the main heading to **Camp Information**.
   - Open contact.html and apply the template. Copy and paste the *Contact Us* heading into the Page Heading region. Change the color to the green used to the page heading on index.html.

9. Activate index.html and create a navigation bar as follows:

- Delete the table-style navigation bar at the bottom of the page.
- Insert a blank line below the main heading for the new navigation bar.
- Create the following navigation bar elements: **home**, **info**, **news**, **contact**.
- For each element, find and insert the corresponding image file in the Lesson 3 Data folder, such as ⊙ t_home_up.png and ⊙ t_home_ovr.png. Save all images in your graphics folder.
- Link each element to the appropriate page in the site.
- Make sure to create a horizontal navigation bar that does not use a table.

10. Save the navigation bar as a library item and then insert it on registration.html (delete the table style nav bar first) and also on the page template. (You may want to use a code view to make sure the navigation bar is inserted between the two editable areas.) Update all template files.

11. Activate index.html and create an image map on the photo that links to the info.html page. The alternative text for the image map should read **Click here for registration information!**

12. Save all pages, and then preview the index.html page in the browser. Test all links in the navigation bar and image map. The Camp Information page should look similar to Illustration A.

13. Open the Copyright library item and modify the text color as desired and then save the item and update all files.

14. Close all open pages and exit Dreamweaver.

Illustration A

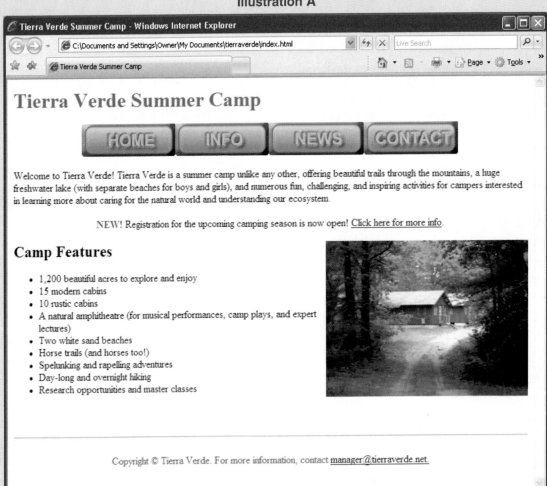

Exercise | 29

Application Exercise

Application Skills In this exercise, you will continue to work on the Classmate Connections Web site. You will add graphic images to the site and create a navigation bar that you can insert on all pages.

DIRECTIONS

1. Start Dreamweaver and open the classmate_connections Web site.

2. Create a folder in the site to hold your site graphics.

3. Open index.html. Insert at the top of the page the ◉ home_class.jpg image from the Lesson 3 Data folder and save the image in your site. Add appropriate alternate text.

4. Align the image on the left and add an H Space value of 10.

5. Increase the indent of the bulleted list to correct the overlap.

6. Choose a page background color of #669999 and set the opacity at 50%.

7. Open groups.html. At the beginning of the opening paragraph, insert the ◉ class01.jpg image from the Lesson 3 Data folder. Add appropriate alternate text. Create a link from this graphic to the addme.html page. (Set the border to 0 if necessary to remove the link outline.) Add this image to your Assets panel favorites. Set the background to #669999.

8. Open the addme.html page and format the page heading as Heading 1. Set the background color to match the other pages. Add the ◉ class02.jpg image. Right-align it. Add an H Space value of 10.

9. In the Files pane, navigate to the ◉ addme_form.doc and copy and paste it into the classmate_connec-tions site.

10. On the addme.html page, create a link from the phrase *your parent's signature on file* to addme_form.doc.

11. Add a Design Note to the addme.html page that sets the status to draft and reminds you to add the Add My Info button, as well as the online content form, to this page. Click to have it open automatically when you view the page.

12. Click to create a template from the current page. Name it class_pages. Add a Student Name editable region, a navigation bar region, and para-graph region. Create three pages based on this template:

   ▪ A directory.html page with the page heading **Student Directory** and a page title of **Student Directory**. In the Student info region, add **Sara R.** and make it a bullet point. Add a second bullet that says **Ben S.**, and format this item as a bullet as well. This will be a list of par-ticipating students as the site grows.

   ▪ A sara_r.html page with the page heading and page title **Sara R**. In the Student info region, add **Awaiting permission info before posting**.

   ▪ A ben_s.html page **with Ben S** as the page heading and title. Copy the text from Sara's Student info region and paste it in Ben's.

13. Link the two bullet points on the directory.html page to the student pages. Save and close the new pages and the template.

14. Return to index.html and delete the table-style navigation bar.

15. Create a new navigation bar, adding elements for **home**, **addme**, **groups**, **pages**, and **links**.

16. Add the buttons from the Lesson 3 data folder for the up and over states for each button. Save the buttons to the images folder in the site. Link the elements to their respective pages. (Link the Pages button to the directory.html page, and leave the Links page unlinked for now.) Do not format the navigation bar as a table.

17. Select the navigation bar on the page and save it as a library item. Center the navigation bar and resave. Update linked files when prompted.

18. Add the navigation bar from the library to the class_pages.dwt file. Update pages.

19. Display groups.html. Replace the table-style nav bar with the one you just saved to the library. Save the page. Add the nav bar to addme.html as well.

20. Detach the template from directory.html, sara_r.html, and ben_s.html, and add the nav bar from the library to those pages. Save all open pages.

21. Click index.html and preview the site. Check all links. Your home page should look something like the page shown in Illustration A.

22. Close all pages and exit Dreamweaver.

Illustration A

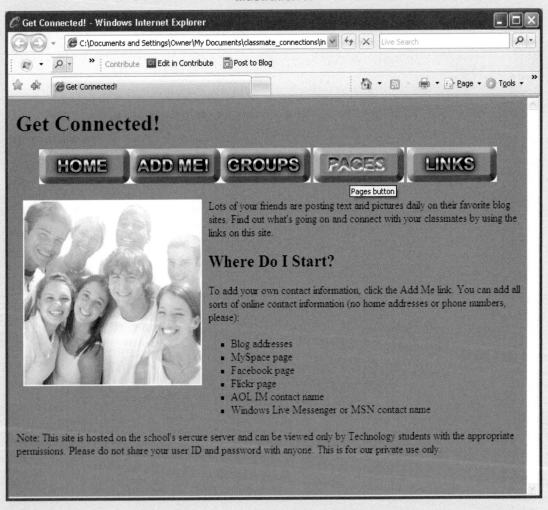

Exercise | 30

Curriculum Integration

Application Skills Your biology class is about to begin a unit on endangered species, and your instructor has asked the class to create a Web site containing information on endangered species in your state. To make sure the contributions are uniform, the class will use several of Dreamweaver's Starter pages. Before you begin this project, gather the following information:

- Locate a list of species identified as endangered in your state (or a neighboring state if you can't find information for your state).

- Choose one of the species from the site to be the focus of your contribution to the Web site.

- Find pictures of several of the species on the list, including the one you are focusing on, and save them to your computer.

- Review how to open one of Dreamweaver's Starter pages; these pages can be accessed from the Start page.

DIRECTIONS

Define a new site with the name endangered. Create your first page for the site using the Starter Page (Theme) page identified as Lodging – Home Page. This page will be your general introduction to the topic of endangered species in your state. Save the page as intro.html. As you save the page, create a new folder to contain the images and other files associated with the page. Change the page title to a more appropriate title.

Replace the main heading on the page with a title such as **OHIO ENDANGERED SPECIES**. Select the image at the left side of the page and delete it.

Insert one of the images you saved in place of the picture you just deleted. Resize the picture to fit in the space used by the default picture (your picture should be about 230 pixels wide and a corresponding height). Resample the image after resizing, and adjust brightness and contrast as necessary. Be sure to supply alternative text for this and any other images you add to the site.

If you'd like to add special effects to the image, click the Edit button to open the file in Fireworks. Apply the settings you want, save the image, and return to Dreamweaver.

Replace the placeholder text below the image with a brief description of the new image and a link to the page where you found the picture as a credit line.

Replace the heading to the right of the image with new text, and then replace the placeholder text below the heading with some general remarks about why you think the species have become endangered in your state.

Create a second page using the Starter Page (Theme) page identified as Lodging – Product Page. Save the page using the name of your chosen species, and save any associated files in the images folder. Give the page an appropriate page title.

If you have located several pictures of your species that are roughly the same size and orientation, create a rollover image: Insert the pictures on the page to adjust size, contrast, brightness, or sharpness and resample as necessary. Then create the rollover image in the placeholder supplied for an image.

Replace the main heading on the page with the same main heading you used on the previous page. Change the subheading to the name of your species, and use the third-level heading for the species' Latin or scientific name if available.

Replace placeholder text with some facts about your species and why it is endangered.

Create a link from the *Home* text below the main heading that returns a site visitor to your intro page. On the intro page, delete all placeholder link text except the first (*OUR ROOMS*) and change the text to the name of your species. Create a link to the species page.

Save all pages and view them in the browser. Test links.

Close all open pages and exit Dreamweaver.

Exercise | 31

Critical Thinking

Application Skills In this exercise, you continue to work on the Web site you started for the non-profit organization you're interested in. You will create a template and a new page based on the template, add images to the site and format them, and work with the site's navigation bars.

DIRECTIONS

- Create a template for your Web site to make it easy to add new pages to the site. Create at least one new page using the template and insert content on the page.

- Add a graphic background to at least one page, using either an image or a background color.

- Edit the image in Fireworks to set the opacity and add any special graphical touches to the image.

- Add an image to at least one page, using clip art or a photo you located on the Web or prepared in Fireworks. Resize the image(s) as necessary and position them as desired on the page(s). Be sure to save the images in a folder in your site and add alternative text.

- Create a set of buttons in Fireworks, with at least two states (such as up and over) for each button. Create a navigation bar with links to any pages you added, and then save the navigation bar as a library item. Insert the new library item on all pages.

- You may wish to detach the navigation bar library item from the page that has a background color so you can adjust or remove the fill color of the table to match the page background. (Use the Tag inspector to do so.)

- Create any additional links necessary to and from your new pages(s).

- Preview the site in the browser.

- Save all open documents and close them.

- Exit Dreamweaver.

Lesson | 4

Work with Tables and Forms

Skills Covered

- About Tables
- Create a Table
- Insert Text and Images in Table Cells
- Adjust Table Structure

Software Skills A table on your Web page provides one of the best ways to organize and align your graphics, text, and other objects on the page. You can design a table to be an obvious part of the page—to show up as an object itself—or you can make it invisible so that it simply holds the page elements in place.

Design Skills Tables not only add structure to your page; they also add continuity. As a designer, you want all the pages in your site to have a similar look and feel. Adding tables to your pages—specifically, creating one table and using it on multiple pages—helps add that consistent feel to the pages you design.

Application Skills In this exercise, you will add a table to the GardenScape site to organize information. You will change the table structure and insert text and graphics in the table cells.

TERMS

Cell The intersection of a row and column.

Cell padding The space between a cell's content and its border.

Cell spacing The space between cells.

Columns Vertical sections of the table.

Merge cells The process of combining several cells to create one larger cell.

Rows Horizontal sections of a table.

Split cell The process of dividing a single cell into multiple rows or columns.

NOTES

About Tables

■ You use tables on your pages to organize and align elements on your page. A table is a grid made up of **rows** and **columns**. A table can consist of only a few rows and columns, or you can use it to organize an entire Web page.

■ Although you can use other, more elaborate ways of organizing Web page data, tables provide the most dependable framework for Web page layout. All browsers can display the HTML codes used to create tables, so if you want to make sure that your page layout will work for all visitors, structure it using a table.

   ✔ *You will use a table to create a page layout in Exercise 34.*

■ After you insert a table on a Web page, you can restructure it very easily. Change the look of a table by adjusting row height or column width, adding or deleting rows or columns, or merging or splitting **cells**.

Create a Table

■ Create a table on a Web page using Insert bar options or a menu command. Position your insertion point where the table should appear and then use one of these methods:

   ● Click the 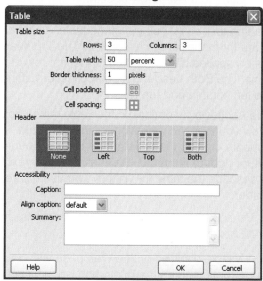 Table button from the Common or Layout tab of the Insert bar.

   ● Use the Insert>Table command.

   ✔ *You can also draw a table in Layout view. You will work with Layout view and table drawing tools in Exercise 34.*

■ The Table dialog box opens after you perform either of these actions (see the illustration at right). In this dialog box, you can specify several kinds of information for the new table.

   ✔ *The Table dialog box shows the settings chosen for the last table. Make sure you check all settings in the Table dialog box before clicking OK.*

■ Your first task in this dialog box is to specify the numbers of rows and columns for the table.

   ✔ *These values aren't set in stone, however; you can add to or remove rows and columns in the table after you create it.*

■ You can also specify a width for the table as it is being created. You can do this two ways—by entering the number of pixels or by entering a percentage. Type a width in the Table width box and choose to measure that width either as a percentage of the page width or in pixels.

Table dialog box

■ Using the percentage value in the Table width text box allows you to maintain the ratio of table-to-page text when the page is viewed in different types of browsers. Using pixel values ensures that the table will be exactly the same physical size in any browser or screen resolution.

   ✔ *Current Web standards prefer percentage widths over exact table sizes, so that a table's content can "flow" according to the size of the browser window.*

■ Either measurement option is appropriate for tables used to format the entire Web page. A pixel value, however, is the best choice for tables that you don't want to be resized in the browser.

■ You can also change the border thickness in the Table dialog box. The default value is 1. Border thickness is measured in pixels.

   ✔ *Leaving the Border thickness box empty results in a borderless—or invisible—table that can be used to format an entire Web page or other data.*

■ If you want to set the spacing used within the cells, you can insert values for **cell padding** and **cell spacing** when creating the table. Cell padding is the distance between cell text and a cell border. Cell spacing is the amount of space between cells.

   ✔ *You can change these values at any time after creating a table using the Property inspector.*

- Use the Header options in the Table dialog box to apply basic formatting to some areas of the table. The None header option doesn't apply any special formatting to the first row or column of the table. The Left header option applies bold, centered formatting to the first column of the table, as indicated in the thumbnail in the dialog box. The Top header option applies this formatting to the first row of the table. The Both header option applies formatting to the left column and top row.

- The Accessibility options in the Table dialog box allow you to insert a caption for the table that appears outside the table grid at the top, bottom, left, or right of the table. Use the Summary text box to describe the table for visitors who use a screen reader.

  ✔ *The text you insert in the Summary box does not display in the browser.*

- A new table displays on the Web page with default border options (see the illustration below) if you have specified a border thickness. The table is selected when inserted.

- Note the green lines and text above the selected table and table columns. The top line tells you the table width as a percentage or pixel value (depending on how you specified the table width when creating it). If you set specific column widths, the lines above each column give you that information.

- This table width information can be toggled on and off using the 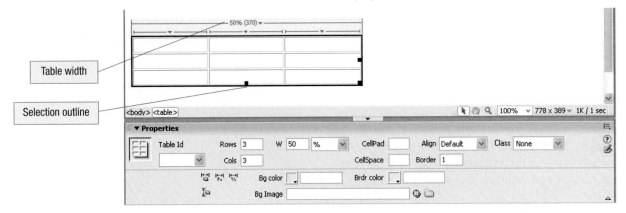 Visual Aids list on the Document toolbar.

- The table and column width lines also display small green downward-pointing arrows that, when clicked, display either the table header menu or the column header menu. These menus give you quick access to commands that allow you to select the table or restructure the table by adjusting column widths and spacing, inserting new columns at the left or right, and so on.

- While the table is selected, you can also use the Property inspector to make a number of changes to the table:
  - Name the table if desired.
  - Change the number of rows and columns in the table.
  - Change the width and/or height of the table in percentage of page width or pixel measurements.
  - Specify the cell padding and cell spacing.
  - Change the border width (or delete the border measurement to remove the borders completely).
  - If the table is less than the full page width, you can use the Align list to center, left align, or right align the table in the page.

- In the expanded portion of the Property inspector, you will find properties relating to the table's appearance. You can change column widths and row heights, and add border and background colors—or use a picture as a table background. (Individual cells can have backgrounds, too.)

  ✔ *You will learn about borders and backgrounds in the next exercise.*

Insert Text and Images in Table Cells

- To enter text in a table, click in a table cell and begin typing. Press the ⇥ Tab key or an arrow key to move from cell to cell in the table.

- Format text in a table cell normally, using the buttons and other options in the Property inspector. You can change font style, size, and color; adjust alignment; and even insert links in table cells.

- You can also insert an image in any table cell using the same procedure you use to add an image to a Web page. If the image is larger than the table cell, the cell automatically expands to accommodate the image.

New table on Web page

Adjust Table Structure

■ After you have added the basic table structure to the Web page, you can make a number of changes to it to accommodate the data you want to add.

■ As you adjust table structure, you will find it helpful to display the History panel so you can view your adjustments. You also can easily undo a series of actions from this panel if you decide you don't want to keep the changes you've made.

Select Table Elements

■ Before you can change the table, you need to select a portion of the table or the entire table. Use these guidelines for selecting table elements:

● Select a single cell by clicking in it.

● Select a column using the column header menu (see the following illustration). Or, position the pointer so that it touches the top edge of the column. When the pointer becomes a solid black arrow, click the mouse button to select the column. You can also select a row this way— position the pointer so that it touches the left edge of the row and click.

Use the column header menu to select a column

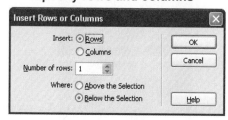

● To select noncontiguous elements, such as cells, rows, and columns in a table, hold the Ctrl key and make the desired selections.

● To select the entire table, use the table header menu or click on any outside border with the sizing pointer. Or click inside the table and then click the <table> tag in the tag selector on the left side of the status bar.

  ✔ *You can also select the entire table by right-clicking anywhere in the table, pointing to Table, and clicking Select Table.*

Change Cell Width and Height

■ You can easily resize column widths or row heights by clicking on a column or row border and then dragging it to the desired size. You can also resize table elements precisely in the Property inspector in order to fit graphics, text, and other objects.

■ Change the size by clicking in a cell and typing a value in the W (Width) and/or H (Height) box in the expanded Property inspector. All cells in the column change when you enter a new width, and all cells in a row change when you enter a new height.

  ✔ *If you want the cell value in percentages rather than in the default pixels, type a percent sign (%) after the value. You can also use the pixel-to-percentage conversion buttons in the expanded Property inspector.*

■ If you aren't happy with the width and height changes you made, you can select the table and use the ⊟ Clear Column Widths or ⊞ Clear Row Heights buttons on the expanded Property inspector. Clear Row Heights returns any rows to their default height. Clear Column Widths reduces the column width to fit exactly the widest entry in the column.

  ✔ *You can also find these commands on the table header menu or use Modify>Table>Clear Cell Heights or Clear Cell Widths to adjust row height and column width in a selected table.*

Insert and Delete Rows and Columns

■ You may need to add or delete rows and columns after you have created a table. You can insert a new row as you are adding content to a table by simply pressing the Tab key when you are in the last cell of the table.

■ To add a new row elsewhere in the table or a new column, use the commands on the Modify>Table submenu:

● Click Modify>Table>Insert Row to insert a new row above the currently selected cell.

● Click Modify>Table>Insert Column to insert a new column to the left of the currently selected cell. You can also use the column header menu to insert a new column to the right or left of the currently selected cell.

● Click Modify>Table>Insert Rows or Columns to open the Insert Rows or Columns dialog box (see the following illustration) where you can specify a number of rows or columns and their position.

Specify rows and columns

  ✔ *You can also access these commands by right-clicking in a cell and then pointing to Table on the shortcut menu.*

- If you prefer to use toolbar buttons to insert rows and columns, you can find them on the Layout tab of the Insert bar.
- To delete a row or column, select it and then press Delete.

Split and Merge Cells

- As you add data to your tables, you may find that you need to split the data in some cells and merge others. You can easily split or merge cells to make room for headers or labels or add other design elements.
- When you **split cells**, you break one cell into two or more cells in a column or row. When you **merge cells**, you combine more than one cell to create a single, larger cell.
- To split a cell, select the cell and then click the ⬚ Splits cell into rows or columns button on the Property inspector (or use the Modify>Table>Split Cell command). The Split Cell dialog box opens so that you can split the cell into the desired number of rows or columns (see the illustration at the bottom of this page).
- To merge cells, select the cells and click the ⬚ Merges selected cells using spans button on the Property inspector (or use the Modify>Table>Merge Cells command).

Span Rows and Columns

- The Modify>Table submenu also features commands for merging columns or rows so that they span across one or more columns or down one or more rows. In the following illustration, for example, the text has been set to span down one row.

Text spans down one row

Fall Specials		

- Use Modify>Table>Increase Row Span or Increase Column Span to span rows or columns.
- Choosing a span command causes the current cell to merge with the one to its right (if you span columns) or below it (if you span rows). You can increase the span by choosing the command again.
- Use the Decrease Row Span or Decrease Column Span command to reduce the number of rows or columns spanned.
- Spanning is much the same as merging, but it is easier to do "on the fly" than merging. If you decide you want text to span three columns rather than two, for example, just increase the span. Decreasing the span is also easier than splitting a cell you have already merged.

  ✔ *You can achieve interesting effects with tables if you do some experimenting. For example, you can nest a table within a table cell to provide additional layout options.*

Split cell into rows or columns

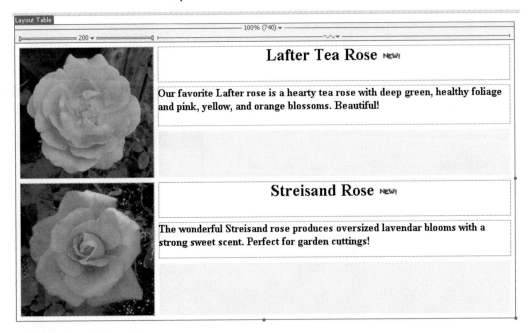

PROCEDURES

Create a Table (Ctrl + Alt + T)

1. Position the cursor at the point you want to create a new table.
2. Click **Insert** .... Alt + I
3. Click **Table** .... T

OR

- Click **Table** button ⊞ on the Common (or Layout) tab of the Insert bar.

In the Table dialog box:

1. Specify the number of rows and columns.
2. Specify the width as a percentage of the page width or in pixels.
3. Enter the border thickness and cell padding and spacing values.
4. Specify header option.
5. Add a caption, if desired, and choose the position of the caption.
6. Add Summary text for accessibility.
7. Click OK .

Align Table

1. Select entire table (see *Select Table Elements* below).
2. Click the **Align** list arrow in the Property inspector.
3. Select the desired alignment.

Insert Text and Images in a Table

- Click in a cell and begin typing.
- Use Tab ⇄ or an arrow key to move from cell to cell.
- Use buttons and features in the Property inspector to change the format, font, size, font style, color, and alignment of text.

To insert images in table cells:

1. Click **Insert** .... Alt + I
2. Click **Image** I

OR

- Click the 🖼 **Image** button on the Common tab of the Insert bar.

In the Select Image Source dialog box:

1. Navigate to the location of the image and select the image.
2. Click OK .

OR

- Drag the image from the site's images folder or the Assets panel.

Select Table Elements

- Click in a cell to select it.
- To select noncontiguous cells, press and hold Ctrl, click in the first cell, and then click other cells.
- To select a column or row, position the mouse pointer just above the column or just to the left of a row. The pointer becomes a solid black arrow. Click the mouse button to select the column or row. Alternatively, click the column header menu and click **Select Column**.
- To select a table, click the table border or click in the table and then click the <table> tag in the tag selector on the status bar.

OR

- Click the table header menu and click **Select Table**.

Change Cell Width and Height

- Drag a column or row border in the direction you want to resize it.

OR

1. Click in a cell to resize it.
2. Expand the Property inspector, if necessary.
3. Type the desired width in **W** text box on the Property inspector.
4. Type the desired height in **H** text box on the Property inspector.

Return to Default Row Height

- Select the table and click the 🖼 **Clear Row Heights** button on the Property inspector to restore the default row height, or click the table header menu and select **Clear All Heights**.

Return to Default Column Width

- Select the table and click the 🖼 **Clear Column Widths** button on the Property inspector to set the column width to accommodate the widest entry in the column, or click the table header menu and select **Clear All Widths**.

Delete Rows and Columns (Ctrl + Shift + M, Ctrl + Shift + -)

1. Select the row or column you want to delete.
2. Press Delete.

Insert Rows and Columns (Ctrl + M, Ctrl + Shift + A)

1. Position the cursor in the cell below which you want the new row to appear or to the right of the new column.
2. Click **Modify**.................`Alt`+`M`
3. Point to **Table** ....`T`
4. Click **Insert Row**................`N`

   OR

   Click **Insert Column**............`C`

   OR

   a. Click **Insert Rows or Columns** ....`I`
   b. Select **Rows** ....`Alt`+`R`
      or **Columns** ....`Alt`+`C`
   c. Type or choose the number of rows or columns you want to add.
   d. Click **Above the Selection**.................`Alt`+`A`
      or **Below the Selection**.................`Alt`+`B`
   e. Click `OK` .

   OR

1. Position the cursor in the cell.
2. Click the column header menu and select **Insert Column Left** or **Insert Column Right**.

   OR

■ Use buttons in the Layout tab of the Insert bar to insert a column to the left or right or insert a row above or below.

Split Cells (Ctrl + Alt + S)

1. Click in the cell you want to split.
2. Click **Modify**.................`Alt`+`M`
3. Point to **Table** ....`T`
4. Click **Split Cell**................`P`

   OR

■ Click the 🗘 **Splits cell into rows or columns** button on the Property inspector.

In Split Cell dialog box:

1. Select **Rows** ....`Alt`+`R`
   or **Columns** ....`Alt`+`C`
2. Type or choose the number of rows or columns you want to create.
3. Click `OK` .

Merge Cells (Ctrl + Alt + M)

1. Select the cells you want to merge.
2. Click **Modify**.................`Alt`+`M`
3. Point to **Table** ....`T`
4. Click **Merge Cells**.................`M`

   OR

■ Click the ▦ **Merges selected cells using spans** button on the Property inspector.

Span Text in Rows and Columns

1. Click in the cell you want to span.
2. Click **Modify**.................`Alt`+`M`
3. Point to **Table** ....`T`
4. Click **Increase Row Span** to span down one row...........`R`

   OR

   Click **Increase Column Span** to span to right across one column...............`A`
5. Repeat to span additional rows or columns.

To remove span:

1. Click in the cell you want to change.
2. Click **Modify**.................`Alt`+`M`
3. Point to **Table** ....`T`
4. Click **Decrease Row Span** ....`W`
   or **Decrease Column Span**......`U`
   to remove span.

EXERCISE DIRECTIONS

1. Start Dreamweaver and open the gardenscape site.
2. Open specialties.html.
3. Press Enter to add a line space and type the following paragraph:

   GardenScape designers have been trained in a variety of design areas. Whether you are interested in creating or maintaining a natural habitat, a fine landscape, a water garden, or a wildflower meadow, our designers can assist you in all phases of your project. The following table shows you the range of our designers' specialties.

4. Press Enter to create a new paragraph.
5. Create a new table at the insertion point that includes 5 rows and 4 columns. Set the table width at 75 percent of the page width. Set the border thickness at 1 if necessary. Insert the following summary text:

   This table shows the various specialties of GardenScape landscape designers.

6. Click OK to create the table.
7. In the selected table on the page, drag the border between the two columns to the left until the left column header reads about 15%. Resize the second column to be 111 pixels wide.

8. Center the table.

9. Format the table heading area:

   - Click in the first cell and type **Designer Specialties**.

   - Click to the left of the text. Insert the 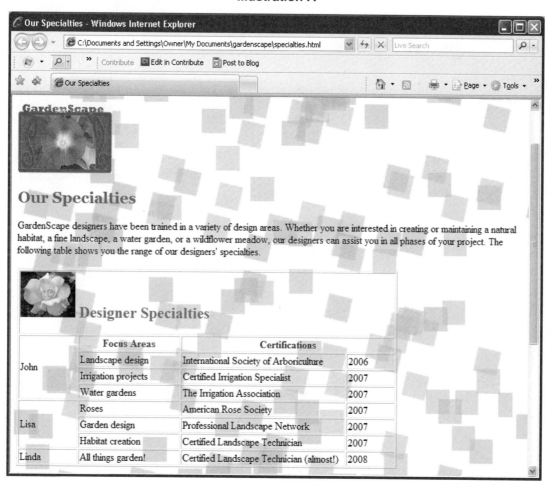 rose.jpg image from the Lesson 4 Data folder and save it in your images folder. Add the alternate text **rose photo**.

   - Resize the image so it is 88 pixels wide and 70 pixels high. Resample the image. Use Bottom alignment.

   - Use the column span command to make the heading span all columns.

   - Format the text as Heading 2 and change its color to #339933. Insert a space between the image and the heading.

10. Using Illustration A as a guide, insert text in the next three rows of the table as follows:

    - Type **John**, **Lisa**, and **Linda**, one in each of the rows in the left column of the table.

    - Click in the cell to the right of *John* and use the split cell feature to split each of the remaining three columns into four rows.

    - In the top row to the right of John, type **Focus Areas** in one column and **Certifications** in the other.

    - Merge the cell containing *Certifications* so that it covers the remaining two columns

    - In the row with *Lisa* in the left column, split each of the three cells into three rows.

    - Adjust column width as necessary to display the certifications on one line.

    - In the last row, enter the information as shown, leaving the cells as they are.

11. Format the table as follows:

    - Use Illustration A as a guide for boldfacing and centering table text.

    - Adjust column widths for the split columns as necessary to look attractive.

12. Save the page and then preview it in the browser. The table should look similar to Illustration A.

13. Close any open pages and exit Dreamweaver.

Illustration A

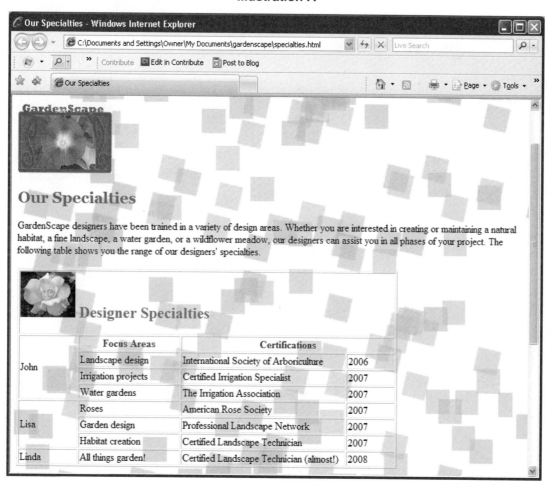

ON YOUR OWN

1. Start Dreamweaver and open the java2go site.

2. Open contact.html and locations.html.

3. On contact.html, copy the muffin image and the page heading and paste them on locations.html.

4. Change the heading to **Visit all our locations!**.

5. Press Enter to insert a new paragraph and type the following text:

   Wondering what's going on around town? Take a look at what's jivin' this month!

6. Create a table to contain the following information. Use your own judgment about how to set up the data and format the table information.

STYLE	LOCATION	DATES
Caribbean music		
The Seabirds	E 10th	8/13-8/14
Jambo	Main St	8/15-8/16
Jazz night		
Fresco	Pier Two	8/21
Berkewaft	E 10th	8/22
Acoustic		
Sally J	Main St.	8/22-8/23
Open mic		
Come one, come all!	Pier Two	8/29

7. If you have access to clip art files, locate a picture of a drum, instrument, or singer and add it to a cell in the table. Adjust size as necessary (don't forget to resample and save the image in your site).

8. Center the band names in the first column.

9. Save changes and preview the page in the browser.

10. Make any necessary revisions to the table, then close all open pages and exit Dreamweaver.

Skills Covered

- **Modify Table Borders and Backgrounds**
- **Import Table Data**

- **Sort Table Data**
- **Insert Table-Related Tags**

Software Skills Use table borders and backgrounds to emphasize portions of a table. If you have tabular data stored in another application, you can import it to create a table in Dreamweaver. After importing the data, you can sort it.

Design Skills You can use design elements—such as borders and backgrounds—to help your tables stand out on the page. Adding table-related tags gives you increased control over the tables you create.

Application Skills In this exercise, you enhance the table you created in the last exercise, import tabular data to create a new table, and sort the table.

TERMS

Delimited format A format for saving application data that uses characters such as commas, tabs, or colons to separate columns of data.

Delimiters The characters used to separate data items.

NOTES

Modify Table Borders and Backgrounds

- New tables usually display a single, 1-pixel default gray border and no background (the page background displays in the table cells). To improve the look of a table, you can modify the weight and color of the table borders and add a color or background image to the table or cells.

Set Border Colors

- Note that by default a Dreamweaver table displays a border around each cell as well as a border around the table to give a three-dimensional look. You have two options for applying color to these borders:

  - You can use a single color for all borders in the table.

  - You can set one color for the outside table border and another color for individual cells in the table. (Or give each cell its own border color, if desired.)

  - ✔ *Cell border colors may not appear the same way in all browsers. See the information on targeting browsers in Lesson 8.*

- To set table border colors, first select the entire table and then click ▢▾ Brdr color to open the color palette and pick the color.

  - ✔ *You can also type the hexadecimal value for any color in the provided text box or select a color already used in the site from the Colors category in the Assets panel by first clicking on the color box and then clicking on the desired color in the Assets panel with the eyedropper tool.*

- To set cell border colors, click in the cell to which you want to apply the color. Click ▢▾ Brdr to display the color palette and click the color you want to use.

- You may need to experiment with border colors to find a combination that looks good without overwhelming the table text.

  - ✔ *Empty cells may not display all border lines when viewed in a browser. To prevent this, insert an invisible object such as a nonbreaking space by selecting it from the Characters list or by pressing* [Ctrl] + [⇧ Shift] + *the Spacebar.*

Add Background Color to Cells

- You can add color to cell backgrounds in a table to draw the visitor's eye to information you want to emphasize. You can add a color background to one cell, a row, a column—or the entire table.

- Select the table element you want to add color to and then click ▢▾ Bg color (the Bg color option is available when the entire table is selected) or ▢▾ Bg (the Bg option is available when a cell, column, or row is selected) on the Property inspector. Then choose a color from the color palette using the eyedropper.

- Applying a background color to an entire table will fill not only the cells but the small spaces between inner and outer borders. You can override the table background color by applying color to individual cells, but the table background color will still show in the border spaces.

- Take care when choosing background colors for table cells. A dark color may make text difficult to read. If you want to use a dark cell background, change the text color to white, light gray, or light yellow to contrast with the background.

Insert Background Image in Cell

- You can select background images for your table or individual cells to add visual interest in much the same way that you add background images that tile for entire Web pages.

- Select the table elements you want to format using the background image. In the Bg box on the Property inspector, type the path to the image, or use the ⊕ Point to File icon or ▢ Browse for File button (or Background URL of cell button) to locate the image.

  - ✔ *If necessary, expand the images folder in the Files list before using the ⊕ Point to File tool.*

- You can insert any Web graphic into a table cell or cells, from texture GIFs, to a JPEG photograph, to a custom Fireworks image (PNG format). If the image is smaller than the cell, it will be tiled inside the table cells just as images on page backgrounds are tiled. Make sure, however, that the image you choose does not make any text in the table difficult to read.

Import Table Data

- You can create simple tables directly on the Web page, but for more involved projects, you may want to use existing data from a word processing program or spreadsheet. Importing data for your table can help eliminate data entry errors or save you the trouble of retyping long columns of numbers.

- Data you import must be saved in a **delimited format**. That means that the columns of data must be separated by **delimiters** such as commas, tabs, semicolons, or colons.

  ✔ *Dreamweaver can use spaces as delimiters, but you may need to do a lot of cleanup on the table if you are importing text with spaces between words.*

- Most spreadsheet and word processing applications allow you to save a file in a delimited form. Save a word processing document using the TXT format or a spreadsheet using the CSV format.

- These formats save only the data, so any formatting such as fonts and font styles will not be imported. This formatting can be applied easily in Dreamweaver.

- Use the File>Import>Tabular Data command or the Insert>Table Objects>Import Tabular Data command to import the data into a new table. Either option displays the Import Tabular Data dialog box (see the following illustration).

Import Tabular Data dialog box

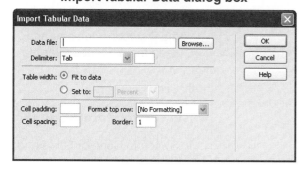

- Use the ⬚ Browse... ⬚ button to locate the file to import. If necessary, choose from the Delimiter list the delimiter format used in the file you want to import.

  ✔ *Dreamweaver will recognize some common file types such as CSV and set the delimiter automatically.*

- Similar to the process of creating a table from scratch, when you import table data, you can choose formats such as size, cell padding, cell spacing, and border width.

- Note in the illustration of the Import Tabular Data dialog box that Dreamweaver will also fit the table cells to the imported data and allow you to choose a font style for the top row.

Sort Table Data

- You can sort table data by row or column to further organize your data. Arranging data in alphabetical or numerical order may be easier for site visitors to read and understand.

- To sort data in a table, click in the table and use the Commands>Sort Table command to open the Sort Table dialog box (see the following illustration).

Sort Table dialog box

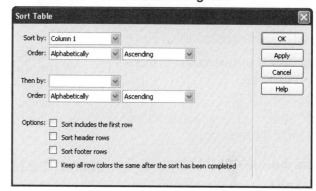

- Select a column to sort by (or select more than one column) and choose to sort Alphabetically or Numerically. You also can set the direction of the sort as Ascending (A to Z, 1 to 10) or Descending (Z to A, 10 to 1).

- If you want to leave the first row out of the sort process so that it is not sorted with the remaining rows, make sure the *Sort includes the first row* checkbox is *not* selected.

- The *Sort header rows* and *Sort footer rows* options apply to special tags that contain one or more rows used to repeat the headers or footers of tables that will print on more than one page. They are not covered in this book, but typically you would not want to sort them.

- Select *Keep all row colors the same after the sort has been completed* if you want to keep row attributes intact after a sort.

- You cannot sort data in a table that has spanned columns or rows. If you know you want to sort data and also want to create spanned columns or rows, sort the data first.

Insert Table-Related Tags

- Dreamweaver provides tools for editing—and even creating—tables in Show Code and Show Code and Design views. The Insert>Table Objects command displays a submenu of tags for creating rows (TR), headings (TH), data (TD), and captions (Caption).

- To use these commands, you must switch to one of the code views.

PROCEDURES

Set Border Colors

To set border colors for the entire table:

1. Select the entire table.
2. Set the same-color borders in the Property inspector:
   a. Click ⬛ **Brdr color**.
   b. Select a color from the palette with the eyedropper.

To set a border color for cell(s):

1. Click in the cell or select multiple cells.
2. Click ⬛ **Brdr**.
3. Select a color from the palette with the eyedropper.

Add Background Color to Cells

1. Click in the cell you want to add a background color to or select the table or group of cells.
2. Click ⬛ **Bg color** or ⬛ **Bg** and select the color you want to use for the background.

   OR

   ▪ Type the hexadecimal value for the color in the box to right of color box.

Insert a Background Image in a Cell

1. Click in the cell you want to add the background image to, or select the table or group of cells you want to change.
2. Type the address for the background image in the **Bg** or **Bg Image** box.

   OR

   a. Click 📁 **Background URL of cell** button on the Property inspector and navigate to the image.
   b. Select the image and click ⬚ OK ⬚ .

Import Table Data

1. Position the insertion point at the location for the imported table.
2. Click **File** .... Alt + F
3. Point to **Import** I
4. Click **Tabular Data** .... T

   OR

1. Click **Insert** .... Alt + I
2. Point to **Table Objects** .... A
3. Click **Import Tabular Data** ... T

In the Import Tabular Data dialog box:

1. Type the path to the data file or click ⬚ Browse... ⬚ and navigate to the data file.
2. Specify a delimiter, if necessary.
3. Set the table width, cell padding, cell spacing, border width, and format for the top row, if desired.
4. Click ⬚ OK ⬚ .

   ✔ *The data file must be saved as delimited text, with columns separated by a delimiter such as commas, tabs, semicolons, or colons.*

Sort Table Data

1. Click in the table you want to sort.
2. Click **Commands** .... Alt + C
3. Click **Sort Table** .... S
4. Choose column(s) to sort by.
5. Specify an Alphabetical or Numerical sort.
6. Choose an Ascending or Descending sort.
7. Select the options to include the first row in the sort and keep the attributes after the sort.
8. Click ⬚ OK ⬚ .

Insert Table-Related Tags

1. Switch to Code or Code and Design view.
2. Click **Insert** .... Alt + I
3. Point to **Table Objects** .... A
4. Click the desired tag to insert it in the code view pane.

EXERCISE DIRECTIONS

1. Start Dreamweaver and open the gardenscape site.

2. Open contactus.html. Position the cursor in the line above the *Returning Merchandise* heading. Press Enter to add a line space.

3. Import the tabular data from ◎ contact.txt. Use a comma delimiter, and set the format of the top row to bold. Click OK.

4. Complete the table formatting as follows:
   - Change the table border width to 2. Set a border color of #663399.
   - Adjust the size of the table so that all data can be viewed easily.
   - Fill the subject heading cells (such as *For Questions About, Contact*, etc.) with background color # 666699 and change the font color to #CCFFFF.
   - Select all remaining cells, excluding the first row, and apply the background image ◎ flowers.jpg from the Lesson 4 Data folder. (Save the file in the images folder.)

5. The background image is interesting, but it makes the text too difficult to read. Remove the background image and change the background color to #CCFFFF.

6. Sort the table data in ascending order according to the first column. Do not include the first row in the sort.

7. Adjust text formatting and alignment if necessary.

8. Insert a new column to the left of the first column. Type the following text in the first cell of the new column:

Contact our designers today for help with your garden projects!

9. Format the text so that it matches the other headings in the row.

10. Span this text down all rows in the column.

11. Adjust the first column width to 85 pixels, and adjust other column widths to best fit their data, if necessary.

12. Adjust the font color, if necessary.

13. Switch to Show Code and Design view. Locate the first table tag, <table border="*x*">. (Your border value may vary, depending on the table format you chose.)

14. In the code pane, click to the right of the <tr> tag and use the Insert>Table Objects menu to insert a caption tag. Insert the caption **Contact Our Designers** between the opening and closing caption tags.

   ✔ *If you have trouble inserting the caption because of a message about locked code or a template, detach the copyright notice from the library and try again.*

15. Format the caption in bold. Your table should look similar to Illustration A.

16. Save and close any open pages and exit Dreamweaver.

Illustration A

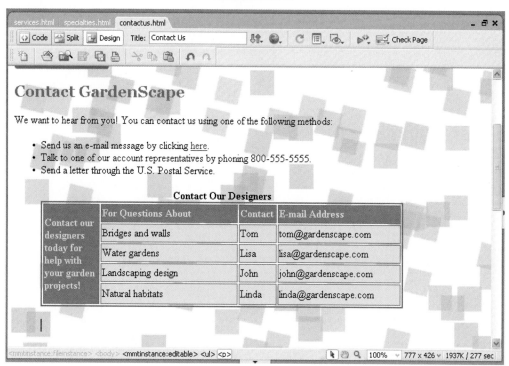

ON YOUR OWN

1. Start Dreamweaver and open the yardart site.

2. Open favorites.html and detach this page from the template, if necessary.

3. Import the tabular data in ⊙ favorites.txt from the Lesson 4 Data folder to create a table below the paragraph text.

4. Sort the data by artist name and then by art type (specify both sort criteria at the same time in the Sort Table dialog box).

5. Modify and format the table as desired. For example, you may want to:

   ■ Apply a background color to the entire table and/or column heading cells.

   ■ Apply a specific cell color to all cells with the value "yes".

   ■ Apply a table format to the entire table.

   ■ Resize the table and adjust column widths as needed.

   ■ Adjust cell padding and cell spacing.

   ■ Eliminate or modify the table borders.

6. Preview your finished table in the browser, and then make any adjustments you think necessary.

7. If desired, apply similar formats to the table on contact.html.

8. Close the page and exit Dreamweaver.

Skills Covered

➤

- ■ **Use a Table for Page Layout**
- ■ **Work in Layout Mode**

- ■ **Format Layout Cells**

Software Skills Using a table for page layout allows you to create a sophisticated design that you can be certain will appear in all browsers. Use Dreamweaver's layout tools to draw the table and its cells. Working in Layout view makes it easier to add content to a layout table.

Design Skills You can use a layout table to set the design for an entire page or a portion of page. Layout tables give you added control over the size, shape, and complexity of a table you create.

Application Skills In this exercise, you create a new page for the GardenScape Web site and organize the page content using a layout table.

TERMS

AP elements Elements on the page that are absolutely positioned.

Autostretch A Dreamweaver feature that adjusts a table column automatically to full browser window width.

Expanded Tables mode A Dreamweaver view that gives you an enlarged view of table contents.

Layout mode A Dreamweaver view that enables you to create layout tables.

NOTES

Use a Table for Page Layout

- Tables are useful not only for organizing data on a Web page but also for laying out a page's content. One advantage to using a table for page layout is that all browsers can display tables. Laying out a page with a table enables you to create a complex page design without using sophisticated layout features such as frames or **AP** (absolutely positioned) elements.

  ✔ *You will learn how to create frame pages and AP elements in the next lesson.*

- Creating a table for page layout involves the same process as creating a table to organize data, except that you work on a larger scale to fill the page. For best results, maximize the Document window and collapse unnecessary panels before you begin creating the page layout.

- Make sure that the table uses the full page width (100 percent of page width). You can then insert rows or columns and merge as necessary to create the areas where you can insert text and images.

- You can apply color and design to the page creatively by adding a background color or image to specific table cells. When laying out an entire page, you will probably not want to use table borders, but applying a cell border to an individual cell can draw attention to its content.

Work in Layout Mode

- To create a layout table, you need access to Dreamweaver's layout tools, available on the Layout tab of the Insert bar.

- The Layout tab offers two buttons that allow you to choose a layout mode.

  - Standard mode gives you access to more advanced tools you can use for creating and restructuring a standard table, adding form functionality, and working with frames.

    ✔ *You will work with Standard mode in Lesson 6.*

  - **Expanded Tables mode** enlarges a table structure so that you can more easily work with the contents of the table cells. This mode does not represent the way a browser will display the table, so be sure to return to Standard mode before completing your work on a table to make sure all content displays the way you want it to.

- To create a layout table, you must be in Layout mode. Use the View>Table Mode>Layout Mode command to change to Layout mode. In this mode, you have access to the 🖼 Draw Layout Table and 🖼 Draw Layout Cell tools that you can use to draw the layout table structure.

- The first time you switch to **Layout mode**, Dreamweaver displays the dialog box shown in the following illustration to give you further information about Layout mode.

  ✔ *If you don't want to see this message each time you switch to Layout mode after you start Dreamweaver, select the* Don't show me this message again *checkbox.*

Layout mode message box

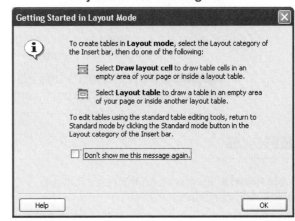

- Creating a layout on a page using a layout table and layout cells (see the illustration at the top of the next page) gives you a great deal of flexibility in inserting and positioning cells precisely where you need them within the table.

- After you create a layout table and layout cells, you can move or resize cells by dragging. You can specify exact dimensions for cells or let them "stretch" to conform to the browser window's size.

Draw a Layout Table

- Begin a new page layout by drawing a layout table. You can create a table the full size of your page, or you can create several different layout tables on a page. You can also create one layout table within another.

  ✔ *You can draw a layout cell without first drawing a layout table; Dreamweaver will automatically create the layout table to surround the layout cell.*

Layout mode showing layout table and layout cells

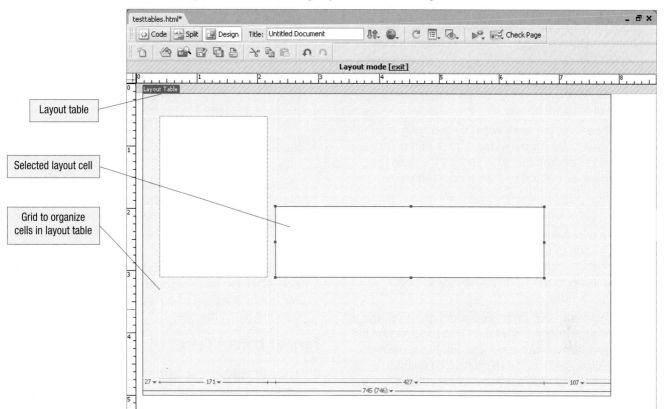

- Draw a layout table by clicking the ⬚ Draw Layout Table button from the Layout tab of the Insert bar and then use the crosshair pointer to drag the outline of the table on the page. This procedure is the same as drawing an object in a program such as Illustrator. The area in which you want to draw the layout table must be empty.

- To help you size layout objects, Dreamweaver displays dimensions near the right side of the status bar as you draw.

- The new layout table displays a green border with sizing handles and a green tab containing the label *Layout Table*. The table's width in pixels is shown in the table header area at the top or bottom of the table. The table area itself is light gray.

- You can modify the table width by dragging a sizing handle or you can use the Width and Height boxes in the Property inspector to set exact measurements. You can also adjust cell spacing and cell padding values just as you do in a standard table.

- If a layout table appears on a page by itself, you do not have to take any special step to select it. Because the table is the only object on the page, it is selected by default.

- Once you insert cells in the table, the table itself is deselected. If you have inserted the table on a page with other content (or within another layout table), you can deselect the table by clicking on other page content.

- To select the table again, click on its green outline or its green tab.

Draw Layout Cells

- Use the same general method to draw layout cells. Click the ▦ Draw Layout Cell button from the Layout tab of the Insert bar and use the crosshair pointer to draw the cell anywhere on the page or within the layout table.

- Dreamweaver automatically creates a grid of rows and columns in the remaining portion of the layout table relative to the inserted cell (see the previous illustration). You can use this grid to guide you in adding other cells.

- The changes you can make to a layout cell depend on whether the cell is *active* or *selected*.

- To make a cell *active*, click in it. An active cell displays a light blue border and a white background. When a cell is active, you can add content to it by typing text at the insertion point or by pasting text. Insert graphics in the cell just as you would in a standard table.

- To *select* a layout cell, move the pointer on the border (the border turns red when the pointer is on it) and then click the border. When selected, the cell border displays sizing handles on the light blue border.

- When a cell is selected, you can change its background color and the horizontal and vertical alignment of its content.

- Modify a selected cell's width by dragging its border or by using the Property inspector's Width and Height boxes. You can also specify the Autostretch option for a selected cell, as discussed next.

Use Autostretch

- Tables and columns within tables can be sized to fixed widths or you can use the **Autostretch** feature. Autostretch allows a table column (or the entire table) to resize automatically to fill the browser window.

- You may often use both fixed-width columns and an Autostretch column in a table. Use fixed widths for columns that contain cells you want to remain the same size, such as those containing images, a menu, or links. Use the Autostretch column for text that can wrap easily in the table.

  ✔ *Only one column in a table can be set to Autostretch.*

- Fixed-width columns display the width in pixels in the cell's column header in the table border. Autostretch columns display a `-⌃⌄▼-` zigzag line in the column header to indicate that the size can change.

- To create an Autostretch column, select a cell in the column and click the Autostretch option in the Property inspector. Or, click the column header and choose Make Column Autostretch.

- If you have not used the Autostretch feature previously in the current site, Dreamweaver asks whether you want to create a spacer GIF file to insert in the fixed-width columns (see the illustration in the next column). The spacer image prevents fixed-width columns from resizing, allowing the Autostretch column to adjust freely in the browser window.

Dreamweaver suggests a spacer file

- The default option is to create the spacer image file. If you select this option, Dreamweaver will create the file for you and allow you to save it in your Web site. You can save the spacer image with your other images.

- You need to create a spacer file only once in a Web site. After you have created the file, Dreamweaver will not prompt you to create one in any other layout table in the site.

Format Layout Cells

- You can apply some formats to layout cells in Layout view using the Property inspector. You can, for example, adjust cell width and height, apply a background color, and set both horizontal and vertical alignment. You can also prevent text from wrapping in the cell, which is a good choice if you have a list of links in a cell that you want to display on one line.

- You can apply standard table formats to layout cells by clicking the Standard button from the Layout tab of the Insert bar to display the layout table as a standard Dreamweaver table.

- You then have access to the same formatting options as for a standard table, such as cell borders and backgrounds, fonts and styles, and so on.

PROCEDURES

Switch to Layout Mode (Alt + F6)

1. Click **View** ....Alt+V
2. Point to **Table Mode** ....T
3. Click **Layout Mode** L

   ✔ *When you are finished working in Layout mode, click the **Standard** button.*

Draw a Layout Table

1. Click the 🖻 **Draw Layout Table** button in the Layout tab of the Insert bar.
2. Hold down the mouse button and drag the crosshair pointer to create the outside border for the table.
3. Release the mouse button when the table is the desired size.

Draw a Layout Cell

1. Click the 🖽 **Draw Layout Cell** button in the Layout tab of the Insert bar.
2. Hold down the mouse button and drag the crosshair pointer to create a cell.
3. Release the mouse button.

   ✔ *If you have not already created a layout table when you draw a layout cell, Dreamweaver will automatically create the table for you.*

Modify the Layout Table or Cell Dimensions

1. Click the outside border of the table or cell to select it.
2. Drag a border to resize it.
   OR
   ▪ Use the Width and Height boxes in the Property inspector to set exact dimensions.

Use Autostretch

1. Select the cell you want to Autostretch.
2. Click the **Autostretch** option in the Property inspector.
   OR
   ▪ Click the down arrow in the header at the top of the column you want to Autostretch and click **Make Column Autostretch**.
3. Choose **Create a spacer image file** in the Choose Spacer Image dialog box.
4. Click OK .
5. Save the spacer image in your site's images folder.

EXERCISE DIRECTIONS

1. Start Dreamweaver and open the gardenscape site.
2. Open a new, blank HTML page. Save the page as roses.html with the page title **Our Favorite Roses**.
3. Create the page layout table shown in Illustration A on the next page, as follows:
   ▪ Switch to Layout mode. Draw a layout table the full width of the page, or about 750 pixels wide if you are working on a large monitor.
   ▪ Draw a layout cell in the upper-left corner of the layout table that is 200 pixels wide and 125 pixels high. (You can see the measurement as you draw at the right side of the status bar.)
   ▪ Draw the remaining cells as shown in Illustration A. Use the following height values for the remaining cells: Cell 2, 50; Cell 3, 75; Cell 4, 125; Cell 5, 50; Cell 6, 75.
   ▪ Make the right column an Autostretch column.
   ▪ Select the table and set cell spacing at **7**.

4. Add content to the layout table as follows:
   ▪ In Cell 1 (see Illustration A on the next page), insert the ⊙ lafter.jpg image from the Lesson 4 Data folder. Save the image in your images folder and add the alternate text **Photo of lafter rose**.

      ✔ *Click in another cell to readjust the cell size around the photo.*

   ▪ In Cell 2, enter the phrase **Lafter Tea Rose**. Apply the Heading 2 format and center the text.
   ▪ In Cell 3, insert the text **Our favorite Lafter rose is a hearty tea rose with deep green, healthy foliage and pink, yellow, and orange blossoms. Beautiful!**. Format the text as Heading 4.
   ▪ In Cell 4, add the ⊙ streisand.jpg image from the Lesson 4 Data folder. Save the image to your images folder, and add **Photo of streisand rose** as alternate text.
   ▪ In Cell 5, type the text **Streisand Rose**. Apply Heading 2 and center the text.

- In Cell 6, add the text **The wonderful Streisand rose produces oversized lavender blooms with a strong sweet scent. Perfect for garden cuttings!**.

5. Resize the image in Cell 4 to match the size of the image in Cell 1.

6. In the Files panel, navigate to the Lesson 4 Data folder and copy the ⊙ new.gif file. Paste the file in the images folder of your site.

7. Drag new.gif to the end of the text in Cells 2 and 5. Add a space between the text and the *new* icon in each heading.

8. Drag the bottom border of Cell 3 upward until it fits closely around the text. Then drag Cell 6 upward about a half an inch. If two new cells appear below the cell you moved, remove them in Standard view. Your layout table should resemble the one shown in Illustration B.

9. Open index.html and position the cursor just before the *A Few Project Ideas* heading at the top of the page. Press Enter and type **See Our Newest Roses!**, apply the Heading 4 format, center the text, and add new.gif, separated by spaces, to either side of the text. Link this text to roses.html.

10. Save changes. Preview the page in the browser and check the link to the Roses page.

11. Close the browser.

12. Close any open pages and exit Dreamweaver.

Illustration A

Layout Table		
	750 (751) ▾	
200 ▾	550 ▾	
Cell 1	Cell 2	
	Cell 3	
Cell 4	Cell 5	
	Cell 6	

Illustration B

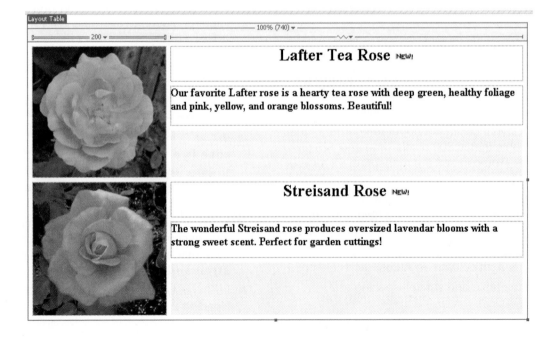

ON YOUR OWN

1. Start Dreamweaver and create a solutions folder to hold the files you work with in this exercise.

2. In the Start window, click Starter Page (Theme) in the Create from Samples area and select the sample page named Lodging – Text Page. Save the file as starter.html in your solutions folder and copy all required files to that location.

3. Switch to Layout mode and view the various layout tables and cells that were used to create this text page.

4. Open a new, blank HTML page and save it in your solutions folder as mytext.html. Using information about the Starter page's layout tables and cells you gather from the Property inspector, recreate the page:

   - Select layout tables and cells to determine their size and then duplicate those sizes and approximate positions in your page.

   - You can attempt to duplicate colors, or use your own. Note that some elements in the Starter page are formatted using CSS codes, but you can determine attributes by viewing the HTML code for Starter page elements.

   - If you do not know how to insert some elements, such as the fine white horizontal lines between layout cells at the top of the page, you can copy the code from the Starter page and insert it in the code of your page.

5. You may find it helpful to create elements in this order:

   - First apply a page background color for the color that surrounds the main layout table and forms the background of the Web site name layout cell. Alternatively, you can add a background image to the page to create a unique effect.

   - Create the main layout table that organizes the entire page. It is about 550 pixels high and is an Autostretch column.

   - Create a layout table in the center of the page that is 440 by 450. Then insert the layout cell that contains the page name and the layout cell that contains the page text.

6. You can insert background colors for the layout cells in layout mode, but you should switch to Standard mode to apply colors to the spacer cells around the layout cells.

7. Insert text placeholders to indicate what kind of content goes in each layout cell. You may want to add the site title, a page title, copyright information, and page update information.

8. Save your page and view it in the browser. Make any changes necessary, and then save and close the page.

9. Use the Files panel to access your solution files and delete the Starter page you used as a guide.

10. Exit Dreamweaver.

   ✔ *You probably learned while doing this exercise that even a relatively simple layout design can take quite a bit of tweaking to get right!*

Skills Covered

Software Skills Creating a form in Dreamweaver is a simple process that uses many of the skills you already have, such as inserting and formatting text. Dreamweaver enables you to add different types of form fields for collecting various kinds of information. To best serve all the visitors to your site, you can create an accessible form that meets current XHTML coding standards.

Design Skills Being able to add different types of elements on your page is one part of developing good design skills. Creating and adding forms that are easy for site visitors to use improves the effectiveness of your site and helps you gather the type of information you need.

Application Skills In this exercise, you will add an accessible form that includes a number of common form field types.

TERMS

Form An interactive area on a Web page that allows a visitor to supply information or answer questions.

Form field An object, such as a text field or check-box, that is inserted in a form to gather a specific type of data.

Form handler An application that processes the form data and displays it in the Web application.

Initial value In a form field, the text or value that will appear in the form field by default when the form page is opened in a browser.

Jump menu A menu that supplies a list of values which, when clicked in the browser, takes a visitor to a specific Web page.

Label In a form, text that identifies a field (for example, the Last Name label identifies the field that collects a visitor's last name).

Value In a form field, the actual result that will be sent to the server after the visitor types text or makes a choice.

NOTES

About Forms

- You can use a **form** to collect information from visitors to your Web site. Forms can be simple or complex, ranging from simple address or registration forms to surveys, contact information, feedback, searching, ordering products, or even online job applications.

- Forms can vary greatly, but they all share the common purpose of gathering data. Forms consist of a form area in which you insert form fields to collect the information.

- Dreamweaver forms can include a variety of fields, such as text boxes, radio buttons, submit buttons, and more.

- You can build a form on an HTML page or on a specific server-type page such as ASP or PHP. The type of page you use for a form depends on the server technology you will use to process the form.

- In many cases, you will not have a choice in what technology to use—it will be determined by the server on which you intend to put your site files. Before you build a form for a real-world site, make sure you know how the form data will be processed by your server.

- *Form data* is the information gathered on the form visitors fill out. You have a number of options for viewing and storing form data. You can specify that it be sent to you via e-mail, or you can send the data to a database for future use. You can also set up a page in your site to display form data in HTML format.

Create a Form

- You can create a form by using commands on the Insert>Form menu or by using buttons from the Forms tab of the Insert bar.

- It is a good idea to insert a descriptive paragraph or caption above the form to make sure your site visitors understand the purpose of the form. You can also use this paragraph to give specific instructions for filling out the form.

- Click to place the cursor where you want the form to begin. Choose the Insert>Form>Form command, or click the ☐ Form button from the Forms tab of the Insert bar.

  ✔ *The first time you choose this command or tool, a message box appears telling you that View>Visual Aids>Invisible Elements must be checked before the form will be visible on the page. Click OK and then choose that command to display the red checked outline for the form.*

- A red dashed outline appears on all sides of the insertion point and as wide as the page. This outline marks the borders of the form. The Property inspector allows you to specify information about the form (see the illustration below).

- Name the form using the Form name text box. If you know the path to the script or application file that will be used to process the form data, you can enter it in the Action box.

- The Method list choices are used to define the way the form data will be handled. If you are not sure what method will be used by your server, leave the setting as POST (the default setting for a new form).

Properties for a new form

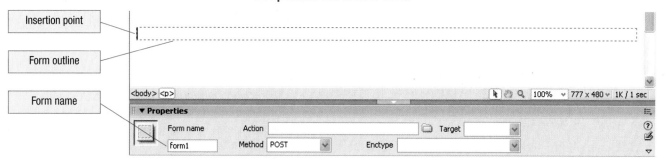

207

- Forms that collect sensitive data, such as personal data and credit card information, also require advanced properties. The Enctype drop-down list lets you specify the type of data encoding that is submitted to the server for processing. The Target drop-down lets you choose a window in which to display data returned by a form handler application.

- If you want to create an orderly form, you can insert a table directly in the form area. Using a table allows you to align labels and form fields and make sure that that the fields and labels are aligned on any browser.

- After you set up the form area, you are ready to enter form objects: **labels** and **form fields**. Labels are text words or phrases that tell a visitor what kind of information to enter. Form fields are the boxes and buttons visitors use to enter information on the form.

- Dreamweaver supplies a number of different form fields you can add to a form, but you are likely to use these field types most often:

  - *Text fields* allow the visitor to type text in a box. A text field can consist of a single line or multiple lines.

  - *Radio buttons* allow the visitor to choose one option from a group of options.

  - *Checkboxes* enable a visitor to select one or many options from a group of options.

  - *List/menu fields* give visitors a list or menu of options to choose from.

  - *Buttons* and *button groups* perform a specific action when a visitor clicks them.

Handle Accessibility Issues

- By default, Dreamweaver prompts you to make your forms accessible to those using screen readers, just as you were prompted to supply alternate text when inserting images so they could be described by a screen reader.

  ✔ *Dreamweaver is set to prompt for accessibility information for forms, frames, images, and media objects. You can deselect any of these options in the Preferences dialog box if you prefer not to supply accessibility information for them. To ensure that you are creating a site that reflects current standards in Web design, however, leave the accessibility settings as they are and provide the information as prompted.*

- To make a form accessible, Dreamweaver uses the <label> tag to supply information about each form field that is then read in a text-only browser or by a screen reader. The <label> tag allows you to associate the form's label with its other coding (such as name and value) so that a visitor using a screen reader can easily understand how your form is structured.

- To create an accessible form, first make sure that Form objects is selected in the Accessibility category of the Preferences dialog box. Then insert a form field in a form, as described in the following sections for each type of field. Dreamweaver displays the Input Tag Accessibility Attributes dialog box, shown in the following illustration.

Input Tag Accessibility Attributes dialog box

- In the ID box, supply a name for the new field. Although you can choose to leave this blank for now (and fill it in later using the Property inspector), it's important that you name each field on the form. The script or application used to handle the form data uses these field names—as well as the name you give to your form—to store data correctly. The field name should be only one or two words. If you use two words, join them with an underscore, such as first_name.

- Type the label to be associated with the form field in the Label box. You can use the Position options to set the label before the form field (that is, to the left of the field) or after the field (to the right of the field).

- Choose a style for how the <label> tag is associated with form elements.

  - The *Wrap with label tag* option encloses the form field name within the <label> tags, as shown in the following illustration. Note how the label (*First Name*) and the field name ("first_name") display between the <label> and </label> tags.

Code showing the Wrap with label tag style

```
<form id="newform" name="newform" method="post" action="">
  <label>First Name
  <input type="text" name="first_name" id="first_name" />
  </label>
</form>
```

- The *Attach label tag using 'for' attribute* option attaches the label tag to the form field using the 'for' attribute, as shown in the following illustration. Note that the <label> tag uses the 'for' attribute to identify the specific tag ("payment") and encloses the label text (*Credit Card*). When this accessibility option is used, a visitor can click either the radio button or its label to select the form element. For example, in the form shown in the following code, a visitor could click either the Credit Card button or the Credit Card label to choose the payment option.

Code showing the Attach label tag using 'for' attribute style

```
<form id="form1" name="form1" method="post" action="">
  <input type="radio" name="radio" id="payment" value="payment" />
  <label for="payment">Credit Card</label>
</form>
```

✔ *The* Attach label tag using 'for' attribute *is the preferred accessibility option, because it makes it easier for visitors to select an option. However, browsers vary in their support for this functionality, so be sure to test in your target browsers before using this option.*

- You can also choose the *No label tag* option if you don't want to use the <label> tag for a particular field or in a particular form.

■ After you complete the Insert Tag Accessibility Attributes dialog box, the new form field appears in the form. You must still supply specific information for the field, such as its name, size, and value. The following sections walk you through the process of adding the required information for the most common form field types.

Insert Single-Line Text Fields

■ Single-line text fields are used to hold a small amount of text data that can appear on one line. You might use a text field to gather names, e-mail addresses, and street addresses.

■ Insert a single-line text field using the Insert>Form> Text Field command. Or, click or drag the ▭ Text Field button from the Forms tab of the Insert bar. Supply accessibility information when prompted.

■ Dreamweaver inserts the default text field. Click in the field to select it so you can modify its properties. Use the Property inspector to display and modify properties for the field, as shown in the illustration below.

✔ *You will know the field is selected when you see* <input#first_name> *appear in the status bar at the bottom of the work area.*

■ If you opted not to name the field by entering a field name in the ID box on the Insert Tag Accessibility Attributes dialog box, be sure to name the field by typing it in the field name box in the Property inspector.

■ You can specify how many characters wide the field should be, as well as how many characters it can hold.

■ If your data is being stored in a database, you will need to make sure that your fields are not incompatible with the size and type of data used by the database.

■ If you want the field to show an **initial value** (text that displays each time the form is opened, such as *Type full name here*), insert this text in the Init val box in the Property inspector.

■ The Password option is selected for text boxes in which passwords are typed so that onlookers cannot see the form user's password, which appears as a series of black dots.

Single-line text field

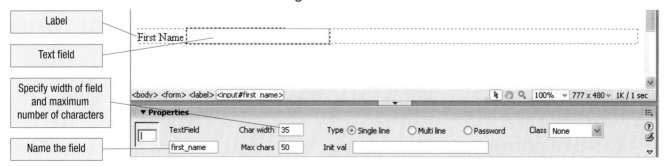

Insert Radio Buttons

- Radio buttons are small circles that visitors click to select a single option from a group of options. Radio buttons allow simple selections to supply data. If you have ever participated in an online poll, you have used this kind of form object.

- Insert a radio button using the Insert>Form>Radio Button menu command. Or use the 🔘 Radio Button item from the Forms tab of the Insert bar. Be sure to use the *Attach label tag using 'for' attribute* style option, so that all visitors can select the option using the radio button or its label.

- Dreamweaver inserts the radio button and the Property inspector shows properties for the radio button field (see the following illustration).

Radio button field

Radio button field | Value returned if selected

Add to mailing list? ⬡

Radio Button list | Checked value Yes | Initial state ○ Checked ● Unchecked

- Radio buttons are generally inserted in groups. (Creating grouped buttons is discussed in the next section.)

- If you insert more than one radio button to gather responses on a particular area of your form, all radio buttons in the group must have the same name. Only the **value** changes for each button. The value entered in the Checked value box is the data that will appear in the form results.

- For example, if you create a group of three radio buttons for a credit card field, each button will be named card_type, but one button will have the value *MasterCard*, another will have the value *Visa*, and the third may have a value such as *Discover*.

- If a visitor selects the *Visa* radio button, the form results will show an entry of *Visa* for the card_type field.

  ✔ *Some servers will not correctly process data in which more than one field element has the same name, as described above for radio buttons. In this case, you may need to redesign a form so that all fields have a unique name.*

- If you want one of the radio buttons to be selected as a default value each time the form opens, select the Checked option for Initial state. Visitors will still be able to change their selection even if one radio button is selected by default.

Insert Radio Groups

- A radio group allows you to create two or more radio buttons quickly either on separate lines or in a table.

- Insert a radio button group using the Insert> Form>Radio Group command. Or, click the 📇 Radio Group button from the Forms tab of the Insert bar. Either command opens the Radio Group dialog box shown in the following illustration. Note that Dreamweaver will not open the Input Tag Accessibility Attributes dialog box for a radio group; the *Wrap with label tag* option is used automatically for this type of form field.

Radio Group dialog box

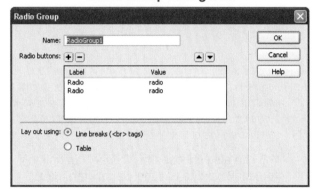

- In the Radio Group dialog box, you can enter a name for the radio group. In the Radio buttons list, two buttons are created by default, with default labels and values. Labels display to the right of each button in the form. The value is the data that will be sent to the server when the form data is recorded.

- To customize the button labels and values, simply click on the label name or value and enter your own information. Values should be similar to item labels, with no spaces or capital letters.

- Use the ➕ button to enter additional labels and values (or simply press Tab to create a new label). Click the ▲ and ▼ buttons to change the radio group order.

- To remove a list item, select the item and click the ➖ button.

- You can lay out a radio group either in separate lines or in a table by selecting the desired *Lay out using* option.

Insert Checkboxes

- Checkboxes are much like radio buttons, but checkboxes can stand alone in a form or be grouped to allow visitors to make more than one selection from several options. Use the *Attach label tag using 'for' attribute* accessibility option to make it possible for a visitor to click either the checkbox or its label to select the field.

- Insert a checkbox using the Insert>Form>Checkbox command. Or, use the ☑ Checkbox button from the Forms tab of the Insert bar.

- Dreamweaver inserts the checkbox and the Property inspector displays properties for the field (see the top illustration below).

- Name the checkbox as you would for any other form field if it is standing alone in the form. If you are offering visitors a number of selections for the same form item, give each checkbox the same name, as when creating radio buttons, to create a group of checkboxes.

- For grouped checkboxes, make sure each checkbox has a unique value. This value is usually similar to the label used for the checkbox. Because a visitor can select more than one checkbox, the form results can show multiple values for the checkbox field name.

- As for radio buttons, you specify whether checkboxes are checked by default when the form opens.

  ✔ *Checkboxes are usually not checked by default. This keeps visitors from unintentionally choosing an option.*

Insert Lists and Menus

- Dreamweaver's List/Menu field allows you to place several options on a scrollable list or drop-down menu. Visitors click the list or menu to display choices and then select one (or more, if you allow multiple selections).

- Lists and menus are generally used for three or more options. For fewer options, use radio buttons or checkboxes.

- Use a list or menu to save room in a form. Because the options are stored in one field rather than in multiple radio buttons or checkboxes, the number of selections on the form is reduced, which simplifies the look of the form.

- Insert a list or menu using the Insert>Form>List/Menu command. Or, use the ▤ List/Menu button from the Forms tab of the Insert bar.

- Dreamweaver inserts the List/Menu field and the Property inspector displays properties for the field (see the bottom illustration below).

- The List/Menu field is only a few characters wide when you first add it. The field will resize as you add choices to the menu.

- Name the field as you would for other form fields (if you didn't enter a name in the Input Tag Accessibility Attributes dialog box). Then choose whether to create a menu or a list:

  - A menu displays a single choice by default and drops down when clicked to display a menu of choices. Visitors can select only one choice.

  - A list can display more than one choice by default, and visitors can scroll the list to see additional choices. Visitors may be allowed to select more than one choice.

Checkbox field

List/Menu field

- If you choose to create a list, you can specify the height of the list (that is, how many items will display by default) and select the Allow multiple checkbox to let visitors choose more than one option from the list.

- For both menus and lists, you must create the choices visitors will see on the menu or list. Click the [List Values...] button to open the List Values dialog box (see the following illustration).

Add choices in the List Values dialog box

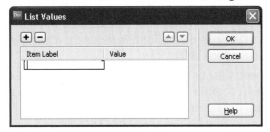

- Type the item labels (the actual list items visitors will see in the form) and a value for each label. As in other form objects, the value is the data that will be sent to the server when the form data is recorded.

- Use the ⊞ button to enter additional labels and values (or simply press Tab to create a new label) and the ▲ and ▼ buttons to change the list order.

- To remove a list item, select the item and click the ⊟ button.

- If desired, you can select one of the choices to appear in the list or menu box (if Height is set to 1). Expand the Property inspector, if necessary, and click the desired label in the Initially selected box (see the illustration at the bottom of this page) in the expanded Property inspector.

- If you do not select one of the choices to appear initially, Dreamweaver displays the first choice in the list when the form is opened in the browser.

- You can insert another type of list/menu field in a form called a **jump menu**. A jump menu supplies a list of values that, when clicked in the browser, takes a visitor to a specific Web page.

- Insert a jump menu using the Insert>Form>Jump Menu command or use the ▢ Jump Menu button from the Forms tab of the Insert bar.

- In the Insert Jump Menu dialog box (see the following illustration), you specify text for each URL you want to include on the menu. Then type the URL itself, or use the [Browse...] button to browse to the location of the page you want to open.

Specify properties for a jump menu field

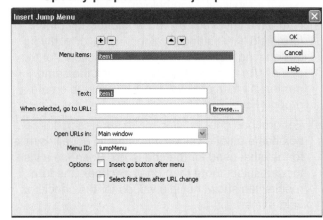

- You can also specify where to open the page and a name for the menu, and you can choose to add a go button after the menu that visitors can use to make the jump. If you have included a general instruction such as *Choose an item below* as the first option on the menu, you can select the *Select first item after URL change* to display this informational item again after a visitor has selected one of the other URLs on the list.

  ✔ *You will notice that large professional sites often include both navigation bars and jump menus when they want to give visitors the options to finding subpages within major categories.*

Select an item for default display

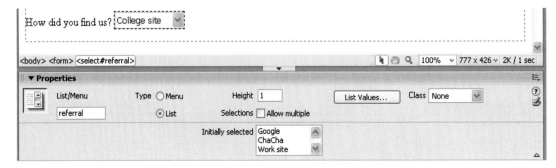

Insert Multiple-Line Text Fields

- As you have already learned, text fields are used for single-line entries. Text fields can also be set to allow for multiple-line entries. You can use a multiple-line text field to request more information from site visitors or allow them to answer questions in a longer format.

- Use a Text field to create a multiple-line text field. In the Property inspector, select the Multi line option. The Property inspector then activates additional properties for the multiple-line field (see the top illustration below).

- You can also shortcut this process somewhat by using the Insert>Form>Textarea command, or by using the 📝 Textarea button from the Forms tab of the Insert bar. This action inserts a multiline text area in the form so that you don't have to select the Multi line option in the Property inspector.

- As for other Text fields, you must specify a name. You can also specify a width in characters and the number of lines visitors can use for their comments.

  ✔ Defining the character width and number of lines allows you to limit user responses to a reasonable length.

- You can change the way text wraps in the multiple-line text field, but the Default option is suitable for most form uses.

- The Init val text box allows you to enter initial value text to ask a question or make a request.

Insert Buttons

- After you add all the fields you need on the form, you also need to give your site visitors a way to send the information they have provided. Use Dreamweaver's Button fields to create Submit and Reset buttons.

- Insert a button using the Insert>Form> Button command. Or, use the 🔲 Button item on the Forms tab of the Insert bar.

- Dreamweaver inserts a Submit button by default (see the bottom illustration below). Generally, you will want to accept the default properties for this button.

Specify properties for multiple-line text field

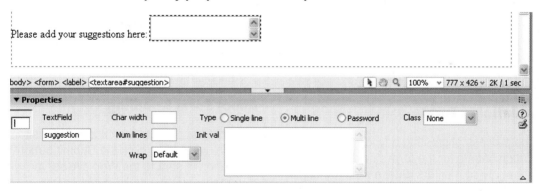

Dreamweaver inserts Submit button

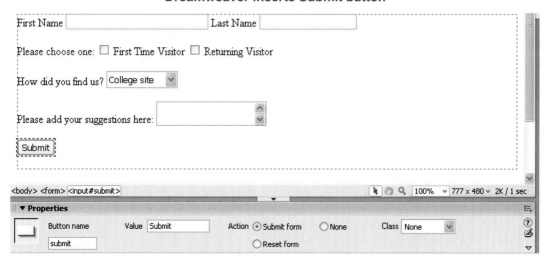

- To insert another button to be used for resetting or clearing the form, use the same procedure. You will then need to change the button's name to reflect its purpose, change its label, and choose the appropriate action (Reset form for a Reset button).

  ✔ *Dreamweaver will name this button* Submit *as well; you can change the name of the button by typing a new name in the Value box in the Property inspector. You can also right-click the button, choose Label, type a new label for the button, and click OK.*

- You may not need a Reset button on your form. Most users can simply modify the fields they want to correct rather than starting over. Because users may accidentally click the Reset button instead of the Submit button, you may decide to use only the Submit button on your form.

About Spry Form Fields

- The Form tab on the Insert bar shows several additional tools you can use to insert form fields with names such as Spry Validation Text Field and Spry Validation Checkbox.

- The Spry framework is new in Dreamweaver CS3. Dreamweaver offers a number of Spry widgets, including form tools, that provide interesting dynamic effects for Web pages.

- The Spry form tools allow you to insert interactive form elements that change color as a visitor enters the correct type of data.

  ✔ *You will work with Spry widgets in Lesson 6.*

About Validating a Form

- Part of the process of creating any form is supplying validation criteria for the form's fields. Validation ensures that a visitor enters data in required fields and inserts the correct type of data in fields where the format of the data makes a difference.

- In Dreamweaver, you can use behaviors to validate fields, or you can insert Spry form fields that have validation features built in to the field code.

  ✔ *You learn more about validation options in Lesson 6.*

Test a Form

- After creating a form, you need to test it to make sure the fields are set up correctly. If your form is linked to a script or application, you can display the form in the browser and fill in the form fields. Your form results will show you whether you need to modify your fields or values.

- Even if you don't have a script or form handler for your form, you should preview it in the browser to check its appearance. By entering sample data in the form, you can determine whether your text fields are wide enough or positioned logically on the form.

About Dynamic Data

- *Dynamic data* is data that is not fixed but changes depending on a visitor's action on the site. For example, when a visitor clicks a particular radio button, a subset of optional fields can be displayed on the form.

- Form fields can be linked to database recordsets to display dynamic data in a form field that can help a visitor choose options in the form. For example, a list field can draw its list items from a database, so that the designer does not have to enter into the List Values dialog box a long series of entries. When a product line changes, the database can be modified and the form can remain the same.

- To create dynamic data and recordsets, you must establish a link to a database.

About Form Handling

- What happens to the information visitors add to a form when they click the Submit button? The information is sent to the Web site server, where it is processed by a script or application on the server.

- The server may then send information back to the client (the Web server) or perform some other action that the form requests, such as interacting with a database server to store or retrieve information.

- The illustration at the top of the next page shows this process in a simplified form. Keep in mind that not all form data proceeds to a database. Some designers set up forms to return results by e-mail, and some forms are set up to request input from a database.

How a form is processed

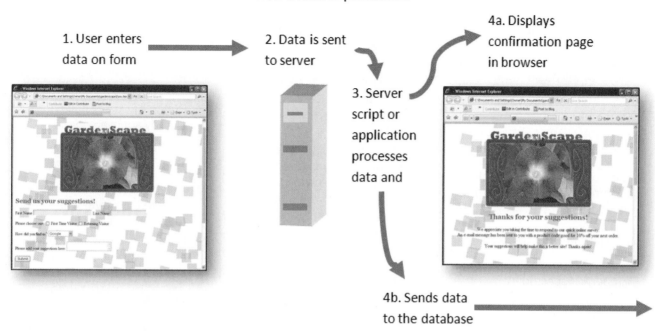

1. User enters data on form

2. Data is sent to server

3. Server script or application processes data and

4a. Displays confirmation page in browser

4b. Sends data to the database

- A program that controls the process of dealing with form data is called a **form handler.**

- Dreamweaver does not include a default form handler that you can use to process or store information from your forms, but the program includes powerful tools to help you create the connections you need in order to handle your form data.

- Some Web hosts offer generic scripts you can customize for your form. If a generic script is not available, you may need to write a script from scratch or download one of the thousands of scripts available on the Internet.

- Scripting languages include Perl, VBScript, JavaScipt, ColdFusion Markup Language, and PHP.

- A form may also require that the Web server communicate with an application server if an application is necessary to process the form data. When you build a form on an ASP page, for example, you need a server that uses ASP technology to handle the form.

- The IIS built into recent Windows versions is not only a Web server but also an application server that can handle both VBScript and JavaScript. You can use the IIS not only to test a form but to set up a connection to a database that allows you to send data to and retrieve data from the database.

PROCEDURES

Create a Form Area

1. Position the cursor at the point the form will begin.
2. Click **Insert** .... `Alt`+`I`
3. Point to **Form** .... `F`
4. Click **Form** .... `Enter`

   OR

■ Click or drag the **Form** button ☐ from the Forms tab of the Insert bar.

To set the properties for the form:

■ Type the form name in the Property inspector.

■ Type the script or application file name in the **Action** box, or click ☐ and navigate to location of script.

■ Specify the method, if necessary.

Create an Accessible Form

1. Click **Edit** .... `Alt`+`E`
2. Click **Preferences**... `P`, `P`, `Enter`
3. Click the **Accessibility** category.
4. Make sure **Form objects** is selected.
5. Click `OK` .

After selecting a form element to insert:

1. Type a name for the field.
2. Type a label for the field.
3. Select a style for the <label> tag:

   ■ Use the *Wrap with label tag* to enclose all information about the field, including the label, inside the <label> </label> tags.

   ■ Use the *Attach label tag using 'for' attribute* to make it possible to click either the label or a button or checkbox to select the field.

   ■ Use the *No label tag* if you do not want a label attached to a field.

4. Select a position for the label **Before form item** or **After form item**.
5. If desired, provide a key combination in the Access box that can be used to access the element.
6. If desired, specify a number in the Tab Index box to indicate the order in which the field will become active when the Tab key is pressed to move through the form.
7. Click `OK` .

Insert a Single-Line Text Field

1. Click **Insert** .... `Alt`+`I`
2. Point to **Form** .... `F`
3. Click **Text Field** .... `T`

   OR

■ Click or drag the **Text Field** button ☐ from the Forms tab of the Insert bar.

To set the properties for the text field:

1. Click the Text field to select it.
2. Type a name in the TextField box if you have not already supplied one.
3. Type the value in Char width field for the width of the field (optional).
4. Type the value in Max chars for the maximum number of characters allowed (optional).
5. Type the value in the Init val field that will display as the initial value (optional).

Insert Radio Buttons

1. Click **Insert** .... `Alt`+`I`
2. Point to **Form** .... `F`
3. Click **Radio Button** .... `R`

   OR

■ Click or drag the **Radio Button** button ☐ from the Forms tab of the Insert bar.

To set the properties for the radio button:

1. Click the radio button to select it.
2. Type the name in the Radio Button box if you have not already supplied one.

   ✔ *In a group of radio buttons, all buttons should have the same name.*

3. Type the value you want to send to the server when the radio button is selected.
4. Select **Checked** as the initial state to show the radio button selected by default (optional).

Insert a Radio Group

1. Click **Insert** .... `Alt`+`I`
2. Point to **Form** .... `F`
3. Click **Radio Group** .... `G`

   OR

■ Click or drag the **Radio Group** button ☐ from the Forms tab of the Insert bar.

To set the properties for the radio group:

1. Specify the items for the radio group in the Radio Group dialog box:

   a. Type a group name in the Name box.

   b. Click **Radio** in label column and replace the text with desired label.

   c. Press `Tab` and type a value.

   d. Click ⊞ to add items to the list or ⊟ to remove items.

   e. Click ▲ or ▼ to reorder the list.

   f. Select the desired **Lay out using** option:

      ■ Click **Line breaks** to place the radio buttons on lines with <br> tags.

      ■ Click **Table** to place radio buttons in a table.

2. Click `OK` .

Insert Checkboxes

1. Click **Insert** ....`Alt`+`I`
2. Point to **Form** ....`F`
3. Click **Checkbox** ....`C`, `Enter`

   OR

   ▪ Click or drag **Checkbox** button ☑ from the Forms tab of the Insert bar.

To set the properties for the checkbox:

1. Click the checkbox to select it.
2. Type a name in the Checkbox name box if you have not already supplied one.

   ✔ *In a group of checkboxes, all boxes should have the same name.*

3. In the Checked value box, type the value you want to send to the server when checkbox is selected.
4. Select the **Checked** initial state to show the checkbox selected by default (optional).

Insert a List or Menu

1. Click **Insert** ....`Alt`+`I`
2. Point to **Form** ....`F`
3. Click **List/Menu** ....`L`

   OR

   ▪ Click or drag **List/Menu** button ▦ from the Forms tab of the Insert bar.

To set the properties for the list or menu:

1. Click the list/menu field to select it.
2. Type the name in the List/Menu box if you have not already supplied one.
3. Select **Menu** or **List**.

   ▪ For **List**, specify number for **Height** and, if desired, select **Allow multiple** checkbox.

4. Specify the items you want to include in the list:

   a. Click `List Values...` .

   b. Type a label for the first item.

   c. Press `Tab ⇆` and type a value.

   d. Click `+` to add items to the list or `−` to remove items.

   e. Click `▲` or `▼` to reorder the list.

   f. Click `OK` .

5. Set initial selections by expanding the Property inspector, if necessary, and choosing the item from the **Initially selected** list.

Insert a Multiple-Line Text Field

1. Click **Insert** ....`Alt`+`I`
2. Point to **Form** ....`F`
3. Click **Textarea** ....`A`

   OR

   ▪ Click or drag the **Textarea** button ▤ from the Forms tab of the Insert bar.

To set the properties for the text area:

1. Click the multiple-line text field.
2. Type a name in TextField box if you have not already supplied one.
3. Type a value for the field width if desired.
4. Type a value for the number of lines in text box if desired.
5. Type an initial value if desired.
6. Change the wrap option if desired.

Insert Buttons

1. Click **Insert** ....`Alt`+`I`
2. Point to **Form** ....`F`
3. Click **Button** ....`B`

   OR

   ▪ Click or drag the **Insert Button** button ▭ from the Forms tab of the Insert bar.

To set the properties for the button:

1. Click a button to select it.
2. For a Submit button, leave all default properties as they are.
3. For a Reset or other button:

   a. Type button name.

   b. Type label to appear on button.

   c. Select the **Reset form** action for Reset button.

EXERCISE DIRECTIONS

1. Start Dreamweaver and open the gardenscape site.
2. Create a new blank HTML page and name it form.html. Save it in the site root folder.
3. Drag gardenscape_logo from the Library to the top of the page. Center the image.
4. Press Enter and type **Send Us Your Suggestions!** and format the text as Heading 2 and assign the color #009999.
5. Add the following single-line text fields:
   - First Name (first_name, character width 35, maximum length, 50)
   - Last Name (last_name, character width 35, maximum length, 50)
6. Add the text **Please choose one:** and insert two checkbox fields:
   - First Time Visitor (first_time, Unchecked)
   - Returning Visitor (returning, Unchecked)
7. Add the text **How did you find us?** and create a list field with the following list values:
   - Google (google)
   - ChaCha (chacha)
   - Work site (work)
   - College site (college)
   - Other (other)
8. Insert the multiline text box:
   - Press Enter and add the text **Please add your suggestions here:**.
   - Insert a Textarea field with the ID **suggestion**. Use the *Wrap with label tag* option.
   - Specify a width of 50 characters and 5 lines.
   - Insert a line break after the text to move the field to a new line below the label.
9. Insert a Submit button:
   - Move to a new paragraph and insert a Button field.
   - Specify *No label tag* and make no changes to the button's properties.
10. Save your changes to this page and preview it in a browser. Your form should look similar to Illustration A.
11. Enter sample data in the form to make sure the fields are large enough for a typical entry. You do not have to click the Submit button when testing.
12. Close the browser and all open pages and exit Dreamweaver.

Illustration A

ON YOUR OWN

1. Start Dreamweaver and open the yardart site.

2. Create a new page based on the yardart.dwt template and name it mailing.html. Add the page title **Mailing List**.

3. Detach the page from the template, and drag the navigation bar from the Library to the top of the page.

4. Add an appropriate heading. Below the heading, insert text explaining the form and add a link to the contact.html page.

5. Insert an accessible form on the mailing.html page. Use your judgment about what information to gather with this form, but you should use as many of the form field types that you learned about in this exercise as you can.

   - Be sure to name each field and supply labels and values as needed.

   - Add a Submit and a Reset button to the form.

6. On contact.html, add a sentence after the contact list that gives site visitors a chance to sign up for the mailing list. Be sure to add the link to the mailing.html page.

7. Close all open pages and exit Dreamweaver.

Exercise | 36

Summary Exercise

Application Skills In this exercise, you will import tabular data to create a calendar for the Tierra Verde Summer Camp site.

DIRECTIONS

1. Start Dreamweaver and open the tierraverde site.
2. Open beachtime.html. Detach the page from the template if necessary.
3. Delete the *Text in progress* placeholder and import the Word text in the ⊙ beachtext.doc file from the Lesson 4 Data folder. Modify the page as necessary after importing by adjusting paragraph tags, formatting the list as bullets, and applying a new font or format if necessary.
4. On a blank line below the new information, import the tabular data in ⊙ calendar.txt from the Lesson 4 Data folder. Set the table width to 700 pixels.
5. Modify the table as follows:
   - Format the month name as Heading 1.
   - Change the font of the table data if necessary to match the font on the page.
   - Merge all cells in the first row.
   - Boldface and center the day headings.
   - Boldface and right align the day numbers.
   - Merge cells vertically to create the calendar blocks, so that there are no borders between the dates and the cell or cells below. You can use Illustration A on the next page as a guide to how to merge cells in the table. (Check this illustration carefully; for the first week of June you merge two rows, and for the remaining weeks you merge three rows.)
   - Use Top vertical alignment for all cells that have dates.
6. Break lines in the events, if desired, to reduce the size of some columns.
7. Format the text of the events as desired.
8. Format the table cells and borders as desired.
9. Preview the table in the browser. Make any necessary changes to the table layout.
10. Close all open pages and exit Dreamweaver.

Illustration A

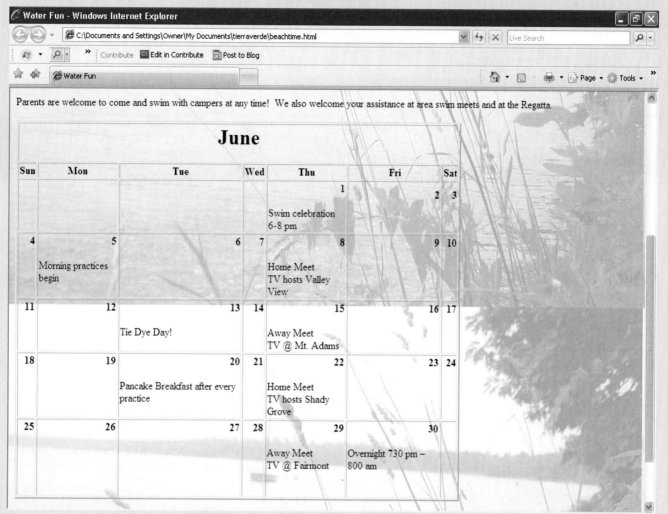

Application Exercise

Application Skills In this exercise, you will add an interest inventory form to the Classmate Connections site.

DIRECTIONS

1. Start Dreamweaver and open the classmate_connections Web site.

2. Open addme.html. Below the last paragraph on this page, insert a new heading that says **Interest Inventory**.

3. Below the heading, type the following text:

    Let us know what your interests are by filling out this form. We'll use the information to match you with others who share your interests.

4. Create a new page based on the classmate_connections template and name it inventory.html. Detach the new page from the template.

5. Type **Interest Inventory** at the top of the page, and insert the following text:

    Please fill out this form and click Submit to share your information.

6. Insert a form and add the following fields. Create an accessible form that uses <label> tags. Be sure to name each field appropriately:

    ■ A text field named First Name (first_name, character width 25, maximum 35).

    ■ A list field named Class (add the values Period 1, Period 3, Period 6).

    ■ A series of checkbox fields with the text Choose your interests (click all that apply): preceding the checkbox fields. Add checkboxes for Movies, Music, Technology, Photography, Books, Crafts, Performance Arts, Sports, and Other.

    ■ Add a Submit button.

7. Preview the form in the browser to make sure all fields work correctly.

8. On the Add Me page, create a link from the text *filling out this form* to the form page.

9. Create a confirmation page that will open when the form is submitted, and set the Action on the form page to display the confirmation page (type the name of the confirmation page in the form's Action box).

10. Preview the home page, test the link to the form page, and submit a form to test the confirmation page.

11. Save and close all open pages.

12. Exit Dreamweaver.

Exercise | 38

Curriculum Integration

Application Skills For your American History class, you have been assigned the task of creating a Web page that shows how many Americans have died in various wars throughout American history. To present your research, you will create a Web page, format it using a layout table, and insert your findings in tabular form within one of the layout cells. Before you begin this project, locate:

- A Web site that gives information on deaths in all the wars in which Americans participated

- A historic war picture you can use to illustrate the site

DIRECTIONS

Create a new site with an appropriate name. Create a new HTML page and save it in the site with the name warcasualties.html.

Create a layout table to organize the page layout. You may want to review some of the Starter pages for ideas on how to lay out the page and use color blocks for effect.

Insert an appropriate page heading in a layout cell. Create a cell to hold the data on war deaths. Within this cell, create a table to organize the data you found. Use your judgment on what data to present. You may want to include the number of service personnel who participated in the war and the number of nonfatal casualties as well as deaths. It might be interesting to determine what percentage of the total number of service members were killed in battle in each war. You may also wish to sort the table to show which wars were the costliest in terms of American lives lost.

Format the table as desired to make the data attractive and easy to understand.

Draw a layout cell above or below the table to explain the data in the table.

Draw a layout cell somewhere in the layout table to hold the war image you located. Below the image, draw another layout cell to hold a caption for the picture.

Save the page and view it in the browser.

Close the page and exit Dreamweaver.

Exercise | 39

Critical Thinking

Application Skills In this exercise, you continue to work on your personal Web site. Add a form to the Web site to gather information from visitors.

DIRECTIONS

■ Open your personal Web site and display the home page.

■ Add text somewhere on the page to give visitors the chance to complete a survey form related to the site's subject. For example, you may survey club members on activities they would like to engage in or create a mailing list form for new members.

■ Create a new page, if desired, to contain the form. (Modify navigation bar or links as necessary to accommodate the new page.) Use a layout table if desired to organize the page content. Insert an appropriate heading and text indicating any special instructions needed to fill out the form.

■ Add a form to the page. You can choose to create an accessible form if desired. Use as many different types of form fields as you can. Name each field appropriately and supply the necessary labels and values.

■ Test the form in the browser to make sure all fields are working correctly.

■ Close all open pages and exit Dreamweaver.

Lesson | 5

Work with AP Elements, Frames, and Styles

Skills Covered

■ About AP Elements

■ Create AP Elements

■ Size and Position AP Elements

■ Use the AP Elements Panel

■ Name AP Elements

■ Add Content to AP Divs

Software Skills AP elements make it possible for Web designers to create overlapping or perfectly aligned images, text boxes, and other objects. Newer browsers support AP elements, giving designers an alternative to using tables to lay out a Web page.

Design Skills AP elements not only enhance the appearance of a Web site, they also enhance its functionality, directing the visitor's eye to important content, links, images, and so on. Knowing how to use AP elements gives you as a designer further control over the appearance and placement of items on the pages you design.

Application Skills In this exercise, you reconfigure one of the Web pages in the GardenScape site by using AP elements to give the page more visual interest.

TERMS

Anchor point An invisible object that marks the location where an element has been inserted.

AP div An absolutely positioned <div> tag that controls a block of content on a page.

AP element An AP (absolutely positioned) element is a page element that has been assigned an absolute or fixed position on a page.

NOTES

About AP Elements

- An **AP element** is any HTML element on a Web page that has been positioned absolutely; that is, it has been assigned specific coordinates on the page. The element will appear at that precise spot on the page no matter which browser is used to view it.

- The most commonly used AP element is the **AP div**, an HTML element that controls a block of Web page content, but any HTML element can be an AP element. An absolutely positioned image, for example, is an AP element.

  ✓ *AP divs are called* layers *in previous versions of Dreamweaver.*

- AP divs can contain text, graphics, multimedia objects such as sounds, and even other AP divs. You can overlap them for creative layouts (see the following illustration) or convert them to a table.

Portion of Web page containing AP elements

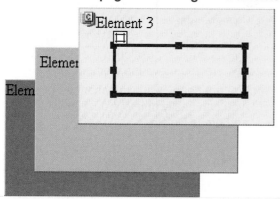

- One advantage of using AP elements is that, because they can be positioned precisely on a Web page, your creative design will look the same on any browser that supports AP elements.

  ✓ *AP elements require Netscape 4.0 or Internet Explorer 4.0 and higher.*

- One disadvantage of using AP elements is that if they aren't specifically supported by a browser, their position and display could be undependable. If you plan to use AP elements extensively in a Web site, test them rigorously in your target browsers to make sure that the AP elements and their contents display the way you want them to.

  ✓ *The CSS coding used to fine-tune AP elements so they display correctly in all browsers can be complex. You will learn more about CSS coding in this lesson; you can also find information about both CSS coding and working with AP elements by searching online.*

Create AP Elements

- AP elements fall into two general categories: HTML objects such as graphics or tables that you want to position absolutely, and AP divs.

- Different methods are used for creating these two types of AP elements.

Position Any Object Absolutely

- To position any object absolutely, you must create a CSS (cascading style sheet) rule that specifies the type of positioning and the page coordinates for the object.

- Create the rule in the CSS Rule dialog box, as shown in the following illustration. The Positioning category in this dialog box allows you to specify absolute positioning and indicate where the object will be positioned on the page.

CSS Rule dialog box

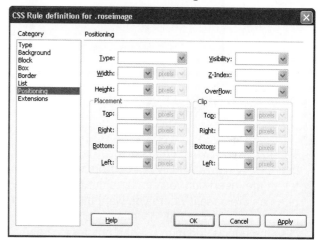

- You will learn how to create new CSS rules in Exercise 44.

Insert AP Divs

- You can insert an AP div on a Web page using any of three methods:
  - Insert an AP div using a menu command.
  - Drag an AP div from the Layout tab of the Insert bar.
  - Draw an AP div using the Draw AP Div button from the Layout tab of the Insert bar.

- To use a menu command to insert an AP div, place the insertion point where you want the element and use the Insert>Layout Objects>AP Div command.

  ✔ *You don't have to place the element exactly where you want it, because you can drag the AP div to any point on the page you want it to appear.*

- Dreamweaver inserts a default-sized AP div at the position of the insertion point, as well as an AP element 🖺 **anchor point** to show where the element was inserted (see the following illustration).

  ✔ *If you don't see an anchor point when you create an AP div, choose the Edit>Preferences menu command and make sure that Anchor points for AP elements is checked on the Invisible Elements page.*

New AP div on Web page

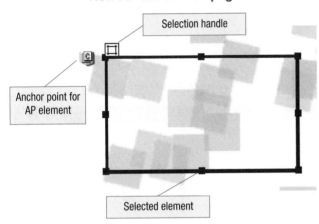

Selection handle

Anchor point for AP element

Selected element

- The remaining two methods of inserting an AP div use the 🖺 Draw AP Div button from the Layout tab of the Insert bar. You can drag the button to the page and release it where you want the element to insert a default-sized AP div element. Or, you can click the button and then use the pointer to draw the element the desired size.

  ✔ *As when drawing a layout cell, you can see the measurements as you draw an AP div by looking near the right side of the status bar.*

Size and Position AP Elements

- You can easily adjust the size and location of an element by dragging. Or, you can use the Property inspector to size and position an element precisely using pixel measurements and coordinates.

- Before you can change the size or location of an element, you must select it. Select an AP element by clicking its anchor point, selection handle, or outside border.

Drag to Resize or Relocate

- The easiest way to resize an AP element is to click one of the handles on its selected border and drag in the direction you want to resize. This method may not be suitable, however, for AP elements that are absolutely positioned graphics, because it resizes the graphic as well.

- You can also use dragging to move AP elements to new positions after they have been inserted. Drag the selection handle or click on the outside border of the element and drag with the four-headed arrow pointer.

- Dreamweaver places a <div> tag at the location where you insert an AP element. This tag will remain in its original position in the HTML code no matter where you move the element.

- If you are not happy with your changes to an element, you can easily delete it. Just select the element and press Delete.

Size and Position AP Elements Precisely

- To size or position an element precisely, use the Property inspector. You can use the Property inspector to set width and height measurements and coordinates for the top-left corner of the element (see the following illustration).

Use Property inspector to size or position precisely

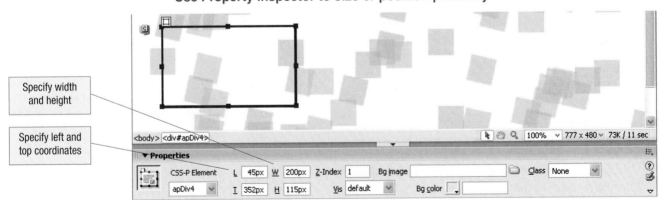

Specify width and height

Specify left and top coordinates

- The L (Left) coordinate measures the distance from the left edge of the page. The T (Top) coordinate measures the distance from the top of the page. Using these positioning coordinates ensures that an element will appear at the same location in any browser.

- Measurements are in pixels (px) by default. You can also use percentages for size measurements or picas (pc), points (pt), inches (in), millimeters (mm), centimeters (cm), or percentages (%) for the positioning coordinates by using the common symbol or abbreviation for each measurement.

- Your ability to reposition AP elements freely will depend on whether you have enabled overlap. You can control overlap in the AP Elements panel.

  ✔ *You will learn more about overlap in the next exercise.*

Use the AP Elements Panel

- After you have inserted multiple AP elements on a page, you can use the AP Elements panel—a panel in the CSS panel group—to work with the AP elements on your workspace. Launch this panel using the Window>AP Elements menu command.

- The AP Elements panel (see the following illustration) shows the names of all AP elements on the page and the order in which they are stacked (the Z column). Note from the illustration that this panel shows not only AP divs but other objects that you have positioned absolutely.

  ✔ *When you create your first few AP elements, their Z numbers reflect the order in which the AP elements were created. As you change the stacking order, the Z number reflects an element's position in the stack.*

AP Elements panel and AP elements

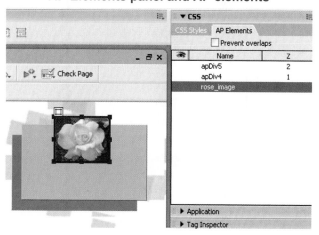

- The AP Elements panel changes as you work with AP elements. When you *activate* an element by clicking anywhere inside it, the element's name is boldfaced in the AP Elements panel. An active AP div is ready for you to enter text or an image and has an insertion point at the left side.

- When you select an element, the element name is highlighted with a color band in the AP Elements panel. You can select an element by clicking its name in the AP Elements panel. This feature is helpful when your page contains many overlapping AP elements.

- Selected elements display a heavy border with sizing handles. The border color adjusts according to any background color you have added to the element to create a contrast.

- As you learned earlier, CSS rules are required to position objects absolutely. For this reason, AP elements display not only in the AP Elements panel but also in the CSS Styles panel, as shown in the following illustration.

  ✔ *At the top of the CSS Styles panel, you see two buttons. Click All if necessary to see the AP elements on the current page. So display the elements in the current page that have been styled using CSS elements, click Current.*

AP elements display in the CSS Styles panel

- If you need to modify settings for an AP element, you can do so in this panel in the same way you modify CSS styles.

Name AP Elements

■ When you have a number of AP elements on a page, you can help yourself remember what each one contains by naming the elements.

■ Name an element by typing a name in the CSS-P Element text box on the Property inspector. As you create names, they appear in the AP Elements panel (see the illustration at the bottom of this page).

✔ *You can also double-click on the name of the element in the AP Elements panel and change the name there, or right-click the selection handle or anchor point of a selected element, choose ID, and then type the element name in the Change Attribute dialog box.*

Add Content to AP Divs

■ AP divs can contain any type of HTML content that you can insert on a Web page. Besides adding text or images, you can format an AP div with a background color or image.

Insert Text

■ To insert text in an AP div, click inside the AP div to activate it and begin typing at the insertion point. The AP div behaves very much like a text box in a word processing application. For example, as you resize the AP div, the text wraps to conform to the new shape.

■ When you first click in a new AP div to add text or other content, the insertion point will be the same size as the AP div's height and the current format will be listed as None. You can simply begin typing to enter unformatted text, or change the format in the Property inspector to Paragraph or a heading format.

■ You can also insert text in an AP div by cutting or copying it from another location and then pasting it in the AP div. After inserting and formatting the text, you can resize the AP div to fit neatly around the text (see the following illustration).

Enter text in an AP div by typing

* Tea roses * Shrub roses *
Climbing roses * Teacup roses *
Container roses * Fragrant roses
* Award-winning roses * More
roses than you've ever seen in
one place! * Healthy roses *

■ Notice in the previous illustration that text begins in the upper-left corner of the AP div, with no padding between the edges of the AP div and the text. This can make text in an AP div look somewhat crowded if the AP div has a background color.

Name each element

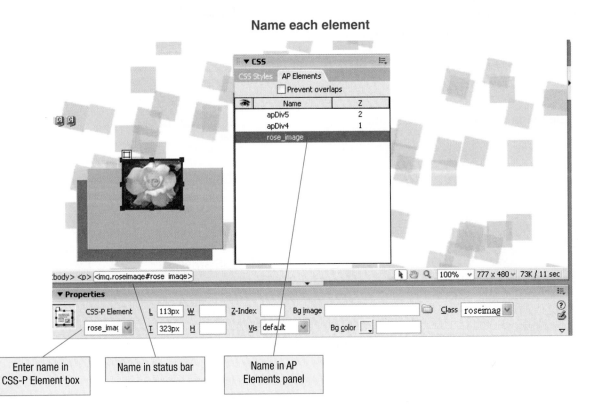

Enter name in CSS-P Element box

Name in status bar

Name in AP Elements panel

■ You can improve the look of text in an element by adding padding, just as you do in a table. To add padding to the top, left, right, or bottom of an element, you must use CSS rules. You will learn how to add padding to AP elements in a later exercise.

Insert Images

■ Inserting an image in an AP div is no different from inserting it on any Web page. Activate the AP div by clicking in it and then use the Insert>Image command or the ▣▾ Image button from the Common tab of the Insert bar to insert the image.

■ An image in an element may be formatted just like any image on a Web page (see the following illustration). You can resize the image, change its alignment, add a border to it, and so on.

Insert image in AP div

Add Background Color or Image

■ Using the Property inspector, you can add color and background images to an AP div to provide contrast with the background of the Web document.

■ You must select an AP div to display properties for background color or image in the Property inspector.

■ Use the ▣▾ Bg color button to display the familiar palette of background colors. Use the Bg image box to type the name of the image to use, or click the Browse for File button to navigate to the background image file.

PROCEDURES

Insert AP divs

1. Position the cursor where you want the AP div to appear.
2. Click **Insert** .... `Alt`+`I`
3. Point to **Layout Objects** .... `Y`
4. Click **AP Div** .... `A`, `Enter`

   OR

   ■ Drag the **Draw AP Div** button 📰 from the Layout tab of the Insert bar to the Document window and release the mouse button.

   OR

1. Click the **Draw AP Div** button 📰 on the Layout tab of the Insert bar.
2. Draw the AP div at the size and location you want.

   ✔ *Check the size as you draw near the right side of the status bar.*

Select an AP Element

■ Click the AP element anchor point 📟 .

■ Click an element selection handle.

■ Click the outside border of the element.

Drag to Resize or Relocate

To resize an element:

1. Select the element.
2. Click a square handle on any side of the selected element and drag in the direction you want to resize it.

To move an element:

1. Select the element.
2. Click a selection handle or the outside border.
3. Drag the element to new location.

Size and Position AP Elements Precisely

To resize precisely:

1. Select the element.
2. Type the exact width in the **W** text box in the Property inspector.
3. Type the exact height in the **H** text box in the Property inspector.

To position precisely:

1. Select the element.
2. Type the measurement from the left edge of the page in the **L** text box in the Property inspector.
3. Type the measurement from the top of the page in the **T** text box in the Property inspector.

Display AP Elements Panel (F2)

1. Click **Window** .... Alt + W
2. Click **AP Elements** L

Name AP Elements

In the AP Elements panel:

1. Double-click the element name.
2. Type the new name.

In the Property inspector:

1. Select the default name in the **CSS-P Element** box.
2. Type the new name.

In the Document window:

1. Right-click the element's selection handle or the anchor point.
2. Click **ID** in the shortcut menu to open the Change Attribute dialog box.
3. Type a new name in the **Id** text box.
4. Click **OK**.

Insert Text in AP Div

1. Activate the AP div by clicking inside the AP div.
2. Begin typing at the insertion point.

   OR

   ■ Paste the cut or copied text at the insertion point.

Insert Images (Ctrl + Alt + I)

1. Activate the AP div by clicking inside the AP div.
2. Click **Insert** .... Alt + I
3. Click **Image** I

   OR

   ■ Click the **Image** button 🖼▾ from the Common tab of the Insert bar.

In Select Image Source dialog box:

4. Navigate to the location of the image, select it, and save it in the current Web site.
5. Create alternate text if desired.

In Dreamweaver:

   ■ Format the image as you would on any Web page.

Add Background Color or Image

To insert a background image:

1. Select the AP div.
2. Click in the **Bg image** box on the Property inspector and type the path to the image.

   OR

   ■ Click the **Browse for File** button 📁 in the Property inspector and navigate to the image.

To add a background color:

1. Select the AP div.
2. Click the **Bg color** button and select a color from the palette.

   OR

   ■ Type a hexadecimal value for the color in the **Bg color** text box.

EXERCISE DIRECTIONS

1. Start Dreamweaver and open the gardenscape site.
2. Open 💿 projects.html and save it to the site root of the current site.

   ✔ In this exercise, you will create and format AP divs to hold the page's text paragraphs. You will complete the layout in the next exercise.

3. Click to the left of the first text paragraph on the page.
4. Use the Insert menu to insert a new AP div. Name this AP div **intro**.
5. Select the first paragraph on the page and cut it by right-clicking and selecting the Cut command from the shortcut menu.
6. Activate the intro Intro AP div and paste the cut text into the AP div. Set the format to None if necessary to remove the automatic space above the paragraph.

7. Resize the element to be 600px wide and 70px high.

   ✔ You do not have to be exact about the size and width. You will set the sizes precisely later in the exercise.

8. Draw a second AP div below the intro AP div, making it about 250 pixels wide and 100 pixels high. Name this AP div project1.
9. Move the AP div so that the left edge of the AP div begins in the center of the page.
10. Add a background color to this AP div using #99CCCC.
11. Draw a third AP div about 250 pixels wide below the intro AP div and aligned with the bottom of the project1 AP div; position it so the right edge of the div aligns with the center of the page. Name this AP div **project2**.
12. Apply a background color of #669966 to the AP div.

13. Draw a fourth AP div below the project2 AP div and name it **project3**.

14. Apply a background color of #669999 to the AP div.

15. Draw a final AP div below the project3 AP div and name it **link**. Apply the background color #99CC99 and center it on the page.

16. Make the following adjustments to size and position in pixels:

    ◼ For the intro AP div, set Left to 9px and Top to 295px.

    ✔ Note that the AP div will be positioned different depending on whether you enter **px** after the value or not. To ensure that the elements are positioned consistently, be consistent in specifying (or not using) the px measurement.

    ◼ For the project1 AP div, set Left to 350px and Top to 390px. Set Width to 400px and Height to 115px.

    ◼ For the project2 AP div, set Left to 15px and Top to 515px. Set Width to 400px and Height to 115px.

    ◼ For the project3 AP div, set Left to 390px and Top to 640px. Set Width to 400px and Height to 115px.

    ◼ For the link AP div, set Left to 175px and Top to 779px. Set Width to 450px and Height to 51px.

17. Save the page and preview it in the browser. The top of the page should look similar to Illustration A. For now, don't worry about the overlapping text. This page obviously still needs some work; in Exercise 40, you will move the existing text into the AP divs and finalize the layout.

18. Close the browser and any open pages.

19. Exit Dreamweaver.

Illustration A

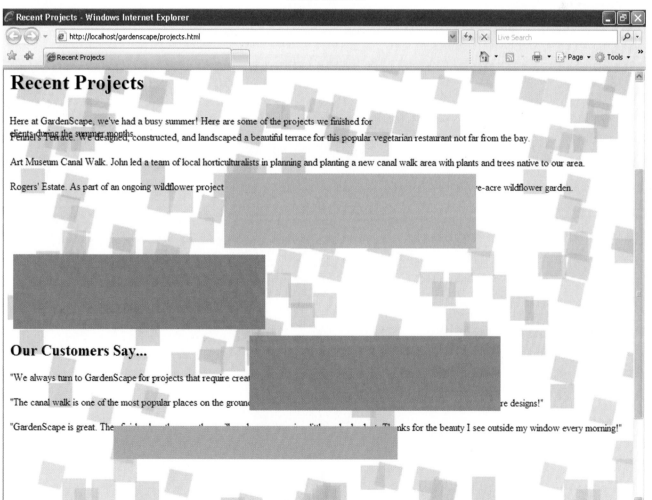

ON YOUR OWN

1. Start Dreamweaver and create a new Web page for a subject of your choice.

2. Practice creating AP divs on the page, using the three methods of inserting AP divs.

3. Position the AP divs by dragging to create a pleasing layout.

4. Add content to the AP divs. Try typing text, pasting text, and inserting both background and other images.

5. Modify some AP divs with background colors.

6. Save the Web page in your solutions folder with a name such as elementpractice.html.

7. Close all open pages and exit Dreamweaver.

Skills Covered

- Manipulate AP Divs
- Control AP Element Visibility
- Advanced AP Element Properties
- Convert AP Divs to Tables

Software Skills You can work with AP divs to adjust or modify the layout of your Web pages. You can change the order of the AP elements and place AP divs within other AP divs to organize content. You can also hide and display AP elements as needed using the AP Elements panel.

Design Skills Learning how to manage the AP divs on your page gives you further control over the display and organization of your page content.

Application Skills In this exercise, you add content to AP divs, adjust visibility to make it easier to add content, and change the order of the AP divs to finalize the layout.

TERMS

Child AP div The nested AP div.

Parent AP div The AP div in which you insert a nested AP div.

Stacking order The order in which AP elements are added to a page. The lowest number is at the bottom of the stack.

Z-index The numbering sequence of the stacking order of AP elements on a page.

Manipulate AP Divs

■ You can work with multiple AP divs on a page to create special effects. For example, you can insert AP divs within AP divs to hold related content or images. Before you begin manipulating AP divs, you need to decide whether you want your AP elements to overlap on the page.

Set Overlap Options

■ By default, Dreamweaver allows you to overlap AP divs. This means that you can drag one AP element on top of another or partially obscure one AP element with another.

■ For some layouts, you will want to prevent AP elements from overlapping. For example, when text in one AP div describes images in another AP element, you will want to make sure the AP elements don't overlap.

■ You control AP element overlap in the AP Elements panel. If you click the Prevent Overlaps checkbox, the AP elements will not be allowed to overlap.

Change Stacking Order

■ When you overlap AP elements, you may need to adjust the **stacking order**. AP elements are stacked on a page in the order they are created, from the first AP div (designated by default as apDiv1) on the bottom to subsequent AP divs on top (see the following illustration).

Stacked AP divs on a page

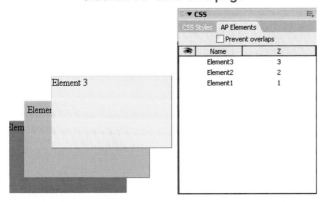

■ The stacking order is also called the **Z-index**. The bottommost AP element is given a Z-index number of 1, and subsequent AP elements receive incrementally higher numbers. To change the stacking order of an AP element, you change its Z-index number.

✔ It is possible to assign the same Z-index number to more than one AP element.

■ You can change an AP element's Z-index number by clicking it in the Z column of the AP Elements panel and typing a new number. Or, type a new stacking order number in the Z-Index box on the Property inspector.

■ You can also change stacking order by selecting an AP element name in the AP Elements panel and dragging it to the desired level in the AP Elements panel's stack.

Nest AP Divs

■ Just as it sounds, a *nested* AP div is an AP div inserted inside an existing AP div. The same methods you use to insert an AP div on a Web page can be used to insert an AP div in another AP div.

✔ If you draw the AP div with the Draw AP Div button crosshair, you must press Alt to nest the new AP div if nesting is turned off in AP Elements preferences in the Preferences dialog box.

■ The AP div in which you insert a nested AP div is called the **parent AP div**. The nested AP div is called the **child AP div**. The child AP div's anchor point appears within the parent AP div, and the child AP div is indented underneath the parent AP div in the AP Elements panel (see the following illustration).

Nested AP div created in Element3

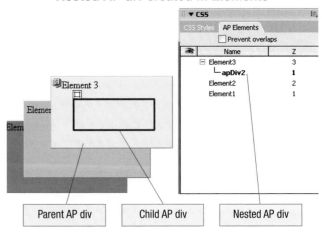

| Parent AP div | Child AP div | Nested AP div |

■ Even though it is created within a parent AP div, the child AP div does not have to remain within the parent AP div. It can be moved outside of the nested AP div without ceasing to be a nested AP div.

■ Click the minus sign next to a parent AP div in the AP Elements panel to hide child AP divs. Click a plus sign to display child AP divs.

- You can click on the nested AP div's name in the AP Elements panel and drag it out of the parent AP div to break the nested relationship.

- To create or restore nesting in the AP Elements panel, press Ctrl and then drag the AP div's name over the name of the desired parent AP div. When the parent AP div is outlined—selected—release the mouse button to create the nesting relationship.

- Nested AP divs can be stacked in the AP Elements panel just like other AP divs. A nested AP div can even be nested within another nested AP div.

- You can also nest or restore nesting in the Document window by clicking the AP div's anchor point and then dragging it inside the target parent AP div, releasing the mouse button when the anchor is in the desired position. The nested AP div—or its anchor—can be dragged into its final position as desired.

- A child AP div inherits certain properties of the parent AP div, such as the visibility setting (see the next section for more information on visibility).

Control AP Element Visibility

- Making an AP element invisible helps you work on one AP element at a time.

- Controlling visibility also allows you to set up sophisticated interactive effects in which elements switch or display and disappear as a result of a visitor's actions.

    ✔ *You use behaviors to create effects like these. You learn about behaviors in Lesson 6.*

- You can control AP element visibility from the AP Elements panel or the Property inspector.

- To hide an AP element in the AP Elements panel, click to the left of the AP element's name. This displays the closed eye icon 👁. When the eye is closed, the AP element is hidden (see the following illustration).

Element2 and the child AP div are hidden

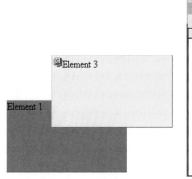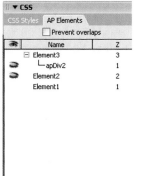

- Note in the previous illustration that Element2 and the child AP div inserted within Element3 are hidden.

- Click the closed eye icon 👁 next to the AP element to show a hidden AP element. The closed eye icon changes to an open eye icon 👁.

    ✔ *To hide or show all AP elements at the same time, click the eye column heading until the desired view is achieved. To reset to the blank default mode, click on the individual eye icon until it is removed.*

- Using the Property inspector gives you greater control over visibility settings for nested AP divs. Select an AP div and click the Vis list arrow on the Property inspector to see a list of visibility attributes.

    - Select *hidden* to make the AP div and its contents invisible.

    - Select *visible* to make the AP div and its contents visible.

    - Select *inherit* to determine the AP div's visibility based on the parent AP div's visibility setting.

    - The *default* setting typically provides the same attributes as the *inherit* setting.

- Using the Vis list, you can set a child AP div's visibility to differ from that of its parent. For example, you can make the child AP div visible while the parent AP div is hidden.

    ✔ *You can also change the visibility of a child AP div in the AP Elements panel.*

Advanced AP Element Properties

- With an AP element selected, click on the expansion arrow of the Property inspector to see advanced settings that control the appearance and functionality of AP divs in different browsers (see the illustration at the top of the next page).

- The Overflow property controls an AP div's behavior when the AP div's content is larger than its size. Choose from the following options:

    - Select *visible* to increase the AP div's size so that all content is visible. The AP div expands down to contain all text or images.

    - Select *hidden* to maintain the AP div's size and crop any content that does not fit. No scroll bars are provided.

    - Select *scroll* to add scroll bars to the AP div regardless of whether the contents exceed the AP div's size.

    - Select *auto* to make scroll bars appear only when the AP div's content exceeds its boundaries.

        ✔ *Scroll and auto settings do not display in the Document window. You must preview the AP div in a browser to see the scroll bars.*

Advanced AP element properties

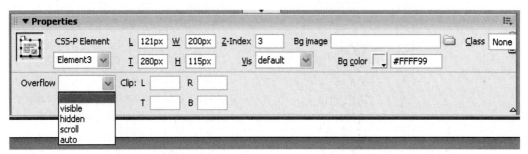

- Use the Clip settings to control the size of AP element content by specifying in pixels (or another measurement system) how much content to remove from each side of the AP div. This is useful when an image is too large for an AP div. You can crop parts of an image that do not contribute to your page.

Convert AP Divs to Tables

- Pre-version 4 browsers do not support AP elements. However, Dreamweaver offers an option to convert an AP div layout to a table so that the page can be viewed by any browser version.

  ✔ *Before converting an AP div layout to a table, you must unnest nested AP divs and make sure AP divs do not overlap.*

- To convert AP divs to a table, use the Modify>Convert>AP Divs to Table command.

- The Convert AP Divs to Table dialog box (see the following illustration) gives you a number of options for the conversion.

Convert AP Divs to Table dialog box

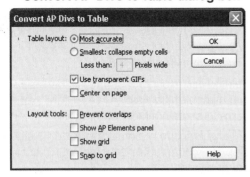

✔ *Most accurate creates a table cell for every AP div. Additional table cells are created to replace the original spacing between AP divs.*

- *Smallest: collapse empty cells* specifies that the AP divs' edges should be aligned if they are positioned within the number of pixels entered in Pixels wide box. This option results in a table with fewer empty rows and columns.

- *Use transparent GIFs* fills the table's last row with transparent GIFs. This allows for tables that are consistent in appearance from browser to browser.

  ✔ *Transparent GIFs are invisible GIF images used to adjust layout.*

- *Center on page* automatically centers the new table in the page.

- The resulting table layout may still need some work to merge cells and reposition content (see the following illustration), but this option is faster than recreating a layout.

AP divs converted to a table

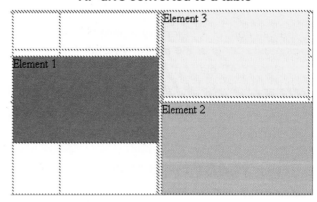

- It is also possible to convert a table to AP divs. In this process, each cell becomes an AP div.

238

PROCEDURES

Set Overlap Options

1. Display the AP Elements panel.
2. Select the **Prevent overlaps** checkbox to prevent overlap.

   OR

   Clear the **Prevent overlaps** checkbox to allow overlap.

Change Stacking Order

In the AP Elements panel:

- Click the **Z-index** number and type the new number.
- Select the AP element name and drag it to a new position in name list.

In the Property inspector:

- Select the **Z-Index** number, type a new number, and press [Enter] or click in the Document window.

Nest AP Divs

1. Select the AP div that will become the parent element.
2. Insert the child AP div by clicking the AP div in which you want to nest the child AP div; then choose Insert>Layout Objects>Ap Div.

   ✔ If you have trouble creating the nested div, choose Edit>Preferences to display the Preference dialog box and click the AP Elements category. Make sure the Nest when created within an AP div option is selected.

3. Format the nested AP div as you would any other element.

Change Visibility

To hide AP element:

1. Select the AP div you want to hide.
2. Click to the left of the AP div name in the AP Elements panel to display the ☞ icon.

   OR

   Click **Vis** list arrow in the Property inspector and select **hidden**.

To show a hidden AP element:

- Click the ☞ icon in the AP Elements panel.

   OR

- Click the **Vis** list arrow in the Property inspector and select **visible**.

To give a child AP div a parent AP div's visibility setting:

- Click the **Vis** list arrow in the Property inspector and select **inherit**.

Convert AP Divs to Table

1. Reorganize any nested AP divs and adjust AP divs to prevent overlap.
2. Click **Modify**.................[Alt]+[M]
3. Click **Convert**.......................[C]
4. Click **AP Divs to Table** ....[A]
5. Select the options for the table.
6. Click [OK].

EXERCISE DIRECTIONS

1. Start Dreamweaver and open the gardenscape site.
2. Open projects.html.
3. Display the AP Elements panel and clear the Prevent overlaps checkbox if necessary.
4. Hide all AP divs except project1.
5. Select and cut the first project paragraph.
6. Paste the cut text into the project1 AP div. Select the None format to remove the automatic space above the paragraph in this and all other AP divs.
7. Cut the client information for the Art Museum Canal Walk. Make the project2 AP div visible and paste the text into this AP div.
8. Cut the text for Rogers' Estate. Hide the project2 AP div and make the project3 AP div visible.
9. Paste this text into the project3 AP div.
10. Make all AP divs visible.

11. Select the intro AP div and set a background color of #99CC99.
12. Add the "stripe" AP div down the center of the page as follows:
    - Clear the Prevent overlaps checkbox in the AP Elements panel.
    - Create a new AP div with a Left setting of 300px, a Top setting of 370px, a Width of 130px, and a Height of 443px. The AP div should overlap the left edge of the project1 AP div about one inch. (See Illustration A.)
    - Name the AP div **stripe** and add background color of #CCFFCC.
13. Change the stacking order so the stripe AP div has a Z-index number of 1.
14. Create a nested AP div within the link AP div, position it on the left side of the div, and name the child AP div **rose**.

15. Insert the rose.jpg image from the images folder in the rose AP div, adding the alternate text **Contact us link**. Resize the picture to 80 by 68 pixels, and then resize the picture AP div to fit closely around the image.

16. Create another nested AP div within the link AP div to the right of the picture. Name the AP div **linktext**.

17. Type the following text in the linktext AP div:

   Click here to contact us about your next project!

18. Create a link from the "Click here" text AP div to contactus.html.

19. Increase the height of the link AP div to 71px.

20. Click to the left of the Our Customers Say heading and press Enter three or four times to create more space below the link AP div.

21. Save your changes and preview the page in the browser. Your page should look similar to Illustration A. If the AP divs do not automatically expand in the browser to fit the text, you can delete the Height measurement for each AP div in the Property inspector to allow the AP div to expand in your browser.

   ✔ Note that the text is too close to the edges of the AP divs. You will find out how to fine-tune text position in an AP div when you learn about style sheets in Exercises 42 and 43.

22. Close any open pages and the browser and exit Dreamweaver.

Illustration A

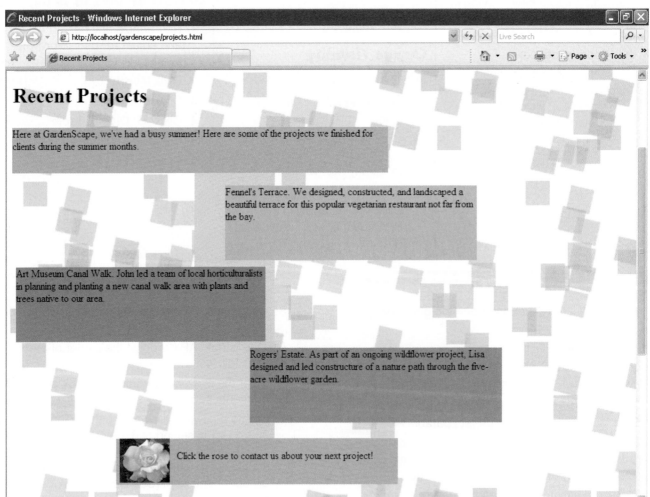

ON YOUR OWN

1. Start Dreamweaver and open the practice page you created in the last On Your Own exercise.

2. Reposition AP divs as desired to overlap, or add an AP div such as the unifying stripe in the previous Exercise Directions.

3. Change stacking order to display all AP divs attractively.

4. Create at least one nested AP div.

5. Practice with the visibility and overflow settings. (Remember, you can view scroll settings only in the browser.)

6. Save your page and preview your page in the browser, and then make any final adjustments to the layout in Dreamweaver. Use the Property inspector to size and position AP divs absolutely.

7. If desired, convert your layout to a table. (You must make sure no AP divs overlap to use this feature.)

8. Save your page with a name such as elementpractice-2.html.

9. Close any open pages, and exit Dreamweaver.

Exercise | 42

Skills Covered

- About Frames Pages
- Create a Frameset
- Work with Frames
- Add Content to Frames

- Add Frame Borders
- Resize Frames
- Set Frame Target for Links

Software Skills A frames page enables you to display several Web pages at the same time in specified areas on the page. You can set up links in a page in one frame to open pages in another frame or create many other kinds of layouts and uses for frames. Dreamweaver's tools make frames page building easy. You only need to plan the layout and choose the content.

Design Skills Knowing how to design and work with frames pages is a valuable part of a designer's skill set. You may not use frames in many of the designs you create, but it's helpful to know how to incorporate content from different pages onto a single page when the need arises.

Application Skills In this exercise, you turn an existing page into a frames page. You will learn how to create a frameset and add and name frames for the page.

TERMS

Frame A container for Web page content that is displayed within a *frameset*.

Frameset A container for HTML frames.

Source The page you want to display in a particular frame.

NOTES

About Frames Pages

- The term *frames page* is used to describe a page that contains several **frames**. Frames are regions on an HTML page that contain a specific HTML page.
- In Dreamweaver, a frames page is known more properly as a **frameset**. The frameset has a name and a page title, but its only content is the frame definitions.
- Each frame in a frameset contains a page that has its own name and page title. Pages displayed in frames consist of text, images, and links just like any other Web page and can be formatted with backgrounds, styles, and other effects.

Create a Frameset

- You have several options for creating a new frameset:
  - Insert frames manually in a new or existing document to create a new frameset.
  - Use a page design from the Framesets category on the Dreamweaver Welcome Screen window to create a new frameset with frames in place.

Insert Frames Manually

- You have two options for inserting frames into a new or existing document:
  - Use the Insert>HTML>Frames command and select the frame(s) you want to insert.
  - Click the [   ] Frames button from the Layout tab of the Insert bar to display the list of frame options. Select one to insert.
- Both options allow you to insert a single frame, such as a left or top frame, or several frames at once, such as the Left and Nested Top Frames option, which inserts both a left and top frame designed to fit together.
- The Frames list on the Insert bar can be more helpful if your page already has some content. Existing content is represented by the blue area of the thumbnail, with new frames shown as white areas (see the following illustration).

Frames list offers basic and complex frame layouts

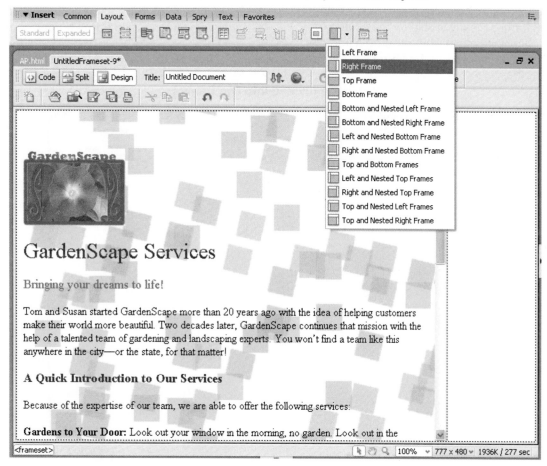

- If you have specified in the Preferences dialog box that you want to be prompted to enter accessibility information for frames, the Frame Tag Accessibility Attributes dialog box displays immediately after you select a new frame option for a page. Use this dialog box to set a title for each frame in the frameset (see the following illustration).

Frame Tag Accessibility Attributes dialog box

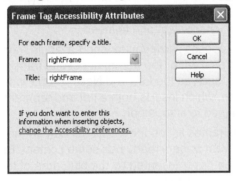

- Click the Frame list arrow to display each default frame name (such as mainFrame) and then type a meaningful title for the frame in the Title text box. The title attribute is used by a screen reader to identify each frame.

- When you insert a new frame in any page, Dreamweaver shows the new frames and any existing content in a new frameset, with the borders between frames clearly visible on the screen (see the following illustration). You can drag a frame's border to adjust the size of the frame.

- You can further divide a frame into additional frames using the Modify>Frameset menu command to display a submenu of split options.
  - Split Frame Left and Split Frame Right insert a border that divides the current frame in half vertically.
  - Split Frame Up and Split Frame Down insert a border that divides the current frame in half horizontally.

  ✓ *Create only two or three frames in a frameset. More than three frames can make the page look confusing.*

- The distinctions between these split directions are more relevant if a frame already contains content. The existing content always moves into the new frame, so choose the split type that will keep your content where you want it.

  ✓ *If you inadvertently choose the wrong split type, simply use the Edit>Undo command to reverse the split.*

Use a Frameset Page Design

- Another way to create a frameset is to use one of the page designs from the New Document or Welcome Screen's Frameset category. The New Document dialog box offers fifteen frameset choices similar to those listed on the Frames button's drop-down list.

- Selecting one of these page designs opens a new page with the specified frame borders in place.

New page divided into two frames

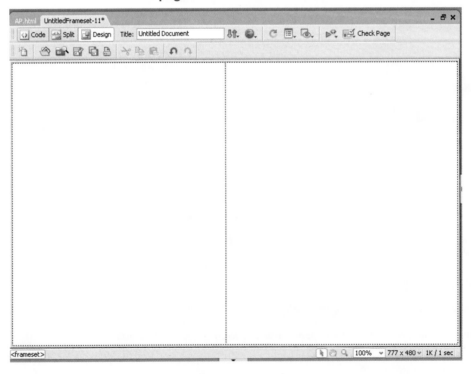

Work with Frames

- To work with frames, you need to know how to activate and select frames, name frames, and save frames and framesets.

Activate or Select a Frame

- Some operations, such as adding content, require the frame to be active. Other operations, such as changing frame properties, require the frame to be selected.

- To *activate* a frame, simply click in it to position the insertion point. When a frame is active, you can add and format content, save the frame's page, and apply page properties such as background color and a page title.

- To *select* a frame, hold down the Alt key and click in the frame. The frame's borders show a dotted outline to let you know the frame is selected (see the illustration at the bottom of this page).

- When you select a frame, the frame's properties—such as the frame's name, source, and border options—appear in the Property inspector.

- The distinction between activating and selecting is extremely important when you are working with frames. If you find you cannot perform a specific operation, check the Procedures section at the end of this exercise to determine whether you should activate or select a frame.

Name a Frame

- It's good practice to name the frames you create (or change the default names Dreamweaver supplies). Even if you have already supplied a title, you still need to provide a name for each frame. Name and title attributes serve different functions in the code.

- It is especially important to name frames if you want to link from one frame to another because you must specify the name of the frame in which the linked page will open.

- Name a frame using the Property inspector. Select the frame, click in the Frame name text box, and type the desired name. Name the frame something that reflects the content or function of the frame. A frame that holds a logo at the top of a page, for example, might be named **logo**.

rightFrame is selected

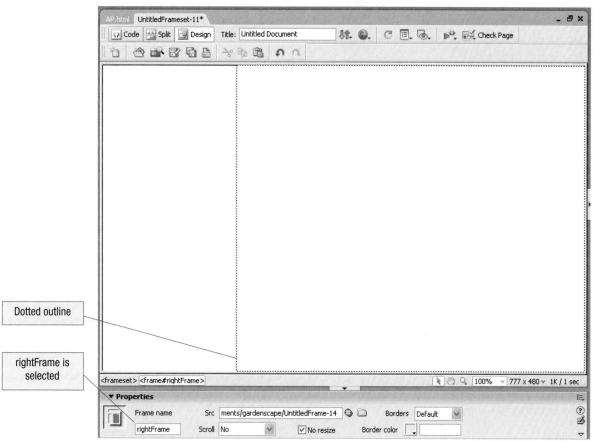

Save Framesets and Frames

- Saving a frameset and its frames pages can be confusing the first time you do it, because the frameset page itself and each frame's page must be named and titled separately.

- The easiest way to save the frameset is to use the File>Save Frameset menu command. This command saves only the frameset, not the frame pages within the frameset.

- After saving the frameset, be sure to give the frameset page a title in the Page Properties dialog box. If you choose the Modify>Page Properties command directly after saving the frameset, you can be certain the page title applies to the frameset, not one of its frames.

  ✔ You can also type a new page title in the Document toolbar's Title box.

- If you intend to create new content in a frame, you must also name and title the page in that frame. You can do so by clicking in the frame to activate it and choosing the File>Save Frame command.

- As you work with the frameset, use the File>Save Frameset command often to save changes to the frameset and its frames. You can also save changes to a specific frame by clicking to activate it and then pressing Ctrl + S.

  ✔ You can also save changes to all frames at once using the File>Save All command.

  ✔ Remember, if the page name within parentheses in the title bar shows an asterisk, changes have been made since the last save. This is your signal to save again.

Add Content to Frames

- You have two choices for adding content to a frame in a frameset:
  - You can simply begin typing in the frame to insert content in the frame, or you can paste text that has been copied or cut from another location.

    ✔ Remember, you must activate a frame before you can add content to it.

  - You can link the frame to an existing Web page. When the frameset is opened, that Web page appears in the frame.

- If you intend to link a frame to a Web page, you can make the process easier by creating that Web page before creating the frameset.

- As you begin to add content to frames, you will find the Frames panel useful as you work with the frames. The Frames panel (see the following illustration) shows the frame layout of the frameset and the names you have assigned each frame.

Frames panel

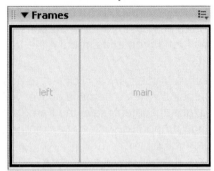

- You can quickly select any frame in the frameset by clicking the corresponding frame in the Frames panel. This operation can be faster than the Alt + click method of selecting a frame.

Set Frame Source

- If you want an existing Web page to open in a frame, you must specify that page as the frame's **source**. Specify a frame source in the Property inspector.

- Select the frame to link to a source and type the address of the source page in the Src text box on the Property inspector. You can also click the 🗀 Browse for File button and navigate to the source page.

  ✔ Or, click the 🌐 Point to File icon and drag it to the desired source page in the Files panel.

- Dreamweaver assumes that you will choose a Web page from the current site folder, but you can select a page at any Internet address.

- The Src text box displays the name of the source page and the page immediately opens in the selected frame (see the illustration at the top of the next page).

- The Src text box will not be empty when you begin this operation. It will contain a placeholder name (such as UntitledFrame-2) for the HTML document set up in the frame when the frame was created.

- If you choose to create a new Web page in the frame, you rename this default placeholder name when you save the frame's page.

Link frame to source page

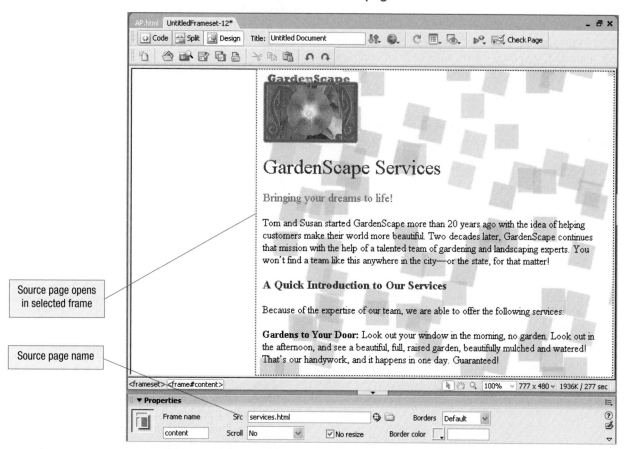

Source page opens in selected frame

Source page name

Web Design Connection

Frames—Pro and Con

Web designers are divided on the overall desirability of frames. Because not all browsers have frames capability, you may be limiting the usability of your site by adding framesets. On the other hand, adding frames can increase the effectiveness of your page by giving readers the ability to navigate through several pages all displayed in a single page.

Find Frames Online

Use the Internet to search for Web sites that use frames in an effective way. Notice how the site designers use the frames structure to enhance the navigational structure of the site. Save the pages you find to your Favorites folder.

Add Frame Borders

- You can add a colorful border to a frame to help set it off visually from the rest of the page.

- Begin by selecting a frame (press Alt and click the frame you want to add the border to). In the Property inspector, set Borders to Yes and type a color value (or choose one from the color selector box).

- You can increase the width of the border by specifying a value in the Border Width box.

  ✔ Click the border of the frame you want to change to display the Border Width box in the Property inspector.

Resize Frames

- You can easily change the width of frames on your frames page. Select the frame you want to change by pressing [Alt] and clicking the column. Make sure the border of the frame is selected.

- In the Property inspector, increase or decrease the value in the Column box. You can also change the measurement, if you choose, from Pixels (the default) to Percent (which displays the frame width as a specific percentage of the browser window) or Relative (which displays the frame sized in relation to the additional frames on the page).

Set Frame Target for Links

■ A common use for frames in a frameset is to insert links in one frame that open pages in other frames. For example, you may insert a list of links such as a table of contents in a frame at the left side of a page. Clicking a link in the left frame opens a page in the main frame of the frameset.

■ When you create a link from text or an image in one frame that will open a page in another frame, you must tell Dreamweaver in which frame to open the page. You use the Target list options (see the illustration at the bottom of this page) in the Property inspector to do that.

■ To set up a link from one frame to another, follow this procedure:

● Select the text or image that will be used for the link.

● In the Link text box in the Property inspector, specify the page that will open when the link is clicked.

● Click the Target list arrow to display a list of the frames in the current frameset (see the illustration below).

● Select the frame in which you want the page to open.

■ In addition to the frames in the current frameset (such as main, contents), the Target list includes four other default targets: _blank, _parent, _self, and _top. Use these targets as follows:

● Choose the _blank target to open the linked page in a new browser window while also keeping the current browser window open.

✔ This is a good choice if you are linking to a page outside your Web site.

● Choose _parent to open the linked page in the current frameset, replacing all frames.

● Choose _self to open the linked page in the frame that also contains the link, replacing all content in this frame.

● Choose _top to open the linked page in the outermost frameset, replacing all frames.

■ If you have only one frameset on a page, _parent and _top function in the same way. If you have more than one frameset in a page, _parent replaces the frameset of the current frame and _top replaces all framesets on the page with the linked page.

■ Consider the use of each frame on your page as you set up links. If you have a frame that functions as a contents area, it should never display other content. The main frame on the page should be used to display the main content of the site.

✔ Target settings are most important when working with frames. You can, however, use the _blank Target setting with any link on any kind of Web page to open the linked page in a new browser window.

Select a target for link

PROCEDURES

Create a Frameset

In a new, blank page or an existing document:

1. Click **Insert** .... [Alt]+[I]
2. Point to **HTML**..................... [H]
3. Point to **Frames** .... [S]
4. Click the desired frame option, such as **Left**, **Right**, **Top**, **Bottom**, **Bottom Nested Left**, etc.

   OR

1. Display the Layout tab in the Insert bar, if necessary.
2. Click [▣ ▾] to display list of frame options.
3. Click a predefined frame layout from the drop-down list.

   OR

1. In the Welcome Screen window, click **Framesets**.
2. Select the desired option from the Framesets list.
3. Click [Create].

   OR

1. Click **File** .... [Alt]+[F]
2. Click **New**............................ [N]
3. Click **Page from Sample**.
4. Click **Frameset** in the Sample Folder list.
5. Select the desired option from the Sample Page list.
6. Click [Create].

Specify Accessibility Tags for Frames

In the Frame Tag Accessibility Attributes dialog box:

1. Click the **Frame** list arrow to display a frame in the current frameset.
2. Type a new title for the frame in the **Title** text box.
3. Repeat steps 1 and 2 until all frames have new titles.
4. Click [OK].

Modify a Frame by Splitting into Additional Frames

1. Click **Modify**.................. [Alt]+[M]
2. Point to **Frameset**.............. [F]
3. Click the desired type of split:
   - Split Frame **Left** .... [L]
   - Split Frame **Right**.......... [R]
   - Split Frame **Up** .... [U]
   - Split Frame **Down** .... [D]

Activate or Select a Frame

To activate a frame:

- Click anywhere in the frame to position the cursor.

To select a frame:

- Press [Alt] and click in frame.

  OR

- Click the frame name in the Frames panel.

To select a frameset:

- Click any frame border in the frameset, if borders are displayed.

  OR

- Click the border that surrounds frames in Frames panel.

Name a Frame

1. Select a frame to name.
2. Click in the **Frame name** text box and type a one-word name.
3. Press [Enter] or [Tab ⇆].

Save and Title a Frameset (Ctrl + S)

Immediately after creating frameset:

1. Click **File** .... [Alt]+[F]
2. Click **Save Frameset**............ [S]
3. Type a name for the frameset.
4. Click [Save].
5. Click **Modify**.................. [Alt]+[M]
6. Click **Page Properties**.......... [P]

7. Click the **Title/Encoding** category.
8. Type a page title.
9. Click [OK].

Save a Frame (Ctrl + S)

1. Activate the frame you want to save.
2. Click **File** .... [Alt]+[F]
3. Click **Save Frame**................ [S]
4. Type the desired page name.
5. Click [Save].

Save Changes to Frames

1. Click **File** .... [Alt]+[F]
2. Click **Save All** .... [L]

Display Frames Panel (Shift + F2)

1. Click **Window** .... [Alt]+[W]
2. Click **Frames** .... [M]

Add Content to a Frame

- Activate the frame and type text or paste text that has been cut or copied from another location.
- Modify the frame's page properties as for any other Web page.

Add a Border to a Frame

1. In the Frames panel, click the border of the frame ..... [Alt]+click
2. In the Property inspector, set **Borders** to Yes.
3. Choose a **Border color**.
4. Type a **Border width** .... [Alt]+[W]

   ✔ Note there are two different sets of options that appear in the Property inspector. If you've selected the border of the frame properly, you will see the Borders, Border color, and Border width boxes.

Resize a Frame

1. Select the border of the frame you want to change in the Frames panel
2. In the Property inspector, select **Value** .... `Alt` + `V`
3. Type the value for the width of the frame.
4. Change the measurement, if you like, by choosing **Units** .... `Alt` + `U`

   OR

   ■ Click the line between frames.
   ■ Drag the line in the direction you want to resize the frame.

Set Frame Source

1. Select the frame to link to source.
2. Click in the **Src** box on the Property inspector and type the address of the source page.

   OR

   ■ Click **Browse for File** button 🗀 on the Property inspector and navigate to the source page.

   OR

   ■ Click **Point to File** button 🌐 on the Property inspector and drag it to the desired source page.

Set Frame Target for Links

1. Click in the link to select it.
2. Specify the page you want to link to.
3. Click the **Target** list arrow and select a frame name from the current frameset or a default target such as _blank, _parent, _self, or _top.

EXERCISE DIRECTIONS

1. Start Dreamweaver and open the gardenscape site. You will create a new frameset page with a contents frame at the left to hold links that will open the Web site's pages in a main frame. You will name the frameset index.html so it will operate correctly as the site's home page.

2. Make the following preparations:

   ■ Open index.html and cut from the page the series of links beginning with *Meet Your Designers!*

   ■ Create a new blank HTML page and paste the cut links on the page. Save the page as contents.html with the page title **Contents**.

   ■ Change the page title for the index.html page to **Welcome to GardenScape**.

   ■ Save and close contents.html and index.html.

   ■ In the Files panel, rename index.html as home.html. Do *not* update links because you will create a new index.html page.

3. Open home.html. If necessary, display the Layout tab of the Insert bar.

4. Display the Frames list and click the ⬜ Left Frame button to create a new frame to the left of the current page content. Change the title of *mainFrame* to **main** and the title of *leftFrame* to **contents**.

5. Save the new frameset as index.html and supply the page title **Welcome to GardenScape**.

6. Name the new frame **contents** and the frame that holds existing text **main**.

   ✔ Remember, specifying a title is not the same as specifying a name. Use the Property inspector to supply a name for each frame.

7. Select the contents frame and set its source as contents.html. The links you cut from the previous index.html page open in the frame.

8. Highlight the text *Meet Your Designers!* at the top of the Contents frame and set the Target to **main**. This tells Dreamweaver to display the linked page in the main frame of index.html. Repeat for each of the links in the Contents frame.

9. Add a border to the contents frame. Specify a width of 4 for the frame and apply the color #99CCCC.

10. Save your changes and preview the page in the browser. Test the links. Adjust the frame width if necessary. Your page should look similar to Illustration A shown at the top of the next page.

11. Close any open pages and exit Dreamweaver.

Illustration A

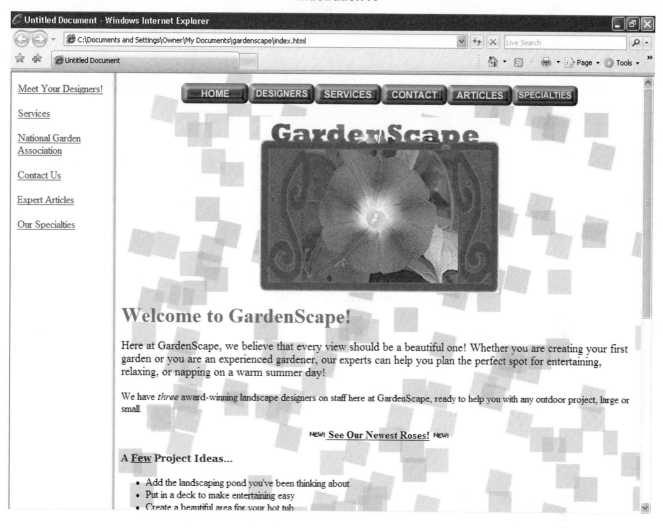

ON YOUR OWN

1. Start Dreamweaver and open the following pages in the sports_info subfolder of the Lesson 5 Data folder ⊙: home.html, soccer.html, basketball.html, football.html, and links.html.

2. Create a new blank HTML page and apply the Left Frame option on the Insert bar. Change frame titles to **links** for the left frame and **main** for the main frame.

3. Save the frameset as index.html with the title **Sports Info**.

4. Name the left frame **links** and the main frame **main**.

5. Set the sources for each frame as follows:
   - Link the *links* frame to links.html.
   - Link the *main* frame to home.html.

6. Create a link for each of the following on the links.html page:
   - Link *Soccer* to soccer.html.
   - Link *Basketball* to basketball.html.
   - Link *Football* to football.html.

7. Select each text link in the links.html page (in the links frame) and set the Target to main.

8. Save all open pages and preview the pages in your Web browser. Be sure to test the links.

9. Close the pages and the browser and exit Dreamweaver.

Skills Covered

- About Styles and Style Sheets
- Use the Property Inspector to Create Internal CSS Styles
- Use the CSS Styles Panel to Create Internal CSS Styles

- Apply Internal CSS Styles
- Edit Internal CSS Styles
- Dreamweaver CSS Reference

Software Skills Use styles to create formatting rules that can easily be applied to other pages in the Web site. You can create internal Cascading Style Sheet (CSS) styles using the Property inspector or the CSS Styles panel and use the CSS Styles panel to apply and edit styles.

Design Skills Cascading Style Sheets give you a great amount of flexibility in designing Web pages and sites, enabling you to create styles that you can use again and again throughout your site or in a variety of projects.

Application Skills In this exercise, you create a new Web site and then create, apply, and edit CSS styles for the site. You will also redefine a standard HTML tag to change the site's appearance.

TERMS

Cascading Style Sheets (CSS) A collection of saved design style properties that you can apply easily to elements in your Web site. CSS is an HTML 4.0 specification that is supported by current browsers.

Style A rule that specifies how to format an HTML element such as text, an image, or a specific tag.

Style sheet A collection of styles created for a page or Web site.

NOTES

About Styles and Style Sheets

- A **style** is a *rule* that contains instructions on how to format an HTML element. A style may be applied to text (like styles in a word processing program such as Word) or to other HTML elements such as images, AP divs, or frames. You can also create styles that apply to specific HTML tags such as the horizontal rule tag or a heading tag.

- A collection of styles created for a page or a Web site is called a **style sheet**. Using a style sheet, you can format a number of HTML elements quickly and easily. Dreamweaver supports **Cascading Style Sheets (CSS)**, style sheets developed specifically for use in Web design.

- There are several advantages to creating and using styles and style sheets:

  - Working with styles is efficient: You can create style rules once and use them many times on a page or throughout a Web site. If you need to edit a style, you can change it in one location and the change is made throughout the site.

  - Styles give you more formatting options than HTML: Using styles, you can easily apply borders to any side of a paragraph, position images or blocks of content absolutely, specify space between lines of text, and apply other options that cannot be achieved with standard HTML coding.

- Styles are not as code-intensive as HTML: Styles take up less room in a document's code than HTML, which means the page's file size is smaller and it will often load more quickly. This is especially true for tags such as <font>, which require a number of attributes and values each time a designer wants to adjust text appearance on a page.

- You have several options for creating and applying styles in Dreamweaver:

  - Create *internal (embedded) CSS* styles that are stored in the Head section of a page and can be applied only to text on that page.

  - Create an *external CSS* containing one or more styles that can be linked to all pages in a Web site.

    ✔ *You will work with the first option in this exercise, and you will work with external style sheets in the next exercise.*

  - Create *inline styles* within specific tags in an HTML document. Inline styles are not recommended, and Dreamweaver offers a utility for converting them to style sheets.

    ✔ *You will learn more about inline styles and conversion options in the next exercise.*

- There are several ways to create an internal CSS style. One of the easiest is to use the Style box on the Property inspector. Or you can use the CSS Styles panel in the CSS panel group or the Text>CSS Styles menu command. These options are discussed in the following sections.

Use the Property Inspector to Create Internal CSS Styles

- By default, Dreamweaver collects all the formats you apply to text or a paragraph and displays them in the Style box on the Property inspector (see the illustration at the bottom of this page). Formats are applied to a default style name, such as *style1*.

- For Dreamweaver to display style formats in the Property inspector, you must select *Use CSS instead of HTML tags* in the Preferences dialog box's General settings.

  ✔ *You deselected this option earlier in the course to learn about applying HTML formats.*

- Font size options differ when you are using CSS tags. Rather than employing the 1 through 7 sizes common in HTML formatting, CSS styles use sizes that look more like those available in a word processing program: 9, 10, 12, 14, 16, 18, 24, and 36. You can also select a unit of measurement for the font size, including pixels, points, inches, centimeters, millimeters, and percentages.

- You also have the option of using descriptive font sizes, such as xx-small, small, medium, and large, or smaller and larger.

- To save a new style using the Style box, click its list arrow and select Rename from the pop-up menu. Then, in the Rename Style dialog box (see the illustration at the top of the next page), type a new name for the style.

Dreamweaver displays formats that can be saved as styles

253

Rename a style

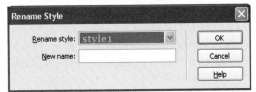

- The Results panel opens with the Search tab active to show you the code of the style and indicate that the style has actually replaced the formats you used to create it.

- The new style information is stored in the Head section of the document enclosed between the <style> </style> tags. The style name appears in the CSS Styles panel.

- A style you create this way can be used only on the page on which it is created, but it can be used anywhere on that page, as many times as desired. You will learn later in this exercise how to apply internal CSS styles.

Use the CSS Styles Panel to Create Internal CSS Styles

- You can also create CSS styles using the CSS Styles panel in the CSS panel group. The CSS Styles panel is designed to help you easily create, apply, and manage CSS styles.

  ✔ *The CSS Styles panel offers many more options for creating styles than the Property inspector. It's a good idea to use the CSS Styles panel for all but the simplest styles.*

- The CSS Styles panel (see the following illustration) lists all CSS styles (also called *rules*) that have been defined for or linked to the current page.

A new CSS style displayed in the CSS Styles panel

- To create a new CSS style using the CSS Styles panel, click the ⊞ New CSS Rule button in the CSS Styles panel to open the New CSS Rule dialog box (see the following illustration).

New CSS Rule dialog box

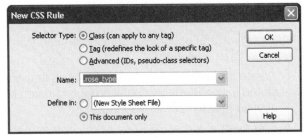

- You can also access this dialog box using the Text>CSS Styles>New command, if you are more comfortable working with menus.

- First provide a name for the new style. Custom CSS style names must begin with a period (.). If you forget to insert the period at the beginning of the style name, Dreamweaver will add it for you automatically. The name must then begin with a letter, and it can consist of only letters and numbers.

- Then choose the type of style to create:

  - The *Class (can apply to any tag)* option allows you to create a style you can apply to any HTML element. For example, if you define a class style to add 15 pixels of padding, you can apply it to an image as well as a paragraph.

  - The *Tag (redefines the look of a specific tag)* option allows you to choose a specific HTML tag (such as h1) and modify the tag with your own formats.

  - The *Advanced (IDs, pseudo-class selectors)* option lets you define formats for a specific combination of tags or tags that contain the ID attribute.

    ✔ *The term* selector *in the New CSS Rule dialog box refers to the terminology of CSS rules. A rule consists of the selector, which is the name of the styled element, and the declaration, which defines the style's attributes.*

- Dreamweaver allows you to define a style for the current document only (that is, the current page only) or create a new style sheet file in which to store new styles.

- If you choose the option to define styles in a new style sheet file, Dreamweaver allows you to name and save the style sheet to create an *external style sheet*.

  ✔ *You will learn more about external style sheets in the next exercise.*

Define a New Class Style

■ If you chose to create a new class style, clicking OK in the New CSS Rule dialog box opens the CSS Rule definition dialog box for your new style (see the following illustration). You can define formats in eight different categories.

Define formats for new style

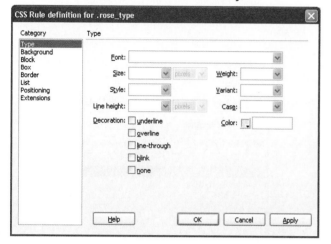

■ You will use the options in the Type category most often when creating new text formats. You can select the desired font, size, style, weight, and color, as well as "decorations" such as underlines or a blink feature. Note that you can also specify line height to add space between lines that can give text a less crowded look.

■ Use the Background category to set a background color or image for the style. If you select a background image, you can tile it on the page using the Repeat option in the Repeat list.

■ Use the Block category to set vertical and horizontal alignment options. You can also create indents in this category.

■ The Box, Border, List, Positioning, and Extensions categories offer additional settings to fine-tune the style: create box shapes for content, add borders to any or all sides of the style object, create custom list settings (such as bullet characters you specify), position an object absolutely, or apply extensions that insert page breaks or change the look of the cursor.

■ After you have finished selecting options for the new style rule, the style name displays in the CSS Styles panel. Information about an internal style is stored in the Head area of the document, as shown in the following illustration.

Internal styles stored in the Head section of the page

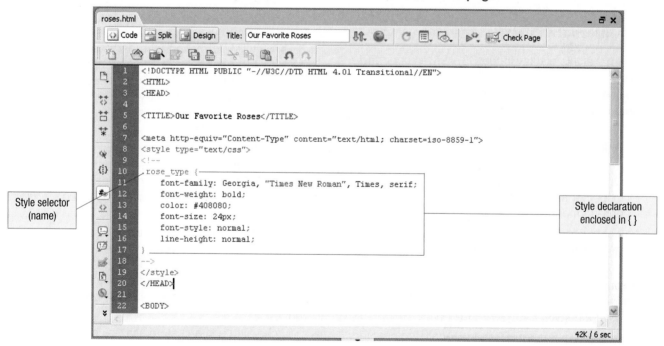

Redefine HTML Tags

- You can modify standard HTML tags to format elements uniquely for a page or Web site. To redefine an HTML tag, choose the *Tag (redefines the look of a specific tag)* option in the New CSS Rule dialog box. Instead of supplying a name for a new style, you select the tag you want to redefine from the Tag list (see the following illustration).

Choose HTML tag to redefine

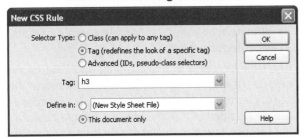

- Choose formats for the HTML tag in the CSS Rule definition dialog box, just as when creating a class CSS style.

- Redefined HTML tags are stored in the Head section of the page along with other internal styles created for that page.

- As with an internal class style, if an HTML tag is redefined for a specific page, it displays its new formats *only* on that page.

Apply Internal CSS Styles

- Internal styles display in the CSS Styles panel. To apply a style to text, click in or select existing text or position the insertion point where you intend to begin typing new text. To apply a style to an object such as an image, select the object. Then:
  - Right-click the style name in the CSS Styles panel and select Apply.
  - Or, click the Style list arrow in the Property inspector and select the style name from the pop-up menu.

- You can also apply a style from within the CSS Rule definition dialog box using the Apply button.

- If you mistakenly apply a style, click the Style list arrow and select None from the pop-up menu to remove the style.

- After you redefine an HTML tag, apply the new tag just as you would apply the HTML format. Apply paragraph and heading formats from the Property inspector's Format list, for example, or apply a redefined unordered list tag using the Unordered List button on the Property inspector or the Text>List>Unordered List command.

Edit Internal CSS Styles

- The CSS Styles panel makes it easy to edit a custom CSS style rule. Select the All button to show all styles available for the current document. The following illustration shows that two new styles have been created, .rose_type and .bodytext, and the h3 tag has been redefined.

  ✔ The <style> heading above these new styles is a default style sheet name used if you do not create a named style sheet.

Different styles in the CSS Styles panel

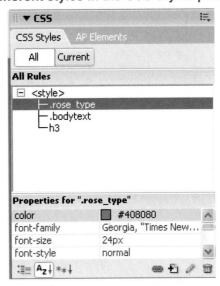

- To see style information for a particular element, click on the element in the document and select the Current button. The CSS Styles panel changes to show a summary of the style information for that element and tells you in which rule each attribute is defined.

- Both the All and the Current version of the CSS Styles panel display a Properties pane at the bottom of the panel. The Properties pane displays all properties that apply to the currently selected rule or element.

- Modify any of these properties by clicking in the box to the right of the property and selecting a new option from those available. Changes to a rule's properties are immediately displayed in the Document window for elements styled with that rule.

- You can also edit a custom style by double-clicking the rule in the CSS Styles panel or by clicking the rule and then clicking the Edit Style button to open the CSS Rule definition dialog box. After you make changes and close the dialog box, all text formatted with that style updates immediately to show the new formats.

Dreamweaver CSS Reference

■ Cascading style sheets are a complex subject. You can get additional help with CSS styles on the Reference panel. Choose the Help>Reference menu command. In the Results window, click the Book list arrow and select O'REILLY CSS Reference, and then choose a style you want information on (see the following illustration).

Learn more about CSS

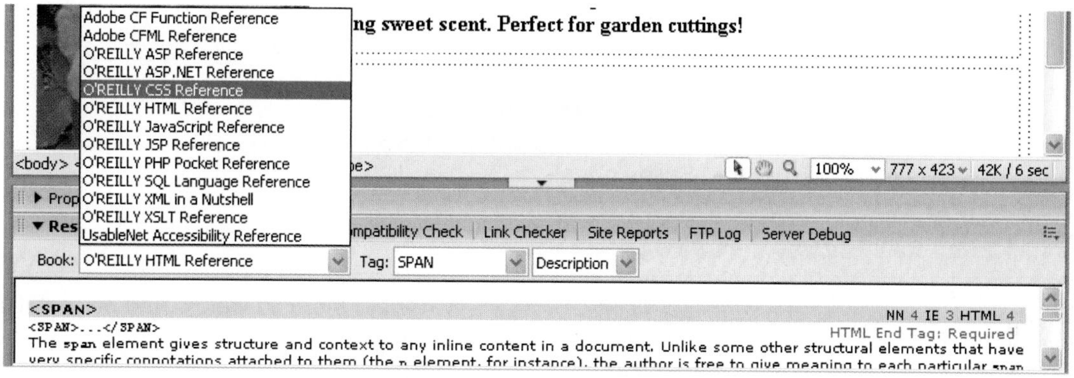

PROCEDURES

Create Internal CSS Styles for the Current Page Only (Ctrl + Shift + E)

1. Format the text or element as desired to display formats in the Style box on the Property inspector.
2. Click the **Style** list arrow and select **Rename**.
3. In the **New name** box, type a name for style.
4. Click [OK].

OR

1. Click **Text**.....................[Alt]+[T]
2. Click **CSS Styles** ....[C]
3. Click **New** ....[N], [Enter]

OR

■ Click **New CSS Rule** button 🔁 on the CSS Styles panel.

In the New CSS Rule dialog box:

1. Choose the **Class (can apply to any tag)** option.
2. Type a name for the style, preceded by a period.

3. Choose the **This document only** option.
4. Click [OK].
5. Select options from the **Type**, **Background**, **Block** and other categories, as desired.
6. Click [OK].

Apply a Style

1. Click in the paragraph you want to apply the style to, or select the text or object.
2. Right-click the style name in the CSS Styles panel.
3. Click **Apply**.

OR

1. Click in the paragraph you want to apply the style to, or select the text or object.
2. Click the **Style** list arrow on the Property inspector.
3. Select the desired style from the pop-up list.

Remove a Style

1. Click in the text or the object formatted with style.
2. Click the **Style** list arrow on the Property inspector.
3. Select **None** from the pop-up list.

Redefine HTML Tags and Apply

1. Click **Text**.....................[Alt]+[T]
2. Click **CSS Styles** ....[C]
3. Click **New** ....[N], [Enter]

OR

■ Click **New CSS Rule** button 🔁 on the CSS Styles panel.

In the New CSS Rule dialog box:

1. Choose the **Tag (redefines the look of a specific tag)** option.
2. Select a tag from the **Tag** drop-down list.
3. Click [OK].

4. Select the options from the categories in the CSS Rule Definition dialog box.

5. Click in the paragraph you want to style.

6. Display the Property inspector, if necessary.

7. Click a formatting option (such as Format list or Ordered List) and select a redefined HTML style.

Edit CSS Styles

1. Click a rule to edit in the CSS Styles panel.

2. Locate the property you want to change in the Properties pane of the CSS Styles panel.

3. Click in the box to the right of the property and select a new option for property.

   OR

1. Click the rule you want to edit in the CSS Styles panel.

2. Click the **Add Property** link in the Properties pane of CSS Styles panel.

3. Select a new property for current rule.

4. Click in the box to the right of the property and select the option you want to apply to the property.

   OR

1. Double-click the rule you want to edit in the CSS Styles panel.

2. Select new options in the CSS Rule definition dialog box.

3. Click ☐ OK ☐.

EXERCISE DIRECTIONS

1. Start Dreamweaver and open the Preferences dialog box from the Edit menu. In the General settings, select *Use CSS instead of HTML tags.* Click OK.

2. GardenScape is preparing to launch a new Web site that contains online tutorials for popular gardening projects. In this exercise, you will create the new Web site and set up styles for one of its pages. Begin by creating the Web site using the Site Definition wizard in Dreamweaver:

   ■ Define a new site named gardenprojects.

   ■ Do not use a server technology, and choose to edit local copies and upload later.

   ■ Store the files at the same local location you have used for gardenscape, such as C:\Inetpub\wwwroot.

   ■ Select None for the remote server option and do not enable check in/check out.

3. In Dreamweaver, open ⊙ products.html and ⊙ index.html from the Lesson 5 Data folder and save them to the new Web site folder.

4. Set index.html as the site's home page.

5. Click products.html and modify the links and the link names in the navigation bar to point to home.html, tutorials.html, products.html, resources.html, news.html, and contactus.html.

6. Select the phrase *Water Gardening* in the first column of the table and create a new style using the CSS Styles panel:

   ■ Name the style **.tableheads** and specify that the style is for this document only.

   ■ Select Times New Roman font, 12-point size.

   ✔ *Be sure to change the units of measurement for the font size to points, or your text will be very small!*

   ■ Select the bold weight and color #336633.

   ■ Choose the center text alignment from the Block category.

7. After you finish defining the style, apply it to the *Water Gardening* text.

8. Apply the .tableheads style to the *Landscaping* text in the first column.

9. Modify the style as follows using the CSS Styles panel. Notice how the new properties are applied immediately to the table text:

   ■ Select the .tableheads rule in the CSS Styles panel.

   ■ Change the font-family property to the Arial font.

   ■ Change the size to 10 points.

   ■ Change the text-align property to Left.

   ■ In the Properties pane, click in the space to the right of the background-color property. (If necessary, choose the property from the list to add it before clicking in the space.)

   ■ Choose the lightest yellow background color (#FFFFCC).

10. Create a second custom style using the Property inspector's Style box. Use the following formats: Arial font and 10-point size. Rename the style **.tabletext**. (Close the Results panel if necessary after creating the style.)

    ✔ *To create this style, select the first table text entry,* Install a garden pond, *and apply formats to it.*

11. Apply the .tabletext custom style to all entries in the right column of the table.

12. Modify the .tabletext style in the CSS Styles panel to have the lightest blue background (#CCFFFF).

13. Redefine the h1 HTML tag to be Verdana, 36 point, and bold, with the light blue color #CCFFFF.

14. Use the Property inspector to apply the Heading 1 style to the page title above the table.

15. Click to the left of the text paragraph and press Enter twice.

16. You want to add an image as a decorative element for the page. Follow these steps to insert the image and create a style for it:

   ■ Create a new folder in the site with the name images.

   ■ Click at the end of the page title and insert the ⊙reflectivepool.jpg image from the Lesson 5 Data files. Save the image in the images folder and supply an appropriate alternate text.

   ■ Create a new internal class rule named **.imagestrip** and display the Positioning category in the CSS Rule dialog box.

   ■ Choose a Type of absolute, set Width to 230px, set Height to 102px. In the Placement area of the dialog box, set Top to 47 and Left to 510.

   ■ Apply the new style to the image.

17. Save changes and preview this page in the browser. It should look similar to Illustration A.

18. Close any open pages and the browser and exit Dreamweaver.

Illustration A

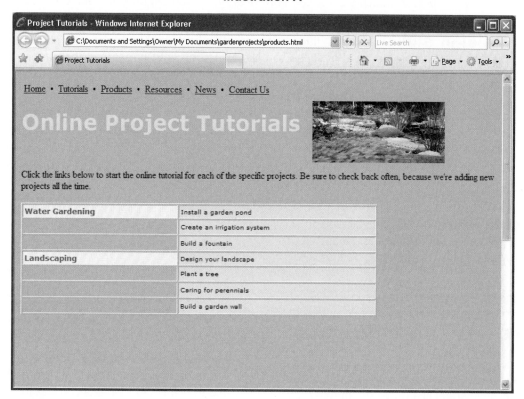

ON YOUR OWN

1. Start Dreamweaver and open the java2go site.

2. Open the recipe.html page and create an internal style to add padding to the right side of the thumbnail muffin image.

3. Create custom CSS styles for this page; for example:

   ■ Redefine the Heading 2 heading to use formatting other than that currently in use.

   ■ Create a style to apply to the introductory paragraph below the heading.

   ■ Create a style that can be applied to the recipe ingredients.

   ■ Create a style that can be applied to the steps. You may want to experiment with line height and indention for this style.

4. Save and view the page in the browser and then make any changes to the formats you think will improve the page.

5. Close all open pages and exit Dreamweaver.

Skills Covered

■ **Create an External Cascading Style Sheet**

■ **Dreamweaver CSS Layouts and Samples**

■ **About Inline Styles**

■ **Manage Styles**

Software Skills You can create an external cascading style sheet that includes styles you can use with any page in your Web site. You can also attach external style sheets to multiple sites. Dreamweaver offers sample style sheets and CSS layouts you can use as they are or customize to fit your own site.

Design Skills The great thing about creating and using external style sheets is that you can create a set of styles you like to use on your pages and then apply them to multiple projects. This adds consistency to your pages and can save you a lot of design time.

Application Skills In this exercise, you create an external style sheet. You then apply the styles to pages in the site and adjust the styles to change the look of your pages.

TERMS

External style sheet A CSS in a text file you attach to a Web page you are creating that includes the style definitions for the elements on the page.

NOTES

Create an External Cascading Style Sheet

■ If you want to apply styles to several Web pages in a site, you need to create an **external style sheet**. An external style sheet is a separate, or external, file that provides the definitions of all the styles used in a Web site. After you create the external style sheet and link it to the site's pages, any change you make to the external style sheet's styles is immediately reflected on all pages linked to the style sheet.

■ External style sheets have the file extension .css. After you create and save the style sheet, you can add styles to it in the same way you create internal styles or redefine HTML tags.

✔ *You cannot simply save a Web page as a .css page. You won't be able to link that file to a Web page and will receive an error.*

Save New External Style Sheet

■ As you have seen already, Dreamweaver allows you to create an external style sheet whenever you use the New CSS Rule dialog box to define a custom style or redefine an HTML tag. You can display this dialog box several ways:

  ● In any document, use the Text>CSS Styles>New command.

  ● Click the ▣ New CSS Rule button in the CSS Styles panel.

■ In the New CSS Rule dialog box, specify the name of the first style for the style sheet or the tag to be modified and make sure (New Style Sheet File) is selected in the Define in section.

✔ *You can create an external style sheet with any page displayed, even one that already contains internal CSS styles. The internal styles, however, will not be included in the external style sheet.*

■ Clicking OK opens the Save Style Sheet File As dialog box (see the following illustration) where you can specify a name for the external style sheet and save it in the current site.

Save an external style sheet in the current site

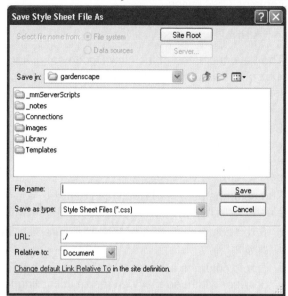

■ After you save the style sheet, its name displays in the CSS Styles panel and the CSS Rule Definition dialog box opens so that you can define your first style. This process can seem a little backward: You must supply the name of a new style before you have even created the style sheet, and after you save the style sheet, you must go back to defining that first style.

■ The external style sheet document displays in the Files panel just like any other page document.

■ The next time you define a new style, you have the option in the New CSS Rule dialog box of creating the style for the current document only or for the external style sheet. The style sheet's name is selected by default in this dialog box.

■ As you define styles for the external style sheet, they are added to the style sheet document. You must save the external style sheet like any other document after you make changes to it.

■ Apply styles from the external style sheet the same way as you add internal CSS styles. If you view the code, you will see that the style information does not appear in a document's Head section, as it does with internal styles, after being applied from an external style sheet.

■ You also edit styles in an external style sheet the same way you edit internal CSS styles: Use the CSS Styles panel's Properties pane to change settings or add new properties to any selected style. These changes, once saved, update automatically on any Web page linked to the style sheet. This enables you to make global changes with one modification on the style sheet.

Attach External Style Sheet to Existing or New Web Document

■ After you have created an external style sheet, you can attach it to existing or new documents in the site. This allows you to use the same styles on all pages to ensure consistency throughout your site.

■ To attach a style sheet to an existing document, open the Web page you want to attach the style sheet to and click the ⊞ Attach Style Sheet button at the bottom of the CSS Styles panel. Or, use the Text>CSS Styles>Attach Style Sheet command. The Attach External Style Sheet dialog box opens, as shown in the following illustration.

Attach External Style Sheet dialog box

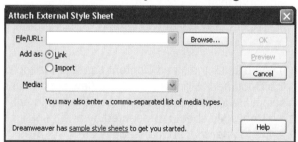

■ Type the name of the external style sheet, select it by clicking the File/URL list arrow to display a list of style sheets, or use the [Browse...] button to locate it in the current site.

✔ *Remember to use all lowercase letters when naming the style sheet.*

■ For most cases, choose the Link option in the Attach External Style Sheet dialog box. If you select the Import option, the styles are directly imported into the document rather than linked to the external file. This option is best for Web documents that might be used outside of the Web site in which the .css file resides.

- You can click the Media list arrow to see a list of target media for the style sheet, such as print, handheld, or Braille. This setting tells Dreamweaver to use the styles only for a particular medium; for example, if the page is to be displayed on a handheld device, only styles for that selection are included. Click the Preview button to display the style sheet's styles in the CSS panel so that you can see which styles will be applied with the style sheet.

- To attach the style sheet to a new document, click the Attach Style Sheet button in the New Document dialog box, specify the desired style sheet in the Attach External Style Sheet dialog box, and allow Dreamweaver to create a relative path to the style sheet until you save the new document.

- The linked style sheet is now available for you to use as you format your document. You can use the styles shown in the CSS Styles panel (or in the Format list on the Property inspector for redefined HTML tags) to apply formats in the same manner you use internal styles.

- The HTML code that controls the link to an external style sheet is stored in the Head section of a page. If you examine the page's code, you will see code similar to this:

```
<link href="styles.css" rel="stylesheet"
type="text/css">
```

- If you display the Head Content panel at the top of the Document window (click View options and select Head Content), you will see the link to an external style sheet represented by a link icon in the toolbar that appears above the work area. Click on the icon to open a Link Property inspector.

- You can have both an external style sheet and internal styles available for a specific Web page (see the following illustration) or even link more than one style sheet to a page.

Dreamweaver CSS Layouts and Samples

- The New Documents dialog box offers several options for creating documents with CSS formatting. Use a Dreamweaver CSS layout or sample style sheet to quickly create a page that already contains CSS styles.

Use a CSS Layout

- The Layout column of the New Document dialog box offers a number of CSS layouts you can use to start a new page. These layouts are new in Dreamweaver CS3.

- Select a layout to see a preview of the page layout with information on how the sections of the page are formatted (see the illustration at the top of the next page).

- The columns of these layouts can be fixed, liquid, elastic, or a hybrid of several of these options.
  - *Fixed* columns have a precise measurement in pixels.
  - *Liquid* columns are measured in percentage of browser width, so they can resize according to the size of the browser window.
  - *Elastic* columns are measured in *ems*, a width measurement that is related to the size of text. If a visitor changes the text size in the browser window, the layout adjusts accordingly.

- A new CSS layout page provides some details on how the page is structured (see the illustration at the bottom of the next page) as well as sample text that you can replace to create the desired page content. The CSS Styles panel contains a list of the styles used to create the page.

CSS Styles panel with internal and external styles

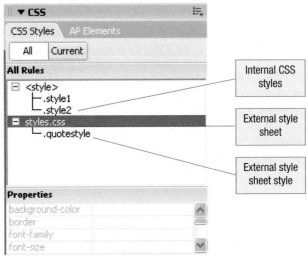

CSS layouts in the New Document dialog box

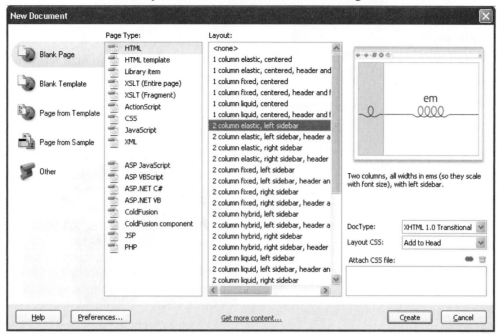

New page with a CSS layout

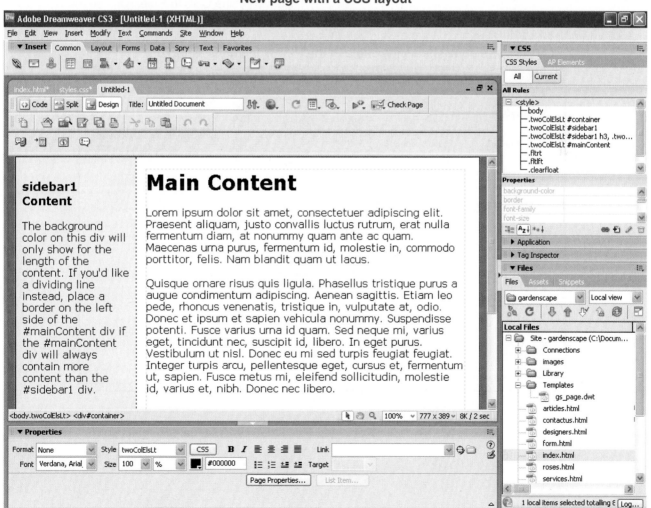

Use a Dreamweaver Sample Style Sheet

- Dreamweaver also offers sample style sheets that you can apply to any Web site. These sample style sheets are available in the New Document dialog box (see the illustration at the bottom of this page).

- These style sheets range from the very simple—style sheets that just apply a specific font—to full designs that offer headings, sidebars, table and link formatting, and so on.

- After you select one of these style sheets, you save it in your site with the desired name and then use its styles the same way you use styles you have defined yourself.

About Inline Styles

- You have learned the two preferred methods of supplying styles for a Web page: creating internal styles on a single page or external styles that can link to many pages.

- It is also possible to create styles within any HTML tag. Such a style is called an *inline style*.

- The following illustration shows an inline style created within a <p> tag.

Inline style that will adjust paragraph size and color

- When a browser applies styles, it gives the highest priority to inline styles. This means that you can use inline styles to override other styles.

- However, the use of inline styles is discouraged in most instances. One of the benefits of using CSS is that the styles are located in one place in a page or style sheet, so that a designer can easily make changes to the styles. Having inline code sprinkled throughout a document defeats the real purpose of using CSS.

- Dreamweaver CS3 provides a handy utility for converting inline CSS to a rule. In a code view, right-click the inline style, click CSS Styles, and then click Convert Inline CSS to Rule. (Or, use the Text>CSS Styles>Convert Inline CSS to Rule command.)

CSS style sheets available in the New Document dialog box

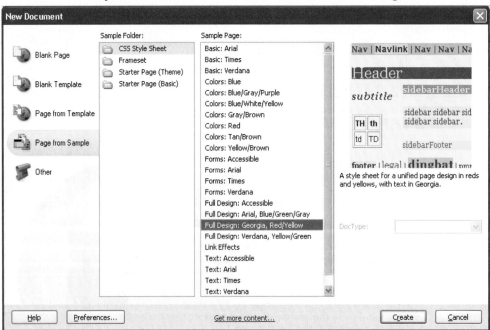

■ Dreamweaver opens the Convert Inline CSS dialog box, as shown in the illustration. Here you can convert the inline CSS to a new class, redefine an HTML tag, or create a new selector. The new CSS can be inserted in an existing external style sheet or added to the Head section of the document to create an internal CSS style.

Convert Inline CSS dialog box

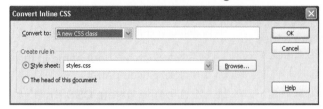

Manage Styles

■ As you might imagine, style sheets give you a lot of flexibility when you are formatting pages in a Web site. You can link an external style sheet to a template so that the styles are applied along with other template elements. Or, you can create custom styles for an editable area in a template.

✔ *You may need to tweak HTML code in the template to make sure that the styles are applied correctly to the editable areas.*

■ One of the great benefits of creating an external style sheet is that it can be used in any number of Web sites. You simply link to the style sheet from any site, saving it in your current site's root folder when prompted.

■ If you have defined internal styles on a page and want to add them to a style sheet, you can easily do so using a new feature, Move CSS Rules. You can right-click a style and select the Move CSS Rules command to move the rule to an existing or new style sheet. You can also duplicate a rule if desired.

■ It is possible to apply more than one style to a text element, but doing so can lead to style conflicts. Style conflicts can give unexpected results because of the way browsers read the conflicting style tags.

■ Browsers use the following rules to resolve style conflicts:

● When two different styles are applied to the same text, browsers display all attributes for both styles, unless the attributes conflict directly (for example, one applies a left alignment and the other applies a right alignment).

● In the case of such a conflict, the browser will display the attribute of the style closest to the text in the HTML code.

● Attributes from CSS styles will override HTML tag styles.

PROCEDURES

Create and Save a New External Style Sheet

To display the New CSS Rule dialog box:

1. Click **Text** .... Alt + T
2. Point to **CSS Styles** C
3. Click **New** .... N , Enter

OR

■ Click **New CSS Rule** button ⊡ in the CSS Styles panel.

In the New CSS Rule dialog box:

1. Type the name for the new style.
2. Select **(New Style Sheet File)** in the Define in section of the dialog box.
3. Click OK .
4. In the Save Style Sheet File As dialog box, type name for the new external style sheet in the **File name** text box.
5. Click Save .

Create a New Style for an Existing Style Sheet

1. Click **Text** .... Alt + T
2. Point to **CSS Styles** C
3. Click **New** .... N , Enter

OR

■ Click **New CSS Rule** button ⊡ in the CSS Styles panel.

In the New CSS Rule dialog box:

1. Type the name for the new style.
2. Click **Define in** and either accept the style sheet name in the Define in box or click list arrow to select another style sheet name.
3. Click OK .
4. Continue the process of defining the new rule, as detailed in the previous exercise.

Attach an External Style Sheet to an Existing Web Document

1. Open page to link to external style sheet.
2. Click **Attach Style Sheet** button ▣ in the CSS Styles panel.
3. Type the path to the style sheet.

OR

a. Click Browse... .
b. Navigate to the location of the style sheet and select it.
c. Click OK .
4. Click OK .

Attach an External Style Sheet to a New Document

1. Click **File** .... Alt + F
2. Click **New** .... N
3. Click **Blank Page** or **Blank Template**.
4. Click a page type.

   ✔ *Not all page types allow style sheets to be attached.*

5. Click the **Attach Style Sheet** button 🖼 at lower-right corner of New Document dialog box.
6. Type the path to the style sheet.
   OR
   a. Click Browse... .
   b. Navigate to the location of the style sheet and select it.
   c. Click OK .
7. Click OK when Dreamweaver suggests making the file:// path.
8. Click OK .
9. Click Create .

Move CSS Rules to New or Existing Style Sheet

1. Display the CSS Styles panel on the page that has styles you want to move.
2. Right-click the style to move.
3. Click **Move CSS Rules** on the shortcut menu.
4. Select an existing style sheet to move the rule to, or choose to create a new style sheet.
5. Click OK .
   OR
■ Drag the style from one style sheet to another.

Delete a Style or Style Sheet

To delete a style:

1. Select style in the CSS Styles panel.
2. Click the **Delete CSS Rule** button 🗑 on the CSS Styles panel.

To delete a style sheet:

1. Select style sheet name in the CSS Styles panel.
2. Click the **Delete CSS Rule** button 🗑 in the CSS Styles panel.

EXERCISE DIRECTIONS

1. Start Dreamweaver and open the gardenprojects site.
2. Open the products.html page. Create a new external style sheet named **gs_styles.css**. Add the following styles to the style sheet:
   ■ Create a class style named **.subhead** that uses Verdana, 24 point, bold, and a dark blue color such as #006699.
   ■ Redefine the H2 HTML tag to use Times New Roman, 24 point, bold, with center alignment and a dark green color such as #009966.
   ■ Create a class style named **.text** that uses Times New Roman, 12 point, and a dark blue color such as #000099.
3. Save the style sheet.
4. Make sure both pages in the Web site are attached to the gs_styles.css style sheet.

5. Apply styles on the pages as follows:
   ■ On index.html, add the heading **A Little About You** following the first paragraph. Apply the Heading 2 format.
   ■ Apply the .text style to the first paragraph on both pages.
6. You have decided the blue body text is not effective. Change the .text style's color to black. Note the style changes on both pages.
7. The H2 format is not quite right. Change the size to 18 and alignment to left. Change the font to Verdana.
8. Save your changes. The Dreamweaver work area should look similar to Illustration A on the next page.
9. Close any open pages and exit Dreamweaver.

Illustration A

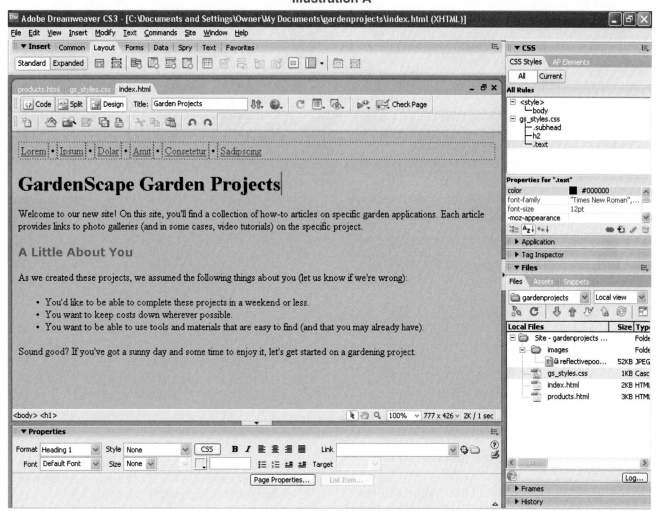

ON YOUR OWN

1. Start Dreamweaver and open the yardart site.

2. Open index.html. Create an external style sheet named **ya_styles.css** and add the following styles to the style sheet:

   ▪ A class style with a name such as **.bodytext** to be used for paragraph text throughout the site. Define this style as desired.

   ▪ Create a **.firsttext** style for the first paragraph on each page.

   ▪ Redefined the h2 and h3 HTML tags for headings in the site.

3. Attach the ya_styles.css style sheet to all the pages in the site except the form (including the template). Apply the styles you have created to the site pages.

4. If the styles don't appear correctly on the text or subheads on your pages, check the code to see whether an inline style has been applied to the text. Delete the inline style and reapply the CSS style.

5. Change the .firsttext and the .bodytext styles to 10 point text.

6. Save and preview the site in the browser to check your new styles.

7. Make any final adjustments to styles.

8. Save and close all pages and the browser and exit Dreamweaver.

Exercise | 45

Summary Exercise

Application Skills In this exercise, you will embellish the Tierra Verde Summer Camp site using AP elements and styles. You will redesign the home page using AP divs and create an internal CSS style to format copyright information throughout the site.

DIRECTIONS

1. Start Dreamweaver and open the tierraverde site.
2. Open index.html. Use AP divs to reorganize this page, as follows:
   - Create an AP div to hold the introductory text below the navigation bar. Cut the text and paste it in the AP div.
   - Create an AP div for the link in the center of the page.
   - Create an AP div to hold the Camp Features heading and the bulleted list that follows the heading.
   - Create an AP div to hold the rule and the copyright info at the bottom of the page.
3. Give each AP div an appropriate name.
4. Change the alignment of the picture to Default so it moves to the left margin. Add a drop shadow effect to this picture as follows:
   - First hide all other AP divs so you can concentrate on the picture.
   - Create an AP div the same size as the picture and give it a name such as **shadow**.
   - In the shadow AP div, add a background color of #999999. The AP div will automatically expand to hold the shadowed rectangle.
   - Nest an AP div inside the shadow AP div that is the same size as the picture, and name it **picture**.
   - Move the picture into the picture AP div. It will look as if it doesn't fit in the element correctly. You may want to save the page at this point and check how it looks in the browser. Adjust the position of the image slightly if necessary so that it fits completely over the gray shadow rectangle.
5. Move and resize the AP divs on the page to create a pleasing organization. Illustration A on the next page shows one possible layout. Check your layout frequently in your browser to make sure AP divs are positioned where you want them.
6. Change the background colors of AP divs as desired. If you add color backgrounds to the divs, consider using CSS padding to create a margin between the text and the layer edges. Adjust stacking order as necessary.
7. Change the colors of links on this page if necessary to contrast well with the AP div colors.
8. The horizontal rule above the copyright information is not very exciting. Use a custom CSS style to reformat the copyright library item as follows:
   - Open the copyright library item for editing.
   - Set up the e-mail address as a link if you have not already done so.
   - Delete the horizontal rule above the copyright text.
   - Create a new CSS style that applies a top border to the text. Name the style appropriately and select formats for the border that will add some punch to this item.

■ You may want to increase the line height of the text so the border does not sit right on top of the text.

■ Apply the new style to the copyright text. Save and update the library item. (You will not see the border on the pages in Dreamweaver.)

9. Preview the site in the browser. You should see the new border on each page of the site.

10. Close all open pages and the browser and exit Dreamweaver.

Illustration A

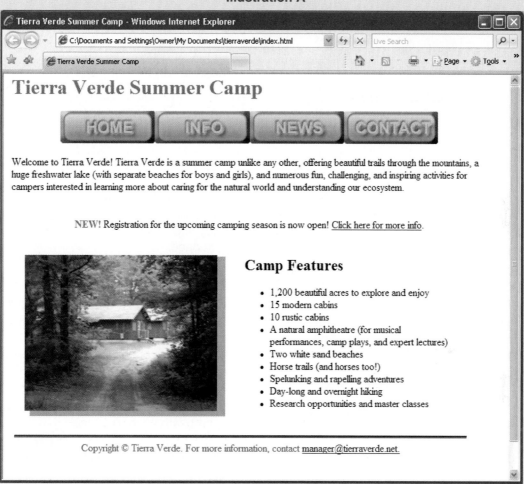

Application Exercise

Application Skills In this exercise, you use framesets to reformat several pages of the Classmate Connections site.

DIRECTIONS

1. Start Dreamweaver and open the classmate_connections Web site.

2. Rename the index.html file as main.html. Do not update pages.

3. Open main.html and delete the navigation bar on this page, as well as the blank paragraph where the navigation bar was.

4. Create a new frameset by splitting this page vertically so the existing text moves into the right frame. Title and name the left frame **navigation** and the right frame **main**. Save the new frameset as index.html with an appropriate page title.

5. Save the new left frame page as navigation.html with an appropriate page title. Format the frame as follows:

   ■ Change the page background of navigation.html to #CC9966.

   ■ Enlarge the navigation frame by clicking the frame border and dragging to the right.

   ■ Create a vertical navigation bar using the buttons you've already added to the images folder.

   ■ In the Modify Navigation Bar dialog box, choose *main* as the target in the When clicked, Go to URL box.

   ✔ *Hint: Don't remember how to create the navigation bar? Choose the Insert>Image Objects>Navigation Bar menu command.*

   ■ Link the buttons to the appropriate pages; make sure the Target is set to *main* in the Property inspector.

6. Preview the index.html page in the browser and check all links from the navigation frame. Your page should look similar to Illustration A on the next page.

7. Rename the directory.html file as links.html. Do not update links. Open the links.html page.

8. Delete the page title and the navigation bar.

9. Create a new frameset by splitting this page vertically so that the existing text moves into the left frame. Name and title the right frame **profiles** and the left frame **links**. Save the new frameset as directory.html.

10. Save the new left frame page as links.html with an appropriate page title.

11. Highlight the first line, *Sara R.* Click Target in the Property inspector and choose profiles.

12. Set the Target for *Ben S.* to profiles as well.

13. Now do some work in the profile frame:

   ■ Set the page background to match the links frame.

   ■ Add a page title of *Student Directory.*

   ■ Create a CSS style that modifies the h1 format in a font style and color that complements the background style. Modify the h2 style as well.

   ■ Create a CSS style sheet called **cc_styles.css** and move the styles you created into the style sheet.

   ■ Create a body CSS style that matches the text used in the links frame. Edit the style and change the padding and margin settings (in the Box category of the CSS Rule definition for body) for Left to 20 pixels.

■ Add the following text below the page heading and apply the body style:

Click one of the student links on the left to display the profile information for that student. Note that not all students choose to display all the information they provide to Classmate Connections. If you choose, you can set your profile so that only your closest friends—or the people in your group—can see your entire profile.

■ Replace the dashes in the text with em dashes by using the Text tab of the Insert bar.

■ Press ⌷Enter⌷ and add **Click here to display Student Links and start browsing!**.

■ Change the color of Student Links to #FFFCC to make it stand out on the page.

   ✔ Notice that changing the color of the phrase adds an inline style to the CSS Styles panel.

■ Create a link between *Click here* and profile.html and set the Target to links.

14. Delete the navigation bar on the remaining pages in the site. Attach cc_styles.css to all pages.

15. Save all pages and then preview the site in your browser and check all links. Make any necessary adjustments to links or frame properties.

16. Save and close all open pages and exit Dreamweaver.

Illustration A

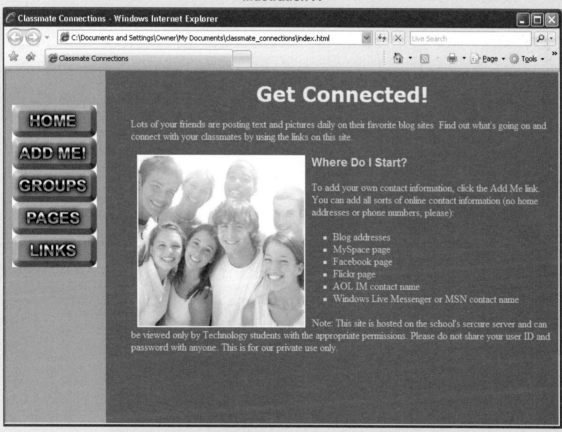

Exercise | 47

Curriculum Integration

Application Skills Your Discrete Math class is studying a curriculum that includes Fibonacci numbers and game theory. You have been given the choice of creating some Web material on either Fibonacci (more properly known as Leonardo of Pisa) or John Nash, who won a Nobel Prize for his work with game theory. Before you begin this project, locate:

■ One or more Web sites that you can use for background information on Fibonacci numbers or game theory

■ Information about Leonardo of Pisa or John Nash, including a picture

You will probably need to use equations in your site. To create superscripts, work in Code view and insert the ^{HTML tag before a superscript number. Close the tag with}. To create subscripts, use . You may then want to change the size of the superscripts and subscripts by selecting them in Design view and adjusting the font size.

DIRECTIONS

Create a new site with an appropriate name. Create a new page with a name appropriate to the subject you have chosen, such as gamehome.html. Then select one of Dreamweaver's external style sheets (you can select one from the New Document dialog box) and save it in the site with an appropriate name. (You may find it easier to use one of the Colors options; the full designs can be difficult for a novice.)

On your first page, insert some biographical information about the subject of your site, including a picture of Leonardo or John Nash. Be sure to indicate why this person is famous in his field. Use the styles from the external style sheet to format elements on the page, and add styles to the style sheet as you need them.

Create a second page that goes into more detail about the chief claim to fame of your subject. If you are working on Fibonacci, explain the concept of Fibonacci numbers and give some examples. If you are working on Nash, explain where game theory stood before he offered his approach to the theory, and explain his theory.

Link the two pages using stand-alone links or a navigation bar.

Test the site in a browser and make sure your equations (if you have used any) display properly.

Close the page and exit Dreamweaver.

Exercise | 48

Critical Thinking

Application Skills In this exercise, you will continue to work on your personal Web site. Create an external style sheet for the site, attach it to all pages, and apply styles to ensure a consistent format throughout the site.

DIRECTIONS

- Open your personal Web site and display the home page.

- Create an external style sheet for the site and save it with an appropriate name. Add styles to the style sheet to control all the text items in the site. You may create new styles or redefine existing HTML tags.

- Link all pages to the style sheet and apply the styles to text elements. You may need to restore defaults on HTML tags before applying redefined tags to show the style sheet formats.

- Test the site in the browser to make sure all the styles are working correctly and look attractive.

- Close all open pages and exit Dreamweaver.

Lesson | 6

Create Dynamic and Interactive Pages

Skills Covered

- About the Spry Framework
- About Spry Widgets
- Insert Spry Validation Widgets
- Create a Spry Menu Bar
- Create a Spry Collapsible Panel
- Create a Spry Accordion
- Other Spry Elements

Software Skills Use the Spry framework to add interesting interactive features to a Web site. Spry widgets allow you to create objects such as menu bars, validation form fields, collapsible panels, and accordions.

Design Skills Part of becoming an effective Web designer involves knowing how to use the resources available to you. You don't need to design everything from scratch—and Spry widgets give you ready-to-use, modifiable interactive elements you can add to the pages you design.

Application Skills In this exercise, you explore Spry widgets and add several to the GardenScape Web site.

TERMS

Spry A JavaScript library containing interactive elements you can add to Web pages.

Validation The process of ensuring that a form field contains an entry, if required, or a specific type of data.

Widget A page element that creates a specific kind of interactive content or carries out a defined function.

NOTES

About the Spry Framework

- **Spry** is a JavaScript library new in Dreamweaver CS3 that allows Web designers to build pages offering interesting interactive options.

- Using the Spry framework, you can add interactive or dynamic tables to a Web page that draw data from XML sources; insert Spry **widgets** such as menu bars, collapsible panels, or form fields with built-in **validation**; or apply Spry effects such as Appear/Fade or Highlight to give page content extra emphasis.

- Spry uses HTML, CSS, and JavaScript to create a variety of fun-to-use page elements. After creating each Spry object, you can customize it by modifying properties in the Property inspector or the CSS Styles panel.

About Spry Widgets

- Dreamweaver CS3 includes a number of Spry widgets that present specific types of information on a Web page. The four Validation widgets, for example, are used to create four different types of form fields, and the Collapsible Panel widget creates an object that displays a panel of text when you click a heading.

- A widget is composed of HTML code that defines the widget's structure, JavaScript that controls the interaction between a visitor's actions and the object, and CSS coding used to format the widget.

- A widget is identified in Dreamweaver by a blue tabbed outline, as shown in the following illustration on the next page. Click the tab to modify or set properties for the widget.

Widget is identified by blue tabbed outline

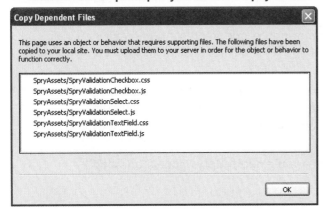

- The first time you save a page after adding a Spry widget (or any other Spry element), Dreamweaver prompts you to copy the files required for the element to your site, as shown in the following illustration.

Dreamweaver prompts you to save Spry files

Copy Dependent Files

This page uses an object or behavior that requires supporting files. The following files have been copied to your local site. You must upload them to your server in order for the object or behavior to function correctly.

```
SpryAssets/SpryValidationCheckbox.css
SpryAssets/SpryValidationCheckbox.js
SpryAssets/SpryValidationSelect.css
SpryAssets/SpryValidationSelect.js
SpryAssets/SpryValidationTextField.css
SpryAssets/SpryValidationTextField.js
```

OK

- These files are stored in the SpryAssets folder and, as indicated in the dialog box, must be put on the server along with pages that use Spry elements to enable them to work properly.

- In the following sections, you will learn about several Spry widgets: Validation widgets, the Menu Bar widget, the Collapsible Panel widget, and the Accordion widget.

Insert Spry Validation Widgets

- You can use Spry Validation widgets to create a form that supplies visual interest to visitors as well as indicating clearly if the form data supplied is not correct.

- The illustration in the next column shows a simple form created with Spry Validation widgets. Color coding and messages are used to give visitors feedback.

  - The green color applied to the Name field indicates the required data has been entered correctly.

  - The light orange color applied to the E-Mail field and the message indicates that the field does not contain a valid e-mail address.

  - The yellow color applied to the Comments field indicates that an entry is being made to the field.

Form created with Spry form fields

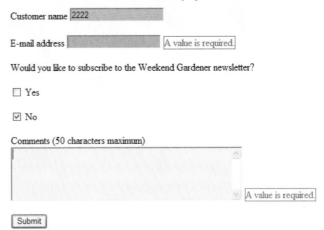

- You can insert Validation widgets from the Forms tab of the Insert bar or the Spry tab of the Insert bar, or use the Insert>Spry command and then select a widget from the submenu.

  ✔ *You can tell which tools are Spry tools because they display a small orange sunburst in the lower-right corner of the tool.*

- Dreamweaver offers four Validation widgets: Text Field, Select, Checkbox, and Textarea. These widgets work in the same way as regular Dreamweaver form fields.

- When you insert one of these widgets, Dreamweaver displays the Input Tag Accessibility Attributes dialog box, just as when inserting a regular form field. Supply a label and any necessary label options, and the field appears in the form.

Set Properties and Validation

- To set properties for a Validation widget, you click the form field just as you would in any Dreamweaver form. The Property inspector supplies the usual properties for the field.

- When you insert a Spry Validation Select widget, for example, selecting the field gives you the standard List/Menu options so that you can supply list items and values.

- When you select a Validation widget's blue tab, options appear in the Property inspector for validating the widget display, as shown in the following illustration at the top of the next page. Validation is the process of specifying the kind of information allowed in a form field and determining whether an entry is required in the field.

- In the Property inspector, you can name the field, select the type of data that must appear in the field, choose a format if you have selected a data type such as Date or Time, provide a pattern to use when inserting data, and supply a hint to help visitors supply the correct information.

Validation options for a Text Field

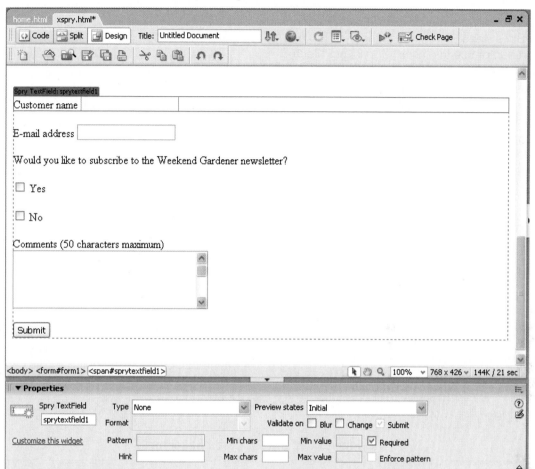

- The validation options displayed differ depending on the Validation widget you add, but you will always have options to name, preview, and validate the widget.

- The Preview states list shows you how the field will look for each state that may apply to the field. Initial, for example, shows the field as it will appear when the form loads. If you have specified that the field is required, you can click the Required option in the Preview states list to see what the field will look like if a visitor fails to enter a value in the field. The Valid option shows you how the field will look if the visitor has entered valid data.

- The Validate on options enable you to select the point at which validation occurs: Blur validates the field when the visitor clicks outside the field, and Change validates the field as the visitor is making a change inside the field. The Submit option is selected by default to validate all fields as the form is submitted.

- Specify a minimum or maximum number of characters to keep entries within a range, and minimum or maximum values if the field requires a numerical entry.

- Select the Required box if you want visitors to supply an entry in a field. If you have supplied a pattern, such as the way a date must be entered, you can select Enforce pattern to require visitors to enter data according to that pattern.

- After you have inserted Validation widgets, you can adjust text formatting or the formats applied to the fields to show various states by selecting the appropriate style rule in the CSS Styles panel and adjusting formats.

Create a Spry Menu Bar

- Add a Spry Menu Bar widget when you want a navigation bar that displays drop-down and pop-out panels that link to pages in a site. If you have a complex site with many related pages, the Menu Bar widget makes it easy for a visitor to navigate among the pages in the site.

- The navigation buttons themselves are created with a complex arrangement of <ul> and <li> tags, and the text and background colors are controlled by CSS styles.

Insert a Menu Bar Widget

■ You can insert a Spry Menu Bar Widget by clicking the ▤ Spry Menu Bar button on the Spry tab of the Insert bar, or use the Insert>Spry>Spry Menu Bar command.

■ In the Spry Menu Bar dialog box, choose whether you want to create a horizontal or vertical menu bar and click ☐ OK ☐. The default menu bar appears on the page. The Property inspector shows the default items in the menu bar, as shown in the top illustration at the bottom of this page.

Specify Menu Bar Entries

■ You can create the button text and links for the menu bar in the Property inspector. The first column, with entries such as Item 1 and Item 2, represents the main menu buttons.

■ Item 1 is selected by default. The boxes to the right of the item columns enable you to enter the text for the button, the page to which the button is linked, and a title for the button, which will appear as a Tooltip when the user positions the mouse over the button.

✔ *Additionally, if you want to specify the frame in which the resulting page will open, indicate it in the Target box.*

■ To create additional choices within items, click the item you want to add options to. Use the ➕ Add menu item or ➖ Remove menu item button to insert or delete a menu item. You can reorder a menu item using the ▲ Move item up or ▼ Move item down button. Enter the properties for those items as you did the main items (see the bottom illustration at the bottom of this page).

■ Notice the # sign in the Link box in the previous illustration. This # sign is called a *dummy link*. Dreamweaver requires an entry in this box, but if you don't want to create a link from a particular button, you can enter the # sign as a placeholder or type **javascript:;** in the Link box. The button will look like a link, and act like a link, but it won't open a page.

✔ *Dummy links can be a great help when creating behaviors, as they allow you to associate events with specific text that you format as a link. You will learn more about behaviors in the next exercise.*

■ If desired, you can click the ☐ Turn Styles Off ☐ button to turn off the CSS button styling and display the menu bar as an outline of links. This can help you better see the navigation structure you're creating for users to follow.

New menu bar and Property inspector

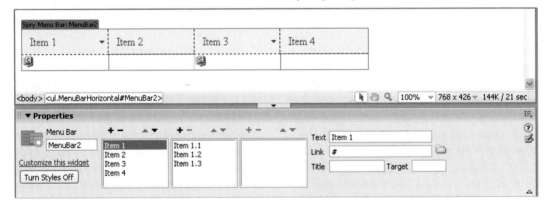

Menu bar properties showing several levels of submenu items

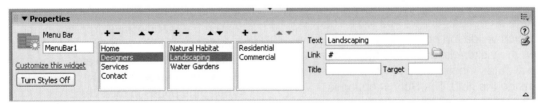

■ If you're new to CSS, the CSS styles required to format a Menu Bar widget can be confusing, but with persistence you'll be able to find the rules required to adjust the colors and text formats of your menu bar.

✔ You can click the Customize this widget link that appears in the lower-left corner of the Property inspector to display Dreamweaver Help on finding and using CSS styles to change the look of your Menu Bar widget.

Create a Spry Collapsible Panel

■ A Spry Collapsible Panel widget inserts a tab and a panel that expands or collapses as you click the tab. The following illustration shows the panel open.

Collapsible Panel widget opens and closes a panel in the browser

Rose of the Month

The Lafter rose is one of our all-time favorites. A fast grower with gorgeous yellow, pink, and salmon petals, the Lafter rose is disease-resistant and easy to grow. And what a scent!

■ When you add a new Collapsible Panel, it will appear by default using the full width of the page, so you may want to insert it in a table cell, as shown in the illustration at the bottom of this page, or add an AP div and insert the Collapsible Panel inside that.

■ Insert the Collapsible Panel widget using the ⊞ Spry Collapsible Panel button on the Spry tab of the Insert bar or the Insert>Spry>Spry Collapsible Panel command.

■ To create the panel content, replace the word Tab with the content you want to appear as the panel's tab, and then insert the panel's content in the Content area.

■ You can choose whether the collapsible panel will be open or closed by default when it displays in the browser. If you enable animation, the text in the panel will appear to scroll down line by line as it appears.

■ As for other Spry widgets, you can, if desired, modify the CSS styles that control tab color and tab and content fonts.

Create a Spry Accordion

■ An accordion is an interactive element that shows and hides panels as you click panel labels. Similar to the Collapsible Panel, you'll want to create this widget in an AP div or a table as well. The illustration at the top of the next page shows an accordion with five labels and panels.

■ Clicking a tab hides any other panels to display only the panel below that head. The opening and closing motion of the panels gives the accordion its name.

■ Insert a Spry Accordion widget using the ⊞ Spry Accordion button or the Insert>Spry>Spry Accordion command.

■ You can type new labels and content directly in the widget. When you have completed the first label and its content, move the mouse pointer near the lower-right corner of the next label to display the eye, as shown in the illustration at the top of the next page, and click the eye to display the next panel.

■ To add or remove panels, use the ⊞ or ⊟ button in the Property inspector. Use the ▲ or ▼ button to change the order of labels and their associated content panels.

Collapsible panel properties

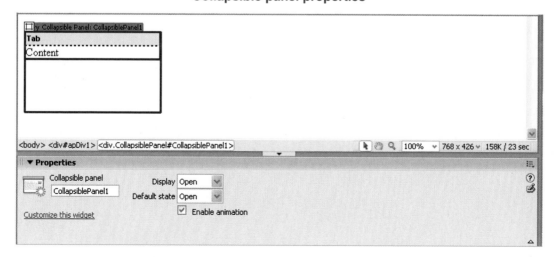

Accordion consisting of five labels and panels

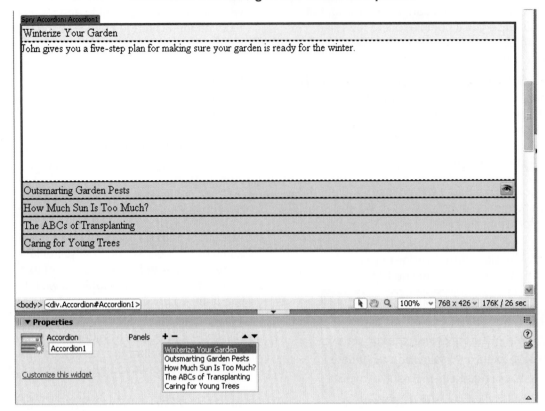

Other Spry Elements

- The Spry tab on the Insert bar offers additional Spry objects you can add to a page.

- The Tabbed Panels widget inserts an object with tabs arranged horizontally at the top and panels associated with each tab for content. Click a tab in the browser to see the content panel for that tab. You insert text in the tabs and content panels as for a Collapsible Panel or Accordion widget.

- The Spry data tools offer you a number of ways to work with an existing XML data set:

  - Spry XML Data Set allows you to create a connection to an XML file that you can then use to create a table or interactive region on a page. This process is similar to creating a database connection for a form.

- Use Spry Region to create an area on a page where you can insert another Spry object, such as a Spry table or repeat list.

- If you want to insert repetitive data, such as a list of values from a data set, you can use Spry Repeat and Spry Repeat List to format the region and display the list. You can set up a Repeat List as a bulleted, numbered, definition, or drop-down list.

- Use Spry Table to insert a table that displays static or dynamic data. You can add sort functionality to allow a visitor to sort table data by heading in the browser.

PROCEDURES

Insert Spry Validation Widgets

To insert a Validation widget:

1. Click **Insert** .... [Alt]+[I]
2. Point to **Spry** .... [S]
3. Select the desired Validation widget:
   - **Spry Validation Text Field** .... [E]
   - **Spry Validation Select** .... [S]
   - **Spry Validation Checkbox** .... [C]
   - **Spry Validation Textarea** .... [X]

   OR
   - Click or drag the desired Validation button from the Spry tab of the Insert bar.

In the Input Tag Accessibility Attributes dialog box:

1. Type a label for the form field and select any label options.
2. Click [OK] .

To copy Spry files to the local site:

- Save the page on which you have just inserted a Spry element and click [OK] to copy dependent files to the site.

To set properties for the field:

- Click the form field within the blue tabbed outline and set properties using the Property inspector as for a regular Dreamweaver form field.

To set validation options:

1. Click the blue tabbed outline around the widget to display widget properties.
2. Select validation options from those offered for each field type. For every Validation widget you should:
   a. Insert a name for the Spry field.
   b. Specify whether the field is required.
   c. Indicate the point at which validation occurs.

Insert a Spry Menu Bar Widget

To insert a Menu Bar widget:

1. Click **Insert** .... [Alt]+[I]
2. Point to **Spry** .... [S]
3. Click **Spry Menu Bar** .... [M]

   OR
   - Click the **Spry Menu Bar** button from the Spry tab of the Insert bar.

In the Spry Menu Bar dialog box:

1. Select **Horizontal** or **Vertical**.
2. Click [OK] .
3. Name the menu bar in the Property inspector.

To set up links for the menu bar:

1. Click the blue tabbed outline to select the widget.
2. Click **Item 1** in the first column in the Property inspector.
3. Type a name for the button in the **Text** box.
4. Insert a link for the button in the **Link** box, if desired.

5. Set up the submenu for the first item, if necessary:
   a. With the first item selected in the first column, click **Item 1.1** in the second column.
   b. Supply a name and a link for the item as directed in steps 3 and 4.
6. Set up a submenu for the submenu item, if necessary:
   a. With the first submenu item selected in the second column, click the **Add menu item** button [+] above the third column to insert an **Untitled item**.
   b. Supply a name and a link for the item as directed in steps 3 and 4.

To adjust menu items:

- Use the [+] or [−] button to add or remove an item.
- Use the [▲] or [▼] button to move an item up or down the list.
- Use the [Turn Styles Off] button if you want to turn off formatting so you can see the navigation outline.

Create a Spry Collapsible Panel

To insert a Collapsible Panel widget:

1. Click **Insert** .... [Alt]+[I]
2. Point to **Spry** .... [S]
3. Click **Spry Collapsible Panel** .... [C], [C], [Enter]

   OR
   - Click the **Spry Collapsible Panel** button from the Spry tab of the Insert bar.

To add content to the Collapsible Panel widget:

1. Select the **Tab** placeholder text and type new tab content.
2. Select the **Content** placeholder text and type new panel content.

To adjust Collapsible Panel properties:

- Type a name for the collapsible panel in the Property inspector.
- Change the Display and Default state options from Open to Closed if desired.
- Deselect **Enable animation** if you don't want the panel's text to scroll into view.

Create a Spry Accordion

To insert an Accordion widget:

1. Click **Insert** .... Alt + I
2. Point to **Spry** .... S
3. Click **Spry Accordion** .... A

   OR

   - Click the **Spry Accordion** button 📇 from the Spry tab of the Insert bar.

To add content to the Accordion widget:

1. Type a name for the accordion in the Property inspector.
2. Select the **Label 1** placeholder text and type new label content.
3. Select the **Content 1** placeholder text and type new panel content.
4. Select the **Label 2** placeholder text and type new content.
5. Move the mouse pointer over the right side of the Label 2 tab until the eye displays.
6. Click the eye to display the Content 2 panel.
7. Replace the **Content 2** placeholder with new text.

To adjust accordion items:

- Use the ⊞ or ⊟ button to add or remove a panel.
- Use the ▲ or ▼ button to move a panel up or down the list.

EXERCISE DIRECTIONS

1. Start Dreamweaver and open the gardenprojects site.
2. Add the following pages to the site from the Lesson 6 Data folder: ◉ index.html, ◉ tutorials.html, ◉ news.html, and ◉ products.html. Save each page in the site.
3. Open index.html and click in the AP div beneath the photo.
4. Insert a Spry Validation Text Field with the following properties:
   - Type the label **E-Mail** in the Input Tag Accessibility Attributes dialog box.
   - In the Property inspector, replace the default text field name with **email**.
   - Choose the Email Address type.
   - Set the Preview state to Initial.
   - Specify that the field is required and choose to validate on Blur.
5. Save your changes, allowing Dreamweaver to store the Spry files in the site, and then preview the page in the browser. Try entering an incomplete address in the E-Mail field to see how you are prompted for information.
6. Select the horizontal navigation bar at the top of the index.html page and delete it.
7. Insert a horizontal Spry Menu Bar widget in that space.

   ✔ *Press Enter if needed to move the page heading out of the way You may also need to click and drag the photo further down the page.*

8. Create the menu bar properties as follows in the Property inspector:
   - Name the menu bar **homemenu**.
   - Click Item 1 and rename the item as **Home**. In the second column, click the ⊟ button to remove the submenu items.
   - Click Item 2 and rename the item as **Tutorials**. In the second column, click the ⊞ button to add three items. Name them **Natural Habitat**, **Landscaping**, and **Water Gardening**. Remove the dummy link in each of the Link boxes for the three items in the second column and type **tutorials.html** as the link for each.
   - Click Item 3 and rename the item as **News**, linking to news.html. Remove the submenu items in the second and third columns.
   - Click Item 4 and rename the item as **Products**. Link the item to products.html.

9. Save the page and preview it in the browser, testing all links. (You will have to use the Back button to return to the home page, because the Home links on the navigation tables are currently incorrect.) Your page should look similar to Illustration A as you select an option from the menu bar.

10. Open the news.html page.

11. Open the ⊙ articletxt.html page.

12. Click news.html and click in the light yellow table cell and insert a Spry Accordion.

13. Insert content for the accordion as follows:

   ▪ Name the accordion **articles**.

   ▪ Copy and paste the information from articletxt.html into the accordion, as follows:

   ▪ Replace Label 1 with the heading **Winterize Your Garden**.

   ▪ Replace Content 1 with the article description.

   ▪ Replace Label 2 with the heading **Outsmarting Garden Pests**.

   ▪ Add that article's description in Content 2.

   ▪ Add three more accordion items by clicking the blue box surrounding the accordion and clicking ⊞ three times in the Property inspector. Add the rest of the information from articletxt.html to complete the set of articles.

14. Save the page, clicking OK to save the supporting Spry files, and preview it in the browser. Click each label to see the color change and the accordion action.

15. Close all open pages and the browser and exit Dreamweaver.

Illustration A

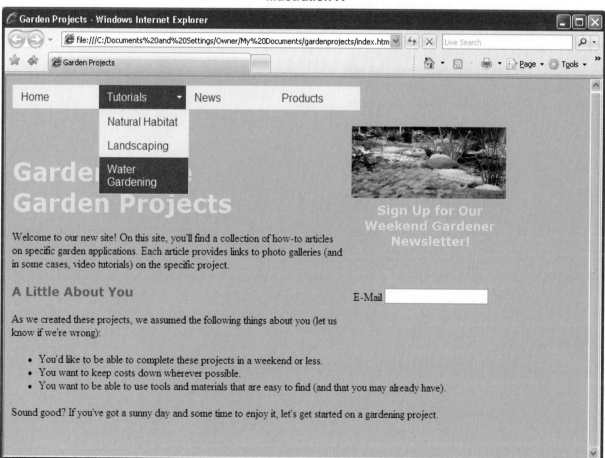

ON YOUR OWN

As you have learned, Spry widgets are formatted using CSS. To become familiar with the CSS formatting, try adjusting some of the formats of the widgets you have inserted in the tutorials site.

1. Start Dreamweaver and open the gardenprojects site.

2. Open the index.html page and view the styles in the CSS Styles panel for the Spry horizontal menu bar. Change the font of the menu bar items as follows:

   ■ Locate the ul.MenuBarHorizontal rule.

   ■ Add the font-family property to the rule and specify the Arial, Helvetica, sans serif font family. You should see all text in the menu bar change to the new font.

   ■ Locate the rule that begins ul.MenuBarHorizontal a:hover and choose a new color that will display when you hover the mouse pointer over the buttons.

   ■ You may also want to change the rule that controls the color of a button when you are hovering over a submenu of that button, ul.MenuBarHorizontal a:MenuBarItemHover.

3. Save changes to all pages and view the page in the browser to see your new styles in effect.

4. Apply the .text CSS style to the menu items, just as you would apply the style to any text: click in the label and apply the style.

5. Open the news.html page and view the styles for the accordion in the CSS Styles panel. Make the following changes:

   ■ Add a property to the .AccordionPanelTab rule to change the font family to Arial, Helvetica, sans serif.

   ■ Add another property to change the font weight to bolder.

   ■ Add the Arial font-family property to the .AccordionPanelContent rule.

   ■ Add the font-weight property for AccordionPanelContent and change it to lighter.

6. Save changes to the style sheet and view the page in the browser.

7. Close all open pages and the browser and exit Dreamweaver.

Exercise | 50

Skills Covered

- About Adobe Flash
- Start Flash and Create a New Document
- Set Document Properties
- Enter Content on the Stage
- Change the Stage View

Software Skills Adobe Flash CS3 is a software program you use to create animations and applications that range from simple (such as an animated logo) to very complex (an interactive game).

Design Skills Being able to add animation, video, and more to the Web pages you create expands your skill set as a Web designer.

Application Skills You will be developing Flash content to include on the GardenProjects Web site. In this exercise, you learn some basic Flash concepts, start Flash, explore the Flash interface, and then exit Flash.

TERMS

Actions Built-in Flash components you can use to animate Flash applications.

Flash Player A program used to run Flash applications.

Frames The basic unit of time used in a Flash animation.

Objects Elements you add to the Stage and animate in Flash.

Stage The central work area of the screen where you create Flash applications.

Timeline The Flash panel at the top of the screen where you arrange, sequence, and set the timing of Flash objects.

NOTES

About Flash

- Use Flash to create Flash applications, to publish applications for use in other programs such as a Web browser, and to play applications on your computer.

- A document file that you create, save, and edit with Flash has a .fla file extension.

- When you publish the file, it is saved with a .swf file extension. You play .swf files using the **Flash Player** program.

- Flash applications are comprised of a series of **frames**, called a **Timeline**. You insert content such as shapes, images, and **actions** on the frames. When you play the application, the frames are displayed in sequence, so that the content appears to change and move.

- This process is similar to creating a flipbook from a simple pad of paper. If you draw a picture on each page in the pad, and then flip the pages quickly, the picture seems to move. A Flash application functions on the same basic principle, with each frame active as a page in the pad of paper.

- Some of Flash's unique features include the following:
  - Flash has a built-in vector-based graphics drawing utility that you can use to draw, edit, and modify shapes.
  - Flash enables you to create both bitmap and vector graphics for use in your animations.
  - You can incorporate interactivity in Flash applications. For example, you can set buttons and images to start actions when clicked, enabling users to access different parts of the application or to start different animations.
  - Flash files download faster and start playing faster than other similar file types because they are smaller and they are streamed, which means they start playing while they are still downloading.

Start Flash and Create a New Document

- Start Adobe Flash CS3 by selecting it in your All Programs menu
- By default, when you first start Flash, the Start page displays, as shown in the illustration below.
- From the Start page, you can open a recent item, create a new item, create an item from a template, or extend the capabilities of your version of Flash by visiting the Flash Exchange Web site.
- If the Start page is not displayed, you can create a new Flash document by choosing the File>New menu command and choosing the document type you want to create in the New Document dialog box, as shown in the illustration at the top of the next page.

Adobe Flash CS3 Start page

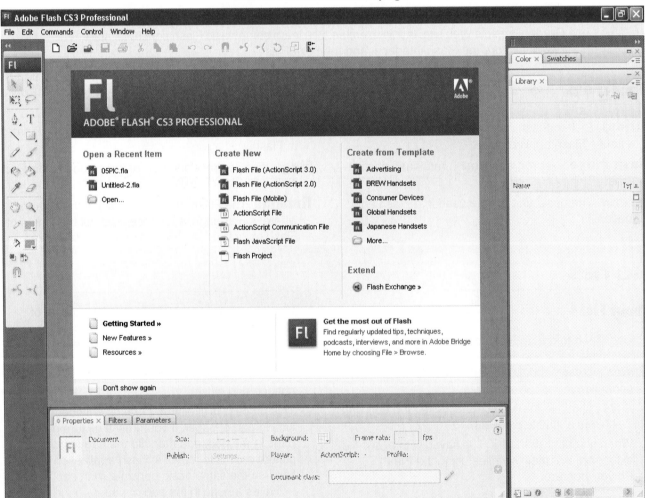

Start a new Flash document

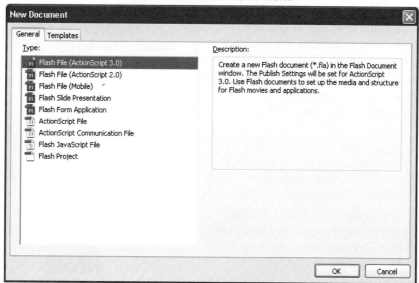

Explore the Flash Window

■ A new Flash document file opens in the Flash window.

✓ *If someone has rearranged the Flash screen on your system, the screen that opens on your computer may not look exactly like the default screen shown in the following illustration.*

■ In addition to typical Windows elements such as a title bar, menu bar, and control buttons, the Flash interface includes the following screen elements.

- *Stage.* The rectangular area where you create content and preview the file.

- *Pasteboard.* The gray area outside the stage, where you store content that you do not want to display when the file plays.

Flash Screen

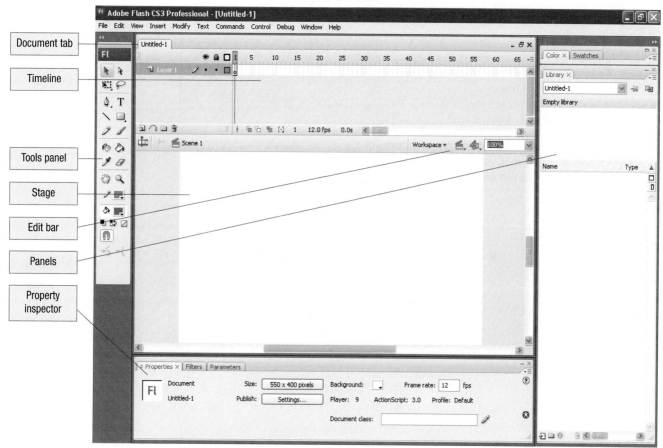

- *Panels.* Panels along the right side of the stage in which you select options to control the behavior or appearance of the selected object. The panel name appears on its title bar. You can collapse or expand panels as needed.
- *Timeline.* A special panel where you organize and control content using layers and frames. The timeline is explored more fully in the next section.
- *Property Inspector.* A panel that displays the most commonly used attributes for the currently selected item. You can view and modify the attributes in the Property Inspector.
- *Toolbars.* Flash displays the Edit Bar by default in the work area. To display the other toolbars, choose the Window>Toolbars menu command and click the toolbar you want to add.

Understand the Timeline

- The timeline is a vitally important part of arranging, ordering, and timing your Flash projects (see the illustration at the bottom of this page).
  - The layers of your Flash document appear in the column on the left side of the timeline.
  - The frames in each layer appear in a row to the right of the layer name.
  - The timeline header shows frame numbers.
  - The playhead moves as the animation plays, showing the current frame (the one displayed on the stage)
  - The timeline status bar shows the current frame number, the current frame rate, and the elapsed time of the current frame.

Learn about the Tools Panel

- The tools panel gives you a collection of tools you use to draw, paint, select, and modify content, and to change the view of the stage.

- Some of the tools are similar to the ones you find in Fireworks CS3; others are unique to Flash.
- Tools that display small arrows in the lower-right corner of the tool offer additional tools behind the currently displayed tool. To display the additional tools, click and hold the mouse button on the tool.
- The tools panel includes tools for selecting **objects**, drawing and painting on the stage, applying color, setting color preferences, and zooming the display, as the following illustration shows. The lower portion of the tools panel displays additional choices that relate to the specific tools you select.

Tools Panel

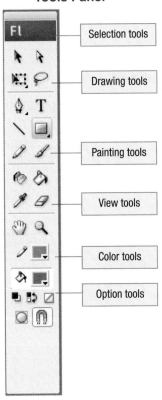

Timeline elements

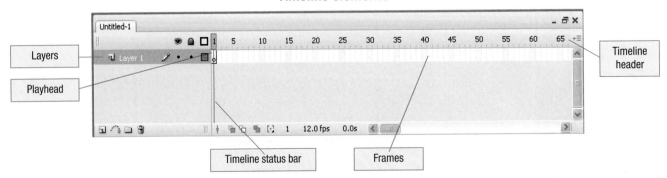

Set Document Properties

- Before you create content in a Flash document, you should set the document properties in the Properties inspector.

- In the Property Inspector, you can set the frame rate (fps), the size of the Stage, and the color of the background (see the illustration at the bottom of this page).

  ✔ *You can also set document properties in the Document Properties dialog box. Display the dialog box by choosing the Modify>Document menu command.*

- Frame rate in Flash is measured in frames per second (fps). The default frame rate is 12.

- By default, Stage size is measured in pixels (px). The default size of the Stage is 550 × 400 px. The minimum size is 18 × 18 px; the maximum size is 2880 × 2880 px.

- You can select a background color from the color palette. The hexadecimal color code for the selected color appears in the code box at the top of the palette when you click [ ].

Enter Content on the Stage

- Adding content in Flash involves using the tools in the Tools panel to draw your objects directly on the Stage. You can also import objects such as pictures, sound, video, or text.

- The quality of objects that you draw may depend on your artistic ability. However, anyone can learn to create basic shapes and apply formatting to enhance content in an application.

- To quickly draw an oval, for example, you select the Oval tool ○ , and then drag the mouse pointer on the Stage.

- Flash displays the shape using the default color settings.

  ✔ *You will learn more about drawing basic shapes in Exercise 51.*

Change the Stage View

- You can close or hide panels you don't need when entering content on the Stage. For example, close the Timeline while drawing objects so that it does not obscure the top of the Stage.

- You can use the Zoom control in the edit bar to change the magnification setting of the Stage.

- Changing the magnification does not affect the actual size of the objects on the Stage. It affects only the appearance of the objects on your screen.

Property Inspector

Stage size | Background color | Current frame rate

PROCEDURES

Start Flash

1. Click ◢ start ◣ / 🖼
   on the Windows
   taskbar................................... ⊞
2. Click **All Programs**.............. Ⓟ
3. Click **Adobe Web Standard CS3**.

   ✔ *If you are using a different suite, the program name displayed in All Programs will vary from the one shown here.*

4. Click **Adobe Flash CS3 Professional**

   OR

   ▪ Double-click the **Adobe Flash CS3 Professional** icon on the desktop.

Create a New Document

1. Start Flash.
2. On the Start page, under Create New, click **Flash File**.

   ✔ *Choose Flash File (ActionScript 3.0) to create a file that reflects the latest Web standards.*

   OR

   ▪ Click the **New** button 🗋 on the main toolbar.

   OR

1. Click **File** .... Alt + F
2. Click **New** .... Ⓝ
3. Click **Flash File**.
4. Click **OK** .... Enter

Set Document Properties

Set the Stage size:

1. Create a new Flash document.
2. Click **Modify** .... Alt + M
3. Click **Document** .... D

   OR

   ▪ In Property Inspector, click the **Size** button.

   ✔ *The Document Properties dialog box appears, with the width value selected.*

4. In the Dimensions setting, type a new Stage width.
5. Press **Tab** .... Tab ⇆
6. Type a new Stage height.
7. Click **OK** .... Enter

Set the Frame rate:

1. Click **Modify** .... Alt + M
2. Click **Document** .... D
3. Click **Frame rate** .... Alt + F
4. Type a new Frame rate.
5. Click **OK** .... Enter

   OR

1. In the Property Inspector, select the current Frame rate.
2. Type a new Frame rate.

Set the Background color:

1. Click **Modify** .... Alt + M
2. Click **Document** .... D
3. Click the **Background color** palette 🔲 .

   OR

   ▪ In Property Inspector, click the **Background color** palette 🔲 .

   ✔ *The mouse pointer changes to an eye dropper.*

4. On the color palette, click the desired color.

   OR

   a. In the Hexadecimal code box, type the code for desired color.
   b. Press **Enter** .... Enter

5. Click **OK** .... Enter

Change the Ruler units:

1. Click **Modify** .... Alt + M
2. Click **Document** .... D
3. Click **Ruler units** .... Alt + R + ↓ , ↑
4. Click desired unit.
5. Click **OK** .... Enter

Draw an Oval on the Stage

1. In Tools panel, click **Oval** tool ◯ .... Ⓞ
2. Position the mouse pointer at the desired location on the Stage.
3. Click and drag to draw the shape.
4. Release the mouse button.

   ✔ *See Exercise 51 for more information on drawing basic shapes in Flash.*

Hide and Display the Timeline

Hide the Timeline:

▪ Click 🖼 Hide/Show Timeline.

   OR

1. Click **Window**.............. Alt , W
2. Click **Timeline** .... M

Display the Timeline:

1. Click **Window**.............. Alt , W
2. Click **Timeline** .... M

Change the Stage View

▪ On edit bar, type desired magnification percentage in **Zoom** box 100% ▾ .

   OR

1. Click **Zoom control** drop-down arrow 100% ▾ .

   OR

   a. Click **View** .... Alt + V
   b. Click **Magnification** .... M

2. Click desired percentage:

   ▪ **Fit in Window** .... W
   ▪ **25%**
   ▪ **50%**............................ %5
   ▪ **100%**........................... !1
   ▪ **200**............................. @2
   ▪ **400**............................. $4
   ▪ **800**............................. *8
   ▪ **Show Frame** .... F
   ▪ **Show All**..................... A

EXERCISE DIRECTIONS

1. Start Flash.
2. Create a new document.
3. Move the mouse pointer over each of the tools in the Tools panel and review the ToolTips.
4. Change the Stage size to 300 × 300.
5. Create a new document and save it with the name S_50oval_xx.
6. Hide the Timeline by clicking 🔳.
7. Open the Document Properties dialog box and change the Background color to light yellow (#FFFFCC).
8. Change the Frame rate to 10.
9. Set the magnification to 50%.
10. Set the magnification to Show All.

11. Select the ⬭ Oval tool by holding the mouse button after clicking the 🔲 Rectangle tool.

   ✔ *Notice that the Property Inspector now displays properties for the oval shape.*

12. In the Property inspector, select a Stroke color of #663333.
13. Change the Stroke fill to #FFCC99.
14. Change the Stroke height to 4.
15. Draw an oval in the upper-left corner of the Stage. Redisplay the timeline. Your screen should resemble Illustration A.
16. Save the changes to the file.
17. Close the file.
18. Exit Flash.

Illustration A

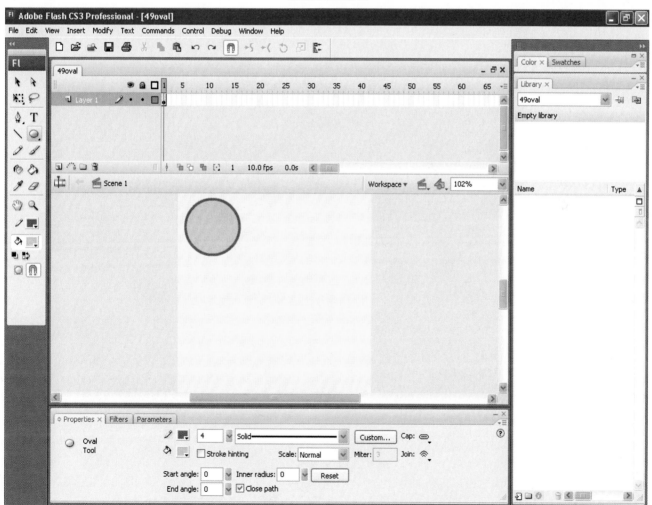

ON YOUR OWN

1. Start Flash and create a new document.
2. Change the size of the Stage to fit dimensions to your liking.
3. Set the background color as desired.
4. Click the drawing tool of your choice.
5. Set the Stroke color, Stroke fill, and Stroke height as desired.
6. Draw a shape on the Stage.
7. Change the view to Fit in Window.
8. Save the file as SO_50sample_xx in your Solutions folder.
9. Exit Flash.

Exercise | 51

Skills Covered

- **Draw Basic Shapes in Flash**
- **Select Objects**
- **Position Objects on the Stage**
- **Transform Objects**
- **Arrange the Stack Order**
- **Group and Ungroup Objects**

Software Skills You are already familiar with the Fireworks drawing tools from an earlier exercise, and using Flash tools is a similar process. Knowing how to draw shapes in Flash is the foundation for the animation and interactivity objects you add to your Web pages.

Design Skills Knowing how to make the most of your Flash drawing and painting tools enables you to create unique, creative drawings that you can then animate and use on your Web pages.

Application Skills In this exercise, you build on your knowledge of Flash by adding, positioning, modifying, and grouping objects in a Flash document.

TERMS

Guides Horizontal and vertical lines you drag out of the ruler to align objects on the Stage.

Snap ring A small black ring displayed on the mouse pointer when the Snap to Objects command has been selected. The ring becomes larger when the object is near a snap location.

Transformation handles Small rectangles around the sides of a bounding box that can be dragged to transform an object.

Transformation point The center point of an object. Sometimes called the *registration point* or *center point*.

NOTES

Draw Basic Shapes in Flash

- Use the tools in the Flash Tools panel to draw shapes, lines, and paths.

- Many of the tools have options that enable you to modify the object before or after you draw. The options become available in the Options area of the Tools panel when you select the tool.

- To draw basic geometric shapes, you use the Line \, Oval ○ , and Rectangle □ tools.

  - The Rectangle Corner Radius options become available in the Property inspector when you select the Rectangle tool. Enter a value if you want to draw a rectangle with rounded corners. The larger the corner radius value, the more rounded the corner. The default is 0, which creates a 90-degree corner.

- The Pencil tool ✎ lets you draw freeform lines and shapes as if drawing with a real pencil. Options for the pencil enable you to adjust the smoothness of the line.

- Similar to the tools in Fireworks, you use the Pen tool ◊ to draw precise straight or curved lines. You also use the Brush tool ✎ to draw as if painting with a paint brush. Options let you control the size and shape of the brush.

- Flash has two drawing models:

  - *Merge Drawing model.* By default, Flash uses this drawing model, which automatically merges overlapping shapes. If you move or delete a shape that overlaps another shape, the underlying shape is permanently altered (see the illustration on the next page).

Drawing with the Merge Drawing model

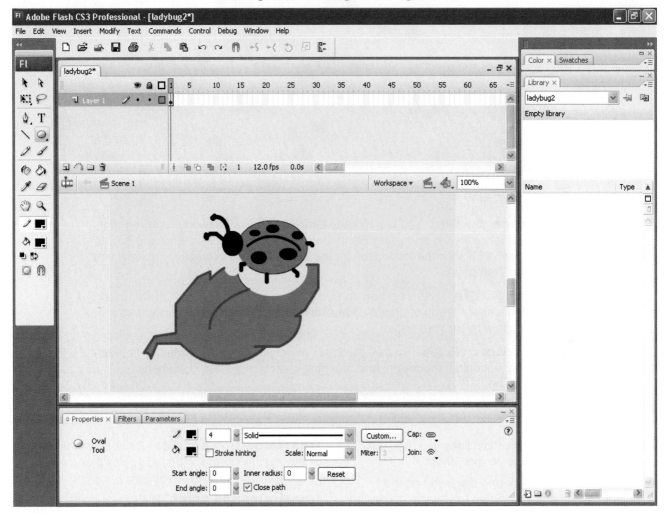

- *Object Drawing model.* This model lets you draw overlapping shapes without them merging or affecting the appearance of other shapes on the Stage (see the illustration at right). You turn the Object Drawing model on or off by clicking the ⬚ Object Drawing tool at the bottom of the Tools panel.

  ✔ *The Object Drawing tool appears only when the Line, Rectangle, Oval, Pen, Pencil, or Brush tools are selected.*

  ✔ *In order for the Object Drawing model to work properly, you must select it before you begin drawing an object.*

- ■ You can combine both drawing models in a single drawing.

Drawing with the Object Drawing model

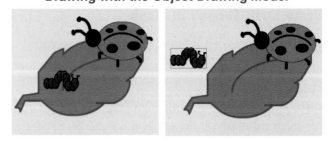

Select Objects

- In order to edit or modify an object on the Stage, you must first select it.
- Use the Selection tool ▶ to select one or more objects.
- You can also use the Lasso tool ♀ to select objects by drawing either a freehand or a straight-edged selection area. The Lasso tool is useful if the object you want to select is very close to a different object.
- When Merge Drawing is active, Flash applies a dot pattern to highlight selected objects to help you identify them on the Stage.
- When Object Drawing is active, Flash displays a rectangular bounding box around selected objects.
- In addition, when Merge Drawing is active, all lines, shapes, and fills are considered separate objects. You must be sure to select all parts of a drawing that you need.
- For example, if you want to move both the stroke and fill of an oval when Merge Drawing is active, you must be sure to select both the stroke and fill. If you select only the fill, and then move it, the stroke remains in its original location.

Position Objects on the Stage

- You can drag selected objects on the Stage to move them to a new location.
- Flash includes visual elements to help you position objects on the Stage, including horizontal and vertical rulers, a grid, and **guides** (see the illustration below).
- Display the rulers and the grid by choose Rulers or Grid from the View menu.
- The unit of measurement on the rulers depends on your selection in the Document Properties dialog box.
- By default, the spacing between grid lines is 18 px, or .25", but you can edit the grid to change the spacing. You can also change the color of the grid lines and remove them when you no longer need them.
- Flash also includes features to help you snap objects to a location on the Stage.
  - To automatically position objects on the nearest grid lines, make the Snap to Grid feature active.
  - By default, the Snap to Objects feature is active so that you can snap an object to the edge of an object already positioned on the Stage.

Tools for positioning objects on the stage

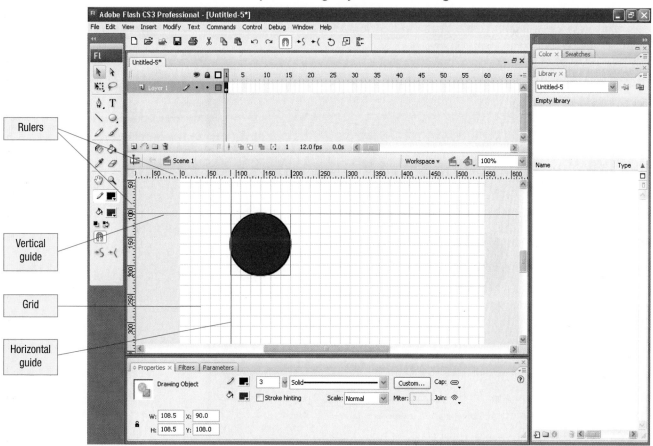

Rulers

Vertical guide

Grid

Horizontal guide

- The Snap Align feature displays a dotted line when you drag an object to a preset distance relative to the edge of another object or to the Stage boundary.

- By default, the dotted line displays when the edge of the object you are dragging is within 18 px of the Stage boundary or within 0 px of an object already on the Stage.

- Snap to Guides automatically snaps an object to a horizontal or vertical guide line.

- When you draw an object with any snap feature active, a **snap ring** displays at the pointer location. When the snap ring increases in size, it means that the object is aligned with the specified location (see the illustration at the bottom of this page).

  - For example, with Snap to Objects, the snap ring increases in size when the object aligns with the edge of an existing object, indicating that you can drop the object to align it with the edge of the object already in place.

  - With Snap to Grid, the snap ring increases in size when the object aligns with a grid line.

  - With Snap to Guides, the snap ring increases in size when the object aligns with a guide line.

- The position of the pointer on the object provides the reference point for the snap ring. For example, if the snap ring displays in the center of an oval, the center of the oval is the point that snaps to the specified location.

Transform Objects

- Use Flash's transformation tools to modify the appearance of an object on the Stage.

- You can rotate, skew, scale, flip, resize, and distort objects.

- When you select the ⊞ Free Transform tool, all transformation options are available. Alternatively, you may select the specific type of transformation you want to perform.

- When you select an object or objects for transformation, a bounding box displays around the selection. **Transformation handles** display around the bounding box and a **transformation point** displays in the center of the selection (see the illustration at the top of the next page).

- The position of the transformation point is determined by the X and Y coordinates, which display in the Info panel or in the Property Inspector. You can move the transformation point by dragging it, or by changing the X and Y settings.

Using Snap to features

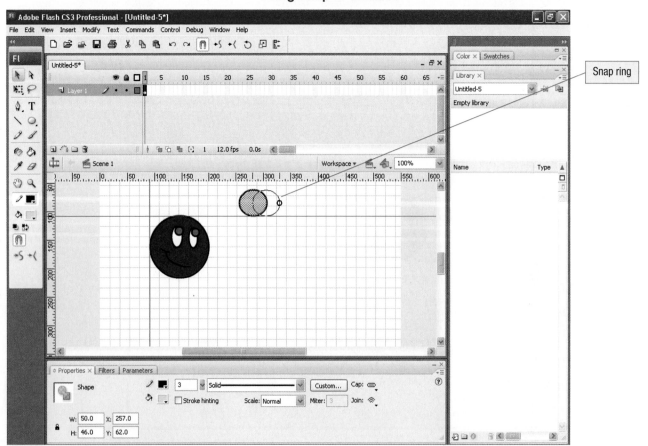

Transformation tools

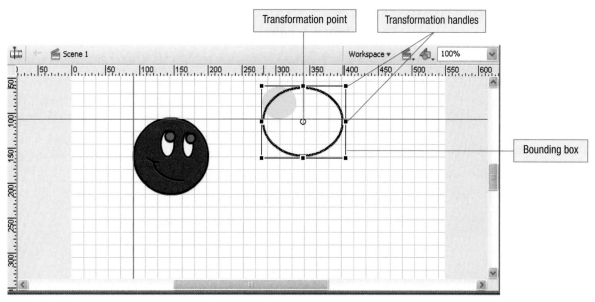

Arrange the Stack Order

- By default, newer objects are stacked on top of existing objects.

- You can arrange the stack order for grouped objects, or for objects drawn using the Drawing Object model in order to move objects forward, backward, behind, or in front of other objects.

- Individual objects drawn using the Merge Drawing model cannot be rearranged.

Group and Ungroup Objects

- Group objects together when you want to modify or transform them as one single object.

- For example, if you draw a face that includes a head, nose, eyes, mouth, and hair, you can group all of the lines and fills comprising the face into a single object so you can quickly select and modify it.

- In addition, grouped objects do not create segments or cutouts when they overlap other objects.

- A bounding box displays around all objects in a selected group, instead of the highlights used to indicate selected Merge Drawing objects. The group's transformation point also displays (see the illustration below).

- You can edit objects within a group without ungrouping them using edit mode. In edit mode, only the objects in the group are available for editing; all other objects on the Stage are dimmed.

Select a group or individual objects

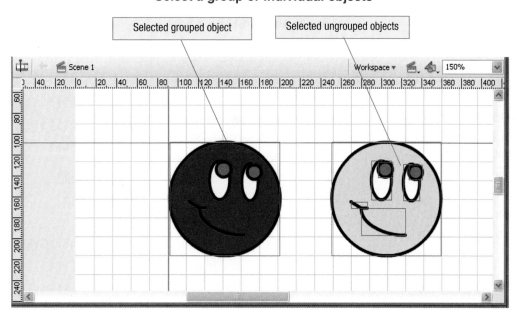

PROCEDURES

Draw Basic Shapes

Draw oval:

1. Click **Oval** tool ⬭ ....[O]
2. Click and drag on the Stage to draw the shape.

Draw freeform lines and shapes:

1. Click the **Pencil** tool ✏ ....[Y]
2. Click the **Smoothness** option button.

   ✔ *The Smoothness option button displays the most recently selected Smoothness option.*

3. Click desired Smoothness option:
   - **Straighten** ⌁ to draw straight lines and shapes.
   - **Smooth** S to draw smooth curved lines.
   - **Ink** ⚡ to apply no modification; in other words, lines display just as you draw them.
4. Click and drag on the Stage to draw the shape.

Draw Paths on Straight Line Segments

1. Click the **Pen** tool ✒ ....[P]
2. Click on the Stage at the desired starting point.
3. Click at each point as desired.
4. Double-click at the last point to end the line.

Draw Paths on Curved Line Segments

1. Click the **Pen** tool ✒ ....[P]
2. Click on the Stage at the desired starting point.
3. Drag to next desired point.
4. Release mouse button.
5. Repeat steps 3 and 4.
6. Double-click at the last point to end the line.

Draw Brush Strokes

1. Click **Brush** tool ✎ ....[B]
2. Click **Brush Mode** option button.

   ✔ *The Brush Mode option button displays the most recently selected Brush Mode option.*

3. Click the desired Brush Mode option:
   - **Paint Normal** ⊙ to paint over existing lines, fills, and blank areas.
   - **Paint Fills** ⊙ to paint over existing fills and empty areas, but leave lines unchanged.
   - **Paint Behind** ○ to paint over blank areas only, leaving lines and fills unchanged.
   - **Paint Selection** ⊙ to paint over selected areas only.
   - **Paint Inside** ⊙ to paint over a fill within a closed shape, leaving the stroke around the fill unchanged.
4. Click **Brush Size** drop-down arrow.

   ✔ *The Brush Size button displays the most recently selected Brush Size option.*

5. Click the desired brush size.
6. Click the **Brush Shape** drop-down arrow.

   ✔ *The Brush Shape button displays the most recently selected Brush Shape option.*

7. Click desired brush shape.
8. Click and drag on Stage to draw shape.

   ✔ *Press and hold Shift key to draw only horizontal or vertical strokes.*

Turn Object Drawing Model On or Off

1. Select desired drawing tool.
2. Click **Object Drawing** option button ⊙ .

   ✔ *The Object Drawing option button becomes available when the Line, Oval, Rectangle, Pen, Pencil, or Brush tool is selected.*

Select Objects

1. Click **Selection** tool ➤ ....[V]
2. Click object to select.

   OR

   a. Click **Lasso** tool ◯ ....[L]
   b. Click and drag to draw a border around the object(s) to select.

   ✔ *With the Selection tool, the border will be a rectangle; with the Lasso tool, the border will follow the mouse pointer, like drawing with a pencil.*

3. Release mouse button.

To select both stroke and fill of merge drawing shape at the same time:

- Double-click in the center of the fill.

To select all objects on the stage:

1. Click **Edit** ....[Alt]+[E]
2. Click **Select All**...................[L]

Use Rulers and Guides to Position Objects

Display the rulers:

1. Click **View** ....[Alt]+[V]
2. Click **Rulers** ....[R]

Display the grid:

1. Click **View** ....[Alt]+[V]
2. Click **Grid**...........................[D]
3. Click **Show Grid** ....[D]

Apply guidelines:

1. Click in the horizontal or vertical ruler.
2. Drag a guide out from the ruler.
3. When the guide is where you want it, release the mouse button.
   OR
1. Click **View** .... Alt + V
2. Click **Guides** .... E
3. Click **Show Guides** .... U

Remove guidelines:

■ Click and drag the guide back to the ruler.
   OR
1. Click **View** .... Alt + V
2. Click **Guides** .... E
3. Click **Clear Guides**.

Turn Snap to Grid On or Off (Ctrl + Shift + ')

1. Click **View** .... Alt + V
2. Click **Snapping** .... S
3. Click **Snap to Grid** .... R

   ✔ A check mark next to the Snap to Grid command indicates that feature is currently on.

Turn Snap to Objects On or Off (Ctrl + Shift + /)

■ Click **Snap to Objects** button 🧲 on main toolbar or in Tools panel options area.

   ✔ Snap to Objects becomes available as an option in the Tools panel when the Selection, Line, Oval, or Rectangle tool is selected.

   OR
1. Click **View** .... Alt + V
2. Click **Snapping** .... S
3. Click **Snap to Objects** .... O

Turn Snap Align On or Off

1. Click **View** .... Alt + V
2. Click **Snapping** .... S
3. Click **Snap Align** .... S

Turn Snap to Guides On or Off (Ctrl + Shift + ;)

1. Click **View** .... Alt + V
2. Click **Snapping** .... S
3. Click **Snap to Guides** .... G

Transform Objects

1. Select the object to transform.
2. Click the ⊹ **Free Transform** tool .... Q
3. Drag a handle in the desired direction.
   OR
■ Drag the transformation point in the center of the object.

Group Objects (Ctrl + G)

1. Select objects to group.
2. Click **Modify** .... Alt + M
3. Click **Group** .... G

Ungroup Objects (Ctrl + Shift + G)

1. Select group.
2. Click **Modify** .... Alt + M
3. Click **Ungroup** .... U

EXERCISE DIRECTIONS

1. Create a new Flash document and save it in your Solutions folder with the name S_51garden_xx.
2. Set the Stage size to 600 × 600.
3. Add a background color of #99FFFF.
4. Hide the Timeline.
5. Display the rulers.
6. Collapse the Property inspector.

   ✔ This gives you more room to work on the Stage.

7. Turn off Snap to Objects and make sure Snap to Guides is on.
8. Set the zoom to Fit in Window.
9. Display a vertical guide 50 pixels (px) from the left boundary of the Stage.
10. Display a vertical guide 50 px from the right boundary of the Stage.
11. Display a horizontal guide 50 px from the top boundary of the Stage.

12. Display a horizontal guide 50 px from the bottom boundary of the Stage.
13. Turn on the grid.
14. Click the ＼ Line tool.
15. Display the Property inspector, and select the color #669900 for the stroke, with a Stroke height of 7.
16. Click on the left vertical guide at the 400px mark and drag the pointer down and to the right, ending at the 200px mark on the bottom horizontal guide.
17. Continue using the ＼ Line tool to create a triangle in the lower-left corner by following the guides.
18. Use the ◇ Paint Bucket tool to fill the shape with #669900.
19. Click the ✏ Brush tool and choose a medium sized brush using the Brush Size tool. Set Smoothing to 60.
20. With #669900 as the color, draw the beginning of a vine emerging from the green triangle. Use Illustration A on the next page as a reference as you draw.

21. Zoom to 150%. Use the ✋ Hand tool to move the vine up into the Stage where you can work with it easily.

22. Click the ✏ Pencil tool and make sure that 🔘 Object Drawing is turned off. Click the ↳ Pencil Mode tool and choose 〜 Smooth.

23. Add a bud to the image by drawing and filling (with the Paint Bucket tool) a green area at the bottom and use the Pencil and Paint Bucket to add a fluorescent pink (#FF00CC). See the large bud in Illustration A for reference.

24. Now add a smaller bud using the shape tools. Click the ⬭ Oval tool and click 🔘 Object Drawing.

25. Set the Stroke color and Fill color to #669900. Draw an oval on the Stage, approximate 40px wide and high.

26. Click the ⤢ Free Transform tool. Click the transformation point in the center of the oval and drag it up and to the right. Move the mouse pointer around the bounding box until you see the pointer

change to a bi-directional arrow. Click and drag to transform the shape and make it look more like a bud (refer to Illustration A). Resize and rotate the shape as needed to make it smaller than the painted bud.

27. Repeat the step creating the flower portion of the bud, using a Stroke and Fill color of #CC66CC. Move this oval and place it so that it overlaps the skewed oval.

28. Click the ↖ Selection tool and select both ovals. Choose the Modify>Group menu command.

29. Click 🔘 to turn off Object Drawing.

30. Move the bud below the larger bud, closer to the stem.

31. Clear the guides and remove the grid.

32. Zoom out to Fit in Window.

33. Save your work.

34. Close the file and exit Flash, unless you are continuing with the On Your Own exercise.

Illustration A

ON YOUR OWN

1. If necessary, open S_51garden_xx from your Solutions folder and resume your work.

2. Redisplay the grid.

3. Add a vertical guide to the 50px position.

4. Use the ╲ Line tool to add a stem to connect the main vine to the new bud.

5. Add another stem that grows up along the vertical guide.

6. Turn on Object Drawing.

7. Use the ⬭ Oval tool to add a cloud in the sky. Change the stroke and fill color before you draw

the shapes for the cloud. Draw multiple ovals, if you like, and group them so that you can work with them as a single object.

8. Feeling creative? Use a variety of shapes to add a bee to the document.

   ✔ *Hint: Zoom up to 400% to work at a detail level when creating the bee.*

9. Turn off Object Drawing, remove the guide, hide the grid, and save your work as SO_51garden_xx.

10. Close the file.

Skills Covered

- **About Animation**
- **About Frames and Keyframes**
- **Work with Frames and Keyframes**
- **View Frames with the Timeline**
- **Preview an Animation**

Software Skills Getting familiar with the Flash tools takes a little practice, but once you have mastered the art of creating images with the Flash drawing tools, you are ready to start creating animated applications. Animations make a Web page or presentation exciting, and Flash makes it easy to create animations. You simply enter content on frames and keyframes, and then preview the animation right on the Flash Stage.

Design Skills Creating an animation is simply a matter of choosing objects you've already drawn in Flash and arranging and modifying them to create a moving story over time. Knowing how to design a simple animation gives you more to offer clients when you design pages for them (and it's also fun).

Application Skills For the GardenProject site, you are going to create a simple animation that plays when visitors arrive at the home page for the first time. In this exercise, you will open an existing file and use frame-by-frame animation to make the image move. You will preview the animation on the Stage, and use different frame rates to see how they affect the animation.

TERMS

Elapsed time The length of time it takes to reach the current frame when the animation plays.

Frame-by-frame animation Animation created by changing the content on each frame in a sequence.

Frame sequence A series of frames beginning with a keyframe and ending with the next keyframe.

Keyframe A frame in which you specify changes in an animation.

Tweened animation Animation in which you specify a starting point and an ending point and let Flash fill in the frames between.

NOTES

About Animation

- Flash provides the tools you need to animate the content you enter in a document so that it moves or changes on the computer screen.

- You create animation by changing the content of frames in a sequence. For example, you can make an object move across the Stage, change its size or color, or even its shape.

- There are two ways to create animation in a Flash document:
  - **Frame-by-frame animation**, in which you manually change content on each subsequent frame. This is best suited for complex animations in which an image changes in every frame instead of simply moving. Frame-by-frame animation increases file size more rapidly than tweened animation.
  - **Tweened animation**, in which you specify the action on the first **keyframe** and the action on the last keyframe and let Flash fill in the frames between the two. Flash varies the object's attributes evenly between the starting and ending frames to create the appearance of movement. Tweened animation is useful for creating movement and changes over time.

    ✔ *Tweened animation is covered in the next exercise.*

About Frames and Keyframes

- A frame is the basic unit used to create an animation in Flash.

- You add a frame by pressing F5 or choosing the Insert>Timeline>Frame menu command. Choose Insert>Timeline>Keyframe to add a keyframe.

- You enter content in each frame, and then display the frames in a sequence to play the animation.

- A frame in which you specify a change in animation, or in which you include frame actions, is called a *keyframe*.

- In frame-by-frame animation, every frame is a keyframe.

- When you add a new keyframe, Flash automatically copies the content from the previous keyframe into the new one.

- In tweened animation, only the first and last frames in a sequence are keyframes.

Work with Frames and Keyframes

- By default, Flash uses frame-based selection, in which you select individual frames in the Timeline.

- You can choose to use span-based selection, in which an entire **frame sequence**—from one keyframe to the next—is selected. The content of the selected frame displays on the Stage.

- You can select a series of frames in the Timeline, but only the first frame in the series displays on the Stage.

- You can insert a frame or keyframe at any location along the Timeline. Right-click a frame to display a context menu of choices for inserting, copying, and cutting frames.

- Since Flash redraws the shapes in each keyframe, you should create keyframes only at those points in the artwork where something changes. Creating extra keyframes may result in unnecessarily large files.

- You can convert a keyframe to a frame, if you decide that a change is not going to take place at that location in the Timeline.

- Delete a frame or series of frames when you no longer need them.

- Copy or move a frame or frame series to a new location on the Timeline to rearrange or reorganize your animation, or to duplicate content from one frame to another.

View Frames with the Timeline

- You can select any frame in the Timeline to display it on the Stage. The location of the playhead indicates the current frame.

- The current frame number, frame rate, and **elapsed time** display on the Timeline status bar.

    ✔ *You can double-click the frame rate on the Timeline status bar to quickly open the Document Properties dialog box.*

- Flash uses visual codes to label frames and keyframes in the Timeline (see the illustration at the top of the next page):
  - A solid circle indicates a keyframe with content.
  - A clear circle indicates a blank keyframe.
  - By default, frames containing content are tinted gray.
  - Tinted frames following a keyframe contain the same content as the keyframe.
  - A clear rectangle marks the last frame in a sequence.

View frames in the timeline

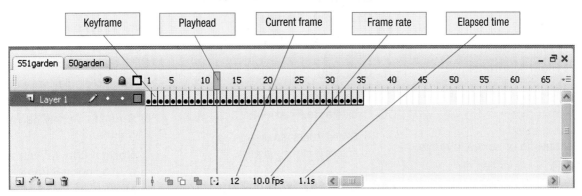

- Using the Timeline options menu, you can modify the Timeline display. For example, you can increase or decrease the height of the entire Timeline. You can also remove the tint, display previews of the contents of frames, or change the width of frames in the Timeline.

Preview an Animation

- To see how an animation looks, you can play it on the Stage.
- Use the commands on the Control menu or the Controller toolbar to play the animation.
- Display the Controller toolbar by choosing the Window>Toolbars>Controller menu command.

PROCEDURES

Select a Frame

- Click frame to select in Timeline.

Select a Frame Series

1. Click first frame in series.
2. Drag to last frame in series.
   OR
1. Click first frame in series.
2. Press and hold **Shift** .... ⏃ Shift
3. Click last frame in series.

Select All Frames (Ctrl + Alt + A)

1. Click **Edit** .... Alt + E
2. Click **Timeline** .... M
3. Click **Select All Frames** .... S

Insert a Frame in the Timeline (F5)

1. Click **Insert** .... Alt + I
2. Click **Timeline** .... T
3. Click **Frame** .... F

OR
1. Right-click frame in Timeline.
2. Click **Insert Frame**.

   ✔ The new frame displays to the right of the right-clicked frame.

Create a Keyframe (F6)

1. Select a frame in Timeline.
2. Click **Insert** .... Alt + I
3. Click **Timeline** .... T
4. Click **Keyframe**.................... K
   OR
1. Right-click frame in Timeline.
2. Click **Insert Keyframe**.

Create a Blank Keyframe (F7)

1. Select a frame in Timeline.
2. Click **Insert** .... Alt + I
3. Click **Timeline** .... T
4. Click **Blank Keyframe** .... B
   OR
1. Right-click frame in Timeline.
2. Click **Insert Blank Keyframe**.

Delete a Frame, Keyframe, or Frame Series (Shift + F5)

1. Select frame, keyframe, or frame series.
2. Click **Edit** .... Alt + E
3. Click **Timeline** .... M
4. Click **Remove Frames** .... R
   OR
1. Right-click frame, keyframe, or frame series.
2. Click **Remove Frames**.

Clear the Contents of a Frame or Keyframe (Alt + Backspace)

1. Select frame or keyframe.
2. Click **Edit** .... Alt + E
3. Click **Timeline** .... M
4. Click **Clear Frames** L
   OR
1. Right-click frame.
2. Click **Clear Frames**.

Convert a Keyframe to a Frame

1. Right-click keyframe.
2. Click **Clear Keyframe**.

Move a Frame or Frame Series

1. Select frame or series to move.
2. Drag to new location on Timeline.

   OR

1. Right-click frame or selected series to move.
2. Click **Cut Frames**.
3. Right-click new location on Timeline.
4. Click **Paste Frames**.

   OR

1. Select frame or series to move.
2. Click **E̲dit** .... Alt + E
3. Click **Ti̲meline** .... M
4. Click **Cu̲t Frames** .... T
5. Select new frame location in Timeline.
6. Click **E̲dit** .... Alt + E
7. Click **Ti̲meline** .... M
8. Click **P̲aste Frames** .... P

   ✔ *Pasted frames replace existing frames in the new location.*

Copy a Frame or Frame Series

1. Select frame or series to copy.
2. Press and hold **Alt** .... Alt
3. Drag to new location on Timeline.

   OR

1. Right-click frame or selected series to copy.
2. Click **Copy Frames**.
3. Right-click new location on Timeline.
4. Click **Paste Frames**.

   OR

1. Select frame or series to copy.
2. Click **E̲dit** .... Alt + E

3. Click **Ti̲meline** .... M
4. Click **C̲opy Frames** C
5. Select new frame location in Timeline.
6. Click **E̲dit** .... Alt + E
7. Click **Ti̲meline** .... M
8. Click **P̲aste Frames** .... P

   ✔ *Pasted frames replace existing frames in the new location.*

Copy Content from a Frame

1. Select content to copy.
2. Click **E̲dit** .... Alt + E
3. Click **C̲opy** C
4. Select destination keyframe.

   ✔ *The destination frame must be a keyframe.*

5. Click **E̲dit** .... Alt + E
6. Click one of the following:
   - **P̲aste in Center** .... A
     to paste copied contents in center of destination keyframe.
   - **Paste in Place** .... P
     to paste copied contents in same position as on original frame.

   ✔ *Copied content replaces existing content on the destination keyframe.*

Move Content from a Frame

1. Select frame.
2. Click **E̲dit** .... Alt + E
3. Click **Cut̲** .... T
4. Select destination keyframe.

   ✔ *The destination frame must be a keyframe.*

5. Click **E̲dit** .... Alt + E
6. Click one of the following:
   - **P̲aste in Center** .... A
     to paste copied contents in center of destination keyframe.
   - **Paste in Place** .... P
     to paste copied contents in same position as on original frame.

   ✔ *Copied content replaces existing content on the destination keyframe.*

Modify the Timeline Display

1. Click **Timeline options menu** ▾☰ .
2. Click desired option:
   - **Tiny** to display vary narrow frames.
   - **Small** to display narrow frames.
   - **Normal** (the default) to display normal frames.
   - **Medium** to display wider frames.
   - **Large** to display very wide frames.
   - **Preview** to display previews of frames sized to fit the Timeline frames.
   - **Preview in Context** to display previews including all white space.
   - **Short** to decrease the height of frames.
   - **Tinted Frames** to turn on or off the gray tint (on by default).

   ✔ *A check mark indicates that the option is on.*

Resize Timeline

- Drag border between Timeline and Stage up or down.

Create Frame-by-Frame Animation

1. Select or create starting keyframe.
2. Create content for first frame in animation.
3. Select next frame in sequence.
4. Create a keyframe.
5. Modify contents on Stage to create next increment of animation.
6. Repeat steps 3 through 5 to complete animation.

Preview an Animation on the Stage

1. Click first frame in the sequence.
   OR
   a. Click **Control** .... Alt + O
   b. Click **Rewind** .... R
2. Click **Control** .... Alt + O
3. Click **Play** .... P

Use the Controller Toolbar

1. Click **Window** .... Alt + W
2. Click **Toolbars** .... O
3. Click **Controller** .... O
4. Click buttons as follows:
   - **Play** ▶ to play animation.
   - **Stop** ■ to stop animation.

- **First Frame** ⏮ to rewind to first frame.
- **Step Back** ◀◀ to go to previous frame.
- **Step Forward** ▶▶ to go to next frame.
- **Last Frame** ⏭ to go to last frame.

EXERCISE DIRECTIONS

1. Start Flash and open ⊙ 52garden. Save the file as S_52garden_xx.

2. If necessary, display the Timeline and hide the rulers and the grid.

3. Decrease the height of the Timeline by dragging the border between the Timeline and the Stage up as far as possible.

4. Set the zoom to Show All.

5. Select frame 2.

6. Insert a keyframe on frame 2.

   ✔ *Flash inserts the content displayed on frame 1 on the new keyframe.*

7. Insert a keyframe on frame 3.

8. Insert a keyframe on frame 4.

9. Insert a keyframe on frame 5.

   ✔ *All frames in the sequence display the same content.*

10. Select frame 2.

11. Deselect all objects, and then select the bee. Move the bee slightly to the right (as though it's flying forward).

12. Select frame 3.

13. Deselect all objects, and then select the cloud and move it a few pixels to the right.

14. Select frame 4.

15. Deselect all objects, and then select the bee and move it to the right and up a little.

16. Continue moving the bee and the cloud for a series of keyframes.

17. Add more keyframes as you go along. When you get to frame 9, copy and paste the cloud on the right so that it enters from the left edge of the Stage. From this point on, move both clouds in subsequent keyframes.

18. Create a flying pattern for the bee.

    ✔ *Hint: Use the Free Transform tool to rotate the position of the bee in the individual frames so that he can dip and turn in his flight path.*

19. Select frame 1.

20. Play the animation.

21. Double-click the frame rate in the Timeline to open the Document Properties dialog box. Change the frame rate from 12 fps to 10 fps.

22. Adjust the zoom to Show All. Return the Timeline to normal height. Your screen should look similar to Illustration A on the next page.

23. Close the file, saving all changes, and exit Flash.

Illustration A

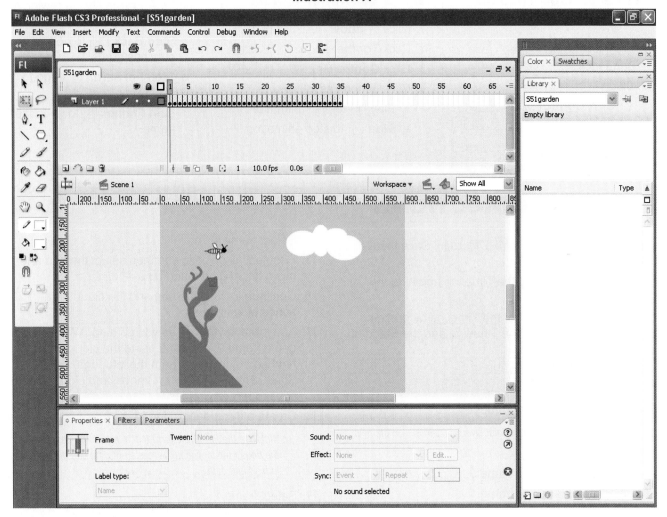

ON YOUR OWN

1. Start Flash and create a new document.

2. Save the document as SO_52myfile_xx.

3. Create an animation of a shape moving across the Stage, using at least 10 frames. For example, you might make an oval or star move from one side of the Stage to the other. Remember to use the Flash tools for positioning, such as for the grid, ruler, and guides.

4. Modify the animation so that the shape also increases in size as it moves across the Stage.

5. Add any other enhancements or transformations that you want in the animation, such as a change in fill or stroke color, or rotation.

6. Try copying or moving frames from one location in the sequence to another.

7. When you are satisfied with the animation, save it and then exit Flash.

Skills Covered

- **About Layers**
- **Work with Layers**
- **Create Graphic Symbols**
- **Add a Symbol Instance**

- **Motion Tweening**
- **Motion Tween Settings**
- **Shape Tweening**

Software Skills   Now that you know how to create a basic animation in Flash, you can explore ways to save time and effort by creating layers, converting objects to symbols, and using tweening to animate objects along a path.

Design Skills   As you've heard throughout this course, part of being a good designer means using your time efficiently and productively. You can use layers and symbols to organize and reuse items in your animations.

Application Skills   This exercise shows you how to use layers, symbols, and tweening to create a simple animation for Tierra Verde.

TERMS

Instance One occurrence of a symbol.

Library A folder in which symbols are stored.

Media assets The content you use to create an application.

Movie clip A symbol comprised of an animated sequence of frames.

Registration point A reference point used to position and transform a group, instance, text block, or bitmap.

Symbol A reusable object used to create content in an application.

NOTES

About Layers

- You can use layers to organize the content of your Flash applications.

- Layers are like clear sheets of paper piled on top of each other—you can see through them, but you can draw, edit, and animate objects on one layer without affecting objects on another layer.

- Each new document contains a single layer, but you can add as many layers as you want. The number of layers you can create is limited only by the amount of memory installed on your computer.

- Layers do not affect the size of your published application.

- Planning your layers before you create an animation can help you keep your objects organized.

- For example, it's a good idea to have a background layer that contains static images that don't change throughout the application. Additional layers might contain one animated object each. Keeping animated objects on separate layers ensures that they don't overlap or segment each other.

- Using separate layers for objects such as sound files and actions makes it easier to find those objects when you need them.

Work with Layers

- The contents of the active layer display on the Stage.

- You can insert a new layer at any time. By default, the new layer becomes the active layer.

- Move layers in the Timeline list to rearrange their stacking order. For example, move a layer up in the list to move it toward the front of the frame.

- It is a good idea to rename layers to reflect their contents. For example, you might name the layer containing static background objects *Background*, as the illustration at the bottom of this page shows.

- You can copy a layer to make an exact duplicate of it. All frames in the layer are copied.

- Delete a layer when you are certain you don't need it anymore.

- Hide layers when you want to work on one layer without being distracted by the content on other layers.

- Lock a layer when you do not want any changes made to it.

- You can also copy and move individual objects and frames from one layer to another.

Layers in the Timeline

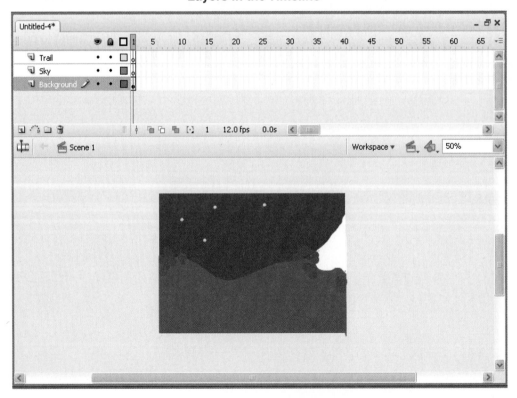

Create Graphic Symbols

■ A **symbol** is a graphic object, **movie clip**, or **button** that you create once and can use many times.

■ You can create a symbol by converting objects already entered on the Stage, or you can create an empty symbol.

■ Any symbol that you create becomes part of the **library** for the current document; you can share symbols among documents.

■ When you create a symbol, it has its own Timeline and Stage, which you can manage just as you manage the document's main Timeline and Stage. For example, you can add layers or keyframes to the symbol's Timeline.

■ You specify the symbol type in either the Convert to Symbol or the New Symbol dialog box, which are virtually the same (see the following illustration).

Convert to Symbol dialog box

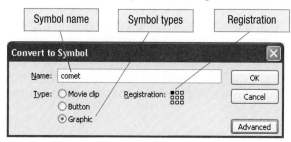

Add a Symbol Instance

■ You can easily add instances of symbols to the currently selected frame. Simply drag the symbol you want to use to the Stage. Flash creates a copy, called an instance, of the symbol and places it in the frame.

■ If you want to modify the original symbol that is saved in the Library, right-click the symbol and click Edit. The symbol opens on the Stage so that you can make changes.

✔ *Note: Working with the Library and instances in Flash is similar to the process you learned in Fireworks.*

Motion Tweening

■ In a Flash animation, the easiest way to create movement over time is to use motion tweening.

■ With motion tweening, you can animate the size, position, rotation, and skew of instances, groups, or type.

■ To create motion tweened animation, you specify the starting properties of an object on the first keyframe and the ending properties of the object on the last keyframe.

■ Flash fills in the frames between the two by evenly adjusting the properties to create the appearance of movement.

■ If you change the number of frames between the two keyframes, or move the object in either keyframe, Flash automatically updates the animation.

■ The easiest way to create a motion tween is by specifying tween properties in the Property Inspector.

■ Alternatively, use the Create Motion Tween command.

■ On the Timeline, intermediate frames in a motion tweened sequence are light blue, with a black arrow across them (see the illustration at the bottom of this page).

■ You can also tween color or transparency.

■ If you want to tween drawing objects, you must use shape tweening.

Motion tweened frames in the Timeline

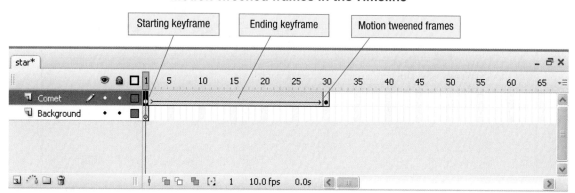

Motion Tween Settings

■ Set motion tween options in the Property Inspector.

■ Motion tween options include the following (see the top illustration at the bottom of this page):

• Scale. Select this check box if you are animating a change in size. There must be a change in size between the starting keyframe and the ending keyframe.

• Ease. Enter an easing value to control the rate of change between tweened frames. By default, the rate is constant.

■ Enter a negative value to begin the tween slowly and accelerate it toward the end of the sequence.

■ Enter a positive value to begin the tween rapidly and decelerate it toward the end of the sequence.

• Rotate. Select an option to control the direction of spin if you are animating rotation.

• Orient to Path. Select this option to orient the baseline of the tweened object to a motion path.

• Sync. Select this option to synchronize the animation of graphic symbol instances with the main Timeline.

• Snap. Select this option to attach a tween object to a motion path by its **registration point**.

Shape Tweening

■ Use shape tweening to animate a change in a shape over time. For example, you can make a square tween into an oval.

■ Shape tweening only works on shapes. You cannot use shape tweening to animate groups, instances, type, or bitmap graphics.

■ You can use shape tweening to animate a change in location, size, and color of a shape.

■ On the Timeline, the frames between keyframes in a shape tweened sequence are light green, with a black arrow across them (see the bottom illustration at the bottom of this page).

■ You set properties for a shape tween in the Property Inspector.

■ Shape tween properties include easing and blend.

• Use Distributive blending when you are tweening shapes with curves and irregular lines.

• Use Angular blending when you are tweening shapes with sharp corners and straight lines.

■ To add elements to a shape during tweening you must insert the new elements on the last keyframe.

■ Shape tweening creates a larger file than motion tweening. You should animate a sequence using a motion tween instead of a shape tween whenever possible.

Motion tween options

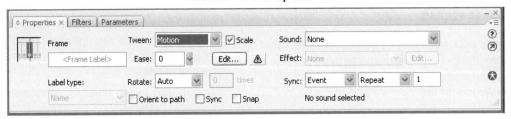

Shape tweened frames in the Timeline

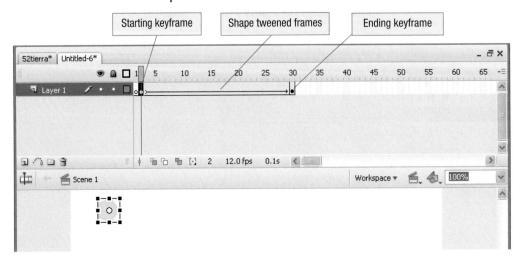

PROCEDURES

Select a Layer

- Click the layer name in the Timeline.

OR

1. Click the first layer name to select.
2. Press and hold **Shift** .... `⇧ Shift`
3. Click the last layer name to select.

OR

1. Click the first layer name to select.
2. Press and hold **Ctrl** .... `Ctrl`
3. Click the next layer name to select.
4. Repeat to select additional layers.

Insert a Layer

- Click the **Insert Layer** button `⊡` on the Timeline.

OR

1. Click **Insert** .... `Alt`+`I`
2. Click **Timeline** .... `T`
3. Click **Layer**........................... `L`

OR

1. Right-click layer in the Timeline.
2. Click **Insert Layer**.

  ✔ *The new layer displays above the active layer.*

Delete a Layer

- Click the **Delete Layer** button `🗑` on the Timeline.

OR

1. Right-click layer in the Timeline.
2. Click **Delete Layer**.

Show/Hide a Layer

- Click in **Show/Hide Layers** column to right of layer's name.

  ✔ *An X displays in the column when the layer is hidden.*

Show/Hide All Layers

- Click **Show/Hide All Layers** icon.

Create a Graphic Symbol from Existing Objects (F8)

1. Select object(s) on Stage.
2. Click **Modify**.................. `Alt`+`M`
3. Click **Convert to Symbol** ..... `C`

  ✔ *The Convert to Symbol dialog box displays.*

4. Type symbol name.
5. Click **Graphic** option button...................... `Alt`+`T`, `↓`
6. Click desired registration point location.
7. Click **OK** .... `Enter`

Create a New Graphic Symbol (Ctrl + F8)

1. Deselect all objects on Stage.
2. Click **Insert** .... `Alt`+`I`
3. Click **New Symbol**................ `N`

OR

  a. Open Library panel.
  b. Click **New Symbol** button `⊞` .

  ✔ *The Create New Symbol dialog box displays.*

4. Type symbol name.
5. Click **Graphic** option button...................... `Alt`+`T`, `↓`
6. Click **OK** .... `Enter`

Insert an Instance

1. Select layer.
2. Select keyframe.
3. Open Library panel.
4. Double-click the folder where the symbol is stored, if necessary.
5. Drag the symbol from the preview area or symbol list onto Stage.

Create a Motion Tween

1. Select a layer in the Timeline.
2. Select the keyframe where you want the tween to begin.
3. Insert or create an instance or group to tween.
4. Select a frame where you want the tween to end.
5. Insert a keyframe.
6. In the ending keyframe, modify the object so it appears as you want it at end of the tween.
7. Select any frame between keyframes.

  ✔ *Tween becomes available in the Property Inspector.*

8. In the Property Inspector, click **Tween Type** drop-down arrow.
9. Click **Motion**.

  ✔ *The Motion tween options become available.*

OR

  a. Right-click any frame between keyframes.
  b. Click **Create Motion Tween**.

10. Set options as follows:

   - Select **Scale** check box to change the size of an object during a tween.
   - Enter a value in the **Ease** box to adjust the rate of change between tweened frames.
   - Select **Rotation options** to animate rotation clockwise, counterclockwise, automatically, or none.
   - Enter a value in the **Rotation count** box to specify how many times you want an item to rotate.

Tween a Shape

1. Select the layer in the Timeline.
2. Select the keyframe where you want the tween to begin.
3. Draw or paste the starting shape.
4. Select the frame where you want the tween to end.
5. Insert a keyframe.
6. Modify the shape on the ending keyframe.
7. Select any frame between keyframes.

   ✔ *Tween becomes available in the Property Inspector.*

8. In Property Inspector, click **Tween Type** drop-down arrow.
9. Click **Shape**.

   ✔ *The Shape Tween options become available.*

10. Click **Ease** box.
11. Enter an easing value.
12. Click **Blend** drop-down arrow.
13. Select one of the following:

    ■ **Distributive** to create an animation in which the intermediate shapes are smooth and regular.

    ■ **Angular** to create an animation that preserves the apparent corners and straight lines of the original object in the intermediate shapes.

EXERCISE DIRECTIONS

1. Open the Flash file 🔘 53tierra from your Data folder. Save the file as S_53tierra_xx in your Solutions folder.
2. Display the Document Properties dialog box and give the file a title of **tierra_logo**.
3. Change the dimensions to 300px by 300px.
4. Change the background color to #003366.
5. Set a frame rate of 10 fps.
6. Add a new layer and name it **comet**.
7. Drag the comet symbol from the Library and place it in the upper-right corner of the Stage. Use Illustration A on the next page as a guide.
8. Use the Free Transform tool to enlarge the instance of the symbol.
9. Click in frame 30 on the Timeline. Add a new keyframe.
10. Make the instance very small and drag it to the lower-left corner of the Stage.
11. Click the first keyframe and, in the Property inspector, click Motion in the Tween list.
12. Press Enter to view the tween in action.
13. Save the file and exit Flash.

Illustration A

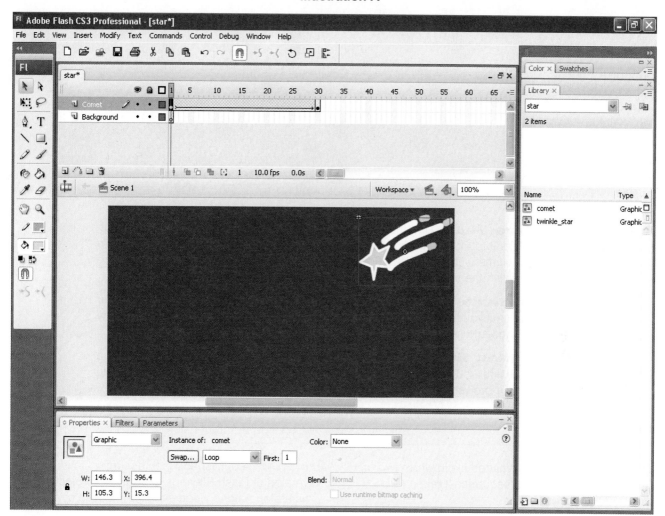

ON YOUR OWN

1. Create a new Flash file and save it with the name SO_myshape_xx.

2. Set the Stage size and background color as you prefer.

3. Click Object Drawing.

4. Click the ⬡ PolyStar tool.

5. In the Property Inspector, choose the same color for the Stroke color and the Fill color.

6. Set the Stroke height to a high value, such as 15.

7. Insert a keyframe and click it in the Timeline.

8. In a corner of the Stage, draw a small polygonal shape.

9. Click a point on the Timeline where you want the end of the shape tween to occur and insert a keyframe at that point.

10. Modify the shape in size, color, and position so that it ends up where you want it.

11. Click the first keyframe, and in the Property inspector, choose Shape for the Tween setting.

12. Preview the animation.

13. Add a layer with objects that animate after the shape has finished tweening.

14. Copy and paste the keyframes for that animation so it repeats three times at the end of the segment.

15. Preview the animation.

16. Save the file and exit Flash.

Skills Covered

- Test a Movie
- Test Download Performance
- Publish a Flash Application

- Publish Settings
- Preview a Published Application
- Export Flash Content

Software Skills Use the Test Movie command in Flash to see how an animation will look to a user viewing it in a Web browser. Test download performance to identify problems with speed and flow. When everything is working properly, you're ready to publish the movie.

Design Skills You never really know how an animation is going to look to your site visitors until you try it yourself. Previewing isn't enough—you need to test the way the movie runs and check download times to make sure they are optimal.

Application Skills In this exercise, you publish the animated logo for the Tierra Verde site. You will select Flash and HTML settings, and then preview the animation in your browser.

TERMS

Animated GIF A .gif-formatted file in which two or more images display in sequence, creating the appearance of animation.

Export To save a file or object created in one program in a format that can be used by a different program.

HTML The acronym for Hypertext Markup Language, which is the programming language used to define and format data for display on the Word Wide Web.

Projector A published Flash document in which a version of Flash Player is stored. The projector plays as a stand-alone video even if the user's computer does not have Flash Player installed.

Publish To create a Web-compatible version of a Flash document file, which can then be stored on a Web server and accessed by users on the Web.

Web browser A software program such as Microsoft Internet Explorer that displays Web pages and allows the user to navigate from one page to another.

NOTES

Test a Movie

- Before you **publish** your Flash application, it's important to test how it will look to a user on the Internet.

- Not every feature in a Flash document can be viewed on the Flash Stage. For example, you cannot play a movie clip instance.

- To view the application as it will look on the Internet, you must use the Test Movie command to export the application to a Flash Player file and display it in a Flash Player window.

- The Flash Player file has the same name as the Flash file, but the three-character file name extension changes from .fla to .swf. For example, a Flash file named dance.fla would become dance.swf.

- The .swf Flash Player file is stored in the same folder as the .fla Flash file.

- In the Flash Player window, the entire animation plays from the first frame to the last frame.

- You may choose to test just the current scene instead of the entire animation.

- If you test a single scene, the frames from that scene only are exported as a Flash Player file. The Flash Player file has the same name as the Flash .fla file, with an underscore and the scene name added. For example, Scene 1 in a Flash file named star.fla would become star_Scene 1.swf.

- By default, the application loops continuously in the Flash Player window. You can use the Control menu options to rewind, play, stop, and forward an animation in the Flash Player window.

Test Download Performance

- To play smoothly over the Internet, each frame in a Flash application must download before the animation reaches that frame.

- If an application reaches a frame that has not yet been downloaded the movie pauses until the download is complete.

- The speed of the download depends on the data transfer rate and the amount of data stored in each frame.

- Use the Flash Bandwidth Profiler to test your animation to locate frames where pauses might occur.

- The Bandwidth Profiler displays a graphic representation of the amount of data that is sent from each frame in the movie.

- The left pane of the profiler has three sections:
  - Movie, which includes information about the dimensions, frame rate, frame size, duration, and preloaded frames by number of seconds.
  - Settings, which has bandwidth information.
  - State, which includes information on the number of frames and loading.

- The right pane of the Profiler shows the Timeline header and a graph.

- The red horizontal line in the graph marks the point at which a frame streams in real time with the selected modem speed.

- You can view a Streaming Graph or a Frame by Frame Graph (see the following illustrations).

Bandwidth Profiler in Streaming Graph view

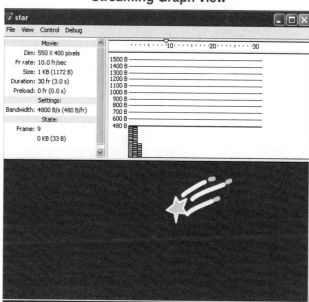

Bandwidth Profiler in Frame by Frame Graph view

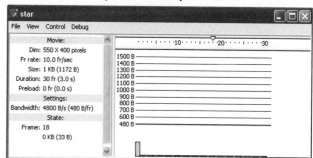

- In the Streaming Graph, frames are represented by alternating light and dark gray blocks, stacked in columns. The height of each block indicates the amount of data being downloaded.
  - In the Frame by Frame Graph, each column represents one frame; any frame extending above the red line might cause a pause in the animation.
- Change the Bandwidth Download settings to see how the animation will play at different modem speeds. For example, you may test the animation as it would play using a 56K modem, a DSL line, or a T1 line.
- If a frame is large enough to impact performance, you can try to optimize it to make it smaller so that it will load faster.
- Typical optimization methods include substituting device fonts for embedded fonts, inserting instances instead of graphics, using vector graphics instead of bitmaps, and deleting unnecessary content.

Publish a Flash Application

- Publish a complete Flash .fla file in Flash Player format so you—and others—can play it on the Web in the Flash Player program.
- When you publish an application, you select options in the Publish Settings dialog box and Flash generates the files required to display the animation correctly.
- By default, when you publish a file, Flash generates an .swf (Flash Player) version of the original .fla file and an **HTML** document that provides the instructions for inserting the Flash application in a **Web browser** window.
- Alternatively, you can publish the .fla file as a Flash stand-alone **projector** or in alternative file formats that display if there is no Flash Player installed on the user's computer. Available formats include .gif, .jpg, .png, and QuickTime.
- If you edit or modify a Flash file that you have published, you must publish it again in order to update the Flash Player file.

Publish Settings

- Select publish settings in the Publish Settings dialog box (see the illustration in the next column).
- Options that you select in the Publish Settings dialog box override options that are set in the application file. For example, if you select red as the background color in the Publish Settings dialog box, then red will display, even if you selected gray in the Document Properties dialog box.

Publish Settings dialog box

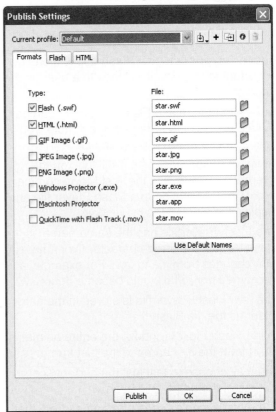

- On the Formats tab in the Publish Settings dialog box you select the type of files you want to generate. By default, Flash (.swf) and HTML (.html) are selected.
- By default, published file names are the same as the original .fla file name, with the appropriate file name extension added, and published files are stored in the same location as the original .fla file.
- You can change the default file name and select a different storage location, if desired.
- In the Publish Settings dialog box, Flash displays a tab for each selected file format so you can select options such as dimensions, color settings, and image control settings.
- On the Flash tab, set image, sound compression, debugging, and file protection options; and select to generate a text file listing the amount of data in each frame of the final Flash Player file, if desired.
- On the HTML tab, select an HTML template, and set parameters specifying options such as how to align the application on-screen, what size window to use, and the background color, as well as playback and quality options.

Preview a Published Application

- Use the Publish Preview command to see how your published movie will look in a Web browser.
- Flash creates a file that you can open in your default Web browser.
- You can also test all interactive options, such as buttons.
- The file may launch automatically in your Web browser, or you may have to use Windows to open it.

Export Flash Content

- **Export** the content of an entire Flash document so you can use it in another program.
- With the Export Movie command, you can save a complete Flash document file in a different movie file format, or as a sequence of still image files.

- You name the exported file and select the file format in the Export Movie dialog box.
- In an exported sequence, each frame is saved as a separate file. That means that if there are 50 frames in an animation, there will be 50 exported files. Numbers are added to the file names to indicate the sequential order.
- Some Flash features may not be supported by the export file type. For example, a movie clip may not display when exported in **animated GIF** format, but may display when exported in QuickTime format.
- Likewise, actions such as those assigned to buttons may not work in all exported file formats.

PROCEDURES

Test a Movie (Ctrl + Enter)

1. Open the document in Flash.

   ✔ If the document contains multiple scenes, be sure the Play All Scenes command is selected on the Control menu.

2. Click **Control**.............. Alt +O
3. Click **Test Movie**.................. M

Test the Current Scene (Ctrl + Alt + Enter)

1. Open the document in Flash.
2. Display the desired scene.
3. Click **Control**.............. Alt +O
4. Click **Test Scene** .... S

Control a Movie in Flash Player

1. Open the document in Flash.
2. Click **Control**.............. Alt +O
3. Click **Test Movie**.................. M
   OR
   Click **Test Scene** .... S
4. Click **Control**.............. Alt +C
   in Flash Player window.

5. Click one of the following:
   - **Stop**..............................Enter
   - **Rewind**............................R
   - **Loop**..............................L
   - **Step Forward One Frame**..........................F
   - **Step Backward One Frame**..........................B

   ✔ If the Controller toolbar is displayed in the Flash window, you can use it to control the movie in the Flash Player window.

Display the Bandwidth Profiler

1. Open the document in Flash.
2. Click **Control**.............. Alt +O
3. Click **Test Movie**.................. M
4. Click **View** .... Alt +V
5. Click **Bandwidth Profiler** .....B
6. Click **View** .... Alt +V
7. Click one of the following:
   - **Streaming Graph** ....S
   - **Frame by Frame Graph** ....F

Change Bandwidth Download Settings

1. Open the document in Flash.
2. Click **Control**.............. Alt +O
3. Click **Test Movie**.................. M
4. Click **View** .... Alt +V
5. Click **Download Settings**.....D
6. Click desired download speed.

Close the Flash Player Window (Ctrl + W)

- Click **Window Close** button ☒.
  OR
1. Click **File** .... Alt +F
2. Click **Close** C

Display Publish Settings Dialog Box (Ctrl + Shift + F12)

1. Open the document in Flash.
2. Click **File** .... Alt +F
3. Click **Publish Settings**.........G

Set File Type Options

1. Display Publish Settings dialog box.
2. Click the Formats tab, if necessary.
3. Click to select or deselect file types:
   - **Flash (.swf)** .... `Alt`+`F`
   - **HTML (.html)** .... `Alt`+`H`
   - **GIF Image (.gif)** .... `Alt`+`G`
   - **JPEG Image (.jpg)** ... `Alt`+`J`
   - **PNG Image (.png)** .... `Alt`+`P`
   - **Windows Projector (.exe)** .... `Alt`+`W`
   - **Macintosh Projector** .... `Alt`+`M`
   - **QuickTime with Flash Track (.mov)** .... `Alt`+`Q`
4. Replace the default file name(s) with new file name(s), if desired.

   ✔ *You must include the correct file name extension.*

5. Click the **Select Publish Destination** icon. To change storage location, if desired, then locate and select desired location and click **Save**.

   ✔ *The default location is the same as the storage location for the original .fla file.*

6. Click **OK** .... `Enter` to save the settings and close the dialog box.

Select Flash (.swf) Publish Settings

1. Display Publish Settings dialog box.
2. Click Formats tab, if necessary.
3. Click to select **Flash** ..... `Alt`+`F` **(.swf)**, if necessary.
4. Replace default file name(s) with new file name(s), if desired.

   ✔ *You must include the correct file name extension.*

5. Change storage location, if desired.

   ✔ *The default location is the same as the storage location for the original .fla file.*

6. Click the **Flash** tab. Click the **Version** drop-down arrow and click the Flash Player version you want to use.

   ✔ *The most recent version is Flash Player 9.*

7. Click the **Load order** drop-down arrow, and then click one of the following:
   - **Bottom up** to load layers from the bottom of the layer list to the top.
   - **Top down** to load layers from the top of the layer list to the bottom.
8. Click **ActionScript version** drop-down arrow and click ActionScript version to use.
9. Select or deselect options to control debugging as desired:
   - **Generate size report** to create a text file listing amount of data in each frame of the published Flash Player file.
   - **Protect from import** to prevent unauthorized users from converting the .swf file back to a .fla file.

     ✔ *You may enter a password to protect the file.*

   - **Omit trace actions** to prevent the Output panel or tab from displaying comments.
   - **Permit debugging** to allow remote debugging.
   - **Compress movie** to reduce file size.
10. Adjust the **JPEG quality** slider to control bitmap compression.

    ✔ *The lower the quality, the smaller the published file.*

11. Click **Audio Stream Set** button to set compression, bit rate, and quality options for streaming audio.

    ✔ *Click OK to return to Publish Settings dialog box*

12. Click **Audio Event Set** button to set compression bit rate and quality options for event sounds.

    ✔ *Click OK to return to Publish Settings dialog box*

13. Select **Override sound settings** check box to override .fla file sound settings.
14. Select **Export device sounds** check box to export sounds suitable for devices.
15. Click **Local playback security** drop-down arrow and then click one of the following:
    - **Access local files only** to let the published files interact with files on the local system, but not on the network.
    - **Access network only** to let the published files interact with files on the network, but not on the local system.
16. Click **OK** .... `Enter` to save the settings and close the dialog box.

Select HTML (.html) Publish Settings

1. Display the Publish Settings dialog box.
2. Click the Formats tab, if necessary.
3. Click to select **HTML** ..... `Alt`+`H` **(.html)**, if necessary.
4. Replace default file name(s) with new file name(s), if desired.
5. Change storage location, if desired.
6. Click the **HTML** tab.
7. Click the Template drop-down arrow and then click desired template.

   ✔ *Flash Only is the default.*

8. Select the **Detect Flash Version** check box to have published file automatically send user to an alternative HTML page if the installed Flash Player version does not match the version selected on the Flash tab of the Publish Settings dialog box.

9. Click **Dimensions** drop-down arrow and then click one of the following:

   - **Match Movie**
     to use the current document size.

   - **Pixels**
     to specify width and height in pixels.

   - **Percent**
     to specify size as a percentage of browser window.

10. Select desired playback options:

    - **Paused at start**
      to pause animation until user action such as a click.

    - **Loop**
      to repeat animation continuously.

    - **Display menu**
      to display shortcut menu when user right-clicks browser screen.

    - **Device font**
      to substitute device fonts for embedded fonts not available on user's system.

11. Click **Quality** drop-down arrow, and then click desired Quality option:

    - **Low**
      to set a low quality and a high processing speed.

    - **Auto Low**
      to automatically increase quality if possible without slowing processing speed.

    - **Auto High**
      to automatically sacrifice image quality to improve processing speed.

    - **Medium**
      to set an intermediate quality and processing speed.

    - **High**
      to set a high quality even if it means slowing processing speed.

    - **Best**
      to display the highest possible quality without regard to processing speed.

12. Click **Window Mode** drop-down arrow and then click desired transparency option:

    - **Window**
      to play animation in its own window on Web page.

    - **Opaque Windowless**
      to display animation over HTML background, without letting the background show through.

    - **Transparent Windowless**
      to display animation over HTML background, letting the background show through transparent areas of the animation.

13. Click **HTML alignment** drop-down arrow and then click desired option for aligning Flash Player window within browser window:

    - **Default**
      to center animation in browser window.

    - **Left**
      to left-align animation in browser window.

    - **Right**
      to right-align animation in browser window.

    - **Top**
      to align animation at top edge of browser window.

    - **Bottom**
      to align animation at bottom edge of browser window.

14. Click **Scale** drop-down arrow and then click desired scale options:

    - **Default (Show all)**
      to fit animation within specified dimensions without distortion.

    - **No border**
      to fit animation within specified dimensions without distortion, cropping if necessary.

    - **Exact fit**
      to fit within specified dimension with distortion.

    - **No scale**
      to prevent the animation from scaling even if the Flash Player window is resized.

15. Click **Flash alignment Horizontal** drop-down arrow and then click desired option for aligning animation horizontally in Flash Player window:

    - **Left**
    - **Center**
    - **Right**

16. Click **Flash alignment Vertical** drop-down arrow and then click desired option for aligning animation vertically in Flash Player window:

    - **Top**
    - **Center**
    - **Bottom**

17. Select **Show warning messages** check box to display error messages if HTML settings conflict.

18. Click **OK** .... [Enter]
    to save the settings and close the dialog box.

Preview a Flash Application in a Web Browser

1. Open your browser.
2. Open the document in Flash.
3. Click **File** .... `Alt`+`F`
4. Click **Publish Preview** .... `R`

5. Click file format to preview:
   - **Default (HTML)** .... `D`
   - **Flash** .... `F`
   - **HTML** .... `H`

   ✔ *Other formats may be available, depending on the options selected in the Publish Settings dialog box.*

6. Change to your Web browser to view the application.
7. Click Web browser's **Close** button to close window when finished.

Publish an Application Using Current Publish Settings (Shift + F12)

1. Open the document in Flash.
2. Click **File** .... `Alt`+`F`
3. Click **Publish** .... `B`

EXERCISE DIRECTIONS

1. Start Flash and open ⊙ 54garden. Save the file as 54garden_xx.
2. Use the Test Movie command to play the animation in a Flash Player window.
3. Disable the Loop command on the Control menu to stop the animation from playing over and over.
4. Rewind and play the animation.
5. Change the display to Frame by Frame Graph. It should look similar to Illustration A.

6. Change the Download Settings to DSL to see how a faster download speed affects performance.
7. Change the Download Settings back to 56K.
8. Close the Bandwidth Profiler.
9. Close the Flash Player window.
10. Display the Publish Settings dialog box and review the settings in each tab.
11. Click Publish to publish the movie.

Illustration A

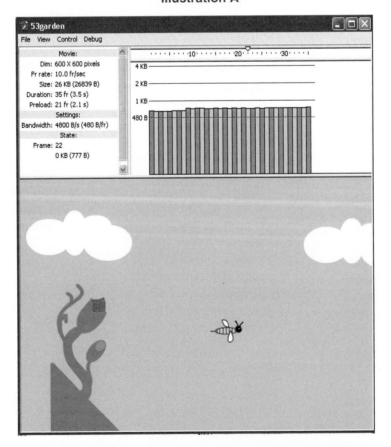

ON YOUR OWN

1. Start Flash and the animation you created in Exercise 53's On Your Own exercise.

   ✔ *If you don't have the previous animation, you can use* ⊙ *SO_54myfile.*

2. Test the movie and view it in the Flash Player.

3. Display the Bandwidth Profiler and test different views.

4. Change the download settings to view it at different speeds.

5. Close the Flash Player window.

6. Slow the video by reducing the Frame rate.

7. Save the file as SO_54myfile_xx.

8. Choose the File>Publish Settings command and select the options appropriate to your use.

NOTE

In the next exercise, you return to Dreamweaver to add your Flash movie to a Web page.

Exercise | 55

Skills Covered

- About Multimedia Files
- Insert a Flash Movie
- Modify and Play a Movie
- Insert Flash Buttons and Flash Text
- Other Multimedia Plugins

Software Skills Multimedia files—sound, action, video, and interactive elements such as games—can add new levels of impact, creativity, and interest to a Web site. Flash objects such as movies and buttons, as well as other kinds of multimedia files such as Shockwave movies and Java Applets, can easily be added to Web documents.

Design Skills Now that you know how to create simple animations in Flash, you can add them easily to your Dreamweaver pages. Remember as you're designing your site that a little animation goes a long way—so choose the best movies and use them sparingly.

Application Skills In this exercise, you will work with multimedia objects such as Flash buttons and text and insert a simple Flash movie in the GardenProjects site.

TERMS

ActiveX Microsoft-developed technology that allows software components to work with other software components regardless of the language used to create them.

Applet Small Java application that can be embedded in a Web page to create interactivity for animations.

Java Programming language that operates on multiple platforms and operating systems.

Multimedia Information presented by video sequences, animation, illustration, and sound.

Plugin Utility program that extends an application's capabilities.

NOTES

About Multimedia Files

■ **Multimedia** files present information in the form of video sequences, animations, illustrations, and sounds. The Media drop-down list on the Common tab of the Insert bar provides buttons for inserting several popular types of multimedia files. These files include Flash movies and objects, Shockwave movies, Java applets, **ActiveX** controls, and **plugin** files. Plugin files require Netscape Navigator plug-ins for Netscape and Mozilla browsers.

■ Although multimedia files add an undeniable punch to Web pages, consider carefully before going all out with sound and video embellishments. Multimedia files can add substantially to the size of the site, which may result in slow downloads that turn visitors off.

■ Moreover, some multimedia objects, such as Shockwave movies, require a visitor to download a player before the object will display. This can be a time-consuming process that many site visitors will not want to bother with.

■ This exercise concentrates on working with Flash, because this application is now so widely used. You will learn in this exercise how to insert Flash movies and how to create Flash buttons and text.

   ✔ *If you have the Adobe Web Design suite installed, you can create your own Flash movies. See Exercises 49 through 53 for more about working with Flash.*

Insert a Flash Movie

■ Adobe Flash files are designed to deliver crisp animations and presentations with relatively small file sizes. Flash files are generally called *movies.*

■ Flash movies can also include sound in the form of MP3. If you want to add sound to your Web site, you can do so by embedding the sound or music in a Flash file.

■ One caveat about using Flash is that it requires Flash Player to display in the browser, and different versions of Flash Player can vary in the kind of content they can display. If you have built a Flash movie that requires a specific version of Flash Player, you should create a message to that effect and a link to allow visitors to download the required version.

■ When you insert a Flash file, Dreamweaver uses two sets of HTML tags to provide support for multiple browsers. The <object> tags are supplied for Microsoft browsers and the <embed> tags are supplied for browsers such as Netscape, Opera, and Mozilla.

■ Flash movies (identified by the .swf extension) can be added to a Web document using menu commands or a button from the Common tab of the Insert bar.

■ Position the insertion point on the page where the movie is to appear and then use the Insert>Media>Flash command.

■ Or, click [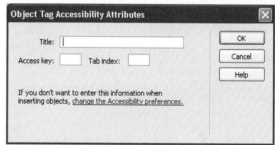] Flash on the Media button's list on the Common tab of the Insert bar.

   ✔ *The movie can be inserted directly in the document or in an AP div in the document.*

■ After you insert the multimedia file and save it in your current Web site, Dreamweaver displays the Object Tag Accessibility Attributes dialog box, as shown in the following illustration. As for images, frames, and forms, this dialog box allows you to supply a title for the media object that can be read by a screen reader.

Object Tag Accessibility Attributes dialog box

■ Once you have supplied a title for the object, Dreamweaver inserts a gray placeholder for the object on the page. If you have the Property inspector displayed, it shows properties for the selected multimedia object (see the illustration at the top of the next page).

■ The size of the placeholder is determined by the original size of the multimedia object. You can change the object's size using sizing handles or the Property inspector.

■ Dreamweaver displays a gray placeholder labeled to identify the media file type. For miscellaneous kinds of plugins, a gray puzzle piece is displayed. More information, specific to the media object or plugin, is also available in its Property inspector.

■ The first time you save the page after inserting the movie, Dreamweaver copies dependent files to your site to run active content. The file is stored in the Scripts folder and must be uploaded with other files for the Flash movie to run.

Flash file placeholder and properties

Flash object placeholder

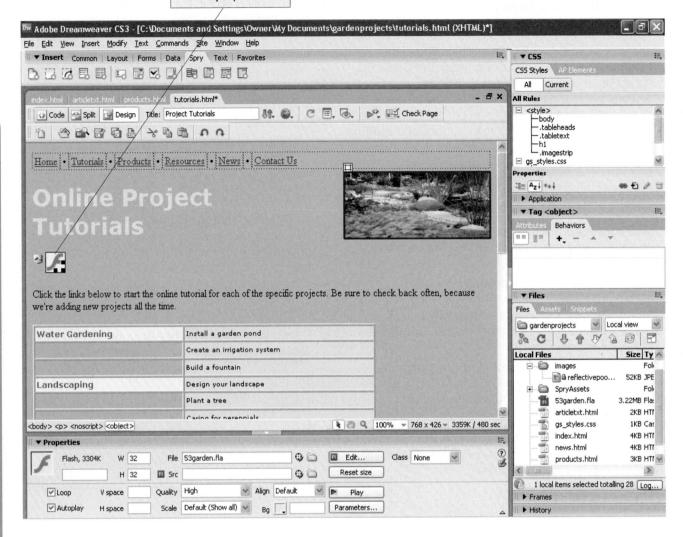

Modify and Play a Movie

- You can use the Flash Property inspector to modify the appearance and performance of the movie in the Web document. Dreamweaver also includes a ▶ Play button on the Property inspector to allow you to play a movie without previewing the page in a browser.

- The Property inspector displays by default several properties that will look familiar to you from other graphic objects (see the previous illustration).

- Use the Name text box to identify the movie for scripting purposes. Specify an exact size for the movie in pixels using the W and H text boxes. You can click the Reset size button after making a sizing change to restore the object to its original size.

- The File text box shows the path to the movie file. You can enter a path in this box, point to the file in the Site or Assets panel, or click the 📁 Browse for File icon to navigate to a file.

- The Edit... button opens Flash so you can edit the movie. Flash will request the original document file, which has the FLA extension. If you know you might need to edit a Flash movie, make sure you have this file as well as the movie file with the SWF extension.

  ✓ When you insert an SWF Flash file, you are inserting a file exported from Flash with properties suitable for embedding in a Web page, not the original Flash file.

- Select the Loop checkbox if you want the movie to play over and over when displayed in the browser. This option is selected by default.

- Select the Autoplay checkbox to play the movie automatically when the page loads. This option is selected by default.

- Use the V space and H space text boxes in the Property inspector to set an amount of white space in pixels above, below, and on both sides of the movie.

- The default Quality setting of High is adequate for most browsers. The other settings (for example, Low) can be used depending on how the movie was made.

- The Scale property sets the scale parameter for the <object> and <embed> tags. This is an advanced setting also determined by how the movie is created in Flash.

- Use the Align options to determine how the movie is aligned in the Web document. You have the same options as for any other image.

- Use the ☐ Bg button to display a color palette you can use to modify the movie's background color (or type the hexadecimal equivalent to the right of the button). The background color appears when the movie is active.

- Click the `Parameters...` button to launch a dialog box that allows you to enter additional movie parameters. These advanced settings are beyond the scope of this book, but you can consult Dreamweaver Help for more information.

  ✔ *The param button on the Media drop-down list inserts a <param> tag using the Tag Editor dialog box. It is used for applying parameters in Code view.*

- Click the `▶ Play` button in the Property inspector to preview the appearance and function of the movie in Dreamweaver. Using this button saves time because you do not have to switch back and forth from the page to the browser to see results of modifications.

- Click the `■ Stop` button to turn off the movie. You must click this button even after the movie stops playing to restore the gray placeholder and make further modifications.

Insert Flash Buttons and Flash Text

- Dreamweaver includes two features that can add visual interest as well as functionality to Web pages: Flash buttons and Flash text. When you use these features, you create your own Flash objects without having to leave Dreamweaver.

Insert Flash Button

- Dreamweaver includes a set of predesigned Flash buttons that you can customize and insert on your Web pages. These buttons are not only graphically interesting, they also provide functional ways to navigate a site. Because you do not have to create the various up, over, and down states in another application, Flash buttons can save you a great deal of time.

- Flash buttons have additional appeal because of their interactive effects. When the mouse pointer is over a Flash button, most buttons change their appearance. Each type of button has its own special effects, such as a color change or a moving part.

- To insert a Flash button, use the Insert>Media> Flash Button command, or click the Flash Button button on the Media list on the Common tab of the Insert bar. Dreamweaver opens the Insert Flash Button dialog box shown in the following illustration.

Insert Flash Button dialog box

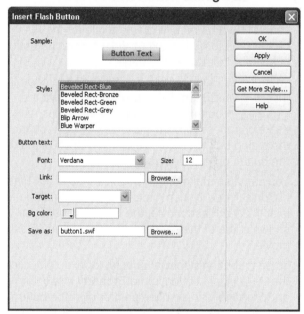

- Choose a button style from the Style list, which offers over 40 different Flash buttons. (Some buttons have the same appearance except for color.) You can then type the text that will appear on the button and choose the font and size for the text.

  ✔ *The buttons can fit only a limited amount of text—typically one or two words. Keep your labels short.*

- Dreamweaver suggests a font and size for each button style. If your system does not have the default font for a particular button, Dreamweaver displays a message at the bottom of the dialog box to let you know you do not have the font. You can then choose a different font from the Font list.

- You can also change the font and size as desired even if your system has the default font. Choose a new font from the Font list and type a new size in the Size box.

  ✔ *The Sample button in the dialog box shows the different styles you choose but not font changes as you choose new settings in the dialog box.*

- Flash buttons are designed to work like links, so you can type in the Link box or browse to locate the page that will open when the button is clicked. You can also specify a target for the linked page.

- If you want to surround the button with a background color other than the default white, use the ☐ Bg color box to choose a new color. The background color displays as a rectangle of color behind the Flash button.

- Dreamweaver suggests a default file name for the Flash button. You can change the default name in the Save as text box if desired.

- If you have specified accessibility for media objects, you will be prompted to create a title for the Flash button (and for Flash text as well) before the button is actually inserted in the page.

- To modify a Flash button, double-click it to open the Insert Flash Button dialog box again or click the ☐ Edit... ☐ button in the Property inspector. As you make changes, you can click the ☐ Apply ☐ button in the dialog box to see the result of your changes on the button on the Web page.

- You can also make some modifications in the Flash button's Property inspector. Because a Flash button is actually a Flash movie, the Property inspector shows some of the same settings as for any Flash movie.

- To see a button's special effects, for example, click the ☐ ▶ Play ☐ button in the Property inspector and then move the mouse pointer over the button to activate the special effects. This saves you the step of previewing in the browser. Press the ☐ ■ Stop ☐ button when you are finished previewing the effects to be able to make further modifications to the button's properties.

Insert Flash Text

- Dreamweaver's Flash text feature allows you to create a short Flash movie that consists of text only. As for a Flash button, you can use this text as a link to another page or Web site, or you can use it simply to create a special text effect on a page.

- Flash text changes color when the mouse pointer rests on it. This effect occurs whether or not the text is linked to another page. Such an effect is called a *rollover* effect, because it occurs when the mouse "rolls over" the object.

- To create a Flash text movie, use the Insert> Media>Flash Text command, or click the ☐ A⚡ ▾ ☐ Flash Text button on the Media list on the Common tab of the Insert bar. Dreamweaver opens the Insert Flash Text dialog box shown in the illustration in the next column.

Insert Flash Text dialog box

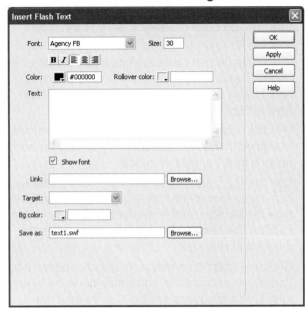

- Choose a font, font size, font style, and alignment for the Flash text object. Use the Color box to select the initial color for the text in the object and the Rollover color box to choose the color that displays when the mouse pointer rests on the text.

- Type the Flash text itself in the Text box. As you can see by the dimensions of this box, you can create a word, phrase, or entire paragraph if desired. Note that the Text box does not have a wrap feature. If you want text in a paragraph to wrap, you must press Enter to start new lines.

- With the Show font checkbox selected, text in the Text box displays in the font you have chosen. Using this feature can help you judge how your Flash text will look on the page.

- As for a Flash button, you can create a link for the Flash text to open, specify a target, and select a background color. You can also save the Flash text object with a file name other than the default shown in the Save as text box.

- Double-click a Flash text object to make further changes in the Insert Flash Text dialog box—or click the ☐ Edit... ☐ button in the Property inspector. As for a Flash button, you can use the ☐ Apply ☐ button to see how your changes look on the page and the Property inspector to "play" the movie.

- Roll the mouse over the text to see the color change take effect after clicking the ☐ ▶ Play ☐ button, and click the ☐ ■ Stop ☐ button when you have finished.

Other Multimedia Plugins

■ You can employ the same techniques used to insert Flash movies to insert Shockwave movies and other plugin types from the Media drop-down list. Click the appropriate button, navigate to the location of the file, insert it, and adjust properties as necessary.

■ Use the 🍵▾ Applet button on the Media drop-down list to insert **Java** applets. An **applet** is a small application that can be embedded in a Web page.

■ For example, an applet can be used to insert Web site counters that tabulate the number of "hits" or visits your site receives, visual effects, games, Web site tools, and so on.

■ Use the 🦊▾ ActiveX button to insert ActiveX components. Formerly known as OLE controls, ActiveX components function like browser plugins to perform specific tasks. They are typically used for buttons, forms, and the like.

■ ActiveX components run only in Windows-based Internet Explorer. They will not work in a Macintosh environment or in Netscape and Mozilla browsers.

■ If you need to insert a file that requires a Netscape plugin to play properly, use the 🧩▾ Plugin button.

■ All of these objects are created in other programs—some of which require programming skills—and are beyond the scope of this course. Your instructor can, however, provide you with, or help you locate, files that you can use.

✔ You can also use a Web browser search engine and type in keywords such as "free Java applets," "free ActiveX controls," and so on to obtain such files to insert in your Web pages.

PROCEDURES

Insert Flash Movie
(Ctrl + Alt + F)

1. Position insertion point where movie should appear on the page.
2. Click **Insert** .... `Alt`+`I`
3. Point to **Media** .... `M`
4. Click **Flash** .... `F`
   OR
■ Click **Flash** button 🗦 from the Media drop-down list on the Common tab of the Insert bar.

In the Select File dialog box:
1. Navigate to the file location.
2. Click the file.
3. Click `OK` .

In Dreamweaver:
1. Store file in current Web site when prompted.
2. Supply a title for the file.
3. Click `OK` .

✔ You can use these steps to insert any media plugin—Java applet, ActiveX, Netscape plugin—on the Media drop-down list.

To copy script files to the local site:

■ Save the page on which you have just inserted media file and click `OK` to copy dependent files to the site.

Play Movie

1. Click the movie to select the placeholder, if necessary.
2. Click ▶ `Play` in the expanded Property inspector to play the movie in Web page.
3. Click ■ `Stop` in the expanded Property inspector to stop playing the movie.

Modify a Movie

1. Click the movie to select the placeholder, if necessary.
2. Change the properties as follows:
   ■ Type name for movie in the Name text box.
   ■ Set exact width and height in the **W** and **H** text boxes.
   ■ Specify or locate media file in the **File** text box.
   ■ Set vertical alignment for movie in the **Align** list box.

■ Change background color using the **Bg** button 🔲 (or type hexadecimal value).

■ Set space above and below and on each side of movie using the **V space** and **H space** text boxes.

■ Set quality in the **Quality** list box.

■ Specify continuous play by selecting the **Loop** checkbox.

■ Set the movie to play when the page loads by selecting the **Autoplay** checkbox.

Insert a Flash Button

1. Click **Insert** .... `Alt`+`I`
2. Point to **Media** .... `M`
3. Click **Flash Button** .... `B`
   OR
■ Click **Flash Button** button 🔲▾ on the Media drop-down list on the Common tab of the Insert bar.

In the Insert Flash Button dialog box:

1. Customize the button:
   - Choose a button style.
   - Enter text to label the button.
   - Select a new font and size, if desired.
   - Type or browse to the page you want to link to the button.
   - Specify the target, if necessary.
   - Select a background color for the button.
   - Save the button with a default or other file name.
2. Click [OK].

In Dreamweaver:

1. Supply a title for the media object.
2. Click [OK].

Insert Flash Text

1. Click **Insert** .... Alt + I
2. Point to **Media** .... M
3. Click **Flash Text** .... T
   OR
   - Click **Flash Text** button [A⧮ ▾] on the Media drop-down list on the Common tab of the Insert bar.

In the Insert Flash Text dialog box:

1. Create Flash text:
   - Choose a font and size.
   - Choose the font style and alignment, if desired.
   - Choose a color for the initial text and rollover color.
   - Type the text for the object.
   - Type or browse to the page you want to link to text.
   - Specify a target, if necessary.
   - Select the background color for text.
   - Save the text with default or other file name.
2. Click [OK].

In Dreamweaver:

1. Supply a title for the media object.
2. Click [OK].

Modify Flash Button or Flash Text

1. Double-click the Flash button or Flash text.
   OR
   a. Click the Flash button or Flash text.
   b. Click [✎ Edit...] in the Property inspector.
2. Change the properties in the dialog box and click [OK].
3. Change other properties in the Property inspector.

EXERCISE DIRECTIONS

1. Start Dreamweaver and open the gardenprojects site.
2. Open ◉ intro.html from the Lesson 6 Data folder and save the page in the current site with the same name.
3. With the insertion point in the blank paragraph below the main head, insert the ◉ garden.swf Flash file from the Lesson 6 Data folder. Save the file in your images folder and supply the title **garden movie**.
4. Name the object **intro** in the Property inspector. Deselect the Loop checkbox.
5. Change the size to W 325 and H 250
6. Click [▶ Play] to play the movie.
7. Click [■ Stop] to stop the movie and display the placeholder again.
8. Save your changes, allowing Dreamweaver to copy dependent files to the site, and preview the page in the browser to see the flash movie play once as the page is loaded.
9. On the intro.html page in Dreamweaver, insert a new paragraph before the last paragraph. Insert a Flash button and customize it as follows:
   - Choose the Glass-Turquoise style.
   - Type the button text **Enter**.
   - Change the font to Arial and the size to 12, if necessary.
   - Type a link to the tutorials.html page in your gardenprojects folder on your hard drive, such as **C:\Inetpub\wwwroot\gardenprojects\ tutorials.html**.

   ✔ Be sure to type the link. You cannot browse to this location and have the text link correctly.

   - Save the button as enter.swf.
10. Close the dialog box and supply the title **enter**. Use the Property inspector to name the button **enter**.
11. "Play" the button: Rest the mouse pointer over the button to see its color change.
12. The button's text is a bit small. Change the size of the label to 14.
13. Preview the page in the browser. It should look similar to Illustration A on the next page.
14. Test the link to the GardenProjects site to make sure you entered the link properly. Use the Back button to return to the intro page.
15. Close any open pages and the browser and exit Dreamweaver.

Illustration A

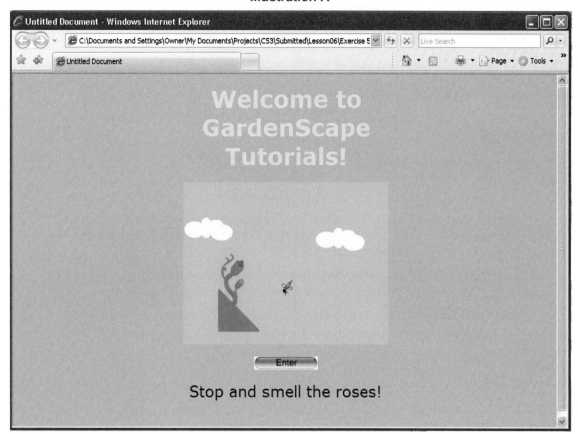

ON YOUR OWN

1. Start Dreamweaver and open the gardentutorial site.

2. Open index.html. You should create a link on this page to the mailing list form—you can use a Flash button for this purpose.
   - Insert the button below the current text with accompanying text to let visitors know they can click the button to open the mailing list form.
   - Choose any Flash button that goes well with the page. Be sure to give the button an appropriate name.

3. Open contact.html. Below the table, insert a new paragraph and type the text **Other Links**. Format the text as Heading 3 in a style and color that matches other headings in the site.

4. Below the heading, insert the following Flash text object:
   - The text should read **Ohio State Extension Services**.
   - Format the text with your choice of font, font size, color, and rollover color.
   - Create the link to **http://extension.osu.edu**.
   - Give the text an appropriate title and name.

5. Open info.html. Insert a Flash movie on this page as follows:
   - Add a new AP div to the page and name it **movie**.
   - Insert in the AP div the Flash movie garden.swf from the Lesson 6 Data folder. Resize the AP div if necessary to fit closely around the movie.
   - Deselect the Loop option for the Flash movie and play it to preview it.
   - Move the AP div to fit under the picture at the right side of the window.
   - Save the page and preview. You may need to adjust the position of the copyright notice or the AP div for your browser.

6. Preview the entire site, checking your new multimedia enhancements on the index.html, contact.html, and info.html pages.
   - ✓ *If you receive a message about Flash stopping an activity, see your instructor for information on how to change settings to allow the Flash text to work.*

7. Close any open pages and exit Dreamweaver.

Skills Covered

- **About Buttons**
- **Create Up and Down States**
- **Create Over and Over While Down States**
- **Add a URL to a Button**

Software Skills Buttons are a special type of Fireworks object. You can add instances of buttons to Fireworks documents and incorporate them as interactive elements on your Dreamweaver pages.

Design Skills Knowing how to create great-looking buttons in Fireworks enables you to design professional sites that users can navigate easily.

Application Skills In this exercise, you learn how to use the Button Editor to create quality buttons you can incorporate on your Dreamweaver pages.

TERMS

Active area The sensitive area of a button that registers and responds when a user positions the mouse pointer on the button or clicks it.

Instances Copies of buttons that you place and use in a Fireworks document.

Mouse event An action that causes a button response; for example, a user positioning the mouse pointer over a button and clicking a button are two examples of mouse events.

Mouse symbol The phrase used to describe the master copy of a button that is stored in the Library panel.

Registration point A marker that shows the center of an object, such as a button.

State The way in which a button appears at different times in relation to a mouse event.

NOTES

About Buttons

- In an earlier lesson, you learned how to add buttons to navigation bars on your Dreamweaver pages. In the last lesson, you found out about Flash buttons on Dreamweaver pages. In this lesson, you learn how to create Fireworks buttons for a variety of states.

- A button **state** is the condition in which the button appears in relation to a **mouse event**. For example, when the user positions the pointer over a button, it could be said to be in an *over* state; when the pointer is not on the button, it is said to be in an *up* state.

- You can create up, down, over, and over while down states for your buttons.
  - An *up* state is the normal state for the button on the page.
  - A *down* state is the state of the button when it is clicked.
  - An *over* state is the state of the button when the user positions the pointer on it.
  - An *over while down* state is the state of the button when it has been clicked and the user hovers the mouse over it.

■ When you design a button, you will create more than one state for each button. It's a good idea to create the button once and then modify it slightly to show a visual difference for each state. The following illustration shows the primary button and then the visual differences added for other states.

Button states

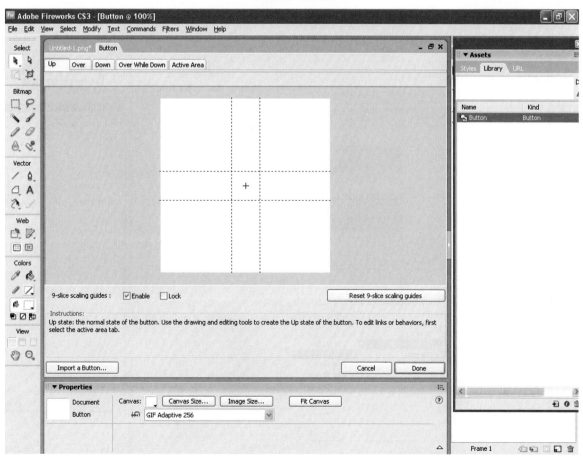

✔ *Note that you do not need to add all four states to all of your buttons. All buttons need at least two states—up and down. Most buttons you'll find on the Web today include an over state so users can see clearly that they have positioned the mouse pointer on the button they want to click.*

■ You use the Fireworks Button Editor to create and work with buttons. Start the Button Editor by choosing the Edit>Insert>New Button menu command. The illustration at the bottom of this page shows the Button Editor.

■ You can create buttons using any of Fireworks' drawing tools. Additionally, you can import buttons from other programs, copy and modify buttons already used on the Web, or edit an existing button.

■ When you create a button in Fireworks, the program adds a master copy of the button to the Library panel. The master copy of the button includes all the properties you want to apply to all instances of a button. For example, the shape, color, shadow, and font used on a button can be saved as part of the master copy, but the link assigned to a specific instance of a button on a page is part of the button instance, not the master copy.

■ You can modify an instance of a button without affecting other buttons; however, if you want to change the properties of all button instances created from a master copy, modify the master version of the button.

■ You can create and save Fireworks buttons for use directly in your Dreamweaver pages; or you can save buttons as jpg, png, or gif files for inclusion on your Web pages.

Button Editor

Create Up and Down States

■ Every button needs an up state.

■ The up state defines the button's appearance when a button is in its normal state on the page.

■ The down state shows the button after the user has clicked it.

■ The down state is optional; however, if you want users to be able to see easily which buttons they have clicked and which they haven't, creating a down state is recommended.

■ In the Over tab, you can use the Copy Up Graphic button in the Button Editor to copy the button into the window so that you can modify it and save it as the over state. You might, for example, change the color of the button to indicate that it has been clicked. (On the Down tab, the button name appears as Copy Over Graphic.)

Create Over and Over While Down States

■ After you create an up state for a button, you can add an over state.

■ The over state shows the user that the pointer is currently over the button.

■ You create an over state in the Over tab of the Button Editor. Click the Copy Up Graphic button to copy the up state to the over state. You can then modify the appearance and save the modified button as the over state.

■ The over while down state shows the way the button appears when the user moves the mouse pointer over the button after it has been clicked. This is an optional state.

Edit Buttons

■ When you want to edit the master copy of the button, called the button symbol, double-click it in the Library.

■ If you want to change an instance of a button rather than the master copy, you can modify the button's settings in the Property inspector.

■ Click the button instance, and the Property inspector shows the properties you can modify, as shown in the following illustration.

✔ You can use filters, the Opacity slider, and Blend modes on button images as you do on other Fireworks images.

Change button instance in the Property inspector

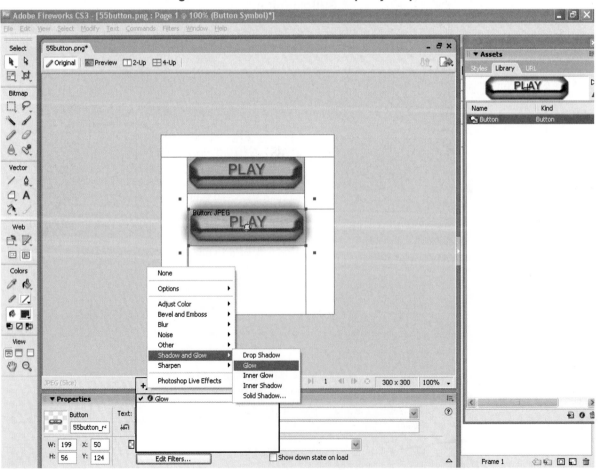

Add a URL to a Button

■ You can add interactivity to your button while you're working with it in Fireworks by adding the URL to the button before you import it. You can also add the links to the button when you add them to your Dreamweaver pages (or when you're creating a navigation bar in Dreamweaver).

■ You can attach a URL two ways in Fireworks:

● To attach a URL to the button symbol (master copy), open the button symbol in the Button Editor, select the Active Area tab, and select the button symbol. Add the URL to the Link text box in the Property inspector.

● To attach a URL to a button instance, click the button instance on the canvas and add the URL to the Link text box in the Property inspector.

PROCEDURES

Create a New Button with the Button Editor (Ctrl + Shift + B)

1. Click **Edit** .... [Alt]+[E]
2. Select **Insert** .... [I]
3. Select **New Button** .... [B]

Create a Button Up State

1. Open the Button Editor by clicking Edit>Insert>New Button.
2. Use the drawing tools to draw the button.
3. Click **Done**.

Create a Button Over State

1. Open the Button Editor.
2. Use the drawing tools to create the up state.
3. Click the **Over** tab.
4. Click **Copy Up Graphic**.
5. Edit the over state.
6. Click **Done**.

Create a Button Down State

1. Open the Button Editor.
2. Use the drawing tools to create the up state you want.
3. Click the **Over** tab.
4. Click **Copy Up Graphic**.
5. Edit the over state.
6. Click the **Down** tab.
7. Click **Copy Over Graphic**.
8. Edit the down state.
9. Click **Done**.

Create a Button Over While Down State

1. Open the Button Editor.
2. Use the drawing tools to create the down state you want.
3. Click the **Over While Down** tab.
4. Click **Copy Down Graphic**.
5. Edit the over while down state.
6. Click **Done**.

Import a Button

1. Open the Button Editor.
2. Click **Import a Button.**
3. Choose the button you want to use.
4. Click **Import**.
5. Edit the button states as necessary.
6. Click **Done**.

Add a Button to the Page

1. Open the Library Panel .... [F11]
2. Drag the button you want to use to the canvas.
3. Release the mouse button.

Edit a Button Symbol

1. Open the Library Panel .... [F11]
2. Double-click the button symbol to open the Button Editor.
3. Change the button as needed.
4. Click Done.

Edit a Button Instance

1. Click the button you want to change.
2. Make any necessary changes in the Property inspector.

Add a URL to a Button

1. Display the button in the Button Editor.
2. Click the Active Area tab.
3. Select the button.
4. In the Property inspector, type the link in the Link text box.
5. Click Done.

EXERCISE DIRECTIONS

1. Open Fireworks and create a new document. Save the document as S_56button_xx.

2. Set the Canvas Size to 300 × 300.

3. Open the Edit menu, choose Insert, and click New Button to open the Button Editor.

4. Display the Rulers by choosing View>Rulers.

5. Choose the ⬜ Beveled Rectangle tool.

6. Click the Styles panel and review the styles displayed.

7. Click the Chrome Misc 014 style and draw a button 200px wide by approximately 50px high.

    ✔ Use the guides in the Button Editor to help you center the button you create.

8. Click the A Text tool and choose Arial, 25pt and #0033CC for the text properties.

9. Click on the surface of the button and type **PLAY**.

10. Click the ✚ Filters arrow in the Property inspector, point to Bevel and Emboss, and click Raised Emboss.

11. Click 🔁 New Symbol and enter the button title **Play**. Click Button for the type, and click OK.

12. Double-click the new button in the Library. In the Convert to Symbol dialog box, click Edit.

13. In the Button Editor, click the Over tab at the top of the screen.

14. Click the Copy Up Graphic button to paste the button in the center of the Button Editor window.

15. Click the button and click ✚ Filters in the Property inspector.

16. Point to Adjust Color and click Hue/Saturation. Increase the Hue to 56 and click OK.

17. Click the Down tab. Create another version of the button with a different color effect for the Down state.

    ✔ Typically a "Down" state is less vibrant than an Up state or Over state, so you may want to use darker colors for a Down state

18. Click Done when you've finished making changes. (You can create an Over While Down state but it's not necessary here.)

19. Click Preview to see how the button will appear on a Web page. Position the mouse pointer on the button and click it; then move it off the button to see how the different states appear.

20. Save and close the Fireworks file.

21. Exit Fireworks.

Illustration A

336

ON YOUR OWN

1. Open Fireworks and create a new document with a canvas size of 250 × 250. Save the file as *SO_56mybutton_xx*.

2. Create three buttons for the **java2go** site: Home, Locations, and Recipes.

   ✔ *If you need to refresh your memory on the color scheme used for that site, open one of the Java 2 Go examples in Windows Explorer.*

3. Create three states for each button: Up, Over, and Down.

4. Preview the buttons in the Button Editor.

5. Save and close the Fireworks file.

Skills Covered

- **About Slices**
- **Draw Slices with the Slice Tool**
- **Modify Slices**
- **Add Rollovers to a Slice**
- **Add a Disjoint Rollover**
- **Remove a Rollover**

Software Skills   Slices and rollovers are useful interactive elements you can add to your Fireworks documents. Slices not only enable you to add features such as pop-up menus, but they also can be used to cut images into pieces that can be loaded progressively.

Design Skills   Slices sound more difficult than they are—slices can be other existing Fireworks documents or pieces of images you are creating. A slice is a portion of a file you use to add interactivity to your document.

Application Skills   In this exercise, you learn how to add slices and rollovers to a Fireworks document.

TERMS

Behavior handle   The handle in the middle of a slice that you use to add rollover effects to a slice.

Disjoint rollover   A type of rollover where a rollover behavior attached to one slice changes the image that appears in a different place on the page.

Frames   A structure in a Fireworks document that allows you to create animations and rollover effects.

Guides   Horizontal or vertical lines that show the edges of objects such as slices

Pop-up menu   A list of choices displayed when a user moves the mouse over an object or clicks a hotspot or slice

Slices   Segments of objects you create and use to add interactivity in other files and sites.

NOTES

About Slices

- You can create slices in your Fireworks image and save those slices as individual files.

- Slices are used most often to add interactivity to your site. You can use slices in special elements, like pop-up menus, or use them to divide up large images into pieces that can be loaded progressively.

- You can draw slices or create them based on existing objects in your Fireworks document.

- Slices always occupy the Web layer of a Fireworks document. You can see this by viewing the Layers panel (refer to the illustration at the bottom of this page).

Draw Slices with the Slice Tool

- Select the ✏️ Slice tool in the toolbar and drag to draw a slice on the image.

  ✔ *If dragging doesn't work, check to see whether you have the Polygon Slice tool selected. You click points instead of dragging when you use the Polygon Slice tool.*

- When you draw slices, Fireworks adds red **guides** to show you the edges of the slices, as the following illustration shows.

Modify Slices

- You can change the size of a slice by using the 🔧 Pointer tool to resize the slice.

- If the slice is layered behind another object, click the 🔧 Subselection tool and then click the item to display the slice.

- You can use the Property inspector to set precise sizing values for the slice.

  ✔ *The values shown in the W, H, X, and Y boxes in the Property inspector are measured in pixels.*

Add Rollovers to a Slice

- In Fireworks, you use **frames** to store the alternate images that create a rollover effect. When the mouse pointer triggers a rollover, the object in one frame is hidden and the object in the other frame is displayed.

  ✔ *The word frame means two different things, depending on whether you are working in Dreamweaver or Fireworks. In Dreamweaver, a frame refers to different areas on a Web page that can display page content. In Fireworks, a frame is an area that displays alternate objects used in rollover effects.*

Guides show the edges of slices

- You can see the contents of only one frame at a time. The rollover simply swaps the view between two frames that occupy the same place on the canvas.
  - Slices are visible across frames, so you can use slices to help position objects in different frames.
  - The easiest way to add a rollover is to click the **behavior handle** in the middle of the slice to display the behavior pop-up menu.
- In most cases, the simple rollover behavior and the swap image behavior act identically:
  - The simple rollover behavior displays the image in frame 1 until the mouse rolls over the slice. At that point, the image in frame 2 is displayed.
  - The swap image behavior allows you to specify which image file or frame is used as the replacement image.
  - ✔ Press F12 to preview interactive features in your Web browser.

Add a Disjoint Rollover

- You can use a **disjoint rollover** to add interactivity at a different position on the page from the spot that triggers the rollover. For example, you could display a larger view of small images as the user moves the mouse across a row of thumbnails.

- Disjoint rollovers can also be triggered by a button or hotspot.
- To create a rollover behavior, drag the behavior handle from the slice, button, or hotspot that you want to use to trigger the rollover behavior onto the slice that contains the images you want to swap.
- For a disjoint rollover, you add the extra frame to the target slice—the slice containing the images you want to swap.

Remove a Rollover

- You can remove a rollover behavior by clicking the blue line from the behavior handle. The dialog box shown in the following illustration appears. Click OK to remove the rollover.

Removing a rollover behavior

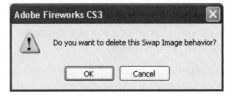

- Remove all rollover behaviors by clicking the behavior handle and choosing Delete All Behaviors.

Behavior pop-up menu

PROCEDURES

Add a Frame

1. Click **Edit** .... [Alt] + [E]
2. Select **Insert** .... [I]
3. Select **Frame** .... [F]

Add a Rollover

1. Draw the object and add a slice to it by clicking [✎] **Slice** and dragging to draw the slice.
2. Click the [▶] **Pointer** tool.
3. Drag the behavior handle and drop it on the slice.
4. Select the frame you want to swap the image from.
5. Click **OK**.

Add a Disjoint Rollover

1. Draw the objects and add slices to them.
2. Click the [▶] **Pointer** tool.
3. Drag the behavior handle from the trigger slice and drop it on the target slice.

Remove a Rollover

1. Click the [▶] **Pointer** tool.
2. Click the blue line for the rollover behavior you want to remove.
3. Click **OK** to confirm deletion.

EXERCISE DIRECTIONS

1. Start Fireworks and open ◉ 57landscape.png.
2. Click the [A] Text tool to select it.
3. Choose 36 point type and the color #FFFF99.
4. Draw a text box on the image and type **Time for a vacation?**.
5. Click the [▶] Pointer tool and click the text box.
6. Select Edit>Copy to copy the text block to the clipboard.
7. Select Edit>Insert>Rectangular Slice to add a rectangular slice to the text block.
8. Select Edit>Insert>Frame to add a new frame. The background image disappears and the slice is highlighted in the workspace.
9. Select Edit>Paste to paste the text block into the new frame.
10. Make sure Frame 2 is selected.
11. Click the [A] Text tool and change the text to **Come out and play**. Make the color #666699.
12. Click the [▶] Pointer tool and select Frame 1 in the Frames panel.
13. Click the slice and display the behavior handle.
14. Drag the behavior handle a short distance and drop it on the slice. The Swap Image dialog box appears.
15. Click OK to swap the image from Frame 2. Your screen should look similar to Illustration A at the top of the next page.
16. Press F12 to view your document in your Web browser.
17. Move the mouse pointer over the text to test the rollover.
18. Close the Web browser.
19. Save your file as S_57rollover_xx.png, and close the file.

ON YOUR OWN

1. In Fireworks, reopen *S_57rollover_xx.png*.
2. Click the 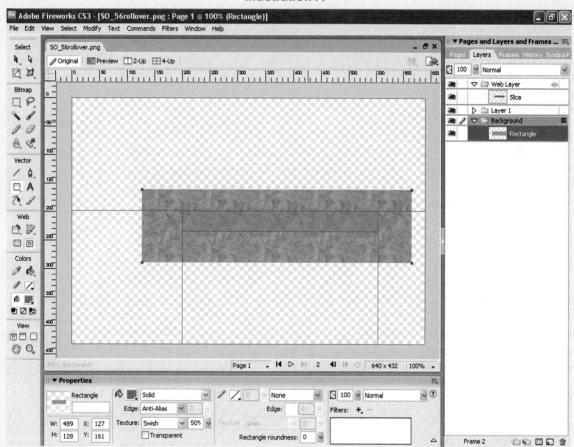 Pointer tool.
3. Select Frame 2 in the Frames panel.
4. Delete the text block from Frame 2.
5. Draw a large rectangle larger than the slice and fill it with a gradient or a texture. Choose a color you like. Your screen will look something like Illustration A.

6. Press F12 to view the document in the Web browser. Notice that only a small portion of the filled rectangle appears. This is the slice at work.
7. Save your work as *SO_57rollover_xx.png*.
8. Close the file and exit Fireworks.

Illustration A

Exercise | 58

Summary Exercise

Application Skills In this exercise, you attach behaviors to some pages of the Tierra Verde site. You also add a Flash movie and create Flash text to link the site to the National Parks Service site.

DIRECTIONS

1. Start Dreamweaver and open the tierraverde site.
2. Create a new intro page to welcome visitors to the site. Name it Intro.
3. Drag the navigation bar from the Library to the top of the page. Center the navigation bar.
4. Click Page Properties and select the background.jpg file from the graphics folder.
5. Press Enter three times to move the cursor down the page.
6. Save the page as intro.html and minimize Dreamweaver.
7. Launch Flash CS3 and open ⊙star.fla.
8. Drag the shootingstar symbol from the Library to the upper-right corner of the Stage.
9. In the Timeline, add a keyframe in frame 30.
10. Click the ꙮ Free Transform tool and reduce the size of the shootingstar image and drag it to the lower left corner of the Stage.
11. Click frame 1 and set Tween to Motion.
12. Press Enter to preview the movie.
13. Save the file in your Solutions folder as S_58star_xx and choose Control>Test Movie to view the movie in the Flash Player.

14. Click File>Publish.
15. Close the Flash file and exit Flash.
16. Maximize Dreamweaver.
17. Choose Insert>Media>Flash.
18. Navigate to your Solutions folder and locate S_58star_xx. Click *Yes* to copy the file to your site root folder.
19. Add **star movie** as the title in the Object Tag Accessibility Attributes dialog box.
20. In the Property inspector, center the Flash place-holder.
21. Click the object and enter the name **starmovie** in the Property inspector.
22. Click the Loop checkbox to clear the check mark.
23. Click Play.
24. Click in the space following the Flash movie object and press Enter to add a new line.
25. Type **Your wish came true! Summer at Tierra Verde!**. Format the text in such a way that it goes well with the design of the site.
26. Save your page and preview it in your Web browser. Your screen should look something like Illustration A on the next page.
27. Close the page and exit Dreamweaver.

Illustration A

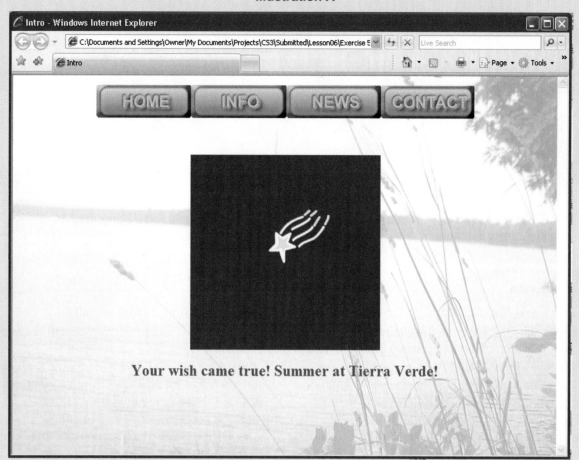

Exercise | 59

Application Exercise

Application Skills In this exercise, you create a montage using rollover slices in Fireworks.

DIRECTIONS

1. Launch Fireworks.

2. Open ⊙ montage.png from the Data folder. This file is a collection of the four primary groups on the Classmate Connections site.

3. Rollovers have been created from slices in each of three areas. You need to create and add the fourth slice, and adjust all the links.

4. Click the ⬚ Pointer tool and click the MUSIC text box.

5. Choose Edit>Copy to place the text on the clipboard.

6. Click Edit>Insert>Rectangular Slice.

7. Click Edit>Insert>Frame.

8. Click Edit>Paste to add the text to the slice.

   ✔ The text is white, so you won't see it until you change the color.

9. Change the text color to #339933 in the Property inspector.

10. Click the 🅰 Text tool and change the text to say **Hear it!**.

11. Click Frame 1 in the Frames panel.

12. Click the ⬚ Pointer tool and click the Music frame.

13. Click the behavior handle and drag it and drop it on the Music frame. In the Swap Image dialog box, click OK to swap the image in Frame 2.

14. Now you need to adjust the other links to images. Display the Swap Image dialog box and adjust the links as follows:

    ■ Movies links to Frame 3.

    ■ Books links to Frame 4.

    ■ Sports links to Frame 5.

15. Save the image and press F12 to preview it in the browser.

16. As you can see, the file is large and will need to be resized when it is imported. Change the image size to 500 × 509 (the second value is adjusted for you). Preview the file again. Your page should look something like Illustration A on the next page.

17. Save the file as S_59montage_xx. Close the file in Fireworks. Exit Fireworks.

Illustration A

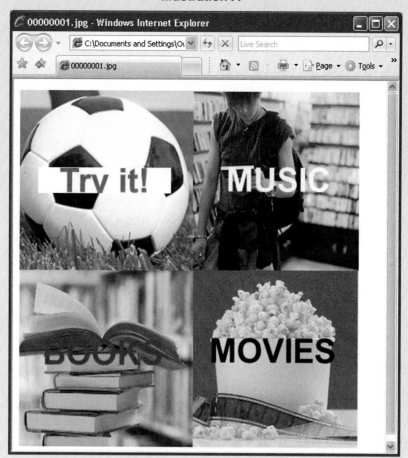

Exercise | 60

Curriculum Integration

Application Skills For your Modern British Literature class, you have been assigned the task of creating a Web page on James Joyce. You will use the Show-Hide Elements behavior to create a timeline of his birth, major works, and death. Prepare for this task by locating the following information:

- Biographical information on James Joyce, including a picture of the author

- Information on when each of his four major works—*Dubliners, Finnegans Wake, Portrait of the Artist as a Young Man,* and *Ulysses*—was published

DIRECTIONS

Create a new site with an appropriate name. Create a new page with a name such as joycetimeline.html and an appropriate page title. You may want to use a table or layers to organize the page.

On your page, insert the picture you found and an appropriate heading. Provide a brief introduction that tells where and when Joyce was born, summarizes his education, and explains where he lived after he left Ireland.

Create small, book-shaped AP divs for each of the four major works and insert in the layer the book title. Format each AP div in a different color. Position the AP divs in a vertical column, in alphabetical order, so that you begin with *Dubliners* and end with *Ulysses*.

Prepare a paragraph summary for each work and position the paragraphs in AP divs to the right of their book layers. You may want to include the first few lines of each book (you can copy this information from books you have on hand or from an online version of the book). At the end of each summary, insert the sentence *When was it published?* Format each of these sentences as a dummy link. (To prevent the browser from jumping to the top of the page each time you click a dummy link, create the dummy by typing javascript:; in the Link box.)

At the bottom of the page, create a table to be used for the timeline itself. Include in the timeline the dates of Joyce's birth, death, and years each major work was published. Illustration A shows one possible layout for the timeline.

Create a copy of each book AP div and position it in the correct location on the timeline. Specify the exact location for each AP div above its year date using the Property inspector.

Attach the Show-Hide Elements behavior to each *When was it published?* link so that when you click the link, the book "disappears" from its original location and displays on the timeline.

Test the site in a browser and make sure your behavior works properly.

Close the page and exit Dreamweaver.

Exercise | 61

Critical Thinking

Application Skills In this exercise, you will replace the navigation bar on all pages of your personal Web site with a Spry menu bar. You will also add behaviors to improve the site.

DIRECTIONS

- Open your personal Web site. Open the Library and delete the navigation bar item.

- Open the home page and remove the existing navigation bar. Replace it with a Spry navigation bar that links to all pages in your site.

- If desired, adjust formats of the Widget to use fonts and colors from your site.

- Copy the menu bar.

- Open each page, including the template page, remove the original navigation bar, and replace it with a copy of the Spry menu bar.

- Test the site in the browser to make sure the menu bars are working correctly and look attractive.

- Display the page that has a form on it. Use actions to validate form fields and add text messages in fields to help visitors fill out the form. (If desired, you may apply Spry Validation widgets to the form's text fields to validate them.) Test the form in the browser to make sure your validation works correctly.

- Close all open pages and exit Dreamweaver.

Lesson | 7

Advanced Graphics and Animation

Exercise | 62

Skills Covered

- **Choose an Output Format**
- **Select the Palette**
- **Choose the Right Number of Colors**
- **Use the Color Palette**

Software Skills When you save images in Fireworks, you need to choose an output format or file type. Depending on the format you choose, you might also need to select the number of colors and the palette.

Design Skills Knowing how to choose an output palette and work with colors is an important part of preparing your images for the Web. Not all your graphics will require this kind of attention, but knowing how to select output colors when you want to control the color display is important.

Application Skills In this exercise, you choose the output format and palette for an image that will be used in the Garden Projects site.

TERMS

8-bit image file format A file format that can contain a maximum of 256 colors.

Optimizing graphics Choosing a color palette to limit the number of colors saved with the image.

Output format The file type of the saved image.

Palette The set of colors used in a Fireworks document.

NOTES

Choose an Output Format

- Your Fireworks files must be saved in a Web-supported format in order for it to be visible in a Web browser. For most graphics that you include on Web pages, you should use the JPEG and GIF formats.

  ✔ *PNG graphics display on the Web as well; however, not all browsers are capable of displaying them. If you want to make sure your images are seen by the greatest number of potential visitors, use JPEG or GIF format.*

- Fireworks enables you to save your graphic files in the following formats:
  - BMP is a common file format used to display bitmap images. BMPs are used primarily on the Windows operating system.
  - GIF is a popular Web format because it typically creates files that are small in size and supported by most browsers. GIF files can contain a maximum of 256 colors, but they can also contain a transparent area and frames for animation, which makes them a flexible format for Web use.
  - JPEG was developed by the Joint Photographic Experts Group and is the best format for scanned photographs, images using textures, gradients, or graphics requiring a greater range of hues than 256 colors allows.
  - PICT is a graphic file format used only on Macintosh systems.
  - PNG (Portable Network Graphics) can support up to 32-bit color, and includes a transparent area. PNG is the default file format for graphics you create in Fireworks; however, not all Web browsers can display PNG graphics.
  - TIFF (Tagged Image File Format) is most commonly used in print publishing and isn't used on the Web.
  - WBMP (Wireless Bitmap) is an output format created for mobile computing devices. WBMP is a 1-bit format, so only two colors are visible: black and white.

Select the Palette

- Even though GIF files can contain a maximum of 256 colors, if your image doesn't use the full range of colors available, you can **optimize** your image by selecting a **palette** that reflects the colors used in the graphic.

- You can choose the palette you want to use for output by choosing the Indexed Palette list in the Optimize panel.

Choose the color palette for output

- Each of the palettes is slightly different:
  - Adaptive is a palette that uses the actual colors in the document
  - Web Adaptive is a palette in which colors that are close to Web safe colors are converted to the closest Web safe color.
  - Web 216 is a palette of the 216 colors common to both Windows and Macintosh computers.
  - Exact contains the exact colors used in the image. If the image contains more than 256 colors, the palette switches to Adaptive.
  - Macintosh contains the 256 colors defined by Macintosh.
  - Windows contains the 256 colors defined by Windows.
  - Grayscale is a palette of 256 or fewer shades of gray.
  - Black and White is a two-color palette consisting only of black and white.
  - Uniform is a mathematical palette based on RGB pixel values.
  - Custom is a palette that has been modified or loaded from an external palette or a GIF file.
- Only those colors that are in the selected palette will appear in the image.
- Any **8-bit file format** uses a color palette, but you are most likely to encounter palettes with GIF files.

Choose the Right Number of Colors

- Fireworks stores information about the selected color palette in the file when you save an 8-bit image file. If your document does not actually use the full 256 colors, you can eliminate the unused colors from the palette and reduce the size of the file.

- The Remove Unused Colors option on the Optimize panel option menu is available only if you have selected an 8-bit output format such as GIF.

- The Remove Unused Colors option is a toggle. A checkmark appears in front of the option when it is selected.

- Fireworks always saves JPEG files in a 24-bit format, so no color palette options are available for JPEG files.

Use the Color Palette

- The Optimize panel shows either the colors that are currently in use or the colors that are in the selected palette. The adaptive palettes show the colors in use, while the set palettes, such as the Web 216 palette shown in the illustration at right, show the colors that are defined for the palette.

A palette in the Optimize panel

- You can click the ⬤ Edit color button to change a color in the palette.

- If you change a color, Fireworks uses that changed color in place of the original color throughout the image. The original image is not changed, however, unless you specifically save the image file over the original version.

PROCEDURES

Choose an Output Format (F6)

1. Click **Window** ....[Alt]+[W]
2. Select **Optimize**...................[O]
3. Click the arrow to open the Export file format list box.
4. Click the format you want to use.

Choose a Palette (F6)

1. Click **Window** ....[Alt]+[W]
2. Select **Optimize**...................[O]
3. Click the format you want to use.
4. Click the Palette arrow to open the Indexed Palette list.
5. Click the palette you want to use.

Remove Unused Colors

1. Click **Window** ....[Alt]+[W]
2. Select **Optimize**...................[O]
3. Click the Options button to open the menu.
4. Click Remove Unused Colors.

View Colors in Document (Ctrl + Shift + X)

1. Click **File** ....[Alt]+[F]
2. Click **Image Preview** ....[R]
3. Click the Format arrow and choose the format you want to use.
4. Click the Palette arrow and click a palette type.
5. Click **OK**.

EXERCISE DIRECTIONS

1. Launch Fireworks.
2. Open the file ⊙ seeds.png from the Lesson 7 Data folder.
3. Choose the File>Image Preview menu command to open the Image Preview dialog box.
4. Notice the file size of the image in the current format. You will find the file size just above the top left corner of the image preview.
5. Choose the GIF format. Notice the file size change, and check the image in the preview window to see whether you notice any change in image quality.
6. Click Palette and choose the Windows palette. Set Loss to 0. Again, notice any file size and quality changes. Your image should look similar to Illustration A.
7. Click OK to close the Image Preview dialog box.
8. Save the file in your solutions folder as S_62seeds_xx.gif. Be sure to choose the .GIF format in the Save As dialog box.
9. Close the file.

Illustration A

ON YOUR OWN

1. Reopen the S_62seeds_xx.gif file you saved in your Solutions folder.
2. Display the image in the Image Preview dialog box.
3. Try selecting the Exact palette to see what happens. Click OK.
4. In the Optimize panel, choose the Grayscale palette and check the file size changes. What happened?
5. Compare the Black and White palette results with the Grayscale palette results.
6. Change the palette to Web 216.
7. Save the file in your solutions folder as SO_62seeds_xx.gif.
8. Close the file and exit Fireworks.

Skills Covered

- **Compress GIF Files**
- **Make Transparent GIFs**
- **Use Interlacing GIFs**

Software Skills GIF files are an efficient option when you are creating content for the Web. Fireworks includes several techniques that enable you to make your GIFs even better.

Design Skills Small file sizes and user interactivity are two big plusses for well-designed Web pages.

Application Skills In this exercise, you continue working with images that can be used on the Garden Projects Web site.

TERMS

Index transparency A type of transparency used commonly with GIF images

Interlacing A method of displaying images progressively—bit by bit—on the screen.

Loss The compression value selected for a file

NOTES

Compress GIF Files

- Even though GIF files tend to be smaller than most other types of image files, it is still possible to compress them somewhat in Fireworks to make them smaller. If you are creating Web pages for dial-up or mobile Web browsers, making file sizes as small as possible can make a big difference for your visitors.

- You use the Loss box in the Optimize panel to set the amount of data that is lost in the GIF file. Higher **loss** (or compression) values result in smaller file sizes, but generally poorer quality.

  ✔ *Because higher loss can mean lower quality images, be sure to weigh out your options and consider your audience before compressing your files.*

Choose the amount of compression

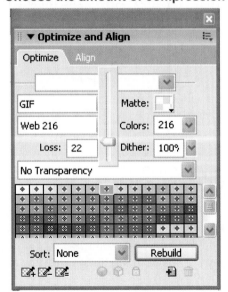

- Use the 2-Up or 4-Up views to see the effects of different compression levels on your image. Click a pane in the selected view and then choose the settings to show in that pane. The illustration at the bottom of this page shows a portion of a GIF image at no compression in the upper-left pane, 33% loss in the upper-right pane, 66% loss in the lower-right pane, and 100% loss in the lower-left pane. Note that the image is zoomed in to 300% to make the differences easier to see.

   ✔ *Fireworks shows compression levels as a percentage of loss, but this terminology is a bit misleading. If the values were truly the percentage of the data that was lost, 100% compression would show a blank image.*

- Viewing 2-Up or 4-Up views also enables you to compare the file sizes at different compression levels. Here the file sizes vary depending on the levels of compression.

- Choosing a compression level always involves a bit of a trade-off. Each image is different and it will take some experimenting to find out how much quality you want to give up in order to get the smallest file sizes.

Make Transparent GIFs

- As mentioned in the last exercise, you can create transparent areas in your GIF images. This makes it possible to create some interesting effects—for example, you could position the GIF on top of another item on your page, allowing the other item to show through the image.

- Making an area of your image transparent does not reduce the size of the GIF, however.

- To make a part of your GIF image transparent, you use the Optimize panel to choose the colors you want to make transparent, as the illustration at the top of the next page shows. The colors you make transparent will allow a background image to show through the color when the image is displayed on the Web.

- Fireworks displays a transparent area using a gray and white checkerboard pattern when you preview the image, as you see in the following illustration.

   ✔ *Notice that because a marbled effect is selected for the outside of the picture frame, the area showing white is also displayed as transparent in the previewed image.*

Comparing compression levels

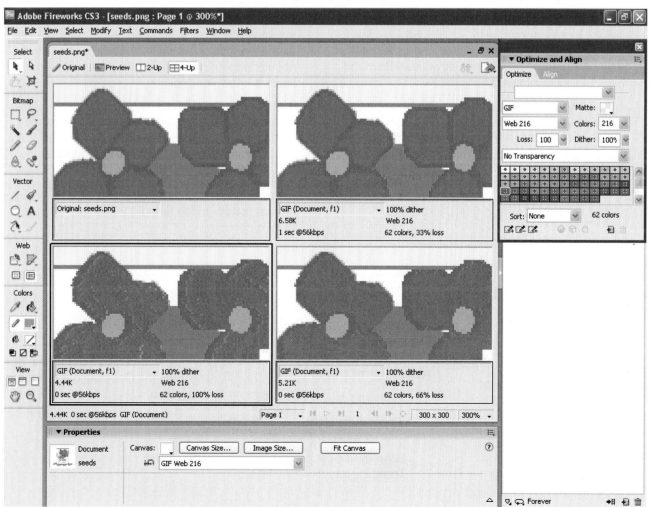

Choose transparency options

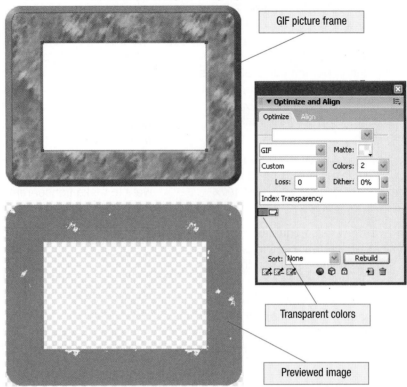

GIF picture frame

Transparent colors

Previewed image

Use Interlacing GIFs

- **Interlacing** makes images appear first as a low-quality image that improves as all of the data in the image file is downloaded.

    ✔ *Interlacing is an option only for GIF and PNG files in Fireworks, but you can use the progressive option discussed in the next exercise to achieve similar results with JPEG files.*

- Interlacing is most useful for fairly large or complex images because it allows users with slow Internet connections to get an idea of how the image will appear without having to wait for the entire image file to be downloaded.

    ✔ *It is important to remember that Web surfers often get impatient waiting for pages to finish downloading. By making lower resolution images appear quickly it is less likely that visitors will click another link before your pages are completely displayed.*

- Interlacing can slightly increase the size of the file, but not usually by an amount that is great enough to be a concern.

PROCEDURES

Select a Compression Level (F6)

1. Click **Window** .... Alt + W
2. Select **Optimize** .... O
3. Drag the Loss slider to the compression level you want.

View Different Compression Levels

1. Click ⬚2-Up **2-Up** or ⊞4-Up **4-Up** just above the canvas.

2. Click the view pane you want to modify.
3. Drag the Loss slider to the compression level you want.

Make Transparent GIFs

1. Click **Window** .... Alt + W
2. Select **Optimize** .... O
3. In the Choose type of transparency list, click **Index Transparency**.

Make Interlaced GIFs

1. Click **Window** .... Alt + W
2. Select **Optimize** .... O
3. Click the **Options** button to display the Optimize panel options menu.
4. Select the Interlaced option.

EXERCISE DIRECTIONS

1. Launch Fireworks if necessary.
2. Open 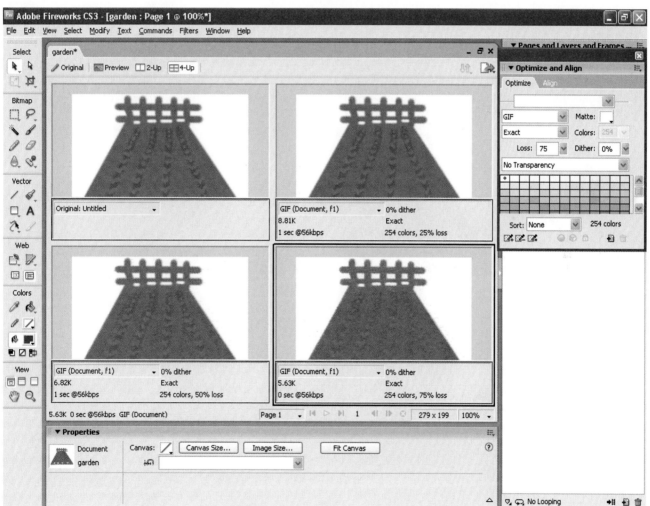garden.gif from the Lesson 7 Data folder.
3. Click the 4-Up icon to display 4 previews of the image.
4. In the Optimize panel, set the Loss (compression) for the upper-right preview to 25%.
5. Set the Loss for the lower-left preview to 50%.
6. Set the Loss for the lower-right preview to 75%
7. Set the zoom level to 200%.

8. Click the upper-left preview image to select it so that you can see the size of the original, uncompressed image just below the lower-left side of the canvas. Compare the image quality for the four previews and their file sizes. Your drawing should look similar to Illustration A.
9. Click the Original icon above the canvas to close the image previews.
10. Preview the file in your Web browser.
11. Save the file in your solutions folder as S_63garden_xx.gif.
12. Close the file.

Illustration A

ON YOUR OWN

1. Reopen the S_63garden_xx.gif file.

2. Zoom the display to 200%.

3. Click [▲ Preview] Preview to preview the image as it will appear on a Web page.

4. In the Optimize panel options menu, select Interlaced.

5. Choose GIF Web 216.

6. In the Optimize panel, change the number of colors to 4.

7. Right-click the second of the four colors in the color table and choose the Transparent option from the pop-up menu. Your image should look similar to Illustration A.

8. Save the file in your Solutions folder as SO_63garden_xx.gif.

9. Close the file.

Illustration A

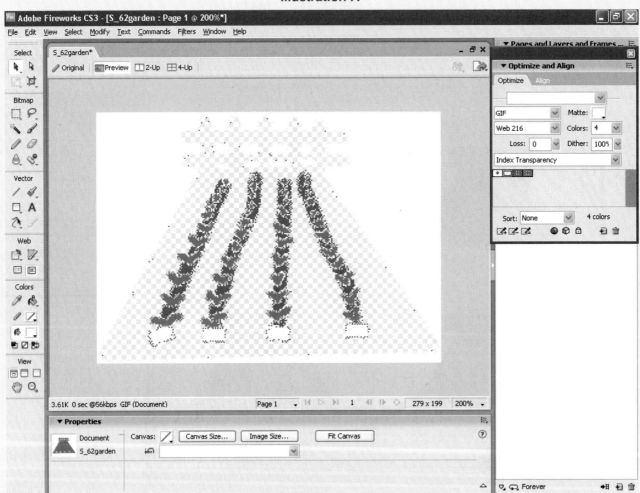

Skills Covered

- **Adjust JPEG Quality**
- **Use Selective JPEG Compression**
- **Adjust Detail Sharpness**
- **Create Progressive JPEGs**

Software Skills JPEG images typically need to be compressed for faster downloading, and Fireworks provides you with some useful tools for controlling how that compression is applied.

Design Skills As a Web designer you are sure to work with JPEG images frequently. JPEG format is the format used most for digital photos. Knowing how to compress JPEG images so that they download quickly is part of creating an efficient site.

Application Skills In this exercise, you learn how to adjust the compression for an entire JPEG image and for selected portions of an image. You also learn how to make sure image details are sharp and load JPEGs progressively.

TERMS

JPEG mask An area within a JPEG image that uses the selective JPEG compression level rather than the compression level in the rest of the image.

NOTES

Adjust JPEG Quality

- JPEG format is ideal for digital photos because it enables you to reduce the size of an image while you adjust the quality of the image. That is, you can greatly reduce the file size without much noticeable effect on the quality.

- JPEG compression works by replacing areas of an image with rectangular blocks that are a single color. When an image is viewed at normal size, there is typically little reduction in quality; but when you zoom the image, you can see the color blocks (see the illustration at the top of the next page).

- You adjust the JPEG compression level using the Quality option in the Optimize panel. Higher values produce better quality.

- Because JPEG compression discards data, you can never recover details that are lost once you save a JPEG image that you have compressed.

  ✔ *Because compressed JPEGs delete any compressed color information, be sure to keep a backup copy of the original JPEG if there's any chance you may want to use the uncompressed version in other things later.*

- JPEG images that are compressed more than once lose even more of the fine details with each compression. It is generally not a good idea to compress an image that has already been compressed.

Color blocks in a compressed JPEG file

Use Selective JPEG Compression

- In most cases, parts of your image are more important than others. For example, in a photo of a person, you will want the face to be as clear as possible but other parts of the image—such as the background—may not be as important to show clearly.

- Fireworks enables you to choose the areas of a JPEG image you want to compress. You can apply an overall JPEG compression level and then set another JPEG compression level for specific areas of the image.

- You apply selective compression by first using a bitmap selection tool to choose the area you want to compress differently than the rest of the image. You then create a **JPEG mask** from the selection and apply the selective compression.

- You use the Selective JPEG Settings dialog box shown in the illustration at right to set the options for selective JPEG compression.

- The Optimize panel has two JPEG quality settings. You use the Quality slider (or text box) to set the compression level for the main part of an image. You use the Selective quality box to set the compression level for the area within the JPEG mask.

Selective JPEG Settings dialog box

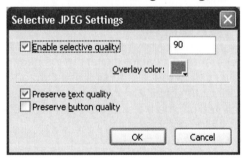

- You can use different types of settings for different purposes:
  - You can set the main quality setting low and the selective quality high to make the area within the JPEG mask as clear as possible while reducing the file size.
  - You can set the main quality setting high and the selective quality low to make the area within the JPEG mask blurry while keeping the rest of the image clear.

Adjust Detail Sharpness

- Reducing the size of JPEG image files always involves trade-offs. You have to give up some detail in order to reduce the file size.

- Depending on the image content, a JPEG image may simply appear blurred or it may look jagged along the hard edges of objects. Fireworks provides two related options for improving the appearance of compressed images:

  - Sharpen JPEG Edges in the Options menu on the Optimize panel makes fine detail and text appear sharper. Choosing this option can increase the file size.

  - Smoothing blurs hard edges. Choosing high values of smoothing reduces the file size in most cases. The following illustration shows an original image (on the left) compared with an image where maximum smoothing has been applied.

Create Progressive JPEGs

- You can choose to make JPEG images appear in low resolution shortly after they begin loading so that visitors will see the image before all of the data is downloaded.

- Progressive JPEG images are similar to interlaced GIF files.

- Using a progressive JPEG download can be an excellent alternative to using extreme JPEG compression, and it gives you the opportunity to use higher quality JPEG images on your Web pages.

- Selecting the Progressive JPEG option on the Options menu of the Optimize panel tends to slightly increase the size of the JPEG file, but for the Web, this slight increase is offset by the faster appearance of the initial image.

An original and a smoothed image

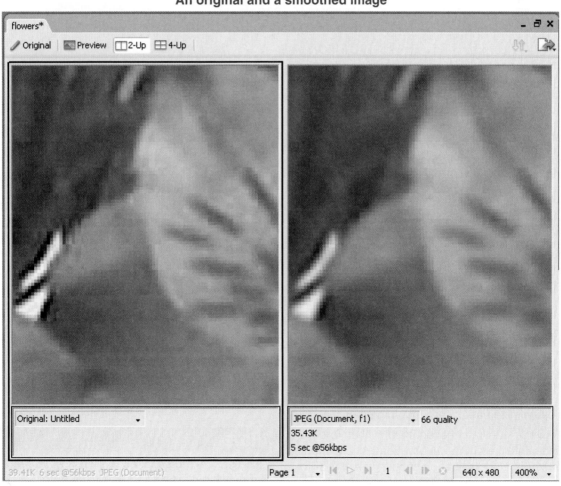

PROCEDURES

Select a JPEG Quality Level (F6)

1. Click **Window** .... `Alt`+`W`
2. Select **Optimize** .... `O`
3. Drag the Quality slider to the quality level you want.

View Different Quality Levels

1. Click `2-Up` **2-Up** or `4-Up` **4-Up** just above the canvas.
2. Click the view pane you want to change.
3. Drag the Quality slider to the level you want.

Apply a JPEG Mask

1. Draw a marquee around the area where you want to apply selective JPEG Compression.
2. Click **Modify** .... `Alt`+`M`
3. Select **Selective JPEG** .... `J`
4. Select **Selection as JPEG Mask** .... `S`

Select a Selective JPEG Quality (F6)

1. Click **Window** .... `Alt`+`W`
2. Select **Optimize** .... `O`
3. Click **Edit Selective Quality Options**.
4. Select the Enable selective quality check box.
5. Type the quality value.
6. Click **OK**.

Sharpen Edges (F6)

1. Click **Window** .... `Alt`+`W`
2. Select **Optimize** .... `O`
3. Click **Options**.
4. Click **Sharpen JPEG Edges**.

Smooth Edges

1. Click **Window** .... `Alt`+`W`
2. Select **Optimize** .... `O`
3. Click the Smoothing arrow.
4. Click your choice.

Select Progressive JPEG

1. Click **Window** .... `Alt`+`W`
2. Select **Optimize** .... `O`
3. Click **Options**.
4. Click **Progressive JPEG**.

EXERCISE DIRECTIONS

1. Open ⊙ daffodils.jpg in the Lesson 7 Data folder.
2. Select the ⬚ Marquee tool and draw a rectangle that encloses both daffodils blossoms.
3. Select Modify>Selective JPEG>Save Selection as JPEG Mask.
4. Click `Preview` Preview.
5. In the Optimize panel, click the Edit Selective Quality Options button to display the Selective JPEG Settings dialog box.
6. Make sure Enable selective quality is selected. Click OK.
7. Set the Quality to 1.
8. Set the Selective quality to 100. Your image should look similar to Illustration A on the next page.
9. Click `Original` Original.
10. Save the file in your Solutions folder as S_64daffodils_xx.jpg.
11. Close the file.

ON YOUR OWN

1. Reopen S_64daffodils_xx.jpg.
2. Click `Preview` Preview.
3. In the Optimize panel, set Smoothing to 8.
4. Click `2-Up` **2-Up** and experiment with different settings until the photo will download in less than 15 seconds. Your illustration should look similar to Illustration B on the next page.

   ✔ You'll find the download statistics for each image below the preview window.

5. Save the file as SO_64daffodils_xx.jpg. Close the file

NOTE

The next exercise takes you back to Flash to create movie clips and button symbols.

Illustration A

Illustration B

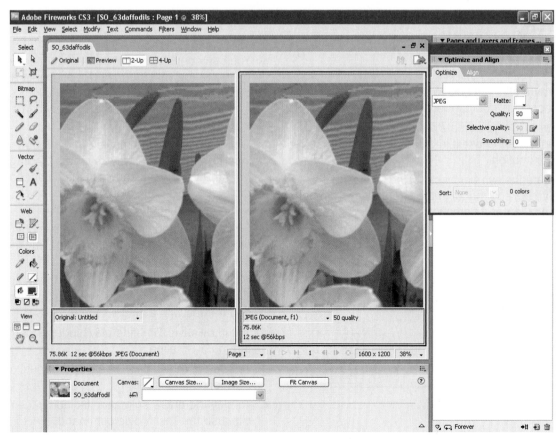

Skills Covered

- **Create a Movie Clip Symbol**
- **Create a Button Symbol**

Software Skills Use a Flash movie clip symbol to store an animation that you need to use more than once in an application. This is very important for keeping file size small, because you store the animation once as a symbol and insert instances when you need them. Use button symbols to create interactive buttons that users can click to navigate in an application. For example, a user might click a button to go to a specific scene in an animation.

Design Skills One of the great things about creating animations and interactive elements in Flash is that you can save them and reuse them easily in other applications. Movie clip symbols and button symbols are the means you use to do that.

Application Skills In this exercise, you learn to create a movie symbol and insert an instance from the Library. Additionally, you create a new button symbol and create the up, over, and down states.

TERMS

Button symbol The original saved button that is stored in the Flash Library.

Movie clip A movie segment.

NOTES

Create a Movie Clip Symbol

- Use **movie clip** symbols to store animated sequences that you can reuse many times.

- For example, if you create an animation of a logo, you might want to use it in different places throughout an animation.

- You create the symbol by choosing the Insert > New Symbol command. In the Create New Symbol dialog box, enter a name for the movie symbol, select Movie clip, and click OK, as the illustration below shows.

Create New Symbol dialog box

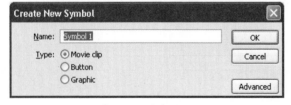

- You can convert an animation sequence you create on the Stage with the main Timeline into a movie clip symbol, or you can create a blank movie clip symbol and then create the sequence in symbol editing mode.

- Once you create the movie clip symbol, you can insert an instance in any keyframe by dragging it from the Library, as shown in the Illustration at the top of the next page; you can even replace the original animated sequence with an instance.

- Since an instance of a movie clip symbol takes up only a single keyframe in the main Timeline, it is an efficient way to minimize file size.

- Movie clips can also help simplify the main Timeline because you can replace multiple layers and frames with a single keyframe.

- The movie clip Timeline plays independently from the main Timeline.

- To see the movie clip Timeline, you must change to symbol editing mode.

- To play the entire animation including the movie clip, use the Test Movie command.

Drag a movie clip from the Library

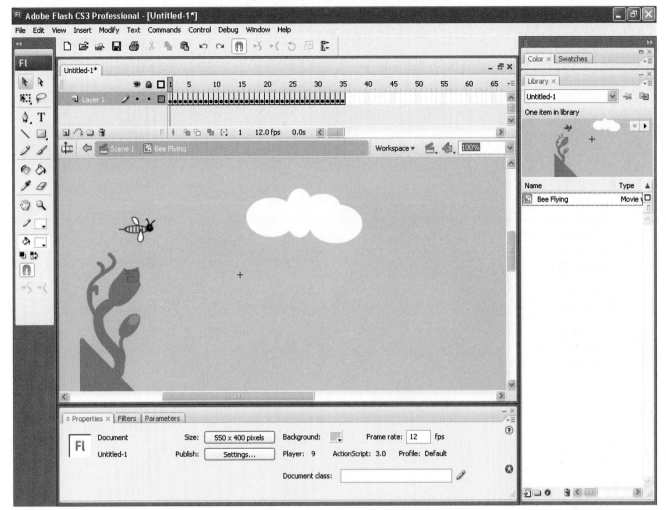

■ When you test the animation, Flash exports the animation to a Flash movie file and plays it in a separate Flash Player window in a continuous loop. The movie file is stored in the same location with the same name as the document file.

Create a Button Symbol

■ Use **button symbols** to create interactive buttons that respond to mouse clicks, rollovers, or other actions.

■ You can convert an existing object on the Stage to a button symbol, or you can create a new button symbol and enter the content in symbol editing mode.

■ When you create a button symbol, Flash creates a Timeline with four frames, corresponding to four button states so you can define each state (see the illustration at the top of the next page):

   ● The Up state is the default appearance of the button.

   ● The Over state is the way the button looks or reacts when the user rolls the mouse pointer over it, or rests the mouse pointer on it.

   ● The Down state is the way the button looks or reacts when the user clicks it with the mouse.

   ● The Hit state defines the area around the button that will respond to the rollover or mouse click. The Hit state is invisible when the movie is played.

■ You may incorporate drawing objects, graphic symbol instances, sounds, and movie clip symbol instances in any button state, but you cannot use a button symbol in another button symbol.

■ Use a movie clip symbol if you want the button to appear animated.

■ When you insert a sound in the button symbol Timeline it is stored with the button symbol so it applies to every instance of the symbol.

■ The button symbol Timeline doesn't actually play; it simply reacts to the user's pointer.

■ By default, buttons are disabled in Flash. You must enable buttons in order to test them on the Stage.

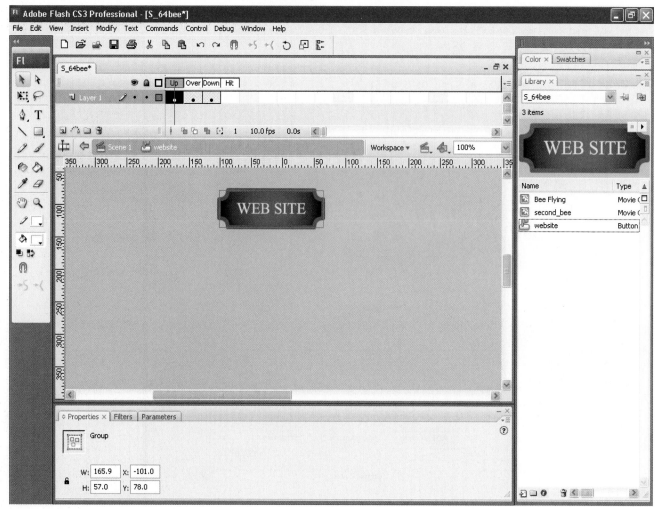

PROCEDURES

Create a New Movie Clip Symbol

1. Deselect all objects on the Stage by clicking outside the stage area.
2. Click **Insert** .... Alt + I
3. Click **New Symbol** .... N
4. Type a name for the symbol in the Name box.
5. Click **Movie clip** button.
6. Click **OK** .... Enter

   ✔ *Flash displays symbol editing mode.*

7. Create animation as you would in main movie Timeline.
8. Save the animation.

Create a Movie Clip Symbol from an Existing Animation

1. Select every frame in every layer you want to include in the movie clip.

   ✔ *To select all frames in all layers, click Edit and then click Select All.*

2. Right-click the selection.
3. Click **Copy Frames**.
4. Deselect all objects on the Stage.
5. Click **Insert** .... Alt + I
6. Click **New Symbol** .... N
7. Type a name for the symbol in the Name box.
8. Click **Movie clip** option button.
9. Click **OK** .... Enter
10. Right-click the keyframe in frame 1 of Layer 1.
11. Click **Paste Frames**.
12. Make changes as needed for the new symbol.
13. Save the file.

Insert a Movie Clip Instance

1. Display the Library panel.
2. Select the keyframe in the Timeline where you want to insert an instance.
3. Drag the movie clip symbol from the Library panel to the Stage.
4. If necessary, insert an ending frame to extend the sequence in the layer containing the movie clip instance.

   ✔ *The movie clip layer should extend as far as the sequences in other layers.*

Create a Button Symbol

1. Deselect all objects on the Stage.
2. Click **Insert** .... Alt + I
3. Click **New Symbol** .... N
4. Type a name for the symbol in the Name box.
5. Click **Button** option button.
6. Click **OK** .... Enter

   ✔ *Flash displays the button Timeline in symbol editing mode.*

7. Select the **Up** keyframe, if necessary.
8. Insert or create the button as you want it to appear when there is no user interaction.

   ✔ *You can use the drawing tools; import files; or insert a graphic, sound, or movie clip instance.*

9. Select the **Over** frame.
10. Insert a keyframe.
11. Modify the content to display the button as you want it to appear when the user positions the mouse pointer over it.
12. Select the **Down** frame.
13. Insert a keyframe.
14. Modify the content to create the button as you want it to display when the user clicks it.
15. Select the **Hit** frame.
16. Insert a keyframe.

17. Use the Oval or Rectangle tool to define an area around the button that will react to a rollover or click.

   ✔ *The Hit area should be at least as large as the button object, and it may be larger. It is invisible on the Stage.*

18. Click **Edit** .... Alt + E
19. Click **Edit Document** .... E

Enable Buttons (Ctrl + Alt + B)

1. Click **Control** .... Alt + O
2. Click **Enable Simple Buttons** .... T, T, Enter

   ✔ *A check mark next to the option indicates that it is already selected.*

Test a Button

1. Enable buttons.
2. Do the following:
   - Move mouse pointer over button on Stage to view Over state.
   - Click button on Stage to view Down state.

Select a Button Instance when Buttons are Enabled

1. Click ⬉ **Selection** tool V
2. Drag selection rectangle around button to select.

Preview a Button or Movie Clip Symbol

1. Display Library panel.
2. Select symbol to preview.
3. Click ▶ **Play** button in Preview area.

   OR

1. Click **Control** .... Alt + O
2. Click **Test Movie** .... M

   ✔ *Animation plays in new Flash Player window.*

3. Click **File** .... Alt + F
4. Click **Close** C
   to close the test window.

EXERCISE DIRECTIONS

1. Start Flash and open the ⊙ 65bee file. Save the file as S_65bee_xx.

2. Select all frames in Layer 1.

    ✔ This is the content you want to convert to a movie clip symbol.

3. Right-click the selection and click Copy Frames.

4. Deselect all objects.

5. Create a new movie clip symbol named **Bee Flying**.

6. Right-click frame 1 of Layer 1 in the movie clip symbol Timeline and click Paste Frames. Your screen should look similar to Illustration A.

7. Play the animation.

8. Close symbol editing mode and return to editing the main document by choosing the Edit>Edit Document menu command.

9. Add a new layer to the Timeline. Click the layer to make it active.

10. Drag the instance of *second_bee* to a point just to the left of the opening pink bud on the Stage.

11. Double-click the instance of the *second_bee* on the Stage.

12. Press Enter to play the animation.

13. Copy all frames in the movie clip Timeline.

14. Click Scene 1.

15. Right-click in frame 1 of Layer 2 and choose Paste Frames.

16. Press Enter to play the animation.

17. Click frame 35.

18. Add a new layer. You will put a button on Layer 3.

19. Deselect all objects and drag the *website* button instance from the Library panel and place it in the bottom center of the Stage.

20. Double-click the button.

21. Select the Over frame and insert a keyframe.

22. Select the instance on the Stage.

23. Modify the color of the instance by ungrouping it and then applying blue (#3300FF) to the ✐ ▣ Stroke Color and a ◊ ▣ Fill Color that uses a blue gradient.

    ✔ You may need to choose Modify>Ungroup more than once before the Properties inspector shows fill and stroke color options.

24. Select the Down frame and insert a keyframe.

25. Modify the color of the instance by applying red (#FF0000) as the stroke and the red gradient for the fill.

26. Return to editing the document.

27. Enable simple buttons.

28. Rest the mouse pointer on the button. The button should tint blue.

29. Click the button. The button should tint red.

30. Test the movie. While it plays in the Flash Player window, you can see how the button reacts to a rollover and to a click.

31. Save all changes to the document. If requested by your instructor, print the last frame in each scene, or print the entire animation.

32. Lock all layers in all scenes.

33. Close the file, saving all changes.

34. Exit Flash.

Illustration A

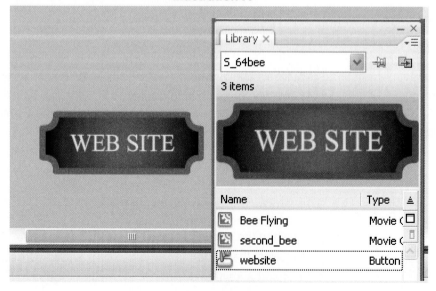

ON YOUR OWN

1. Start Flash and open ⊙ walking in your Lesson 7 Data folder. Save the document as SO_65walking_xx.

2. Create a movie clip symbol from the animation already in the document.

3. Insert a keyframe half way through the movie and insert another instance of the movie clip.

4. Test the animation.

5. Zoom up to 200% view.

6. Create a button symbol that transforms depending on the state. For example, the symbol may increase in size, rotate, or change color in the Over or Down state.

7. Modify the text color as well so the different states are reflected.

8. Insert an instance of the button symbol in the application and then test it. Test the entire animation.

   ✔ Remember to Enable Simple Buttons (in the Control menu) if necessary.

9. When you are satisfied with the results, save the changes and lock the layers.

10. Close the document, saving all changes, and exit Flash.

Exercise | 66

Skills Covered

Software Skills Use the Flash Movie Explorer to examine the contents of an application to quickly locate specific elements such as instances. For example, you can use the Movie Explorer to select all instances of a specific symbol or to select a symbol in the library. You can even use it to print a flowchart of a scene or of the entire application. Apply a Timeline effect to an object in a Flash document to create a complex animation without using a lot of time or effort. For example, use a Timeline effect to add a drop shadow or blur to a circle, or to cause an object on the Stage to appear to explode. Timeline effects may be applied to text, graphics, bitmaps, and button symbols.

Design Skills As your experience with creating movies for Web pages grows, you will design longer and more complex animations. Knowing how to use Movie Explorer and Timeline effects helps you locate and work with items in your movie easily.

Application Skills In this exercise, you use the Movie Explorer and Timeline effects to find and work with elements in the movie clip.

TERMS

Collapse To change the view to hide items. For example, collapse a hierarchical display to hide sub-elements and show only the main element.

Expand To change the view to show hidden items. For example, expand a hierarchical display to show sub-elements branching off the main element.

Hierarchical list A diagram in which elements branch from a main element—the root—to other elements. It is usually used to show how the elements relate to each other. Sometimes called a *tree diagram*.

Symbol definition The content that comprises a symbol.

Timeline effects Predefined animations that come with Flash that you can apply to objects on the Stage.

NOTES

Use the Movie Explorer

- Use the Movie Explorer to view and organize the contents of a document, to locate an element by name, to locate all instances of a specific symbol, or to select elements in the document.

- The Movie Explorer opens in a panel and displays a **hierarchical list** of elements currently used in the document. **Expand** or **collapse** the display to show or hide elements that branch off of other elements (see the following illustration).

Movie Explorer

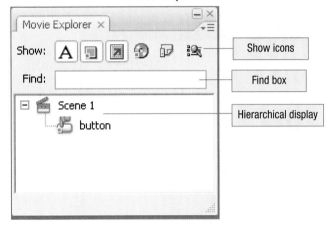

- By default, Flash displays the elements one scene at a time. You may choose to display all scenes.

- You may also choose to display **symbol definitions** in place of movie elements, or you may display both.

- Customize the display by selecting the specific elements you want to view: text; graphics; buttons; movie clips; actions; and imported files, such as sounds, bitmaps, and videos.

- You can also print the Movie Explorer to generate a diagram of the document structure.

- The Movie Explorer is particularly useful for managing large applications and familiarizing yourself with a document created by someone else.

Use Timeline Effects

- **Timeline effects** are built-in animations that you can apply to text blocks, graphics, bitmap images, or button symbols.

- When you apply an effect to an element, Flash moves the element to a new layer or, if there is no other content on the current layer, renames the current layer. The layer name reflects the type of effect you apply.

- Flash also creates a folder in the library for storing the elements required for the effect.

- When you apply a Timeline effect to an object, Flash may convert the object to a symbol. For example, if you animate a drawn circle, Flash converts the circle to a symbol.

- Use the Insert>Timeline Effects menu command to display your choices. The Timeline effects are divided into three submenus:
  - Assistants
  - Effects
  - Transform/Transition

- On the Assistants submenu, you can select either Copy to Grid or Distributed Duplicate:
  - Copy to Grid duplicates a selected object to create a grid of columns and rows.
  - Distributed Duplicate duplicates a selected object by a specified number of times. Each additional object is modified incrementally to achieve a desired result.

- On the Effects submenu, you can select from the following:
  - Blur, which creates a motion blur effect by changing the alpha value, position, or scale of an object over time.
  - Drop shadow, which creates a shadow below the element.
  - Expand, which expands, contracts, or expands and contracts objects over time.
  - Explode, which causes elements of text or a group of objects to break apart, spin, and arc outward.

- On the Transform/Transition submenu, you can select either Transform or Transition:
  - Transform adjusts the position, scale, rotation, alpha, and tint of the selected elements.
  - Transition wipes in or wipes out selected objects by fading, wiping, or a combination of both.
  - ✔ *Not all effects are available for all objects. For example, you cannot apply the Expand effect to drawn objects, but you can apply it to button symbols.*

- When you select an effect from the Timeline Effects menu, Flash displays a settings window in which you preview the animation and select settings and options.

- For example, when you select the blur effect, you may specify options such as the duration in frames and the direction of movement (see the illustration below).

- Update the preview after making changes to see the animation with the new settings.

- On the Timeline, the frames containing the effect are gray. Use the Play command to preview the animation on the Stage.

- You can edit a Timeline effect to change the selected settings, or you can remove the effect completely.

Blur Effect Settings Window

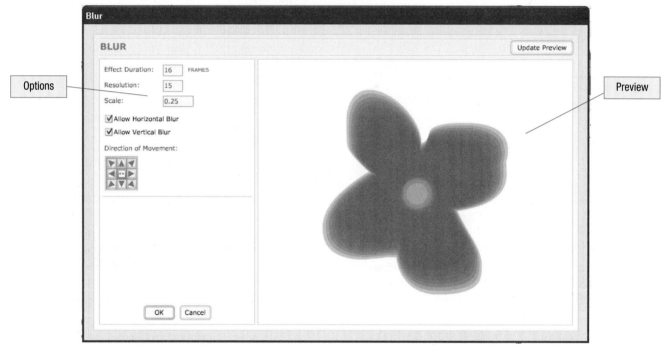

PROCEDURES

Show/Hide Movie Explorer (Alt + F3)

1. Click **Window** .... Alt + W
2. Click **Movie Explorer** .... M, M, Enter
   - ✔ *A check mark next to the Movie Explorer command indicates it is already displayed.*

Show/Hide Elements in Movie Explorer

1. Display Movie Explorer.
2. Click button to show or hide element:
   - **Show text** A
   - **Show movie clips, buttons, and graphics** 🔲
   - **Show ActionScript** ▣
   - **Show video, sounds, and bitmaps** 🔊
   - **Show frames and layers** 🔲

Customize Movie Explorer Display

To select elements to display:

1. Display Movie Explorer.
2. Click **Customize which items to show** button 🔧.
3. Click to select or deselect elements to show:
   - **Text** .... T
   - **Buttons** .... B
   - **Movie clips** .... M
   - **Video** V

- ■ **A**ctionScript.................[A]
- ■ **B**itmaps........................[I]
- ■ **G**raphics......................[G]
- ■ **S**ounds........................[S]
- ■ **L**ayers...........................[L]
- ■ **F**rames.........................[F]
4. Click **OK**............................[Enter]

To change display category:

1. Display Movie Explorer.
2. Click **Customize which items to show** button 🔍.
3. Click to select or deselect category for organizing display:
   - ■ Movie **e**lements...............[E]
   - ■ S**y**mbol definitions.........[Y]
4. Click **OK**...............................[Enter]

   OR

   a. Right-click in the Movie Explorer panel.

   b. Click desired option:
      - ■ **Show Movie Elements**
      - ■ **Show Symbol Definitions**
      - ■ **Show All Scenes**

Expand or Collapse the Movie Explorer List

1. Display the Movie Explorer.
2. Do one of the following:
   - ■ Click **plus sign** to expand list.
   - ■ Click **minus sign** to collapse list.

   OR

1. Right-click an element in Movie Explorer list.
2. Click one of the following:
   - ■ **Expand Branch** to expand current element.
   - ■ **Collapse Branch** to collapse current element.
   - ■ **Collapse Others** to collapse all except current element.

Resize Movie Explorer Panel

- ■ Drag a panel border.

Find an Element in Movie Explorer Panel

1. Display the Movie Explorer.
2. Click in **Find** box.
3. Type element to find.

   ✔ *Flash displays matching element(s) and hides other elements.*

To display all elements:

- ■ Delete all text from Find box.

Use Movie Explorer Options

1. Display Movie Explorer.
2. Right-click element in list.
3. Select option:
   - ■ **Go to Location** to display frame containing current element.
   - ■ **Go to Symbol Definition** to display symbol definition for current element.
   - ■ **Select Symbol Instances** to select all instances of current symbol.
   - ■ **Find in Library** to select current symbol in Library panel.
   - ■ **Rename** to rename current element.
   - ■ **Edit in Place** to edit current element in place on Stage.
   - ■ **Edit in New Window** to edit current element in symbol editing mode.

Print the Movie Explorer List

1. Display Movie Explorer.
2. Right-click in panel.
3. Click **Print**.
4. Select print options in Print dialog box.
5. Click **OK**............................[Enter]

Apply a Timeline Effect

1. Right-click the object you want to animate.

   OR

   a. Select the object to animate on the Stage.

   b. Click **Insert**.............[Alt]+[I]
2. Click Timeline **E**ffects..........[E]
3. Click one of the following:
   - ■ **Assistants**
   - ■ **Effects**
   - ■ **Transform/Transition**
4. Click the desired effect.
5. Select options as desired.
6. Click **Update Preview** to view the animation with the new settings.
7. Click **OK**...............................[Enter]

Edit a Timeline Effect

1. Right-click the object you want to edit on the Stage.

   OR

   a. Select object to edit on Stage.

   b. Click **M**odify.............[Alt]+[M]
2. Click Timeline **E**ffects..........[E]
3. Click **E**dit Effect..................[D]
4. Change settings as desired.
5. Click **Update Preview**.
6. Click **OK**...............................[Enter]

Remove a Timeline Effect

1. Right-click the object you want to edit on the Stage.

   OR

   a. Select the object you want to edit on Stage.

   b. Click **M**odify.............[Alt]+[M]
2. Click Timeline **E**ffects..........[E]
3. Click **R**emove Effect...........[R]

View a Timeline Effect on the Stage

1. Click **C**ontrol................[Alt]+[O]
2. Click **P**lay............................[P]

EXERCISE DIRECTIONS

1. Open the 66flowers in the Lesson 7 Data folder.

2. Insert keyframes at frames 10, 20, 30, 40, and 50. Drag flowers 1 through 4 and place one on the Stage at each keyframe in frames 10 through 40. Place the flowers on the Stage as shown in illustration A. Leave frame 50 blank for now.

   ✔ You will add Flower 5 in frame 50 in the On Your Own exercise.

3. Choose Window>Movie Explorer to display the panel. Review the content; then close the panel.

4. Position the playhead at frame 1.

5. Select Flower 1 on the Stage. Choose the Insert> Timeline Effects menu command.

6. Point to Effects and click Blur. Click OK.

7. Click the next keyframe (notice that the frames changed to accommodate the effect) and select the second flower.

8. Display the Timeline Effects submenu again; this time, point to Effects and select Drop Shadow.

9. Change the Shadow Offset settings to 5 pixels for both the X and Y values.

10. Change the color of the drop shadow to #CC0066.

11. Click Update Preview and click OK.

12. Click the next keyframe, and click the third flower.

13. Choose a Timeline Effect of Expand. Set the Effect Duration to 10 frames, and set the Expand option to Both. Click Update Preview; then click OK.

14. Click the next keyframe and click the fourth flower.

15. Assign a timeline effect of Explode. In the Explode dialog box, set the Effect Duration to 10 frames, set the X value of the Change Fragments Size to 50, and adjust the Final Alpha value to 40%. Click OK.

16. Play the movie clip and notice the way in which the various effects display. The Stage should look something like Illustration A.

17. Save the movie as S_66flowers_xx and close the file.

Illustration A

ON YOUR OWN

1. Reopen S_66flowers_xx and adjust the placement of the items on the Timeline so they appear one at a time.

2. Add a new layer and cut and paste the fifth flower to the new layer.

3. Add a special effect for the fifth flower.

4. Rename the layer to reflect the effect you apply to the flower.

5. Change the frame rate so that you can watch the animation in slow motion.

6. Add a background color to the image.

7. View the Movie Explorer and scroll through the various effects added to the scene. Close the Movie Explorer.

8. Save the animation as SO_66flowers_xx and test it.

9. Close the file and exit Flash.

Exercise | 67

Summary Exercise

Application Skills In this exercise, you create and optimize a logo for the YardArt site using Fireworks and then use it to create and modify a movie clip symbol in Flash.

DIRECTIONS

1. Launch Fireworks.
2. Begin a new document with the size 300 × 300.
3. Select the [A] Text tool, click on the canvas, and type **Yard**.
4. Set the text properties as follows:

   Font: Hobo Std font
   Size: 70px
   Color: FFCC66
   Filter: Bevel and Emboss, Outer Bevel,
   Bevel Edge Shape set to Frame 2, width 12,
   color #FF6633

5. Click below the first text box and type **ART**, setting the properties as follows:

   Font: Hobo Std font
   Size: 75px
   Color: CC0000
   Filter: Bevel and Emboss, Outer Bevel,
   Bevel Edge Shape set to Flat, width 10,
   color #FF0000

6. Layer ART behind Yard so the edges just barely overlap. (Use Illustration A as a guide.)
7. Fit the image to the canvas.
8. Group the objects by choosing the Modify > Group command.
9. Save the object as S_67yalogo_xx.png.
10. Display the Optimize pane by choosing Window>Optimize.
11. Click ⊞4-Up to choose the 4-Up display.
12. Choose a GIF format for the upper-right version of the file and set a Loss value of 10.

Illustration A

13. Choose GIF Web 216 for the lower-right version.
14. Choose JPEG - Better Quality for the lower-left version of the logo.
15. Zoom the display to 200%. Compare the quality of the logos as well as their file sizes and download times.
16. Select the logo in the upper-right corner and pre-view it. Save it as S_67yalogo_xx.gif in your Solutions folder.
17. Start Flash and create a new document.
18. Name the document S_67yalogo_xx, and leave the dimensions as they are. Choose a Background color of #FFFFCC.
19. Click the Insert>New Symbol menu command and create a movie clip symbol, naming it **yalogo_clip**.
20. Choose the File>Import>Import to Stage menu command, navigate to the S_67yalogo_xx.gif file you just created, select it, and click Open.
21. With the image selected, change the width and height to 50 × 50.
22. Position the object in the upper-left corner of the Stage.

23. Add a keyframe in frame 35.

24. Enlarge the object so that it appears in a larger size and centered in frame 35.

25. Select frame 1 and create a motion tween for the logo.

26. Play the animation to see the effect.

27. Click Scene 1 to return to the Stage.

28. Select *yalogo_clip* in the Library list and preview it in the panel at the top of the Library.

29. Insert a keyframe in frame 35 to mark the ending point.

30. Double-click the logo in the top of the Library panel to add it to the Stage.

31. Play the animation.

32. With the playhead set in frame 35, click the object on the Stage and choose Insert>Timeline Effects> Effects>Explode.

33. In the Explode dialog box, set the Effect Duration to 40 frames. Click OK.

34. In the Property inspector, change the Options for graphics setting to Play Once.

35. Test the movie. The clip appears in the upper left of the Stage and zooms to the center; then breaks apart and dissolves to the background color (see Illustration B).

36. Close all open files.

Illustration B

Application Exercise

Application Skills In this exercise, you use Fireworks to create a logo for the Classmate Connections site, animate it in Flash, and add it to your Classmate Connections site.

DIRECTIONS

1. Launch Fireworks and create a new document with a canvas of 300 × 300.

2. Apply a background color of #009999

3. Select the [A] Text tool and set the properties as follows:

   Font: Century Schoolbook
   Size: 96px
   Color: #CCCC66

4. Click in the center of the canvas and type **C**. Select the object.

5. Apply a filter of Bevel and Emboss, Raised Emboss. Increase the Width to 3.

6. Fit to canvas, and save the character as S_68cclogo_xx.gif in your Solutions folder.

7. Exit Fireworks.

8. Launch Flash and create a new file. Add the background color #009999 to the Stage.

9. Create a new movie clip symbol by choosing Insert>New Symbol and entering the name **cclogo** for the symbol. Click OK.

10. Use File>Import>Import to Stage and add S_68cclogo_xx.gif. Change the size of the object to 50 × 50.

11. With the object selected, choose Insert>Timeline Effects>Effects>Expand.

12. In the Expand dialog box, enter the following settings:
    - Effect Duration: 30 frames
    - Shift GroupCenter by: Y: –200 pixels
      Note that entering a minus sign before the 200 is important because it causes the logo to move up from the bottom of the screen.
    - Fragment Offset: 100 pixels
    - Change Fragment Size by: Height: 100, Width: 100

13. Click Update Preview to see the result of the changes.

14. Click OK to add the effect to the object.

15. Copy all frames in the movie clip symbol and click Scene 1 to return to the document. Right-click frame 1 and choose Paste Frames.

16. Click the movie clip symbol on the Stage and drag it to the bottom center of the Stage, as shown in Illustration A on the next page.

17. Press Enter to play the animation.

18. In the Property inspector, set the Options for graphics to Play Once.

19. Create a new layer and add a second instance of the movie clip in frame 10 by pasting the frames into frame 10. Arrange the objects so that the second object zooms to appear beside the first object. Set that object to Play Once.

20. Test the movie and save it as S_68cclogo_xx. Choose File>Publish Settings and click Publish to publish the movie. Exit Flash.

21. Open Dreamweaver and display the navigation.html page.

22. Click above the navigation panel and press Enter to add space.

23. Choose Insert>Media>Flash. Navigate your Solutions folder and locate the S_68cclogo_xx.swf Flash movie. Choose to save it to the site root and add the **cc_logo** object tag.

24. Resize the movie object to W 140 and H 120.

25. Save your changes to navigation.html and close the page.

26. Open index.html and preview the page in your Web browser. The page should resemble Illustration B. Close all open pages.

Illustration A

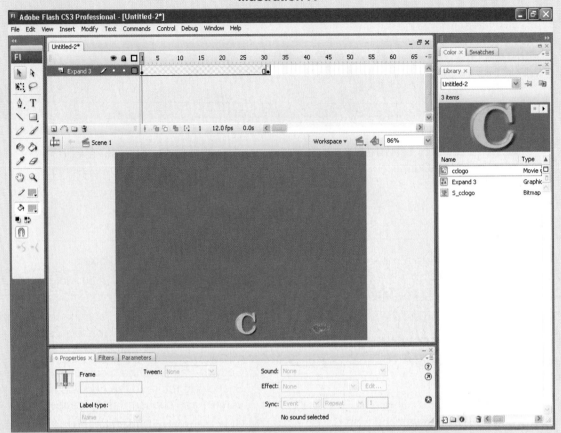

Illustration B

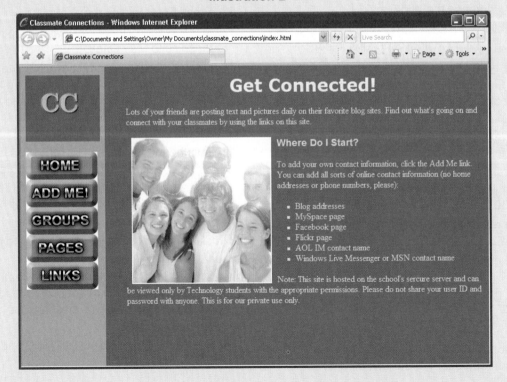

Exercise | 69

Curriculum Integration

Application Skills For your Psychology class, you are creating a Web page that provides the biographical information and foundational theories explored by Carl Jung, the Swiss psychologist. You'll need the following information for the page:

- Background information on Carl Jung, including one or more photos.

- Information on each of the following key ideas: *Collective unconscious; synchroncity; archetypes; introversion*; and *extroversion*.

DIRECTIONS

Create a new site with an appropriate name. Add a new page and name it something like cjung_keyideas.html. If you choose, create a layout table or a standard table to organize the information on the page. Apply formats to the table as desired.

Add content to the page that provides an introduction to each of the key ideas listed above. Be sure to provide links to Web pages where you located the information.

Save the page and minimize Dreamweaver.

Open Fireworks, and open the photos of Jung you found in your search. Crop the photos as needed, add special effects (for example, you might want to use the Drop Shadow or Sharpen filters). Optimize the images so they download quickly and display the highest quality possible. Save the photos and exit Fireworks. (Be sure that you don't use any copyrighted material.)

Launch Flash. Add the Jung photos you optimized to the Library. (You can use the Jung photos in the Lesson 7 Data folder if you were unable to find photos to use for this exercise.) Create a new symbol and name it something like **photobook**. Create a picture frame and, using the Timeline, keyframes, and the Swap button in the Properties inspector, create a photo album that displays the different photos of Jung on a rotating basis. Save the movie clip, test it, and publish it as a Flash movie.

Return to your Jung page in Dreamweaver and insert the movie clip as a media object. Experiment with different placements on the page until you find the right spot for it. Preview the effect in your Web browser. Save and close the file.

Illustration A

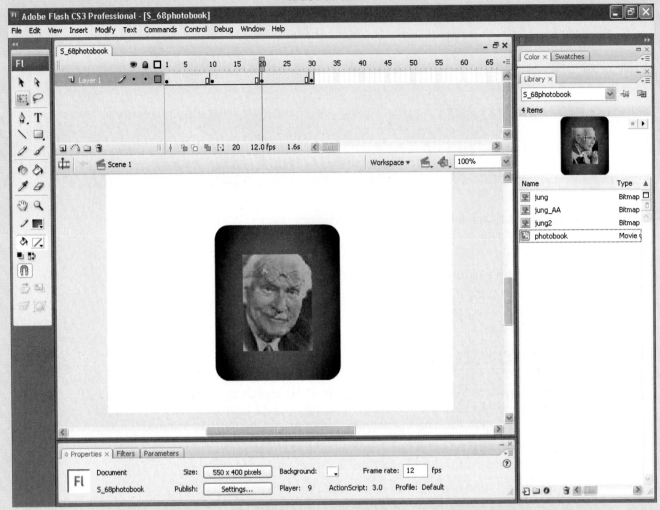

Exercise | 70

Critical Thinking

Application Skills In this exercise, you create and animate a logo for the nonprofit Web site you created.

DIRECTIONS

- Open your nonprofit Web site. Identify a space on the home page where you'd like to add a logo.

- In Fireworks, design a logo that uses the colors you've selected throughout your site.

- Optimize the image so that it downloads quickly and still gives you the quality you want.

- Open Flash and create a new movie clip symbol.

- Import the logo you created in Fireworks and animate it in any way you choose.

- Test the movie and make changes as needed.

- Publish the movie and exit Flash.

- Return to your Dreamweaver page and add the media object to the page. Save the object to the site root and add an object tag. Resize it as needed.

- Preview the page with the animated logo.

- Save all open pages and exit Dreamweaver.

Lesson | 8

Manage and Publish a Web Site

Skills Covered

- **Use Browser Compatibility Check**
- **Check and Modify Links**

Software Skills After creating your Web site, you can use Dreamweaver tools and features to manage the site and publish it to a server. Dreamweaver allows you to check pages for compatibility in a number of browsers and check and modify links to prevent broken links or unlinked pages.

Design Skills You're almost done! The last step in designing a Web site is ensuring that the site appears the way you want it to in multiple browsers, checking the links, and publishing the site.

Application Skills In this exercise, you do some final cleanup on the GardenScape site. You will check links throughout the site and check pages in the site against your specified target browser and make some corrections required by the browser.

TERMS

No new terms in this exercise.

NOTES

Use Browser Compatibility Check

- As you create your Web sites in Dreamweaver, you have some options for tailoring content to specific browsers. The Behaviors panel, for example, allows you to select behaviors that will perform correctly in a target browser version.

- A feature new in Dreamweaver CS3, the Browser Compatibility Check, allows you to check a page to find potential CSS problems that might affect how a page displays across a variety of browsers. Checking compatibility both during and at the end of the site-creation process prevents you from designing pages that cannot be viewed correctly in browsers you wish to support.

- Launch this feature using the File>Check Page>Browser Compatibility command, or click the `Check Page` Check Page button and then click Check Browser Compatibility.

- You can also access the Check Browser Compatibility command by clicking the ▶ Check Browser Compatibility button in the Browser Compatibility Check panel of the Results panel group.

- The Browser Compatibility Check feature automatically checks for compatibility with Internet Explorer 6.0 and 7.0 for Windows and 5.2 for Macintosh, Firefox 1.5, Netscape Navigator 8.0, Opera 8.0 and 9.0, and Safari 2.0.

- You can select which browsers to check by clicking Settings on the Check Page menu. In the Target Browsers dialog box, shown in the illustration on the next page, you can select browsers to check your pages against. For browsers that have a number of versions, such as Internet Explorer and Netscape Navigator, click the version number to see a drop-down menu on which you can select a specific browser version.

  ✔ *Many dynamic features such as behaviors and movies require the most recent browser versions. Keep this in mind when designing pages.*

Choose target browsers to check

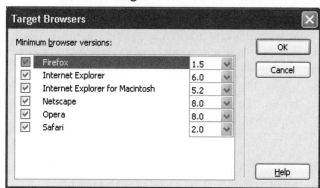

- If Dreamweaver finds errors or problems during a browser compatibility check, the Browser Compatibility Check panel of the Results panel group opens (see the illustration below) with an explanation of the issue.

- The left pane in the Browser Compatibility Check panel lists the line of code of the reported issue and the name of the issue. The circle to the left of the line number indicates visually how likely the problem is to occur: The more filled the circle is, the more likely the problem.

- The issue is described in the right pane, along with a listing of what browser is affected and likelihood. A link at the bottom of the pane takes you to the Adobe CSS Advisor, where you can read more about the problem and how to solve it.

- The Browser Compatibility Check feature can report three levels of issues:
  - Errors that might cause serious visible problems in a browser.

- Warnings about code that isn't supported in one of the target browsers but will cause no serious visible problem.
  - Messages about code that isn't supported but will have no visible effect.

- To select the object affected by a reported issue, double-click the issue in the left pane. You can then determine how the problem might affect that element and make adjustments if necessary.

- If you know the error is related to a specific browser that you don't need to support, you can right-click the issue and select Ignore Issue.

- After you make suggested changes, you can check the page or pages again to make sure the browser errors have disappeared.

- The Browser Compatibility Check feature does not offer a sitewide check. Open each page you want to check and run the check.

- The Browser Compatibility Check panel has a toolbar with buttons that help you manage your results report.
  - In some cases, you may need to stop the browser check before it is completed. To do this, click the ⊗ Stop Report button.
  - Click the ⓘ More Info button to go to the Adobe CSS Advisor for more information on the issue.
  - Because the report you see in the Browser Compatibility Check panel is a temporary file, you may want to save it for you or others to reference in the future. Click the 🖫 Save Report button to save an XML text file of the report in your Web site folder.

Results of browser check

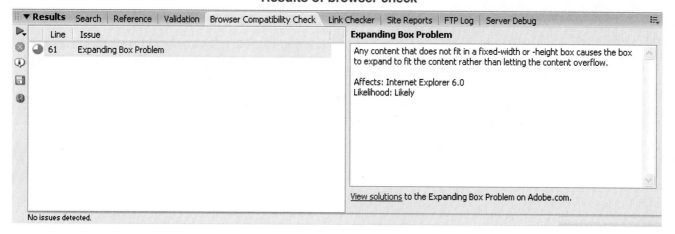

- An HTML document of the report can be created by clicking the ● Browse Report button. The report opens in your Web browser (see the illustration below) and it provides the same information the Results panel shows in an easy-to-read format that you can also print.
- To clear the report in the Browser Compatibility Check panel, right-click anywhere in its report pane and select Clear Results.

Check and Modify Links

- As pages are added to and removed from Web sites, it is all too easy to forget to update or remove links. Maintaining and fine-tuning your Web site's navigation structure are important parts of Web site upkeep.
- Clicking each link on a number of pages to check its source can take a considerable amount of time. Instead, use Dreamweaver commands to speed the process.

Check Links

- Dreamweaver gives you a great deal of flexibility when checking links in a Web site. You can check links from either the Document window or the Files panel—either in its collapsed or expanded form.
- To check links in the current document only, use the File>Check Page>Links command in the Document window. In the collapsed or expanded Files panel, right-click the site name or any file and select Check Links, and then choose Selected Files or Entire Local Site. In the expanded Files panel, use the File>Check Links command.
- To check links throughout the site, you can also use the Site>Check Links Sitewide command in Design view or in the expanded Files panel.
- When you issue a command to check links, Dreamweaver examines the current open document or Web site and lists any link problems in the Link Checker panel of the Results panel group (see the illustration at the top of the next page).

Browser Compatibility Check results report in Web browser document

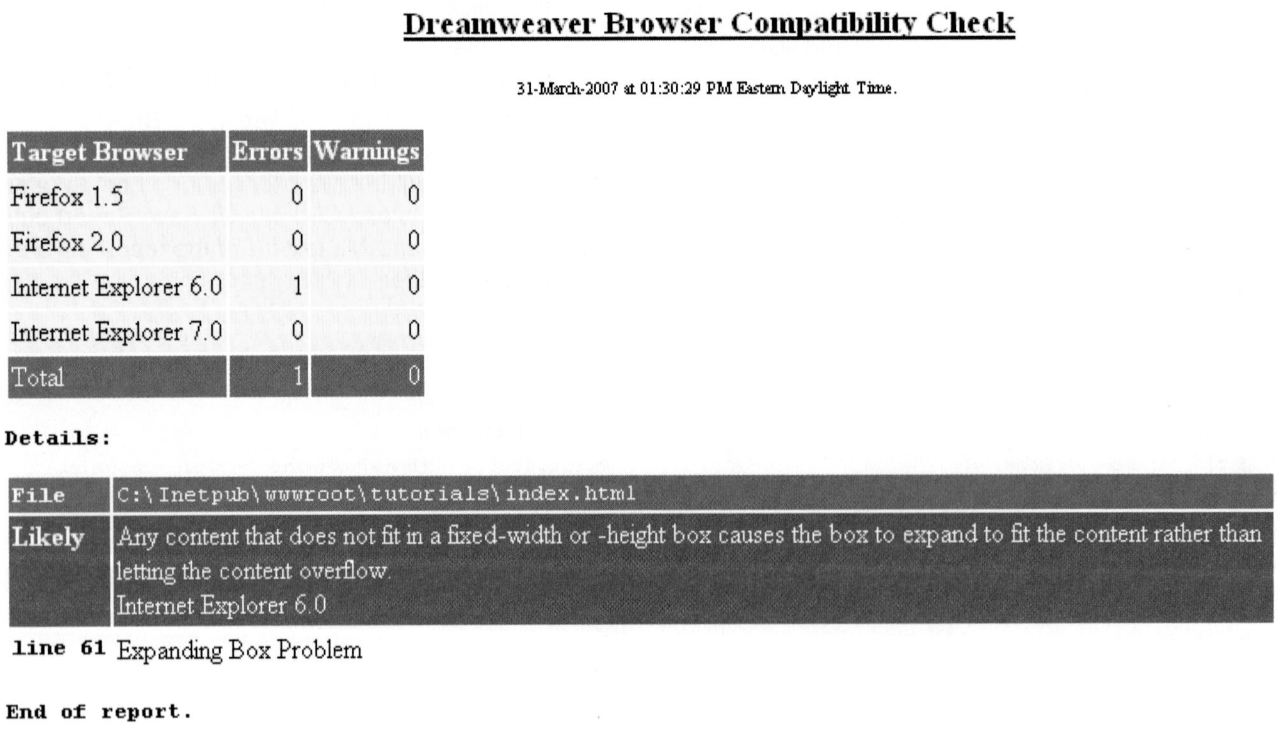

Dreamweaver Browser Compatibility Check

31-March-2007 at 01:30:29 PM Eastern Daylight Time.

Target Browser	Errors	Warnings
Firefox 1.5	0	0
Firefox 2.0	0	0
Internet Explorer 6.0	1	0
Internet Explorer 7.0	0	0
Total	1	0

Details:

File	C:\Inetpub\wwwroot\tutorials\index.html
Likely	Any content that does not fit in a fixed-width or -height box causes the box to expand to fit the content rather than letting the content overflow. Internet Explorer 6.0

line 61 Expanding Box Problem

End of report.

Link Checker panel displays link problems

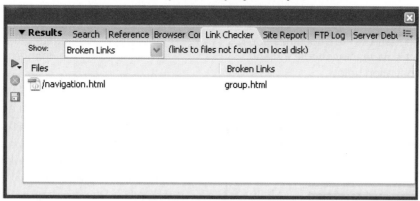

- Dreamweaver displays broken links by default in the Link Checker panel, but you can click the Show list arrow to see lists of external links (links outside the site that Dreamweaver cannot check) and orphaned files (files that are not linked to other files).

  ✔ *Don't be alarmed if the Link Checker shows orphaned files. Files such as style sheets are included in this list.*

- The Link Checker panel features a toolbar from which you can click the ▶ Check Links button and from the drop-down menu select Check Links in Current Document, Check Links for Entire Current Local Site, or Check Links for Selected Files in Site.

- In some cases, you may need to stop the Link Checker before it is completed. To do this, click the ⊘ Stop Report button.

- Because the report you see in the Link Checker panel is a temporary file, you may want to save it for you or others to reference. Click the ⊟ Save Report button to save a .TXT text file of the report in your Web site folder.

Repair Links

- Identifying link problems is just the first step to maintaining links. After you have identified problems, you have a number of options for fixing links.

- To repair a link identified as a problem in the Link Checker panel, click the file name to select it and then click on the link in the Broken Links column to select it. Dreamweaver highlights the link and also displays a 🗀 browse folder icon (see the illustration below).

- You can either type the correct file name for the link or click the folder and navigate to the correct file in the Select File dialog box. When you click OK, you will be prompted to fix any other instances of the same broken link, which Dreamweaver does automatically.

- If your site contains a number of links to a specific file that you want to change to another file, you can use the Change Link Sitewide command to substitute one link for another throughout the site.

Repair a link identified as a problem

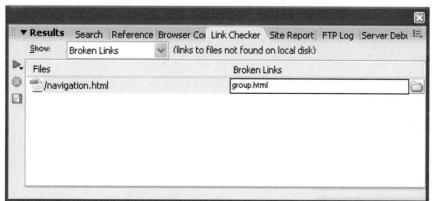

- Issue the Site>Change Link Sitewide command in the Document window or expanded Files window. Dreamweaver displays the Change Link Sitewide dialog box. Type the name of the page links currently point to and the page they should instead point to (see the illustration below).

Change a link sitewide

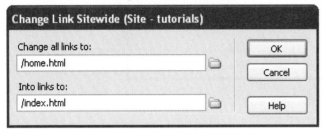

Modify Links in Site Map Pane

- The Site Map in the expanded Files panel window gives you a number of other ways to view and modify links. You can select a page in the Site Map and modify its links using commands on the Files panel menu (or right-click the page and select commands from the shortcut menu).

  - Link to New File lets you insert a link to a new Web document. This allows you to create the document and the link to it at the same time. You supply a file name and page title along with the text of the link.

  - Link to Existing File launches the Select Internet File dialog box in which an existing file can be linked to the selected Web document.

- Change Link launches the Select HTML File dialog box in which a new file can be selected to replace a link. When you change a link, you may be prompted to update other links in the site that are affected by the change.

- Remove Link removes a link and also launches a dialog box that gives you the option of updating links throughout the site that might be affected by the modification.

- Open to Source of Link opens the source file of the link in the Document window with the link text selected for editing.

- Two additional commands help you control the display of linked pages in the Site Map:

  - Use View>Site Map Options>Show/Hide Link to view a portion of the Site Map. You can, for example, hide e-mail links or dependent files by choosing this command to hide them. To display a hidden file again, use the View>Show Map Options>Show Files Marked as Hidden command.

    ✔ *The file name of a hidden file is italicized. Unmark a hidden file by right-clicking it and selecting Show/Hide Link again.*

  - Use View>Site Map Options>View as Root to place a subordinate—or child—Web document at the top of the site map, rather than the designated home page. This allows you to concentrate on links to and from a specific page.

    ✔ *The Site Navigation field above the site map displays the original path from the home page to the page chosen to view as the root. Click once on the home page in the Site Navigation field to return the site map to the original layout.*

PROCEDURES

Select Browsers to Check for Compatibility

1. Click the **Check Page** button 🔲 Check Page in the Document toolbar to display the drop-down list.
2. Click **Settings**.
3. Click in checkbox for desired browser(s).
4. Click version number to display the drop-down list and select the version number, if desired.
5. Click ⬚ OK ⬚.

Run Browser Compatibility Check

1. Open a page to check.
2. Click **File**..................... Alt + F
3. Point to C**h**eck Page .... H
4. Click **Browser Compatibility**..................... B

   OR

1. Click **Check Page** button 🔲 Check Page on Document toolbar.
2. Click **Check Browser Compatibility**.

   OR

In the Results panel group:

1. Click the Browser Compatibility Check tab.
2. Click the **Check Browser Compatibility** button ▶.
3. Click **Check Browser Compatibility**.

In the Browser Compatibility Check panel of Results panel group:

- View report of errors and warnings and read information about making necessary corrections:
  - Click ⊗ to stop the report.
  - Double-click a problem in the report pane to select the problem element.

- Select a problem in the report pane and click ⓘ to read the expanded description.
- Click 🔲 to save the report.
- Click 🌐 to view or print the report in the Web browser.

Check Links (Shift + F8, Ctrl + F8)

To check links on the current page:

1. With desired Web page open, click **File** .... Alt + F
2. Point to C**h**eck Page .... H
3. Click **L**inks L

   OR

1. Right-click page in **Files** list.
2. Point to **Check Links**.
3. Click **Selected Files**.

In Link Checker panel of Results panel group:

- View report in the Link Checker panel:
  - Click ⊗ to stop Link Checker.
  - Click 🔲 to save the report.
  - Repair link if desired.

To check links throughout the site:

1. Click **Site** .... Alt + S
2. Click **Check Links Site**w**ide** .... W

   OR

1. Right-click page in **Files** list.
2. Point to **Check Links**.
3. Click **Entire Local Site**.

   OR

1. Click **Window** .... Alt + W
2. Click **Results**...................... R
3. Click the **Link Checker** panel.
4. Click ▶ in the Link Checker panel and select from the menu:

- **Check Links in Current Document**
- **Check Links For Entire Current Local Site**
- **Check Links For Selected Files in Site**

In Link Checker panel of Results panel group:

- View report in the Link Checker panel:
  - Click ⊗ to stop Link Checker.
  - Click 🔲 to save the report.
  - Repair link(s) if desired.

Repair Links

In the Link Checker panel:

1. Select **Broken Links** from the **Show** drop-down list, if necessary.
2. Click file name to select it.
3. Click link in **Broken Links** column to select it.
4. Type correct link.

   OR

- Click 📁 and select correct file in the Select File dialog box.

Change Links Sitewide

1. Click **Site** .... Alt + S
2. Click **Change Link Sitewide**..................... K
3. In Change all links to box, type / and then type file name of existing link.
4. In Into links to box, type / and then type file name of new link target.
5. Click ⬚ OK ⬚.

Modify Links in Site Panel Map Pane

With the site map displayed in the expanded or collapsed Files panel:

1. Right-click on a page in the site map that displays links.

2. Click one of the options below:
   - Click **Link to New File** to create new document and link at the same time.
   - Click **Link to Existing File** to choose file to link to.
   - Click **Change Link** to replace link with link to another page.

   - Click **Remove Link** to remove link from page (or remove page from site map).
   - Click **Open to Source of Link** to open a page with the link itself highlighted.

EXERCISE DIRECTIONS

1. Start Dreamweaver and open the gardenscape site.

2. Check links throughout the site. If any links appear as broken links, make the necessary corrections and close the Results panel.

3. Change the target browser settings to check only Internet Explorer 6.0 and Firefox 1.5. Run the Browser Compatibility Check to check for any compatibility problems.

4. Save and close all pages and exit Dreamweaver.

ON YOUR OWN

1. Start Dreamweaver and open the gardenprojects site.

2. Check links throughout the site. If you find any broken links, repair them.

3. Specify the Internet Explorer 6.0 browser and another browser such as Mozilla or Firefox.

4. Save and close all pages and exit Dreamweaver.

Skills Covered

■ **Run Dreamweaver Reports** ■ **Validating Web Pages**

Software Skills View reports to help you identify problems in a site and check accessibility for all types of site visitors. Validate your code to help you locate errors in syntax for a number of languages, including HTML and XHTML.

Design Skills Use Dreamweaver reports to ensure that your site is as accurate and accessible as possible. If you are creating the site for a client, printing reports after you finish a site lets your client know the types of errors and accessibility issues you checked for.

Application Skills In this exercise, you continue fine-tuning the GardenScape site in preparation for publishing it. You will view several reports on the site and run the Validator to see whether you have any critical errors in coding on the site pages.

TERMS

No new terms in this exercise.

NOTES

Run Dreamweaver Reports

■ Dreamweaver's Site>Reports command in either the Document window or the expanded Files panel menu bar displays the Reports dialog box (see the illustration at right). From this dialog box, you can run a number of workflow and HTML reports to check your site before publishing it.

■ To run a report, first choose what you want to report on by clicking the Report on list arrow. You can run a report on the current document, the entire current site, selected files, or a folder. Then select the checkbox of the report you want to run and click the Run button.

> ✔ Click the ▶ Reports button in the Site Reports panel in the Results panel group to open the Reports dialog box. You can then select other reports to run.

■ Use the Workflow reports to show what pages a team member has checked out and to find information stored in Design Notes. Selecting one of these reports displays the [Report Settings...] button that allows you to specify further settings.

Reports dialog box

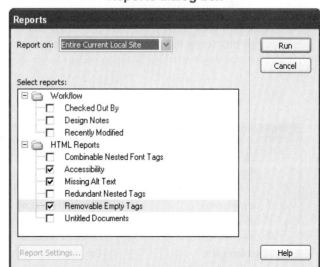

- For example, to find out what files a team member has checked out, click the Report Settings button and type the team member's name in the Checked Out By dialog box. When you run the report, Dreamweaver displays a list of all files checked out by the team member you specified.

  ✔ *You will learn more about checking files in and out in the next exercise.*

- The HTML reports help you locate HTML code problems and oversights such as pages that have no page titles. These reports can help you to locate errors in code you import from other sources.

  ✔ *Several of the HTML reports search for the same kinds of code problems identified in the Clean Up XHTML dialog box.*

- The Accessibility report locates problems that might affect your Web pages when people access them using text-only browsers and browsers designed for the hearing or visually challenged.

  ✔ *You can also check accessibility using the File>Check Page>Accessibility command.*

- One of the primary issues it will alert you to is how images, colors, and sounds and other multimedia files will be interpreted by text-only browsers—including the browsers used in cell phones and PDAs—or browsers that actually "read" the content text to a visually challenged person. The report will tell you, for example, that colors you have applied to text are not essential in a site designed to be read.

- If you supply alternate text for images and accessibility tags for forms, frames, and media objects while creating your pages, you can minimize the number of problems flagged in the Accessibility report.

- The Accessibility report will also analyze your text and warn you if sentences are not in natural English or have other issues that might be a disservice to the physically—and cognitively—challenged.

- You can run reports one at a time to isolate results, or you can select all reports and click Run to check all categories. Dreamweaver displays the report results in the Site Reports panel in the Results panel group (see the illustration below).

- Selecting a file in the report pane and clicking the ⓘ More Info button opens the Reference panel with a discussion of the issues that might occur and suggested ways to fix it. For example, if the information you convey depends on an image file, you will want to add a text description in the Alt text box of the Properties panel.

- To open a page identified in a report, right-click its file name in the File column and then click Open File.

- As in other Results group panels, you can stop running a report by clicking the ⊗ Stop Report button. Click the 🖫 Save Report button to save an XML text file of the report in your Web site folder.

Validating Web Pages

- Use Dreamweaver's Validator feature to locate tag and syntax errors in your code.

- Validator is used much like the other report tools in the Results panel group. You can check one Web page, selected pages or files, or an entire Web site.

- To check the page that is in the Document window, use the File>Validate>Markup command.

  ✔ *If you are validating an .XML page, you use the Validate>As XML command.*

Report results

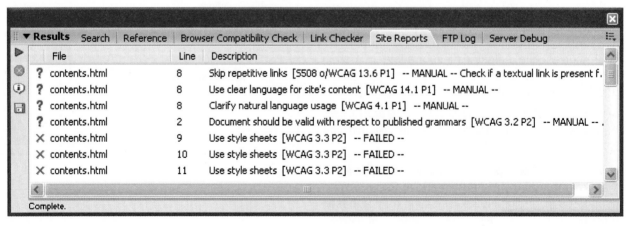

■ The report that is created appears in the Validation panel of the Results panel group, as shown in the illustration below. As with checking links and target browsers, the Validation panel has a ■▾ button on its toolbar that allows you to validate single Web pages, selected pages and folders, and the entire site.

■ There are also buttons to stop running a report, to read more information, to save the report, and to open the report in your browser.

■ Dreamweaver's Validator feature can report errors and warnings that may not require immediate editing or correction. When a problem occurs after you publish your Web site to a remote server, the Validator may provide you with the information that you, your Web server administrator, or your ISP may need to use to repair your Web site so that it looks and functions as expected.

■ Before you use the Validator, you must use the Edit>Preferences command and click the Validator category in the Preferences dialog box. The default setting for Dreamweaver is to validate against HTML version 4.0. You can select and deselect other codes and browsers to validate against.

■ The Options button in the Preferences dialog box opens the Validator Options dialog box, in which the different levels of warnings and error messages can be selected or deselected.

■ It is beyond the scope of this book to cover this advanced trouble-shooting feature at length. In many instances, the reports that the Validator creates will alert you more often to possible or potential problems rather than to anything that you will notice in your site whether locally or published on a remote Web server and accessed by most version 4 or later browsers.

Validation issues to check and correct for an entire site

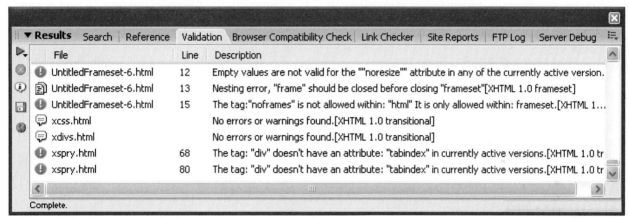

PROCEDURES

Run Dreamweaver Reports

In the Document window or Site panel menu:

1. Click **Site** .... Alt + S
2. Click **Reports** .... T
3. Click the **Report on** list arrow and select subject for the report.
4. Select checkbox for desired report.
5. Click Report Settings... if necessary (for Workflow reports) and supply additional settings for report.
6. Click Run .

7. View report in the Site Reports panel:
   ■ Click ⊗ to stop the site report.
   ■ Select a problem in the report pane and click ⓘ to read the expanded description.
   ■ Double-click a problem in the report pane to open the page in Code and Design views.
   ■ Click 🖫 to save the report.

Validate a Web Page (Shift + F6)

To validate the current page:

1. Click **Edit** .... Alt + E
2. Click **Preferences** .... P
3. Click **Validator** in the Category list.
4. Choose Validator options and click OK .
5. With desired Web page open, click **File** .... Alt + F
6. Point to **Validate**.
7. Click **Markup** .... M

8. View report in the Validation panel:
   - Click ⊗ to stop the Validator.
   - Click 🖫 to save the report.
   - Click 🌐 to view or print the report in the Web browser.

To validate the entire site:
1. Click **<u>Window</u>** .... Alt + W
2. Click **<u>Results</u>** .... R
3. Click the **Validation** tab.
4. Click ▶ in the Validation panel.
5. Choose **Settings**.

6. Choose Validator options and click [OK].
7. Click ▶ in the Validation panel and select from the menu:
   - Validate Current Document
   - Validate Current Document as XML
   - Validate Entire Current Local Site
   - Validate Selected Files in Site

8. View report in the Validation panel:
   - Click ⊗ to stop the Validator.
   - Click 🖫 to save the report.
   - Click 🌐 to view or print the report in the Web browser.

EXERCISE DIRECTIONS

1. Start Dreamweaver and open the gardenscape site.

2. Run a report on accessibility for the entire site.

3. In the report pane of the Site Reports panel, select the first problem shown with a red X and read more information on the problem. You will find that the Accessibility report prefers using relative units in the CSS style sheet; this is flagged for every page of the site that is linked to the style sheet. Double-click the first error showing an X. You'll see that the links in the contents.html that appear in the left navigation panel use deprecated HTML tags instead of CSS styles. To fix the problem:
   - Create a new style named something like .pagelink to format the links in contents.html.
   - Apply the style to the links in the frame.

4. Save changes to the page and run the Accessibility report again. You should not see any problems with CSS styles.

5. There are other accessibility issues you may be able to fix with some study of accessibility guidelines. For now, save the report in your site so you can refer to it later with the name AccessibilityResultsReport.xml.

6. Run the Missing Alt Text report as well. There should be no results that show missing alt tags.

7. Save and close the pages and exit Dreamweaver.

ON YOUR OWN

1. Start Dreamweaver and open the gardenprojects site.

2. Run an accessibility report for the entire local site.

3. Correct as many of the red X problems as you feel comfortable modifying. For example, you may want to:

   ■ Provide metadata for pages that do not have it.

   ■ Adjust style sheet font sizes using relative measurements such as small, medium, and large. Check any pages that show deprecated elements and update the items using style sheets.

   ✔ *Read the information for each problem even if you decide not to fix it.*

4. Run some of the other Dreamweaver reports, such as Untitled Documents and Removable Empty Tags, and fix any problems you find.

5. Run the Validator for the entire current local site, validating against HTML 4.0 and Internet Explorer 4.0 extensions. Read information on some of the tag cautions and warnings.

6. Save all pages and close Dreamweaver.

Exercise | 73

Skills Covered

- **Publish a Web Site on a Server**
- **Copy Files from a Remote Server**
- **Check Files In and Out**

Software Skills You can put files on an FTP, WebDAV, or local server to make them available to visitors. When you configure the site for remote access, you can also enable check out/in to prevent more than one team member at a time from working on a site file. If you need to work on a published file, you can copy it from the remote server to your local server.

Design Skills Knowing a variety of methods for posting and working with Web pages and sites enables you to be flexible enough to provide what your clients need.

Application Skills In this exercise, you will complete your work on the GardenScape site by publishing it to a server. When you set up the remote access for the site, you will enable file check out/in and check out one of the site files.

TERMS

Publishing Copying Web site files from a local computer to a server.

FTP (File Transfer Protocol) A method for copying files to and from servers on a network.

HTTP (Hypertext Transfer Protocol) Fixed set of messages and replies between a browser and server on the Web.

NOTES

Publish a Web Site on a Server

- **Publishing** is the process of copying Web site files from a local computer to the server that *hosts* the site and where visitors can access it. The server to which you copy, publish, or "put" files can be an **FTP** (file transfer protocol) server; a local/network server that can be on your computer or on your network; or a WebDAV **HTTP** (hypertext transfer protocol) server on the Internet.

- Dreamweaver also makes it easy for you to publish your Web site on remote RDS (Remote Development Services) and Microsoft Visual SourceSafe servers. It is beyond the scope of this book to discuss how to configure a connection to these specialized servers. Consult Dreamweaver Help and your Web server administrator or ISP for more information.

- When you created your site as described in Exercise 2, you had the option of selecting and configuring your remote server using the Site Definition wizard. In the following section, you will learn how to use settings in the site Definition dialog box to set up an FTP, WebDav, or local/network server—three of the most common ways to publish a Web site so that it can be accessed on the Internet or on an intranet.

Associating an FTP Server with a Web Site

- Use the Remote Info category on the Advanced tab of the Site Definition dialog box to enter the appropriate settings to publish on an FTP server. You specify the same settings whether you create a site using the Site Definition wizard or create the site using the Site Definition dialog box's Advanced tab, so the procedure discussed here can be used when you first set up your site—or if you need to edit an existing site to specify settings.

■ Use the Site>Manage Sites command to open the Manage Sites dialog box and select the desired Web site. Then click the [Edit...] button.

■ Select the Advanced tab's Remote Info category in the Site Definition dialog box and choose FTP on the Access list. You must then supply the following information:

● Enter the FTP server's address in the FTP host text box. The following illustration shows the proper syntax. You do not need to enter "ftp://" before the address because it is already incorporated.

● In the Host directory text box, enter the name of the folder on the server that contains the site files.

● Most servers require a login name to connect to the server. Enter that name in the Login text box. If you do not enter a login name, a dialog box will request it—and the password—when you attempt to connect to the FTP server.

● Most servers, for security reasons and to prevent hackers from tampering with the Web site, also require a password. If you do not supply a password and click the Save option, a dialog box will request it when you attempt to connect to the server.

■ The options for Use passive FTP, Use IPv6 transfer mode, Use firewall, and Use Secure FTP (SFTP) may need to be selected. Consult with the Web administrator of the FTP server to find out if you need to select these settings.

■ To make sure that your FTP settings work, use the [Test] button to test them. Dreamweaver will then attempt to connect to the FTP server and tell you if the test is successful—or unsuccessful (see the illustrations at the top of the next page).

■ The Remote Info category also allows you to enable file check out/in. File check out/in is discussed in a later section of this exercise.

Set up FTP connection in Dreamweaver

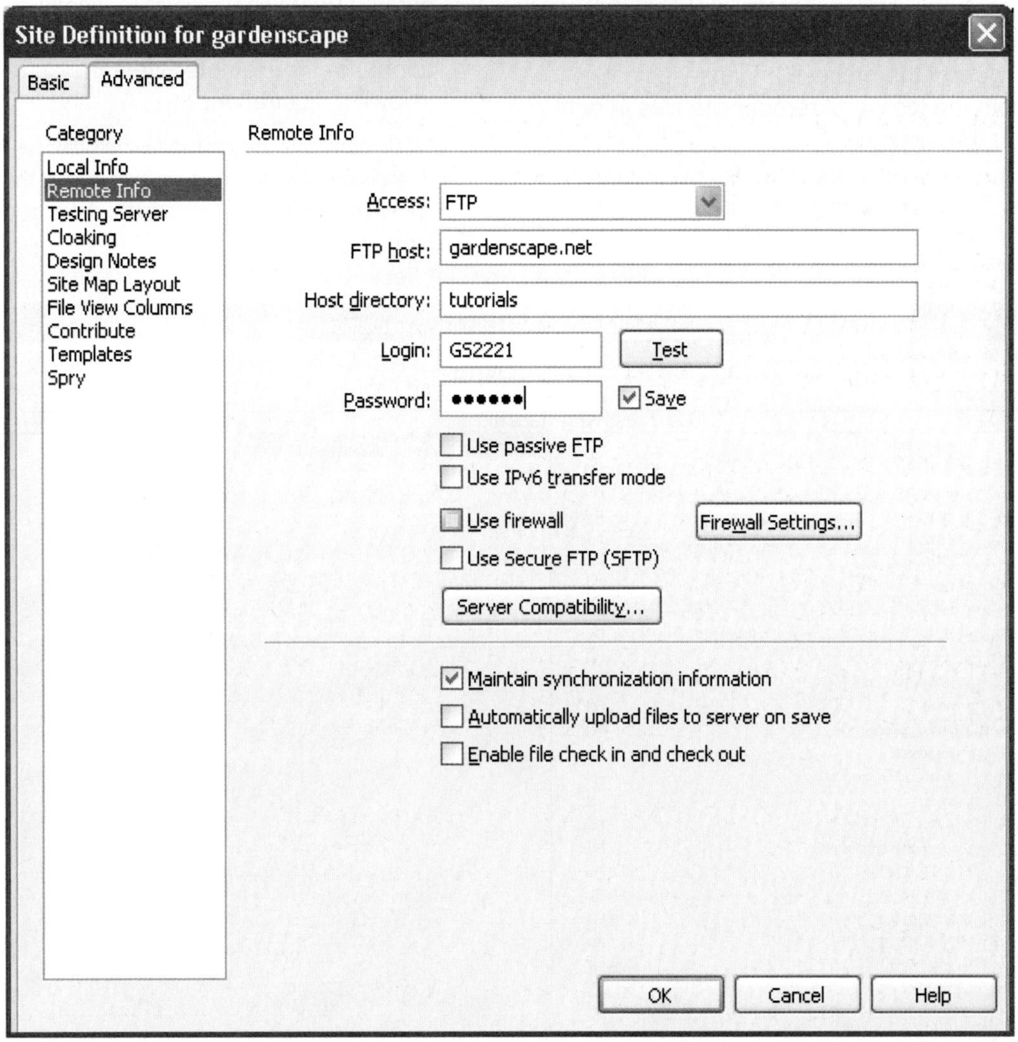

Site Definition for gardenscape	⊠

Basic Advanced

Category
- Local Info
- **Remote Info**
- Testing Server
- Cloaking
- Design Notes
- Site Map Layout
- File View Columns
- Contribute
- Templates
- Spry

Remote Info

Access: FTP

FTP host: gardenscape.net

Host directory: tutorials

Login: GS2221   [Test]

Password: ●●●●●●   ☑ Save

☐ Use passive FTP
☐ Use IPv6 transfer mode
☐ Use firewall   [Firewall Settings...]
☐ Use Secure FTP (SFTP)

[Server Compatibility...]

☑ Maintain synchronization information
☐ Automatically upload files to server on save
☐ Enable file check in and check out

[OK] [Cancel] [Help]

FTP test messages

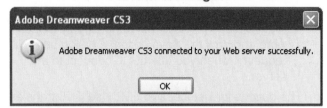

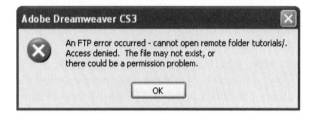

Putting the Web Site on the FTP Server

- Once the FTP settings—or the settings for other kinds of server connections discussed in this exercise—have been specified, the Web site is ready to be copied to the server.

- You can publish your site—or *put* the files on the server, to use Dreamweaver's term—using the Files panel in either its collapsed or expanded form. Using the expanded form, however, gives you the best view of the process because it clearly shows both the local and remote site files in one window at the same time.

- In the expanded Files panel window toolbar, click the ⊟ Site Files button to display the Remote Site pane and then click the 🖧 Connects to remote host button to establish the connection to the FTP server.

- A message box informs you when you have made a connection with a server. If you cannot connect, you will receive messages explaining why. A live connection will be indicated by the 🖧 button.

- In the Local Files pane, select the desired files to be published on the FTP server and drag them onto the host directory folder in the Remote Site pane. Or, you can select the desired files in the Local Files pane and click the ⬆ Put File(s) button in the Files panel toolbar.

  ✔ Typically, you will want to publish all of the contents of the local folder. You can simply select the local Web site's folder at the top of the file tree rather than select files individually. You may need to click Yes to put all of the files.

- The Background File Activity dialog box records the progress of the files that upload from your local server to the FTP server. If you have enabled check out/in, Dreamweaver automatically checks out the files. The process is completed when the files appear in the Remote Site pane as shown in the following illustration.

  ✔ Dreamweaver may ask during this process if you want to include dependent files. Be sure to click Yes, or files such as images will not be transferred to the server.

Files "put" on FTP server

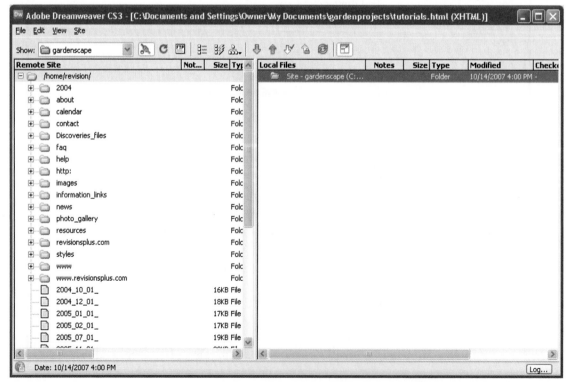

- You can put an open document on the server from the Document window. Click the ⇅ File Management button on the Document toolbar and select Put from the menu. You can also use the Site>Put command.

- Click the ↻ Refresh button if necessary to arrange the folders and files in the Remote Site pane in the same order as the Local Files pane. When you have finished the process of copying files, click ⚲ to disconnect from the server.

- The [FTP] View Site FTP Log button in the expanded Files panel window opens the FTP Log panel in the Results panel group, which displays a log report of all the activity experienced by the FTP server. It can be used for a number of administrative purposes, including security.

- The FTP server administrator or your instructor can supply you with the URL for the Web so that you can see the published Web in a browser.

- You will need to enter the URL in the HTTP address box in the Site Definition dialog box's Local Info pane (see the following illustration).

Associating a WebDAV Connection (HTTP Server) with a Web Site

- If you are going to publish directly to an HTTP site, you can use the WebDAV standard. WebDAV, or Web-based Distributed Authoring and Versioning, uses the Microsoft Internet Information Server (IIS) 5.0 that comes with Windows 2000, Windows 2000 Server, Windows XP Professional, and the like.

- To configure a WebDAV site, you must have its URL and any login and password information that you will need.

- As with configuring an FTP site, you must set up a remote HTTP server by selecting the Remote Info category in the Site Definition dialog box and choosing WebDAV on the Access list. You must then supply the following information in the appropriate text box: the site URL, Login, and Password. (See the illustration at the top of the next page.)

- If you want Dreamweaver to remember your password, select the Save checkbox.

- To publish to a WebDAV server connection, use the same procedures for putting files on an FTP site in the Files panel window. (You may encounter different message boxes.)

Specify URL for published Web site

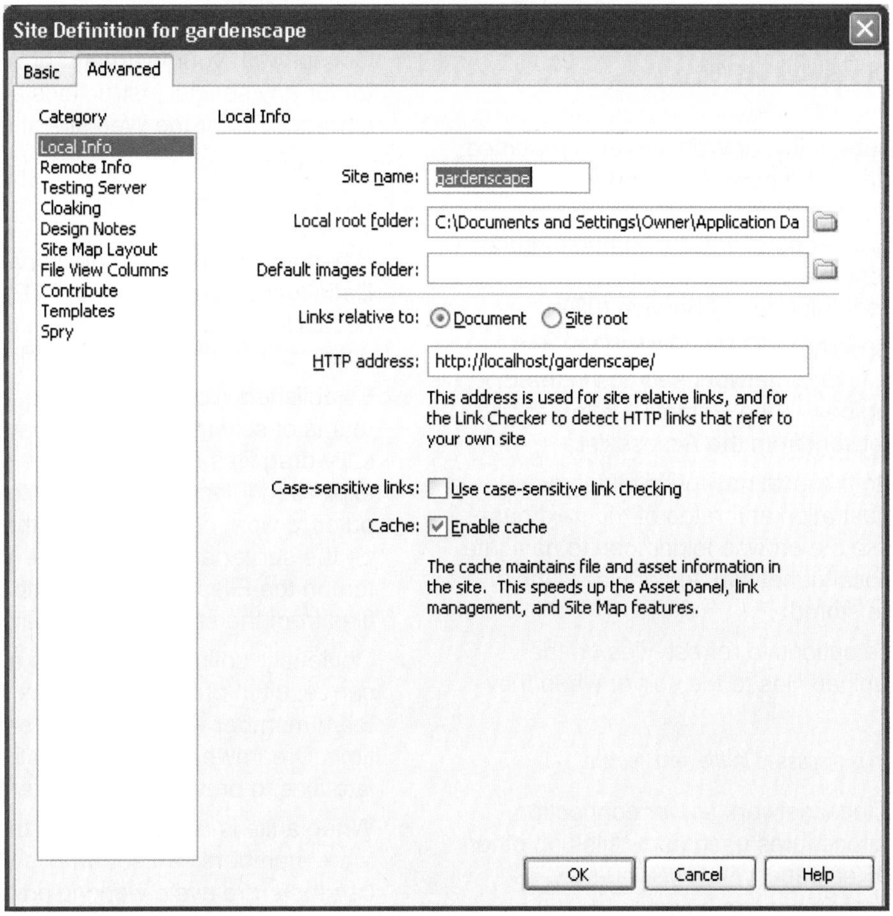

Site Definition for gardenscape

Basic | Advanced

Category — Local Info

- Local Info
- Remote Info
- Testing Server
- Cloaking
- Design Notes
- Site Map Layout
- File View Columns
- Contribute
- Templates
- Spry

Site name: gardenscape

Local root folder: C:\Documents and Settings\Owner\Application Da

Default images folder:

Links relative to: ⦿ Document ◯ Site root

HTTP address: http://localhost/gardenscape/

This address is used for site relative links, and for the Link Checker to detect HTTP links that refer to your own site

Case-sensitive links: ☐ Use case-sensitive link checking

Cache: ☑ Enable cache

The cache maintains file and asset information in the site. This speeds up the Asset panel, link management, and Site Map features.

OK | Cancel | Help

WebDAV Connection dialog box

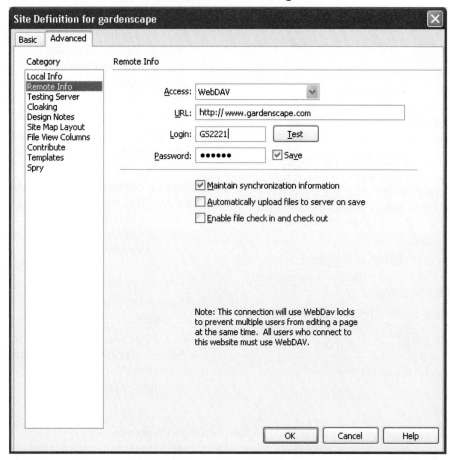

Associating a Local or Network Server with a Web Site

■ You can also publish if your Web server is mounted as a network drive (Windows) or as an AppleTalk or NFS server (Macintosh), or if you are running a personal Web server on your local computer such as Microsoft Personal Web Server (PWS) or Microsoft Internet Information Service (IIS).

■ Just as when specifying FTP and WebDAV settings, you specify local/network settings in the Site Definition dialog box. In the Remote Info category, select Local/Network from the Access list.

■ Type the path to the local network's folder, as shown in the illustration at the top of the next page. You can also use the browse folder icon to navigate directly to the local or network folder where the Web site will be stored.

■ You can choose options to refresh files on the server and to upload files to the server when they are saved.

✔ File checkout/in is discussed in the next section.

■ To publish to a local/network server connection, use the same procedures used to put files on other servers in the Files panel window. (You may encounter different message boxes.)

■ Consult with your instructor or Web site administrator for any special instructions and obtaining the correct URL for the Web site after it is published.

Check Files In and Out

■ When you define a remote server site in the Site Definition dialog box for an FTP, WebDAV, Local/Network, or RDS connection, you have the option of enabling the file check out/in feature.

■ Established Web sites are frequently managed by teams of several members. Team members typically drag files from the remote server in the expanded Files panel window to their local computer to work on the files. Or, they may select files on the server and then use the ⬇ Get File(s) button on the Files panel toolbar to copy the selected files from the server to the local computer.

■ Obviously, unlimited access to a Web site's files can result in problems, such as more than one team member working on the same file at the same time. Dreamweaver's check out/in feature can regulate files to prevent such problems.

■ When a file is checked out on the remote server, all team members can see who is working on it and can therefore avoid working on that file.

Set up local network connection

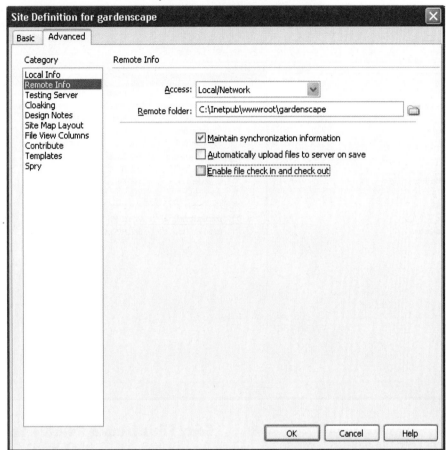

- You enable check out/in in the Remote Info category of the Site Definition dialog box for the FTP, WebDAV, Local/Network, and RDS server connections (see the following illustration). Note that this feature is not active unless a remote server location has been established for the Web site.

Enable check out/in options in Remote Info category

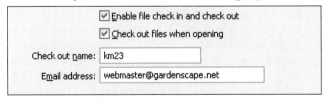

- If you have enabled check out/in, files you put on a remote server are automatically checked out to you at the time you publish them.

- Select the *Check out files when opening* option to automatically check out files when you double-click to open them from the Files panel.

- You can also supply your e-mail address so that team members can send e-mail to you while you are working on checked-out files.

- When you enable check out/in, the 📝 Check Out File(s) and 🔒 Check In buttons are activated on the Files panel's toolbar in both the collapsed and expanded form.

- To check out a file on your computer, select the file (or select more than one file) in either the Remote Site or Local Files pane and use the Site>Check Out command on the menu bar, or click the 📝 Check Out File(s) button on the Files panel toolbar.

  ✔ You can undo the check-out process using the Site>Undo Check Out command, or right-click the checked-out file and select Undo Check Out on the shortcut menu.

- Checking out a file tells others that you are working on the file now. If they open the file, it will be a read-only version.

- When a file is checked out, a check mark displays next to the file's icon in both the Remote Site and Local Files panes (see the illustration on the next page).

  ✔ If the file you check out has dependent files, you will be asked if you want to include them when checking out the file.

Files have been checked out by James Horner

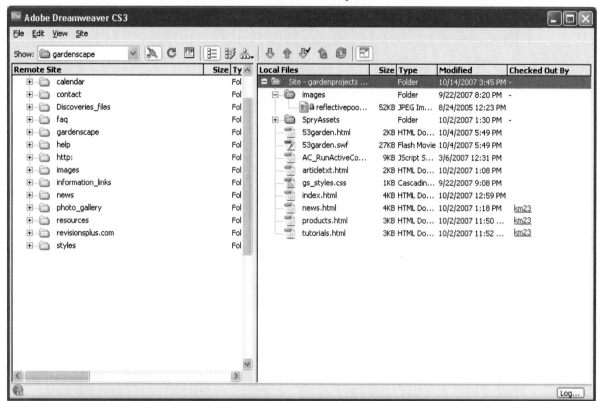

Check mark colors give you additional information about who has checked out a file. You will see a green check mark when you have checked out a file on your computer. A red check mark means the file is checked out by another person on another computer.

The name of the person who checked out the file displays in the Checked Out By column of the Files panel and also displays in the status bar of the Files window when the mouse button hovers over the file name.

When you have finished working on a file, you check it in by selecting the file in either the Local Files or Remote Site pane and using the Site>Check In command. Or, click the 🔒 Check In button in the Files panel toolbar.

Checking in a file makes the file available to other team members. The green check mark in the Remote Site pane is removed and a lock icon displays next to the checked-in file in the Local Files pane.

While the lock icon displays, other team members will see a message box informing them that the file is a read-only file that can be viewed but not changed.

To remove the lock symbol so other team members can open the file, right-click the file and select Turn off Read Only in the shortcut menu.

Copy Files from a Remote Server

You can reverse the publishing process if you need to "get" files from a remote server and copy them to your local site. Select the files you want to copy in the Remote Site pane of the expanded Files panel window and drag them into the Local Files pane. Or click the ⬇ Get File(s) button in the Files panel toolbar.

> ✔ You can get files while working in the Document window by clicking the File Management button on the Document toolbar and selecting Get from the menu.

If the Check In/Out feature is active, dragging a file or files—or using the Get File(s) button—results in a read-only local copy of the file. The file remains available on the remote site for others to check out. If the Check In/Out feature is deselected in the Site Definition dialog box, then copying/getting a file transfers a copy that has read and write privileges.

PROCEDURES

Display Site Definition Dialog Box

1. Click **Site** .... Alt +S
2. Click **Manage Sites** .... M
3. Click name of site to modify.
4. Click Edit... .
5. Click the **Advanced** tab.
6. When finished modifying the site, click Done .

Set Up FTP Connection

In the Site Definition dialog box (Advanced tab):

1. Click the **Remote Info** category.
2. Click the **Access** list arrow .... Alt +A
3. Click **FTP**.
4. Enter FTP settings:
   a. Click in **FTP host** box .... Alt +H and type FTP server address.
   b. Click in **Host directory** box .... Alt +D and type name of folder that holds files.
   c. Click in **Login** box .... Alt +L and type name or code necessary to log in to server.
   d. Click in **Password** box .... Alt +P and type password necessary to log in to server.
   e. Click Test to test the connection.
   f. Select firewall options, if desired.

   ✔ *Select the Save checkbox to avoid having to enter this information each time you log on.*

5. Click OK .

Set Up WebDAV HTTP Server

In the Site Definition dialog box (Advanced tab):

1. Click the **Remote Info** category.
2. Click the **Access** list arrow .... Alt +A
3. Click **WebDAV**.
4. Enter the following information in the proper text boxes:
   a. Click in **URL** box .... Alt +U and type URL for Web site.
   b. Click in **Login** box .... Alt +L and type name or code necessary to log in to server.
   c. Click in **Password** box .... Alt +P and type password necessary to log in to server.
   d. Click the **Save** checkbox .... Alt +V to save password if desired.
5. Test the connection if desired.
6. Click OK

Set Up Local/Network Server

In the Site Definition dialog box (Advanced tab):

1. Click the **Remote Info** category.
2. Click the **Access** list arrow .... Alt +A
3. Click **Local/Network**.
4. Click in **Remote folder** box .... Alt +R and type path to local/network folder.
   OR
   ■ Click 📁 and navigate to folder.

Enable File Check Out/In

In the Site Definition dialog box of FTP, WebDav, Local/Host, and RDS servers:

1. Click the **Remote Info** category.
2. Click the **Enable file check in and check out** checkbox .... Alt +E
3. Click **Check out files when opening** .... Alt +C if desired.
4. Click the **Check out name** box .... Alt +N and type name to be used to identify you.
5. Click the **Email address** box .... Alt +M and type e-mail address.

Put Files on Server

In the expanded Files panel window:

1. Click **Site Files** button ▤ on the Files panel window toolbar to display the Remote Site pane.
2. Click 🔗 on the Files panel window toolbar.
3. Select file, files, or entire root folder in the Local Files pane.
4. Click ⬆ on the Files panel window toolbar.
5. Click OK if necessary to include dependent files.
6. Click 🔌 to disconnect from remote server.

Check File Out
(Ctrl + Alt + Shift + D)

1. Select file in the Remote Site or Local Files pane of the Files panel (expanded or collapsed).
2. Click **Site** .... [Alt]+[S]
3. Click **Check Out** .... [C]

   OR

   Click [icon] in the Files panel toolbar.

Check File In
(Ctrl + Alt + Shift + U)

1. Select file in the Remote Site or Local Files pane of the Files panel (expanded or collapsed).
2. Click **Site** .... [Alt]+[S]
3. Click **Check In** .... [I]

   OR

   Click [icon] in the Files panel toolbar.

   ✔ *To remove the Read Only lock icon from the file, right-click the file in the Site panel and click Turn Off Read Only.*

Copy Files from Remote Server

1. Select file or files in the Remote Site or Local Files pane of the Files panel (expanded or collapsed).
2. Click [icon] in the Files panel toolbar.

EXERCISE DIRECTIONS

1. Start Dreamweaver and open the gardenscape site.
2. Publish your Web site to a server or to a local folder. Put all the files on the remote site.

   ✔ *If you have not yet selected a remote server, your instructor will supply information for putting your Web site files on an FTP, WebDAV HTTP server, or a local network server. If no server is available, create a folder on your hard drive. In the Site Definition dialog box, use the Local/Network server access option and make sure the path to the folder you created appears in the Remote Folder box on the Web Server Info or Remote Info category. Then publish your Web site files to this folder.*

3. Use the Site Definition dialog box to make sure the check out/in feature is enabled for the current site. (Be sure to insert your name where indicated so it will display when you check files out.)

4. Check out the index.html file, if necessary, and rest the mouse pointer on the file name to see your name in the Files window's status bar. Make sure index.html is set as the home page for the site.
5. Run the Checked Out By report to see what files you have checked out.
6. Check in the index.html file. Click in the file and then remove the lock symbol from the local version of the file and any dependent files.
7. Disconnect from the server, if necessary.
8. Close any open pages and exit Dreamweaver.

ON YOUR OWN

1. Start Dreamweaver and open the yardart site.
2. Publish the Web site to a server or local folder, as indicated by your instructor. When you set up remote access, enable the check out/in feature.
3. If possible, ask a classmate to access the site and check out a page so you can see how the site files look when someone other than you has checked out a file.

4. Make a change to at least one file that you have checked out and put it again on the server to update your site.
5. Disconnect from the server, if necessary.
6. Close any open pages and exit Dreamweaver.

Summary Exercise

Application Skills In this exercise, you will do some final work on the Tierra Verde site and then publish the site on a server or at a network location.

DIRECTIONS

1. Start Dreamweaver and open the tierraverde site.
2. Open each page in the site and check browser compatibility using Internet Explorer 6.0 and Firefox 1.5.
3. Check links throughout the site.
4. Run the Missing Alt Text report for the entire site. Because you have been supplying alternate text while adding images to the page, you should not have any results from this report. (If you have missed adding alternate text to any of the site's images, insert it now where indicated by the report.)
5. Run the Untitled Documents report to make sure all pages have titles.
6. Publish the site on the network your instructor indicates. Enable the check out/in feature.
7. Put all files on the remote site.
8. Check out several pages, and then check them back in.
9. Close all open pages and exit Dreamweaver.

Exercise | 75

Application Exercise

Application Skills In this exercise, you finish your work on the Classmate Connections site by running reports and the Validator. You will then put the files on a server or network to be available for site visitors.

DIRECTIONS

1. Start Dreamweaver and open the classmate_connections Web site.

2. Specify several target browsers and run the browser compatibility check on each page in the site. Read any information you receive about browser incompatibilities.

3. Check links throughout the site and fix any broken links you find.

4. Check for missing Alt attributes throughout the site and supply appropriate attributes where needed.

5. Specify that the Validator will check HTML 4.0 and Internet Explorer 4.0 extensions, and then validate markup sitewide.

6. Review the markup problems and fix any that you feel comfortable changing.

7. Publish the site as directed by your instructor and then visit the site using your Web browser.

8. Close the browser.

9. Save and close all open pages and exit Dreamweaver.

Exercise | 76

Curriculum Integration

Application Skills Your Physical Sciences class is studying natural disasters such as earthquakes, volcanoes, and hurricanes. Choose one type of disaster and create several pages on the subject that you can publish on a Web site. Do the following research:

- Locate general information on your natural disaster; for example, what causes a hurricane? What kinds of faults lead to damaging earthquakes? How do volcanoes provide a vent for the magma below the earth's crust?

- Locate graphic files if possible to illustrate your site.

- Locate information on the social impact of your type of disaster, such as the ten costliest hurricanes in terms of lives lost or property damage or the destruction caused by a volcanic eruption.

DIRECTIONS

Create a new site with an appropriate name for your disaster. As you define the site, specify both a local server and a remote server, using information provided by your instructor.

Create a home page for the site with an appropriate name and page title. You may want to use one of Dreamweaver's Starter (Theme) pages to save layout and formatting time.

Insert general information about your natural disaster on the home page, including one or more images you found.

Create a second page for the site that discusses a particular example of your disaster or general information about the destructive impact of the type of disaster. You may want to include additional images or a table of data. Link the pages by inserting or modifying existing links.

Specify Internet Explorer 6.0 and Netscape 8.0 as target browsers. Check each page for browser compatibility.

Run an Accessibility report on the current site. (You may discover, if you used Dreamweaver Starter pages, that even professionally designed sites don't meet every accessibility standard required.)

Validate the markup sitewide.

Put your files on the remote server you identified when you defined the site.

Close any open pages and exit Dreamweaver.

Exercise | 77

Critical Thinking

Application Skills In this exercise, you will complete your work on your personal Web site by running reports and validating code. Then you will publish the site for others to visit.

DIRECTIONS

- Open the personal Web site you have been working on throughout this course.

- Select one or more target browsers for the site and check all pages to see if there are any browser problems you need to fix.

- Check links sitewide and make any necessary changes.

- Run any reports you think necessary to locate problems on the pages.

- Validate the markup throughout the site.

- Specify remote access information for the Web site, using a server or network connection.

- Put all local files on the remote server. Invite several of your classmates to visit your site, if possible, and ask them for feedback on the site.

- Close all open pages and exit Dreamweaver.

Glossary

8-bit image file format A file format that can contain a maximum of 256 colors.

A

Absolute link A link that includes the complete path name in the URL (for example, http://www.yoursite.com). Used for linking to Web sites that are external to your site.

Actions Built-in Flash components you can use to animate Flash applications.

Active area The sensitive area of a button that registers and responds when a user positions the mouse pointer on the button or clicks it.

ActiveX Microsoft-developed technology that allows software components to work with other software components regardless of the language used to create them.

Adobe Bridge A file management application included with the applications that are part of Adobe Web Design, enabling you to view and manage image files.

Alignment Horizontal placement relative to the left and right edges of a page.

Anchor point An invisible object that marks the location where an element has been inserted.

Animated GIF A .gif-formatted file in which two or more images display in sequence, creating the appearance of animation.

Anti-aliasing A technique that smoothes the rough edges of a bitmapped image by adding transitional colors to the pixels along the edges.

AP div An absolutely positioned <div> tag that controls a block of content on a page.

AP element An AP (absolutely positioned) element is a page element that has been assigned an absolute or fixed position on a page.

Applet Small Java application that can be embedded in a Web page to create interactivity for animations.

Assets panel In Dreamweaver, a panel in the Files panel group that displays the "assets" of the site: images, colors, URLs, library items, templates, and other objects used in a Web site.

Attribute A characteristic that is applied to an HTML tag (for example, **align** is one example of an attribute).

Autostretch A Dreamweaver feature that adjusts a table column automatically to full browser window width.

B

Behavior handle The handle in the middle of a slice that you use to add rollover effects to a slice.

Bitmap graphics A type of image made up of individual dots (also known as *pixels*).

Bounding box A rectangular shape that completely encloses a shape and defines the total height and width of the shape.

Brightness The amount of light in an image.

Broken link A link to a page that is not available in the site because it has been deleted, renamed, or not yet created.

Browser A program that enables a user to view and move among pages on the World Wide Web. Examples of popular Web browsers include Internet Explorer, Firefox, Netscape, Mozilla, Opera, and Safari.

Bullet An indicator or simple graphic file used to denote individual points or items in an unordered (bulleted) list.

Button symbol The original saved button that is stored in the Flash Library.

C

Canvas color The color used as the background color for the image you create in Fireworks.

Cascading Style Sheet (CSS) A collection of saved design style properties that enable you to easily apply formats to specific items on your Web pages. CSS is an HTML 4.0 specification that is supported by current browsers.

Cell The intersection of a row and column.

Cell padding The space between a cell's content and its border.

Cell spacing The space between cells.

Child AP div The nested AP div.

Child Page A subordinate page that is an off-shoot of a first-level page (for example, the home page of your site).

Closing switch The / character used in a closing HTML tag (such as </strong>).

Closing tag An HTML tag used to indicate the end of an element. For example, </h1> is the closing tag placed at the end of Heading 1.

Code inspector A Dreamweaver feature that displays the HTML code used to create page elements.

Code view This is the view that shows HTML code. Dreamweaver can show an entire page of code or show both Code view and Design view on a split page.

Collapse To change the view to hide items. For example, collapse a hierarchical display to hide sub-elements and show only the main element.

Columns Vertical sections of the table.

Contrast The difference between the light and dark areas of an image.

Crop Changing the size of an object by removing unneeded parts of the image.

D

Definition list An HTML list type that includes a term set on one line and its description indented below.

Delimited format A format for saving application data that uses characters such as commas, tabs, or colons to separate columns of data.

Delimiters The characters used to separate data items.

Design view This is the default Document window view that shows page content similar to the way it will appear in the browser.

Device Central A feature that allows you to preview various types of content on simulated mobile devices.

Disjoint rollover A type of rollover where a rollover behavior attached to one slice changes the image that appears in a different place on the page.

E

Editable region In a template, an area that an author can change in a page to which the template is applied.

Elapsed time The length of time it takes to reach the current frame when the animation plays.

Element (1) The name of an HTML tag; (2) An item in a Dreamweaver navigation bar.

Expand To change the view to show hidden items. For example, expand a hierarchical display to show sub-elements branching off the main element.

Expanded Tables mode A Dreamweaver view that gives you an enlarged view of table contents.

Expander arrow The small arrow icon at the bottom right of the Property inspector that, when clicked, enlarges the panel to reveal additional properties.

Export To save a file or object created in one program in a format that can be used by a different program.

External style sheet A CSS in a text file you attach to a Web page you are creating that includes the style definitions for the elements on the page.

F

Fill The color, pattern, or texture used in the interior of a shape, arc, or text.

Filters Enhancements you can add to objects in a Fireworks document.

Flash Player A program used to run Flash applications.

Floating panel A Dreamweaver container for tools and properties that is undocked and can be repositioned anywhere in the workspace or closed if desired.

Font A specific design of type (also referred to as a *typeface*).

Font combination Also referred to as a *font family*, a collection of fonts that can be applied to text on a Web page. The browser will display the first font listed in the collection, and if the user's system doesn't have that particular font, the second font is substituted, and so on.

Font style A format applied to a font to change its appearance, such as **bold** or *italic*.

Form An interactive area on a Web page that allows a visitor to supply information or answer questions.

Form field An object, such as a text field or checkbox, that is inserted in a form to gather a specific type of data.

Form handler An application that processes the form data and displays it in the Web application.

Frame A container for Web page content that is displayed within a *frameset*.

Frame sequence A series of frames beginning with a keyframe and ending with the next keyframe.

Frame-by-frame animation Animation created by changing the content on each frame in a sequence.

Frames (1) The basic unit of time used in a Flash animation; (2) A structure in a Fireworks document that allows you to create animations and rollover effects.

Frameset A container for HTML frames.

FTP (File Transfer Protocol) A method for copying files to and from servers on a network.

G

GIF (Graphics Interchange Format) A bitmapped image format designed for on-screen viewing of images.

Group Joining two or more objects so they function as a single object.

Guides Horizontal and vertical lines you drag out of the ruler to align objects on the Stage. Guides can show the edges of objects such as slices.

H

Head An important section of code on your Web page that contains information browsers need in order to display the document, such as the page title and the character set used to create the page.

Hierarchical list A diagram in which elements branch from a main elementthe rootto other elements. It is usually used to show how the elements relate to each other. Sometimes called a *tree diagram*.

History panel A Dreamweaver feature providing visual maps of past work on Web pages.

Home page The first page of a Web site, displayed when a Web site is accessed. The home page typically includes an easy-to-locate navigation panel with links to all main pages on the site.

Hotspot A region on an image map that provides a link to another Web page.

HTML The acronym for Hypertext Markup Language, which is the programming language used to define and format data for display on the Word Wide Web.

HTML (Hypertext Markup Language) The code used to create all Web pages.

HTML tag Formal name for an HTML markup element. HTML tags appear inside angle brackets (<tag>).

HTTP (Hypertext Transfer Protocol) Fixed set of messages and replies between a browser and server on the Web.

I

Image map An image on your Web site that has been linked to other documents or areas of the Web site. An image map can have one or many regions linking to one or many other pages or documents.

Index transparency A type of transparency used commonly with GIF images.

Initial value In a form field, the text or value that will appear in the form field by default when the form page is opened in a browser.

Insert bar A toolbar in the Dreamweaver window that shows categories from which to insert objects into a Web page, including graphics, text features, tables, multimedia objects, etc.

Insertion point The blinking vertical line that shows you where text will appear when you begin typing or an object will appear when you create or insert one.

Instance One occurrence of a symbol.

Instances Copies of buttons that you place and use in a Fireworks document.

Interactive buttons Objects you create and place on your Web site that enable users to interact with your site.

Interlacing A method of displaying images progressively bit by bit on the screen.

J

Java Programming language that operates on multiple platforms and operating systems.

JPEG (Joint Photographic Experts Group) A file format particularly suited for Web graphics, such as photos.

JPEG mask An area within a JPEG image that uses the selective JPEG compression level rather than the compression level in the rest of the image.

Jump menu A menu that supplies a list of values which, when clicked in the browser, takes a visitor to a specific Web page.

K

Key In the Design Notes feature, an identifier for a set of information, such as *status*.

Keyframe A frame in which you specify changes in an animation.

Keywords Words or phrases that describe the site content. Keywords are important because search engines scan and index them, creating the links that bring visitors to your site.

L

Label In a form, text that identifies a field (for example, the Last Name label identifies the field that collects a visitor's last name).

Layout mode A Dreamweaver view that enables you to create layout tables.

Library (1) Dreamweaver feature that stores text, images, or other objects so that you can add them easily on any page in the Web site; (2) A folder in which symbols are stored.

Library items Objects and page elements stored in the Library.

Line break A HTML tag, <br>, that starts a new line but not a new paragraph.

Line length The width of the text line as it appears on your web page.

Link A connection between pages in the same file or different files.

Loss The compression value selected for a file

M

Mask An object that influences the display of other objects by applying a form or shape through which the object is viewed.

Media assets The content you use to create an application.

Merge cells The process of combining several cells to create one larger cell.

Mouse event An action that causes a button response; for example, a user positioning the mouse pointer over a button and clicking a button are two examples of mouse events.

Mouse symbol The phrase used to describe the master copy of a button that is stored in the Library panel.

Movie clip (1) A symbol comprised of an animated sequence of frames; (2) A movie segment.

Multimedia Information presented by video sequences, animation, illustration, and sound.

N

Named anchor A named location in a Web page that is used for links on the same page. Sometimes also referred to as a bookmark.

Navigation bar A set of links to pages in a Web site.

Nest To place one object inside another. HTML tags are often nested.

Noneditable region In a template, an area that is locked so that the designer cannot change its content.

O

Objects (1) Elements such as a forms, images, or multimedia files added to a Web page; (2) Elements you add to the Stage and animate in Flash.

One-sided tag A type of HTML tag that does not require a closing tag. The
 line break tag is a one-sided tag.

Opacity The transparency level of the selected object. An object that is 100% opaque is completely solid, and one that is 0% is transparent.

Opening tag An HTML tag that identifies the start of a new element. The opening tag for a paragraph is <p>.

Optimize Reducing the size of images so that your Web pages will load quickly while displaying the highest possible quality.

Optimizing graphics Choosing a color palette to limit the number of colors saved with the image.

Ordered list A listalso called a *numbered list*whose items must be in a certain order.

Output format The file type of the saved image.

P

Palette The set of colors used in a Fireworks document.

Panel A Dreamweaver container for tools and properties that appears in the Dreamweaver window either alone or as part of a panel group. Panels can be undocked and repositioned anywhere in the workspace or closed if desired.

Panel groups pane The panel on the right side of the Dreamweaver workspace where panels appear by default.

Parent AP div The AP div in which you insert a nested AP div.

Parent Page A first-level page (for example, your home page) to which other subordinate pages are linked.

Path The line that defines the outer edge of a vector object.

Pixels The individual dots that make up a bitmapped image.

Plugin Utility program that extends an application's capabilities.

PNG (Portable Network Graphic) A bitmapped image format designed for easy use of images on the Internet.

Points (1) A common measurement used for fonts. There are 72 points in one inch; (2) Places where vector paths change direction.

Pop-up menu A list of choices displayed when a user moves the mouse over an object or clicks a hotspot or slice

Projector A published Flash document in which a version of Flash Player is stored. The projector plays as a stand-alone video even if the user's computer does not have Flash Player installed.

Property A characteristic that defines the value, appearance, and/or state of an object.

Property inspector A Dreamweaver panel that displays properties for the currently selected object.

Publish To create a Web-compatible version of a Flash document file, which can then be stored on a Web server and accessed by users on the Web.

Publishing Copying Web site files from a local computer to a server.

R

Reference panel A Dreamweaver panel that supplies reference material about HTML tags, CSS, and JavaScript.

Registration point (1) A reference point used to position and transform a group, instance, text block, or bitmap; (2) A marker that shows the center of an object, such as a button.

Relative link A link set within a specific site that does not include the domain name (for example, ../yoursite/file.html.

Remote server A server, such as an FTP or WebDAV server, on which you put or publish your Web site. The remove server is typically the server where the files used to display your Web site are stored.

Resolution The number of dots or pixels per linear unit of measurement. For example, a computer monitor typically displays about 72 pixels per inch.

RGB A common color model that uses a hexadecimal value (for example, #C7C7C7) to communicate a color by the amount of Red, Green, and Blue used to create the color.

Rollover image An interactive effect created by specifying two images, one of which loads with the page and the other that displays when the mouse rolls over the image.

Rollovers areas on a Web page that change in appearance when the mouse pointer passes over them.

Rows Horizontal sections of a table.

RTF Rich Text Format, a text file format that includes formatting information such as font name, size, and attributes like bold.

Rules Horizontal lines added as a design element to a page to help organize the content and add a design element.

S

Sans-serif A type of font in which strokes do not appear at the end of the characters.

Scalable Type of object that can be resized easily without any loss of quality or proportion.

Serif A kind of font in which strokes appear at the end of the characters.

Site Map A diagram that shows you the file structure of your site and enables you to identify any broken links

Slices (1) Areas in an image that react to the mouse pointer; (2) Segments of objects you create and use to add interactivity in other files and sites.

Snap ring A small black ring displayed on the mouse pointer when the Snap to Objects command has been selected. The ring becomes larger when the object is near a snap location.

Snippets Predefined HTML forms, tables, menus, and other Web page scripts that you can insert on your page by using the Snippets panel in the Files panel group.

Source The page you want to display in a particular frame.

Split cell The process of dividing a single cell into multiple rows or columns.

Spry A JavaScript library containing interactive elements you can add to Web pages.

Stacking order The order in which AP elements are added to a page. The lowest number is at the bottom of the stack.

Stage The central work area of the screen where you create Flash applications.

State The way in which a button appears at different times in relation to a mouse event.

Stroke The outline of an object, including characteristics such as weight, color, style, and more.

Style A rule that specifies how to format an HTML element such as text, an image, or a specific tag.

Style sheet A collection of styles created for a page or Web site.

Styles Saved formatting specifications that you can apply to items on your page.

Symbol A reusable object used to create content in an application.

Symbol definition The content that comprises a symbol.

Syntax Rules that govern the use of HTML code and create a connected, orderly system.

T

Tag inspector A Dreamweaver panel that maps and shows the properties of the tags used in a Web page's code.

Template A collection of formats and page elements that can be used to give pages in a Web site a consistent look.

Text blocks Groups of editable text used in Fireworks documents.

Thumbnail A small picture that represents the contents of each layer in the Layers panel.

Timeline The Flash panel at the top of the screen where you arrange, sequence, and set the timing of Flash objects.

Timeline effects Predefined animations that come with Flash that you can apply to objects on the Stage.

Transform To modify by scaling, skewing, rotating, or distorting.

Transformation handles Small rectangles around the sides of a bounding box that can be dragged to transform an object.

Transformation point The center point of an object. Sometimes called the *registration point* or *center point*.

Tweened animation Animation in which you specify a starting point and an ending point and let Flash fill in the frames between.

Typeface A specific family of type that includes alphabetic characters, numerals, and punctuation marks.

U

Unordered list A list that does not have to be in order. Also called a *bulleted list*.

URL (Uniform Resource Locator) Another name for a Web page address, this is the server and path information used to locate documents on the Internet.

V

Validation The process of ensuring that a form field contains an entry, if required, or a specific type of data.

Value (1) The precise instruction for the way in which an attribute should function. (For example, the value for the **align** attribute might be **center.**); (2) In a form field, the actual result that will be sent to the server after the visitor types text or makes a choice.

Vector graphics A type of image that is defined mathematically and drawn as an object on the screen (as opposed to the dots that comprise bitmap images).

W

Web browser A software program such as Microsoft Internet Explorer that displays Web pages and allows the user to navigate from one page to another.

Web page A single file in a collection of files that make up a Web site.

Web site A collection of Web pages and other objects, such as images, that are linked to create a resource dedicated to a particular subject.

Web-safe colors A palette of 216 colors that will display the same in any browser, regardless of the operating system.

Wicket The angle brackets (< >) that surround the HTML tag.

Widget A page element that creates a specific kind of interactive content or carries out a defined function.

Wizard An automated process that provides you with the steps for completing a specific program task. (For example, you will use the Site Definition wizard to set up a new Web site in Dreamweaver.)

Workspace In Dreamweaver, the desktop area where the Document window and panels appear.

X

XHTML (Extensible Hypertext Markup Language) The current version of HTML that combines HTML structure with XML power and flexibility.

Z

Z-index The numbering sequence of the stacking order of AP elements on a page.

Index

typefaces. *See also* fonts
  defined, 38
  modifying, 41

U

Uniform color palette, 353
UNIX-based operating systems, 10
unordered lists
  creating, 51
  defined, 49
updating
  Library items on Web pages, 169
  templates, 161, 163
URLs (Uniform Resource Locators), 67.
    See also links
  Assets panel information on, 155
  Fireworks buttons, adding URLs to, 335
  relative links, 66
  root URL, selecting, 11

V

validating
  forms, 214
  in Spry framework, 277
  Web pages, 394–395
Validator feature, 394–395
values. *See* forms; HTML tags
VBScript for forms, 215
vector graphics, 95, 117
  bounding boxes
    defined, 115
    for ellipses, 116
  defined, 94
  deleting points, 119
  ellipses, drawing, 116
  fill to path, adding, 119
  groups for, 115
  handles for, 116–117
  layers, placing objects on, 128
  lines, drawing, 116
  mask, creating, 129–130
  paths
    fill, adding, 119
    Pen tool for creating, 118
    stroke of path, changing, 119
  Pen tool, creating paths with, 118

points
  adding, changing and deleting, 119
  defined, 115
  in paths, 118
polygons, creating, 116
rectangles, drawing, 116
scaling, 116
stroke of path, changing, 119
tools for, 98
transforming, 116–117
  defined, 115
Vector Path tool, drawing with, 118
Vector Path tool, 118
  in Fireworks, 98
Verdana font, 41
views and viewing
  Design notes, 170
  Fireworks, changing view in, 98
  site map, 75–76
  Web site files, 15
V Space text box, 141

W

WBMP format for Fireworks files, 353
Web Adaptive color palette, 353
Web browsers. *See* browsers
WebDAV Connection dialog box, 402
WebDAV connection with Web site,
    associating, 401–402
Web pages. *See also* frames; home page
  additional pages, creating, 15
  creating, 13–15
  defined, 2
  design guidelines, 16
  existing pages, opening, 14
  fold of, 142
  Library items, inserting, 168
  opening, 4
  previewing, 73
  saving, 14
  titles for, 15
  validating, 394–395
Web-safe colors
  defined, 89
  using, 91
Web sites, 4
  additional pages, creating, 15
  defined, 2

different site, opening, 27
keywords, adding, 24
naming, 10
new site, creating, 9–13
storing, 10–11
summary of new site, 13
testing, 11
viewing site files, 15
Web 216 color palette, 353
wickets. *See* HTML tags
widgets. *See* Spry framework
width. *See also* tables
  of rules, 90
windows
  Bridge window, 135
  Fireworks window, 96
Windows color palette, 353
Window Size list box, 6
wizards
  defined, 9
  new site, creating, 9
  Site Definition wizard, 10
Workflow reports, 393–394
workspace, 4
  defined, 2
  saving layout, 6
wrapping text around Bridge images,
    139–140

X

XHTML (Extensible Hypertext Markup
    Language), 21
  alignment options, 140
  cleaning up code, 61
  defined, 21
XML (Extensible Markup Language),
    Spry XML Data Set, 282

Z

Z-index. *See* AP elements
Zoom Blur filter, Fireworks, 111
zooming
  in Fireworks, 98
  in Flash, 291

SINGLE PC LICENSE AGREEMENT AND LIMITED WARRANTY

READ THIS LICENSE CAREFULLY BEFORE OPENING THIS PACKAGE. BY OPENING THIS PACKAGE, YOU ARE AGREEING TO THE TERMS AND CONDITIONS OF THIS LICENSE. IF YOU DO NOT AGREE, DO NOT OPEN THE PACKAGE. PROMPTLY RETURN THE UNOPENED PACKAGE AND ALL ACCOMPANYING ITEMS TO THE PLACE YOU OBTAINED THEM. THESE TERMS APPLY TO ALL LICENSED SOFTWARE ON THE DISK EXCEPT THAT THE TERMS FOR USE OF ANY SHAREWARE OR FREEWARE ON THE DISKETTES ARE AS SET FORTH IN THE ELECTRONIC LICENSE LOCATED ON THE DISK:

1. GRANT OF LICENSE and OWNERSHIP: The enclosed computer programs and data ("Software") are licensed, not sold, to you by Pearson Education, Inc. ("We" or the "Company") and in consideration of your purchase or adoption of the accompanying Company textbooks and/or other materials, and your agreement to these terms. We reserve any rights not granted to you. You own only the disk(s) but we and/or our licensors own the Software itself. This license allows you to use and display your copy of the Software on a single computer (i.e., with a single CPU) at a single location for academic use only, so long as you comply with the terms of this Agreement.

2. RESTRICTIONS: You may not transfer or distribute the Software or documentation to anyone else. Except for backup, you may not copy the documentation or the Software. You may not network the Software or otherwise use it on more than one computer or computer terminal at the same time. You may not reverse engineer, disassemble, decompile, modify, adapt, translate, or create derivative works based on the Software or the Documentation. You may be held legally responsible for any copying or copyright infringement which is caused by your failure to abide by the terms of these restrictions.

3. TERMINATION: This license is effective until terminated. This license will terminate automatically without notice from the Company if you fail to comply with any provisions or limitations of this license. Upon termination, you shall destroy the Documentation and all copies of the Software. All provisions of this Agreement as to limitation and disclaimer of warranties, limitation of liability, remedies or damages, and our ownership rights shall survive termination.

4. LIMITED WARRANTY AND DISCLAIMER OF WARRANTY: Company warrants that for a period of 60 days from the date you purchase this SOFTWARE (or purchase or adopt the accompanying textbook), the Software, when properly installed and used in accordance with the Documentation, will operate in substantial conformity with the description of the Software set forth in the Documentation, and that for a period of 30 days the disk(s) on which the Software is delivered shall be free from defects in materials and workmanship under normal use. The Company does not warrant that the Software will meet your requirements or that the operation of the Software will be uninterrupted or error-free. Your only remedy and the Company's only obligation under these limited warranties is, at the Company's option, return of the disk for a refund of any amounts paid for it by you or replacement of the disk. THIS LIMITED WARRANTY IS THE ONLY WARRANTY PROVIDED BY THE COMPANY AND ITS LICENSORS, AND THE COMPANY AND ITS LICENSORS DISCLAIM ALL OTHER WARRANTIES, EXPRESS OR IMPLIED, INCLUDING WITHOUT LIMITATION, THE IMPLIED WARRANTIES OF MERCHANTABILITY AND FITNESS FOR A PARTICULAR PURPOSE. THE COMPANY DOES NOT WARRANT, GUARANTEE OR MAKE ANY REPRESENTATION REGARDING THE ACCURACY, RELIABILITY, CURRENTNESS, USE, OR RESULTS OF USE, OF THE SOFTWARE.

5. LIMITATION OF REMEDIES AND DAMAGES: IN NO EVENT, SHALL THE COMPANY OR ITS EMPLOYEES, AGENTS, LICENSORS, OR CONTRACTORS BE LIABLE FOR ANY INCIDENTAL, INDIRECT, SPECIAL, OR CONSEQUENTIAL DAMAGES ARISING OUT OF OR IN CONNECTION WITH THIS LICENSE OR THE SOFTWARE, INCLUDING FOR LOSS OF USE, LOSS OF DATA, LOSS OF INCOME OR PROFIT, OR OTHER LOSSES, SUSTAINED AS A RESULT OF INJURY TO ANY PERSON, OR LOSS OF OR DAMAGE TO PROPERTY, OR CLAIMS OF THIRD PARTIES, EVEN IF THE COMPANY OR AN AUTHORIZED REPRESENTATIVE OF THE COMPANY HAS BEEN ADVISED OF THE POSSIBILITY OF SUCH DAMAGES. IN NO EVENT SHALL THE LIABILITY OF THE COMPANY FOR DAMAGES WITH RESPECT TO THE SOFTWARE EXCEED THE AMOUNTS ACTUALLY PAID BY YOU, IF ANY, FOR THE SOFTWARE OR THE ACCOMPANYING TEXTBOOK. BECAUSE SOME JURISDICTIONS DO NOT ALLOW THE LIMITATION OF LIABILITY IN CERTAIN CIRCUMSTANCES, THE ABOVE LIMITATIONS MAY NOT ALWAYS APPLY TO YOU.

6. GENERAL: THIS AGREEMENT SHALL BE CONSTRUED IN ACCORDANCE WITH THE LAWS OF THE UNITED STATES OF AMERICA AND THE STATE OF NEW YORK, APPLICABLE TO CONTRACTS MADE IN NEW YORK, AND SHALL BENEFIT THE COMPANY, ITS AFFILIATES AND ASSIGNEES. HIS AGREEMENT IS THE COMPLETE AND EXCLUSIVE STATEMENT OF THE AGREEMENT BETWEEN YOU AND THE COMPANY AND SUPERSEDES ALL PROPOSALS OR PRIOR AGREEMENTS, ORAL, OR WRITTEN, AND ANY OTHER COMMUNICATIONS BETWEEN YOU AND THE COMPANY OR ANY REPRESENTATIVE OF THE COMPANY RELATING TO THE SUBJECT MATTER OF THIS AGREEMENT. If you are a U.S. Government user, this Software is licensed with "restricted rights" as set forth in subparagraphs (a)-(d) of the Commercial Computer-Restricted Rights clause at FAR 52.227-19 or in subparagraphs (c)(1)(ii) of the Rights in Technical Data and Computer Software clause at DFARS 252.227-7013, and similar clauses, as applicable.